THE WORLD BANK PARTICIPATION SOURCEBOOK

ESD

Environmentally Sustainable Development

The World Bank
Washington, D.C.

First printing February 1996

ISBN 0-8213-3558-8

Library of Congress Cataloging-in-Publication Data

World Bank participation sourcebook.
      p.   cm. — (Environmental Department papers ; 019)
   ISBN 0-8213-3558-8
   1. World Bank.   2. Economic development projects—Case studies—
Handbooks, manuals, etc.   3. Economic development projects—Citizen
participation—Case studies—Handbooks, manuals, etc.   4. Community
development—Case studies—Handbooks, manuals, etc.   I. World Bank.
II. Series: Environmental management series (Washington, D.C.) ;
019.
HG3881.5.W57W692   1996
338.9—dc20   96-1868
                                     CIP

Cover Design: Tomoko Hirata

Cover Note: The artwork reproduced on the cover is from the Warli tribe, who live in the Sahyadri mountains in Maharashtra state, north of Bombay. These tribal peoples are renowned for their mythic vision of Mother Earth, their traditional agricultural methods, and their lack of caste differentiation.

Photos in Table of Contents: Chapter I, Curt Carnemark; Chapter II, Stefano Pagiola; Chapter III, Ron Sawyer; Chapter IV, Asem Ansari; Appendix I, Deepa Narayan; Appendix II, Curt Carnemark.

CONTENTS

Tables

FOREWORD

Although I joined the World Bank less than a year ago, I have had the privilege of visiting many of our developing country partners in this short period. On every mission, I have made it a point to listen and learn from different in-country stakeholders. Based on my discussions, I am convinced that their involvement and collaboration can not only make our development efforts more effective and sustainable, but can also foster ownership and a sense of belief in the relevance and value of our programs—right down to the community level.

This book presents the new direction the World Bank is taking in its support of participation, by recognizing that there is a diversity of stakeholders for every activity we undertake, and that those people affected by development interventions must be included in the decision-making process.

I personally believe in the relevance of participatory approaches and partnerships in development and am committed to making them a way of doing business in the Bank. I therefore welcome *The World Bank Participation Sourcebook* which shares with Bank staff how they can support participatory approaches. To do this, the authors have turned to participation practitioners within the Bank who contributed their expertise and advice. It is this experience—its successes and frustrations—that is documented on the pages of this book.

I commend Bank staff who are pioneering participatory approaches in the Bank's work. I encourage others to learn from the practical experience of their colleagues in order to produce better results on the ground, improve development efforts, and more effectively reach the poor.

James D. Wolfensohn
President
The World Bank
February 1996

PREFACE

Through participation, we lost 'control' of the project and in so doing gained ownership and sustainability, precious things in our business.

—World Bank Task Manager

Participation is a rich concept that means different things to different people in different settings. For some, it is a matter of principle; for others, a practice; and for still others, an end in itself. All these interpretations have merit. *The World Bank Participation Sourcebook,* however, follows the definition of participation adopted by the Bank's Learning Group on Participatory Development:

Participation is a process through which stakeholders influence and share control over development initiatives and the decisions and resources which affect them.

In writing the *Sourcebook,* we wanted to discover how this could be achieved. As a first step, we turned to our colleagues, who contributed their experience and advice. It is this experience, both successes and frustrations, that we have tried to capture for Bank staff.

The *Sourcebook* is not a policy document on participation; nor is it to be read cover to cover. It also does not seek to persuade anyone (other than through example) to use participatory approaches. It is primarily intended for readers who have already decided to use participatory approaches in their professional work.

How you read the *Sourcebook* is up to you. We hope, however, that it strengthens your ideas about participation and how you do your work. We also hope you agree that the new ways of working presented here can improve projects, contribute to the development process, and help reach the poor.

ACKNOWLEDGMENTS

Participatory approaches to development activities have been pioneered and practiced for many decades by community workers, government bureaucrats, nongovernmental organization (NGO) practitioners, and academics. Indeed, the World Bank is fortunate in being able to draw from the vast body of literature and path-breaking work of the individuals and institutions that have moved participation forward. We are most grateful to development colleagues outside the Bank, whose experiences and support we have relied on in learning how to apply participatory approaches in our work.

The World Bank Participation Sourcebook has been prepared by the Environment Department's Social Policy Division (ENVSP). It was written by a team led by Bhuvan Bhatnagar, Task Manager, and comprising James Kearns and Debra Sequeira. Valuable inputs came from Sandy Granzow, Sue Jacobs, Gillian Perkins, and Jennifer Rietbergen-McCracken. Cristy Tumale, Isabel Alegre, and Nona Sachdeva provided secretarial support. Pamela S. Cubberly edited the manuscript. Jennifer Sterling was responsible for the design and layout. The work was carried out under the general direction of Gloria Davis, Division Chief, ENVSP.

Many other people inside the World Bank provided valuable contributions, advice, and comments. All told, more than 200 Bank staff and consultants contributed directly to the contents of the *Sourcebook*. As a result, the preparation process has resulted in sharing, learning, and a sense of ownership on the part of participating Bank staff.

The *Sourcebook* builds on the work of a Bankwide Learning Group on Participatory Development, which was led over the last four years by David Beckmann and Aubrey Williams and which drew on the contributions of countless Bank staff. Case studies documenting the Bank's experience with participation were contributed by Michael Azefor, Ajit Banerjee, Neil Boyle, Ann Clark, Willy de Geyndt, Jacomina de Regt, Esther Gadzama, Sunita Gandhi, Scott Guggenheim, Charles Gunasekara, Abel Mejia, Makha Ndao, Maria Nowak, Yogendra Saran, Katrine Saito, Turid Sato, Bachir Souhlal, Denise Vaillancourt, and Thomas Wiens.

Twenty steering committees composed mainly of Bank staff prepared background technical papers for the *Sourcebook*. Primary contributors included Charles Antholt, Dan Aronson, Michael Bamberger, Ajit Banerjee, Anthony Bebbington, Lynn Bennett, Mark Blackden, Gabriel Campbell, Tim Campbell, Thomas Carroll, Nat Colletta, Chona Cruz, Shelton Davis, Jim Edgerton, John Frankenhoff, Michael Goldberg, Gita Gopal, David Gow, Hans Jurgen Gruss, Malcom Holmes, N. Vijay Jagannathan, James Kearns, Anirudh Krishna, Andrew Manzardo, Alexandre Marc, Ruth Meinzen-Dick, Augusta Molnar, Deepa Narayan, Andrew Norton, Gillian Perkins, Richard Reidinger, Mary Schmidt, Jerry Silverman, Lars Soeftestad, Tova Solo, Thomas Stephens, Abeba Taddese, Ellen Tynan, Gabrielle Watson, and Willem Zijp. These background papers are being published as Environment Department Papers, and most have been summarized in Appendix II.

The *Sourcebook* was prepared with support from two of the World Bank's central vice presidencies—Environmentally Sustainable Development (ESD) and Human Capital Development and Operations Policy (HCO)—and with resources from the German Gesellschaft für Technische Zusammenarbeit (GTZ) and the Swedish International Development Authority. Thomas Kuby of GTZ also provided substantive support.

In addition to direct contributions to its contents, the *Sourcebook* has benefited from the comments and feedback of several hundred reviewers both inside and outside the Bank. We have taken many of these views and insights into account in revisions. But given the sheer number of responses, it was impossible to incorporate all of them. Fortunately, we do not see this document as the final word. Instead, we envision the *Sourcebook* as a "living" document, which will be updated and revised regularly to reflect our rapidly growing experience in this area. In future editions, we also hope to incorporate contributions from outside the Bank—from donors, NGOs, our government counterparts, and other participation practitioners, all of whom have valuable experiences of their own from which we can learn.

ACRONYMS

ADP	Agricultural Development Project
AIC	Appreciation-Influence-Control
AIDS	Acquired Immune-Deficiency Syndrome
BA	Beneficiary Assessment
CAMPFIRE	Communal Areas Management Programme for Indigenous Resources
CDEEP	Comité Departemental de suivi d'Execution et d'Evaluation des Programmes du Secteur de la Santé
CEF	Caixa Economica Federal
CESW	Country Economic and Sector Work
CFE	Comisión Federal de Electricidad
CIDP	Communal Irrigation Development Project
CIR	Country Implementation Review
CNEEP	Comité National de suivi d'Execution et d'Evaluation des Programmes du Secteur de la Santé
COGEC	Comité de Gestion de la Commune
COGES	Comité de Gestion de la Sous-préfecture
DENR	Department of Environment and Natural Resources
ENVSP	Environment Department, Social Policy Division
ESD	Environmentally Sustainable Development Vice-Presidency
ESMAP	Energy Sector Management Assistance Program
ESW	Economic and Sector Work
EXPACO	Executive Planning and Action Coordination Organization
FACU	Federal Agricultural Coordinating Unit
FENACOAC	Federación Nacional de Cooperativas Agrícolas de Ahorro, Créditos, y Servicios Varios
FONCODES	Fondo Nacional de Compensación y Desarollo
FPC	Forest Protection Committees
GA	Gender Analysis
GDP	Gross Domestic Product
GOS	Government of the Sindh
GTZ	Gesellschaft für Technische Zusammenarbeit
HCO	Human Capital Development and Operations Policy Vice-Presidency
HIV	Human Immunodeficiency Virus
IA	Irrigation Association
ICC	Indigenous Cultural Community
IDA	International Development Association
IFAD	International Fund for Agricultural Development
INDAP	Instituto Nacional de Desarollo Agropecuario
IPAS	Integrated Protected Areas System
IPM	Integrated Pest Management
KWSB	Karachi Water and Sewerage Board

LogFRAME	Logical Framework
LPDR	Lao People's Democratic Republic
LTPS	Long-Term Perspective Study
MOH	Ministry of Health
NGO	Nongovernmental Organization
NIA	National Irrigation Administration
OOPP	Objectives-Oriented Project Planning
O&M	Operations and Maintenance
PA	Poverty Assessment
PAMB	Protected Areas Management Board
PPA	Participatory Poverty Assessment
PPM	Project Planning Matrix
PRA	Participatory Rural Appraisal
PSM	Public Sector Management
RDF	Rural Development Fund
SA	Social Assessment
SARAR	Self-esteem, Associative strength, Resourcefulness, Action planning, and Responsibility for follow-through
SCC	Systematic Client Consultation
SSDP	Sindh Special Development Project
TM	Task Manager
TWUWS	Transportation, Water, and Urban Development Department, Water and Sewerage Division
UNICEF	United Nations Children's Fund
VCC	Village Credit Committee
VCF	Village Credit Fund
W&S	Water and Sanitation
WIA	Women in Agriculture
ZOPP	Zielorientierte Projektplanung (Objectives-Oriented Project Planning)

THE PROJECT CYCLE AT A GLANCE

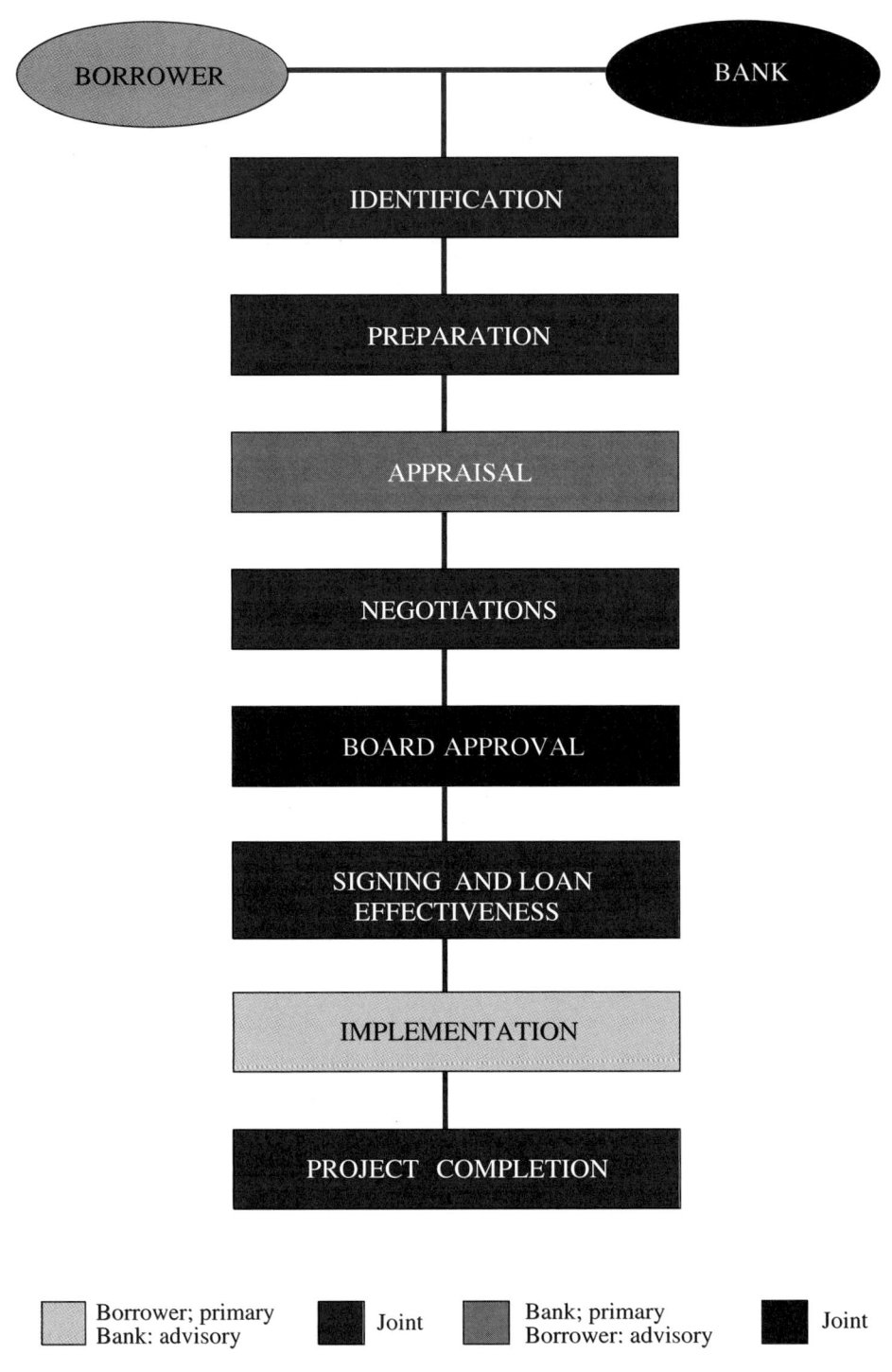

Source: The Task Manager's Handbook, World Bank, 1995

INTRODUCTION

It is not that we should simply seek new and better ways for managing society, the economy, and the world. The point is that we should fundamentally change how we behave.

—Vaclav Havel

We have written the *Sourcebook* for World Bank Task Managers—and those who work with them—to help them support participatory processes in economic and social development.

The *Sourcebook* is not a policy document on participation; nor is it to be read cover to cover. It also does not seek to persuade anyone (other than through example) to use participatory approaches. In preparing it, we are assuming that readers have already decided to use participatory approaches in their professional work. The *Sourcebook* has been formatted so that busy people can pull it off the shelf, consult the table of contents, and quickly turn to the section they need. Chapters are set up in modular form, with reference headings that should allow the reader to dip in and out of the document according to individual interest and need. Readers may also wish to supplement the contents of the *Sourcebook* by reading more detailed information on methods and tools (Appendix I) or the background paper summaries (Appendix II).

WHAT IS IN THE SOURCEBOOK?

Chapter I: Reflections on Participation

Chapter I brings together the key themes and common elements of participation. It also contains our reflections on what we have learned from the examples in Chapter II. We explore what participatory development is and what it means to use participatory processes to plan and implement Bank-supported operations. We also discuss the importance of using participatory approaches in reaching the poor. Although Chapter I is not an executive summary, it does invite you to explore the cases that follow.

Chapter II: Shared Experiences

This chapter contains examples, presented in the first person, of how World Bank staff used or helped others use participatory approaches in Bank-supported operations. We identified these examples through the work of the four-year Bankwide Learning Group on Participatory Development. In making selections, we attempted to cover a variety of countries, sectors, and types of activities. We recognize, however, that we have not even come close to capturing the vast, rich, and varied experiences in participatory development, even within the Bank.

In compiling these case studies, it became evident that each example is *context specific*; therefore, applying what you find useful in these examples to other situations will no doubt require some interpretation and adaptation. You may wish to browse through several of these cases to see what your colleagues are doing before settling on a final approach.

Chapter III: Practice Pointers in Participatory Planning and Decisionmaking

Chapter III draws largely on the experiences presented in Chapter II to guide the reader through the various steps of participatory planning and decisionmaking. These practice pointers provide answers to questions Task Managers may have about using participatory approaches in Bank-supported activities. Given the context-specific and multidimensional nature of participation, the practice pointers give the reader a menu of options for each stage of the participatory process based on actual Bank experiences. This leaves readers free to decide for themselves which examples are most relevant to their own situation and adapt the ideas accordingly.

Chapter IV: Practice Pointers in Enabling the Poor to Participate

The practice pointers in Chapter IV focus on one particular group of stakeholders—the poor—and some of the common barriers to their participation. Chapter IV presents the experience of Bank staff and their government counterparts and shares approaches to strengthening the financial and organizational capacities of the poor. It also discusses ways of creating an enabling environment for the participation of all stakeholders, including the poor.

Appendix I: Methods and Tools

This appendix describes a range of participatory methods, some of which have been used in the Chapter II examples. We have borrowed techniques freely from those who "invented" them and have modified them, when necessary, to fit into the context of Bank-supported operations.

Appendix II: Working Paper Summaries

Steering committees composed mostly of Bank operational staff prepared background papers on participation for the *Sourcebook*. The eighteen papers fall into three categories *(a)* Bank-supported activities and operational tasks, *(b)* sectors, and *(c)* cross-cutting issues. Appendix II contains summaries of these papers and their main findings for readers who want to explore a specific area or issue in greater depth.

CHAPTER I

REFLECTIONS: WHAT IS PARTICIPATION?

Participation is a process through which stakeholders influence and share control over development initiatives and the decisions and resources which affect them.

—Participation Learning Group Final Report

Some readers who know the World Bank well will note that the examples presented in Chapter II differ from their notions of how the Bank normally goes about its work. This difference could be either in style or presentation. In our opinion, however, it is not a matter of style but rather the "stance" adopted by the sponsors and designers in organizing and carrying out the activity. Also different is the explicit recognition and importance attached to description of the *processes* used to plan and implement development activities.

The behavior of those who sponsored and designed the development activities described in Chapter II illustrates what we mean by "stance." For Bank activities, the central government is usually, but not always, the sponsor. In the examples included here, the sponsors and designers take a stance that places them inside the local social system being addressed; that is, they demonstrate a willingness to work *collaboratively* with the other key stakeholders in carrying out the steps required to prepare a project for World Bank financing. Specifically, they do the following:

- Identify the strengths and weaknesses of existing policies and service and support systems; that is, the stakeholders *conduct the analysis and diagnosis collaboratively.*
- Decide and articulate what is needed; that is, the stakeholders *collaboratively set objectives.*
- Decide in pragmatic terms, directions, priorities, and institutional responsibilities; that is, the stakeholders *collaboratively create a strategy.*
- Develop or oversee development of project policies, specifications, blueprints, budgets, and technologies needed to move from the present to the future; that is, the stakeholders *collaboratively formulate project tactics.*

These steps are carried out for all Bank-financed projects, be they traditional projects or projects planned in what we call a "participatory" way. But the key characteristic of a participatory approach is the collaborative stance the project sponsors and designers take in carrying out these steps so that stakeholders *influence and share control* over the decisions that are made.

EXTERNAL EXPERT STANCE

Bank-supported projects have in the past usually been prepared in a different manner. We call this more traditional approach the "external expert stance" to distinguish it from what we are calling the "participatory stance." In the external expert stance, the same activities—setting objectives, diagnosis, and so on—are undertaken to prepare a project for financing. The difference is that in the exter-

3

nal expert stance, the project sponsors and designers place themselves outside the local system they are investigating and about which they are making decisions—even if they happen to come from or live within the local system.

Usually, these externally positioned sponsors and designers are substantive experts in the subject matter they are investigating. *They* determine what the project will look like. They view other stakeholders mainly as sources of information and opinions. Their "expert role" includes collecting information and opinions from the other stakeholders, making sense out of what they collect, and converting all of it into a development strategy or project.

The external expert stance is not a World Bank innovation but an inherent and deeply embedded part of our understanding of how to produce results and the role one plays in producing them.

LISTENING AND CONSULTATION

Even when working in the external expert stance, Bank staff, their government colleagues, and the consultants they hire do consult with and listen to people in the local system. Admittedly, in the past, sponsors and designers may not have always listened to all the people or consulted poor and disadvantaged members of society, but this is changing. Concerted efforts are now being made to consult and listen to all concerned stakeholders. The emphasis of the Bank's Africa Region on systematic client consultation is an example of the changes underway. The inclusion of beneficiary assessments in poverty assessments is another example.

We fully support and advocate consultation and listening—especially with the poor and disadvantaged. But we do not equate this with the process called "participation." Instead, we recognize consultation and listening as essential *prerequisites* for participation, because, no matter how good the sponsors and designers are at consultation and listening, what is still missing is *learning* on the part of the people in the local system. A person who is being "listened to" or "consulted with" does not learn nearly as much as the person doing the listening and consulting.

By focusing attention on "who needs to learn what" in a project and revising our understanding of how learning occurs, we gain insights into the reasons why the behavior change dimensions of Bank-financed projects have run into so many problems. We are also aided in our understanding of what project design changes are needed to enable social change.

SOCIAL LEARNING

In the external expert stance, experts design strategies and projects that require behavior changes on the part of people within a given system. Then they turn these preset specifications over to people who are accustomed to behaving in a significantly different way and have not learned what the experts have learned about *how* and *why* their behavior needs to change. The implementation challenge that arises in such situations hinges, as far as we can tell, on the issue of *learning*. Specifically, how can the people within a local system learn the value and rationale of new social behaviors specified by an expert?

Behind the well-institutionalized practice of specifying new behaviors in reports and other texts is the belief that people learn by reading information about a reality external to them. Under this assumption, it is logical to think that presenting people with a plan is enough to enable them to take new actions effectively. And if the actions taken turn out to be ineffective in practice, then we believe it is necessary to go back and reconstruct our strategy or project or plan.

But, over time, development experience has shown that when external experts *alone* acquire, analyze, and process information and then present this information in reports, social change usually does not take place; whereas the kind of "social learning" that stakeholders generate and internalize during the participatory planning and/or implementation of a development activity *does* enable social change.

As indicated in the Chapter II examples, Bank Task Managers are increasingly supporting processes in which the stakeholders themselves generate, share, and analyze information; establish priorities; specify objectives; and develop tactics. The stakeholders contribute their experience and expertise—for instance, the experience of what it is to be poor or female or the expertise to develop specifications for a new road or educational program. The stakeholders learn and develop a joint purpose together.

SOCIAL INVENTION

This social learning is followed by "social invention." The stakeholders invent the new practices and institutional arrangements they are willing to adopt. In the process, they individually and collectively develop insight and understanding of the new behaviors required to attain the objectives they set. Having all stakeholders work, learn, and invent together reduces the need for the transfer of expert learning from one group of stakeholders to another.

The Task Managers of the case studies in Chapter II say that local people often create the most important parts of the projects. Task Managers make a point of distinguishing between what seem to outsiders to be good ideas and what the local stakeholders invent as practical and expedient ways to get things of value done. The implication is that experts standing outside of the local system often miss possibilities and opportunities that come naturally to its members. The **Chad Education** Task Manager, for example, points out that he had never thought about parent education as an important means of improving child education until the parents themselves proposed it.

Again, this seems sensible. How can experts positioned outside the local system figure out what the people in it are willing and able to change? More important, how can they know the speed and depth with which the local stakeholders are willing to make these changes? If behavioral and organizational changes are necessary, then the people whose behavior has to change should create the change and commit themselves to it.

COMMITMENT

The absence of sufficient "commitment" in many of the projects the Bank finances comes, we believe, mainly from the external expert stance, in which small groups of experts ask the other stakeholders to commit themselves to a project the experts have designed. Even if these stakeholders do so, they often have not learned enough to understand fully the commitment they are being asked to make. Nor have they learned enough to judge their ability individually and collectively to fulfill it. We need to be clear that commitments made under such circumstances cannot be relied on.

Through the participatory process, however, people can make informed commitments, and, by *observing* the participatory process, assessments can be made by Bank and government staff, among others, about the presence or absence of the commitment necessary to ensure sustainability.

In Chapter II, we see how such a network of support and commitment generated by participatory processes can keep a project going in the face of problems. In the **Benin Health** example, a strong network of local health committees was formed during the initial design phase to set the objectives and strategies of the project. This network was able to keep the project going as officialdom continually changed—with four new health ministers in fourteen months and four different notions about what would be good for the people. This is because the process that produced the project was inclusive from the start, therefore gaining broadly based support from all concerned.

Of course, more than commitment is needed. Economic, financial, and technical arrangements must be in place to deliver on these commitments. But if these arrangements exist only on paper or in agreements made without the understanding of those stakeholders who must implement and sustain the project, little will be accomplished.

POPULAR VERSUS STAKEHOLDER PARTICIPATION

When we began preparing the *Sourcebook*, we assumed we would be writing about "popular" participation, that is, participation of the poor and others who are disadvantaged in terms of wealth, education, ethnicity, or gender. It seemed obvious to us to focus on the participation of these poor and disadvantaged groups because, although often the intended beneficiaries, they are usually without voice in the development process.

But, as we started documenting the Chapter II examples, we noted that apart from poor and disadvantaged people who were directly affected, a range of *other* stakeholders for Bank-supported operations existed. These stakeholders could affect the outcome of a proposed Bank intervention or were affected by it; because of this, their participation was critical. In addition to those directly affected by the project, these stakeholders include the following:

- *Borrowers,* that is, elected officials, line agency staff, local government officials, and so on. Governments representing borrower member countries are the Bank's most significant partners in that they are shareholders as well as clients and are responsible for devising and implementing public policies and programs.
- *Indirectly affected groups,* such as nongovernmental organizations (NGOs), private sector organizations, and so forth with an interest in outcomes
- *The Bank,* that is, Bank management, staff, and shareholders

We also noted that, in our Chapter II examples, sponsors and designers of development activities had to work with and through powerful stakeholders to serve the needs of the poorest people. Attempts to bypass powerful stakeholders often resulted in opposition from them; this opposition usually compounded the problem of getting anything useful accomplished.

For these reasons, we shifted our focus from popular participation to *stakeholder participation*—the participation of all relevant stakeholders in the development process. This is a decision that we have made consciously and that will have important implications for the way the Bank works.

But although we argue that all stakeholders must work collaboratively to advance development projects, we recognize that different stakeholders have different levels of power, different interests, and different resources. For these reasons, we also recognize that arrangements are needed to level the playing field and enable different stakeholders to interact on an equitable and genuinely collaborative basis. Appendix I discusses the methods and tools that can be used for these purposes.

Achieving consensus and reconciling key stakeholder differences is not always easy; it may entail risks, such as generating or aggravating conflicts among groups with competing interests and priorities. Dealing with conflict often requires an understanding of the underlying societal interests inhibiting consensus and putting into place mechanisms for dispute resolution and negotiation.

REACHING THE POOR

As the *Sourcebook* examples illustrate, the poor face many barriers on a number of different levels that prevent them from having a real stake in development activities. Reaching and engaging the poor requires special arrangements and efforts by the sponsors and designers that go *beyond* those used to involve government officials and other relatively powerful stakeholders in participatory processes.

Who Are the Poor?

The poor include people in remote and impoverished areas. Women and children make up a large proportion of the very poor, which also includes people marginalized by virtue of their race and ethnicity as well as those disadvantaged by circumstances beyond their control, such as disabilities and natural or man-made disasters. Some of the poorest people live in countries characterized by weak governments and civil strife.

Because the poor are generally less educated and less organized than other more powerful stakeholders, because they are more difficult to reach, and because the institutions that serve them are often weak, interventions targeting the poor must often be small, context-specific, and resource-intensive.

Learning from the Poor

Task Managers, some of whose experiences are cited in Chapter II, are learning a great deal about reaching the poor and engaging them in their own development. Understanding how to do this calls in part for "bottom-up" approaches that begin by involving the poor and learning from them about their needs and priorities.

When we take a look at the types of methods and approaches that work best at the field level for engaging and enabling the poor to participate, we see that these are quite different from the set of techniques used when relatively sophisticated and powerful stakeholders are involved. The Chapter II examples indicate that stakeholder workshops and other planning methods, such as Objectives-Oriented Project Planning (ZOPP)* and Appreciation-Influence-Control (AIC) (see Appendix I for descriptions of both), tend to work well when

---

* From the German term *"Zielorientierte Projektplanung."*

the objective is to gain ownership and commitment on the part of stakeholders such as government officials and staff of international agencies. These examples also demonstrate that workshops can be structured to include the views of the poor, but this requires conscious and careful planning.

But, when the primary objective is to learn from and collaborate with the poor, a different kind of dynamic is involved that calls for a different approach to facilitating participation. These methods should engage poor people and build their confidence, knowledge base, and capability for action. Visual methods that are carried out in the local setting, using local materials and calling on local knowledge and expertise as inputs into project design are often used to good effect.

Building Capacity to Act

Getting the participation of the poor involves a lot more than finding the right technique. It requires strengthening the organizational and financial capacities of the poor so that they can act for themselves. In searching for ways to build local capacity, we found it useful to think in terms of a continuum along which the poor are progressively empowered.

On one end of this continuum, the poor are viewed as beneficiaries—recipients of services, resources, and development interventions. In this context, community organizing, training, and one-way flows of resources through grant mechanisms are often appropriate. Although much good work has been done in this mode, the provision of benefits delivered to people in this way may not be sustainable in the long term and may not improve the ability of people to act for themselves.

As the capacity of poor people is strengthened and their voices begin to be heard, they become "clients" who are capable of demanding and paying for goods and services from government and private sector agencies. Under these changed circumstances, the mechanisms to satisfy their needs will change as well. In this context, it becomes necessary to move away from welfare-oriented approaches and focus rather on such things as building sustainable, market-based financial systems; decentralizing authority and resources; and strengthening local institutions.

We reach the far end of the continuum when these clients ultimately become the owners and managers of their assets and activities. This stage ranks highest in terms of the intensity of participation involved. A question we asked ourselves while preparing the *Sourcebook* was, how can we support and prepare poor people to own and manage assets and activities in a sustainable manner? In part, we found out that the more poor people are involved upstream in the planning and decisionmaking process, the more likely they are to own a development intervention, contribute to it, and sustain it; this alone, however, is not sufficient.

Constraints exist at the policy level that impinge on the rights of people to organize, access information, engage in contracts, own and manage assets, and participate fully as members of civil society. Efforts are needed, therefore, to create an enabling policy environment that allows all stakeholders—especially poor and disadvantaged ones—to be part of the definition we noted at the outset. They too must be enabled to:

...influence and share control over development initiatives and the decisions and resources which affect them.

CHAPTER II

SHARING EXPERIENCES

Photo by Stefano Pagiola

In preparing the *Sourcebook* we discovered that the best way to learn about participation is to *experience it directly*. The second best way is by seeing what others have done in the name of participation, talking to them, and seeking their guidance. This chapter shares the experiences of individuals who supported participatory approaches in Bank operational activities. We have documented these examples to help Task Managers and other interested parties learn about participation from the practical experiences of their colleagues. They are presented in the first-person narrative, most often but not always by Bank Task Managers, the people with overall responsibility for processing Bank-supported projects and policy work.

NO PERFECT MODELS

We do not offer these examples as perfect models of how, for example, to plan a development project in a participatory manner. In fact, we believe that no "perfect model" for participation exists. The form participation takes is highly influenced by the overall circumstances and the unique social context in which action is being taken.

Whatever our initial intuition might have suggested, we observed that participation has many faces and ways of showing up in the multidimensional field of development—a field that embraces many different types of historical, political, cultural, sectoral, and institutional settings.

STILL MUCH TO BE LEARNED

We recognize that the Bank is in the process of learning how to introduce participatory approaches into its work, especially from those practitioners in developing countries who have been practicing participation for many years.

Because the Bank has a great deal to learn about using participatory approaches, you may wonder why we have not gone outside the institution in search of examples. The reason is that, at this initial stage, we feel the *Sourcebook* will be more useful, relevant, and convincing to Bank staff and managers if it is based on actual Bank staff experience with participatory approaches. By highlighting current Bank practices, the *Sourcebook* demonstrates that participation is not only possible but already underway in many Bank-supported activities. We hope to include examples from other organizations in future editions of the *Sourcebook*.

SELECTION BIASES

We selected the following examples from those we came to know through the work of the Bank's four-year Learning Group on Participatory Development. We have included examples of economic and sector work, investment projects, and a country implementation review—all of which were conducted in a participatory manner.

We acknowledge two limitations in the range of examples presented in this chapter. The first is that more of the examples are about participation during preparation and planning than during implementation. This does not mean we think the former are any more important than the latter. In fact, we want to be clear that participation is an *iterative process* that can and should be repeated at every stage of the Bank's project cycle. This "planning bias," however, does reflect that the Bank has only recently made an institutional commitment to supporting participatory approaches and most of the examples from which we had to choose are still in the "honeymoon" phase of the project cycle. Wherever we could, we have tried to include examples of participation during implementation. But beyond this, we will have to wait, watch, and document our experience in this area as it grows.

Perhaps more important, we have found that not all projects can be planned in detail from the outset. Many projects deal with stakeholders or sets of problems for which the exact modalities for achieving the set objectives are unknown at the start. These projects require flexible and iterative planning that can respond to changing situations and new information as it becomes available. Such projects need to be approached in an exploratory mode, in which future stages are planned in light of the outcome of initial interventions.

We have selected several examples because they illustrate how Bank Task Managers adapted a "process" approach for such operations. This entailed *(a)* piloting activities, *(b)* undertaking design concurrently with implementation, *(c)* introducing flexible targets, time frames, and funding mechanisms, and *(d)* encouraging other changes in the existing project cycle and operating procedures. These examples also document a significant shift in stance from emphasizing mechanistic "things" to emphasizing people, processes, and continuous learning.

A second limitation of the *Sourcebook* lies in the preponderance of examples that deal with Bank-financed projects as opposed to policy work. Again, this reflects the realities of Bank experience with participation to date. We hope to add more examples of participatory policy work as our experience grows.

THE MANY FACES OF PARTICIPATION

In selecting these examples, we have tried to reflect the impressive diversity of participatory practices across countries, sectors, and types of activities. For instance, we have included at least one example from each region of the Bank. We have also tried to represent a range of participatory techniques currently being used in Bank-supported operations. We are well aware, however, that for every example we included, many other equally innovative and instructive cases probably exist. We have been told so, in fact, by dozens of Bank staff who are working in a participatory manner in countries, sectors, or activities that have not been included in this edition of the *Sourcebook*.

INTENSITY OF PARTICIPATION

Another important criterion for selection was the *level* or *intensity* of participation illustrated by the examples. This is important because participation is an elastic term that can mean different things to different people in different institutions. All the examples you will read in the *Sourcebook* are situations in which the relevant stakeholders have engaged in *collaborative decisionmaking* as opposed to listening and consultation. In making this distinction, we are emphasizing the point that participation must involve some degree of shared control.

FINDING YOUR WAY THROUGH THE SOURCEBOOK

The map and table on the following pages will guide you to the examples most appropriate to your needs. You may wish to read a few of the examples representing the sector or region in which you work, or you may wish to choose examples based on participatory techniques you have heard about or the type of Bank activity in which you are involved. However you choose to start, you will probably find that reading an example will stimulate your interest in reading others and drawing your own conclusions about what works and what does not.

TABLE 2.1   GUIDE TO SOURCEBOOK EXAMPLES

Country	Sector	Activity	Technique	Starting Point	Stakeholders Involved	Community Organization
Albania	Rural Credit	Project	Generic	Preparation	G, I, D	Village Credit Committees
Benin	Health	Project	SW	Preparation	G, I, D	Village Health Committees
Brazil	Water/Urban	Project	Generic	Three years into Implementation	G, I, D	Homeowner Condominiums
Chad	Education	Project	ZOPP	Preparation	G, I	Parent-Teacher Associations
Colombia	Energy	ESW	AIC	Start of the Study	G, I	NA
Egypt	Natural Resource Management/ Agriculture	Project	PRA	Preparation	G, I, D	Community Resource Management Committees
India	Forestry	Project	ZOPP	Preparation	G, I, D	Forest Protection Committees
Lao People's Democratic Republic	Health	Project	SW	Mid-way through Preparation	G	NA
Mexico	Hydroelectric/ Resettlement	Project	Generic	Preparation	G, I, D	NA
Morocco	Women-in-Development	ESW	PRA	Beginning of Study	G, I, D	NA
Mozambique	Cross-Sectoral	CIR	SW	Start of the Review	G	NA
Nigeria	Agriculture	Project	SW	Preparation	G, I	Women's Groups
Pakistan	Public Sector Management/ Urban	Project	Action Research	Preparation	G	NA
Philippines	Biodiversity	Project	Generic	After Appraisal	G, I, D	Community Management Boards
Philippines	Irrigation	Project	Generic	Before Preparation	G, I, D	Irrigation Associations
Yemen, Rep. of	Education	Sector Adjustment Programs	SW	Preparation	G	Local Schools

Legend: *NA = Not Applicable*   *CIR= Country Implementation Review*   *ESW = Economic and Sector Work*
           G = Government Stakeholders
           I = Indirectly Affected Stakeholders (NGOs, intermediary organizations, technical bodies, and so on)
           D = Directly Affected Stakeholders (those who stand to benefit or lose from Bank-supported operations)

Techniques: *AIC = Appreciation-Influence-Control*   *PRA = Participatory Rural Appraisal*
               ZOPP = Objectives-Oriented Project Planning   *SW = Stakeholder Workshop*

MOROCCO

Through meetings and orientation workshops in participatory methods, TM convinces skeptical government officials to allow local women to participate in formulation of Women in Development strategy paper. Government agrees but stipulates that PRA must be carried out by Moroccans. Government and NGO personnel receive intensive training to undertake PRA in rural villages. Rural women are preparing their own recommendations for inclusion in the sector report.

YEMEN, REP. OF

Once government education officials focus on the quality of education instead of number of classrooms, teachers, and books, attention turns to the local schools. Workshops are used to give voice to headmasters and mistresses, local schools are empowered to create their own quality education programs with central government funding. The network of support generated by the participatory preparation approach keeps the momentum going during a change at the political level.

EGYPT

Bedouin representatives join government officials and consultants on a project design team. Planning sessions and PRA held in Bedouin communities. Separate planning sessions are held for women. Local people develop project implementation arrangements including community action plans.

MEXICO

Negotiations between the government and the Bank break off, in part over the government's reluctance to prepare participatory resettlement plans. When the government returns seven months later, however, the Bank helps CFE, the national power company, to develop decentralized outreach capacity, create appropriate incentives for its staff, and strengthen public accountability mechanisms.

COLOMBIA

When government asks the Bank to help deal with the bankruptcy of its electric power sector, TM responds with the recommendation that Colombians solve the problem themselves through a participatory AIC workshop. Workshop concludes that the main problem is lack of coordination among the many, diverse stakeholders. Workshop leads to the creation of an Energy Board to coordinate the entire sector; however, lack of follow-up limits progress.

The boundaries, colors, denominations and any other information shown on this map do not imply, on the part of The World Bank Group, any judgment on the legal status of any territory, or any endorsement or acceptance of such boundaries.

BRAZIL

Participatory subproject design saves a large loan component targeted at the poor from cancellation. A new procurement approach binds engineering firms and social organizers into joint ventures. Engineers and social organizers negotiate design and management of subprojects with slum dwellers. Women provide leadership in the slums. The Bank integrates structured learning into the project.

BENIN

TM convinces skeptical government officials and villagers of the utility of participatory approaches by holding town hall meetings in remote villages. Once the stakeholders are enlisted, the project is prepared through participatory planning workshops. A result of the effort is that villagers now serve on the boards of national bodies and carry out important local health care delivery responsibilities.

NIGERIA

When studies reveal that women are no[t] benefiting sufficiently from agricultura[l] extension services, the Bank brings repre[sentatives of government ministries an[d] state agriculture line departments togethe[r] in a three-day planning workshop to de[velop action plans for implementation o[f] the extension program. Due to several di[f]ficulties, women farmers are unable t[o] participate directly. Female extensio[n] agents, familiar with and able to represe[nt] the needs of women farmers, serve as su[r]rogates for them in participatory plannin[g] event.

ALBANIA

An urgent need exists to inject cash into impoverished mountain areas and provide employment opportunites. Prior to Bank-financed pilot, TM and Albanian consultants work with rural farming communities to design credit delivery mechanisms suitable for the poor. Sixty-three village credit funds are created as a result.

PAKISTAN

After piloting bureaucratic reorientation of the Water Board, an intervention is made through the preparation of the project to transform the core agencies of the Sindh Province to accomplish policy, financial, and institutional reform. A three-tiered participatory policy planning structure is institutionalized to bring together bureaucrats and politicians from different parts of the Sindh government. Accomplishments in the Sindh are being adopted elsewhere in the country.

INDIA

Bank helps mainstream the Forest Protection Committee approach initiated in West Bengal. Through this approach foresters shift out of a policing role to a social role that provides income to poor people and regenerates the forest. ZOPP workshop brings various government stakeholders together to collaboratively identify institutional changes needed to support participatory forestry.

LAO P.D.R.

Government officials, misunderstanding the Bank's role, thought the Bank prepared and implemented projects, much like NGOs have been doing in Laos. Midway through project preparation, TM used participatory workshops to engender ownership among central, state, and local government stakeholders.

PHILIPPINES

Bank and government undertake a Joint Consultative Appraisal Mission arranged by an NGO on discovering that expert-designed legislation and project overlooked needs and concerns of indigenous communities. NGOs conduct follow-up meetings with local stakeholders and participatory implementation arrangements are inserted into project to give local residents greater control over resources and decisionmaking in subprojects.

PHILIPPINES

In the late 1970s, the Filipino National Irrigation Agency (NIA) learns how to plan and manage communal irrigation schemes collaboratively with local farmers. At the time the Bank makes its first communal loan to NIA, the agency has already "mainstreamed" farmer participation as a standard practice. After verifying that the participatory practice is effective, the Bank TM spends most of his time helping NIA navigate through Bank and central government obstacles.

MOZAMBIQUE

TM assigned to the resident mission brings together the various parts of the government and the Bank to review implementation problems. Government participants develop an intragovernmental network as a result of the workshop. Overall relationships improve, but many implementation problems remain due to difficult country situation. Absence of the full range of stakeholders, especially politicians with the power to affect change, limits effectiveness.

CHAD

Government specifically requests participatory preparation. Preparation time and cost are very low. No women show up at planning sessions, and intermediaries represent their own interests instead of interests of the poor. Implementation arrangements include capacity building for parent associations.

ALBANIA

RURAL POVERTY ALLEVIATION PILOT PROJECT

Maria Nowak is the Task Manager for the Albania Rural Poverty Alleviation Pilot Project.

Photo by Kathryn Funk

Albania is the poorest country in Europe, with an estimated 1992 per capita GDP of under $400.* Amid political and economic turmoil, the centrally planned economy collapsed in 1992, giving way to a democratically elected government and ending Albania's forty-year isolation from the rest of the world. Revolution and reform have resulted in an abrupt transition to a market economy, which has had a dramatic impact on Albania's rural population.

The dismantling of agricultural cooperatives and rapid privatization of land has transformed state farm workers into private land owners whose average holding is a meager 1.4 hectares per family. People were expected to create farms out of their new plots to provide food for their families but have been unable to do so because of a lack of start-up capital to purchase inputs and supplies. Without the necessary tools, inputs, and opportunities, people were surviving on little more than food aid. To make matters worse, rural infrastructure was destroyed during the revolution along with rural organizations in charge of its development and maintenance. The challenge was clear: get village infrastructure up and running, provide employment opportunities for local people, and find a way to inject cash into the most impoverished areas—fast.

LEARNING BY DOING

The government's reform program, including restructuring Albania's entire banking system, would take time to take effect, but in the immediate term we knew that something had to be done to address the desperate situation of farm-

---

* *Unless otherwise indicated in the text, dollars indicate U.S. currency.*

ing families in the mountainous areas. The system had no capacity to lend small amounts to 3,000 small farmers. Given the urgency of the situation, we decided to begin immediately with operational activities. Setting up a formal, traditional, "top-down" structure for operations would have entailed a long, bureaucratic process, so we opted for a quicker, more informal route. We chose to take a "learning-by-doing" approach and train our Albanian counterparts "on the job" and in the field.

In attempting this, we were entering uncharted territory with no prior experience on which to build. Our first objective was to find out what would work. For example, what type of credit delivery mechanism would be most suitable for reaching the poor? A typical Bank-supported project would have undertaken a sector study. But in this case, we couldn't do studies because there was nothing to study! Everything was new. We were operating in a climate with so many unknown factors and uncertainties that adopting an experimental and participatory approach seemed the most sensible way to proceed. In fact, there was really no other way. We needed to work with the villagers to test out different ideas and mechanisms.

This in itself presented a challenge, given that "bottom-up" participation was a completely new approach in a country where everything had been decided at the top. So, not surprisingly, some government officials were skeptical and viewed this approach as a waste of time. After all, "credit delivery is a complex topic," they argued. "What would rural peasants know about such things?" During the course of our discussions, however, we realized that some key people within the Ministry of Agriculture were receptive to this approach. By building an alliance with them, we were able to obtain the support and encouragement needed to proceed.

PARTICIPATORY DESIGN OF CREDIT COMPONENT

In August 1992 we began a small test project with seed money from the United Nations Development Programme and Frères d'Espérance, a French nongovernmental organization (NGO). Before studying, we began *doing*. The availability of flexible funds allowed us to start experimenting and spending money right away. We were convinced that the only way to understand what could work was to see it in action. We wanted to give money to people and observe what happened. This would provide us, we hoped, with the information needed to design a larger pilot project to be financed by the Bank.

We began by advertising in the national newspaper for two Albanian counterparts with experience in microcredit

to join our team. We hired two consultants, one a physics professor at the university and the other an engineer. We took them to the villages to see how they interacted with the farming communities. An important criterion in hiring them was their desire and ability to work in a participatory manner. Given the situation, we realized how important this personal interaction would be to the success of our efforts. I also brought along two foreign consultants to help us design the process. Once the team was assembled, we asked the Ministry of Agriculture to choose a district not too far from the capital to launch the "pre-pilot."

We met first with the district authorities and the commune chiefs who helped us identify the poorest villages. No official village organizations existed at the time, so we met with village "chiefs" and informal village councils of different sorts. We wanted the meetings to be as informal as possible and open to anyone in the village who was interested, so we held them under a tree where passers-by could join us.

It was difficult at first to get things started. Working in an Eastern European context posed all sorts of problems, not the least of which was simply explaining the concept of individual "credit" to the local farming communities, who had never heard of such a notion. Many were initially frightened by the idea of assuming personal risk. It was quite a challenge in the beginning to introduce such foreign concepts as "inflation" or explain why it was necessary to charge "interest" on loans.

These meetings constituted the start of a series of extensive conversations and repeated interactions between groups of villagers and the Albanian members of our team, who were charged with carrying on the process after the rest of us left. The fact that we had money available right away was key. It meant we could start experimenting immediately with the different ideas being proposed. Not only did this expedite the process, it was critical in establishing our credibility among the initially skeptical village communities.

VILLAGE CREDIT FUNDS

We concentrated our efforts on four villages that had shown the greatest interest in collaborating with us. Through repeated visits, we worked with the local people to come up with a design for the credit program. My colleagues and I had certain preconceived ideas about what might work. I had prior experience in Bangladesh with the Grameen Bank and then had worked for more than thirty years in Africa where I also helped to adapt the Grameen model of group-based rural credit to the local context. Later, I had founded an NGO in France to develop credit for self-employment. So I was influenced by my own experiences and was therefore thinking along the lines of a solidarity group-lending approach.

When we introduced this notion to the villagers, however, we were surprised by their response. Although they were enthusiastic about the prospect of receiving credit, they rejected the idea of solidarity groups outright. To them, it too closely resembled the communist system they had just cast away. But, although they were fed up with cooperatives, they were eager to restore village solidarity. So they took *our* idea and adapted it to suit *their* needs. The result was group lending "Albanian style."

Together, we decided on a "village credit fund" (VCF) in which the entire village is held accountable for the loans of its members. In other words, if anyone in the village defaults, the whole VCF could be in jeopardy of being cut off. In hindsight, this approach has proved extremely effective and, thus far, has resulted in a 100 percent repayment rate in sixty-two of the sixty-three VCFs. This is quite remarkable in a country where the repayment rate to formal banking institutions is a real problem.

Designing this credit component was truly an interactive process between our team and the villagers. In one instance, the consultant had just finished explaining the rationale for charging interest on loans and was working with the group to decide collectively on an interest rate. The consultant proposed indexing the interest rate to the price of a cow (which was a commodity of real value within these communities). Again, the villagers did not like this idea. They argued that all cows were not the same and were not worth equal sums of money. After much discussion, it was decided to index interest rates to the US dollar.

VILLAGE CREDIT COMMITTEES

To ensure that decisionmaking control remained at the local level, we jointly decided that each village would elect a three-person "village credit committee" (VCC) to decide who would receive funds and oversee the disbursement and repayment of loans to borrowers. Because the members of the VCC were themselves from the village, they knew the applicants and could assess their creditworthiness based on personal knowledge. The funds were disbursed from the implementing agency, the Rural Development Fund (RDF) (see below) and deposited in tranches directly into local branches of the state-owned Rural Commercial Bank to be accessed solely by the VCCs. An RDF credit officer and a member of the local Rural Commercial Bank played an advisory role on the VCCs.

Eligibility criteria for loans were also developed in conjunction with the villagers. Although funds were not specifically targeted at the poorest families, the VCCs had made a clear agreement that they intended the funds for those least well-off in the villages. The $500 limit on loans "selected out" those better off among the group since the amount was too low for their purposes. Ultimately, however, it was up to the VCCs, which held public meetings, to evaluate loan applications and to decide who in the village would receive funds. Interestingly, many VCCs chose to decrease the amount of the individual loans from $300 to $200, so that more families could receive credit sooner rather than later.

RURAL DEVELOPMENT FUND

It was decided during appraisal that the Rural Poverty Alleviation Pilot Project would be best implemented by an autonomous transition agency that would be outside government. This decision was based on the fact that the existing administration did not have the ability to carry out the project in a participatory manner nor the outreach to interact at the local level with several thousand small farmers. In another country, NGOs may have assumed this role, but in Albania no such NGOs existed. So, in January 1993, the Rural Development Fund (RDF) was established by government decree. As an autonomous agency, it was given the responsibility for implementing both the pilot and subsequent full-scale project. It was given administrative, financial, and technical autonomy and the authority to enter into contracts.

The RDF is governed by a Board of Trustees who are the ministers of the relevant ministries, such as labor, finance, and agriculture and chaired by the deputy prime minister. It is run by an Albanian executive director and an executive committee made up of the heads of the credit and infrastructure departments. The credit program is decentralized with credit officers in every participating district. They attend VCC meetings and follow up on loan repayment. All decisionmaking concerning the VCFs rests at the local level. RDF engineers also work closely with communes and villages in implementing rural infrastructure projects, which constitute the other major component of the program. The RDF has now attracted other cofinanciers including the government of Italy, the European Union, and the International Fund for Agricultural Development (IFAD).

MONITORING AND EVALUATION

Establishing a separate department within the RDF for project monitoring and evaluation has proved difficult. At the beginning, the RDF staff person charged with this responsibility was not open to new methods and ideas and was simply not the right type of person for the job. Subsequent staff have been more open-minded, and some progress is now being made. Midway through the pilot project, we undertook an evaluation in the form of an impact study. The project hired foreign consultants to establish the framework for the study, and a team of Albanians—from the large pool of previous cooperative farm technical staff—were trained and hired to carry out the surveys.

Although the establishment of a separate monitoring and evaluation unit has been slow and difficult, the small credit program itself continues to incorporate participatory monitoring and feedback effectively. For example, through discussions with the villagers and VCC members, it was learned that farmers wanted the loan ceiling raised. In the first phase of the project, most farmers had used their loans to purchase livestock. Now they wanted to invest in larger, more capital-intensive items, such as small tractors, mills, and transport. As a direct response to this feedback, the project was modified and loan ceilings were doubled from $500 to $1,000.

DISTRICT WORKSHOPS

Regular district seminars and workshops have done a lot to promote dialogue, information sharing, and learning among project participants from different areas. The Albanian consultant, who now heads the RDF's credit department, organizes training seminars every two to three months, which bring together VCC members from various districts. These typically two-day workshops are held in a local school with the RDF covering the costs of transport, food, and accommodation for the participants. During these seminars, representatives of the various VCCs make presentations on the way the credit program runs in their villages. They share new ideas and experiments they are undertaking and discuss the obstacles and problems they face.

For example, one VCC went beyond basic credit and started experiments to mobilize savings by soliciting contributions from its members. They received help in setting up the necessary procedures from their district credit officer. I was pleased to learn about this initiative, because we had been planning to introduce a savings component in the next phase of the project in 1995. We have found, however, that introducing new ideas and concepts is much easier when they come from the people themselves. After all, when local people themselves invent practical ways to get things of value done, they are more likely to commit themselves to it. Now that the idea of savings mobilization has been planted by one VCC, it has proved contagious, spreading among communities as other VCCs are eager to introduce the concept in their villages. Local people are starting to really feel that they own the system and, as a result, are willing to take on greater responsibilities and risks.

NEXT STEPS

This project, particularly the provision of credit to small farmers, progressively creates new needs and, therefore, is growing and expanding at a rapid pace. Enabling farmers to purchase livestock has led to the creation of local "animal health associations," financed jointly by the RDF and farmer contributions. These indigenously derived associations, which ensure the vaccination of all livestock, are the first signs of what I think will be a growing trend to diversify activities and a growing demand for technical assistance and larger amounts of capital lending as farmers branch into animal breeding and other related activities. Already, they are moving toward off-farm activities, which are being financed under the credit program.

In response to this, the follow-up to the pilot, the Rural Development Project, which became effective in May 1995, will provide technical support for these new activities through the creation of a microenterprise support department within the RDF to help farmers use the right technology and find markets. The upcoming $12 million project will include the creation of 125 additional "village credit funds" throughout Albania.

TIME AND MONEY

The participatory preparation of the project actually took little time. The first preparation mission was in August 1992, and the project was passed by the Bank's Board in February 1993. A consensus existed among relevant Bank staff that the project was needed quickly, so they agreed that the pre-pilot phase and experience was equivalent to a project appraisal. Supervision of the project, however, has been time consuming. This may partly be due to its participatory nature (which makes supervision more complicated than simply going to a ministry with a checklist), but it also has to do with Albania's transition economy and the fact that RDF has financing from five or six donors.

As for the costs of preparation, our experience has been that participatory preparation costs less than doing expert studies, because participation involves local people rather than many foreign consultants. As mentioned before, the pre-pilot was paid for by the United Nations Development Programme and Frères d'Espérance. The amount allocated for the credit component during the pre-pilot phase was $20,000. The project impact study cost about $60,000, most of which was used to hire a foreign consultant. This was paid out of project funds. The district workshops were very inexpensive.

ON REFLECTION

An added twist to this project is that we are operating in an Eastern European environment. Believe me when I say that it is a completely different and often difficult context in which to work. In this project, we had to introduce western management concepts, but, even after two years of repeated interaction and training, it is clear that the Albanians are still not comfortable with these concepts of management and often insist on doing things their way. For example, our team really took for granted the tradition of writing down and documenting procedures and activities. Albanians, however, have an "oral" culture; they don't understand our fixation on preparing agendas or reports. For them, this information is stored in their heads, and they much prefer to tell you about it than write it down.

Similarly, when it came to recruiting local staff for the project, the Albanians were baffled by our request that job descriptions and selection criteria be drawn up. Furthermore, they were surprised when we began choosing candidates based on their professional qualifications. Again, we had taken this for granted but soon realized that this was not the Albanian way. Instead, people are hired on the basis of their "biography"—in other words, according to the political history of their family over the last two generations. So whether one's uncle was a good communist or one has any relatives in prison is given more importance than professional background.

I am continually reminded that much of what we take for granted simply does not always correspond to any precise concept in the Albanian context. In dealing with procurement and disbursement, I was shocked to discover that when local communes ordered supplies from a state enterprise, the standard procedure was to send a blank check, which would eventually be returned three months later with a fixed price filled in by the state. After so many years in a centrally planned system, competitive bidding and western accounting practices are just not something people can relate to easily.

Trying to apply Bank regulations in such a situation is complicated at best. As a Bank Task Manager, this means you have to be flexible, be willing to compromise and adapt, and learn how business is done "Albanian style." This understanding does not develop overnight, but over time a process of cross-fertilization occurs in which each side learns from the other. I think this is the way it should be.

I also think the reason a great many of these projects fail is that we try to interject our style of doing things into a context that has a completely different history, tradition, and mode of interaction. The reason the Albania Rural Poverty Alleviation Pilot project has worked well and has progressed quickly is because we started small, included local people, and then scaled up over time. This has allowed people to get used to the project, understand it, feel comfortable with it, and claim it as their own. Of course, this is not possible for all projects; for example, you would not build a dam with NGO seed money and piloting. But for this type of rural development project, the "process approach" has really worked well.

BENIN

HEALTH SERVICES DEVELOPMENT PROJECT

Michael Azefor, Task Manager of the first Benin Health Services Development Project, was appointed as the Bank's resident representative in Benin in October 1995. Denise Vaillancourt is the Task Manager of the second project.

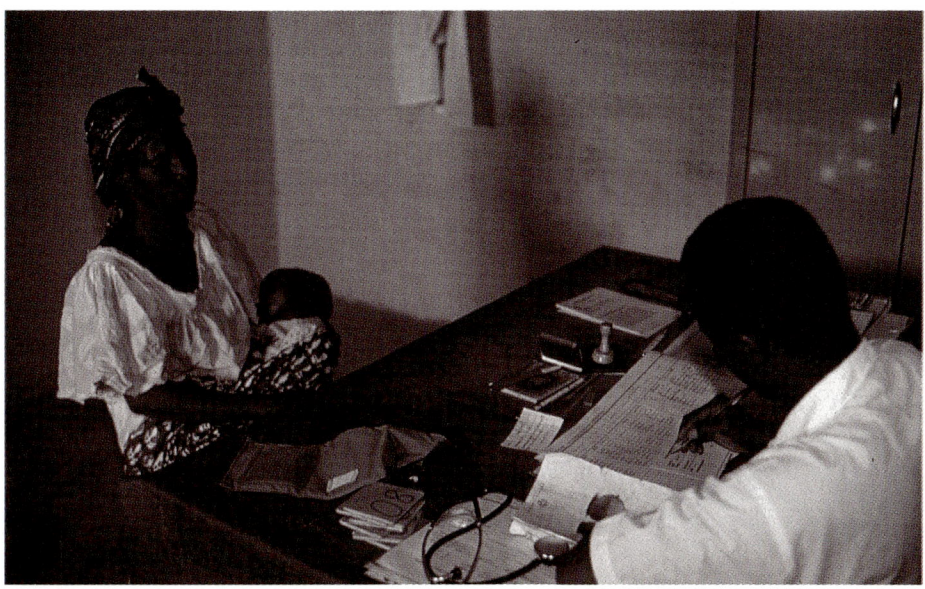

Photo by Curt Carnemark

In 1972 Benin became a leading innovator in primary health care, when it designed—without outside help—a unique, state-of-the-art primary health care system involving rural populations and covering the entire country. By 1986, however, Benin's primary health care ranked among the poorest in Africa.

IDENTIFICATION MISSION

When the government of Benin asked the Bank for help in this area, we suggested we start by finding out why the original strategy failed. In February 1988 I led an identification mission accompanied by a Bank health management specialist and an architect. As agreed in advance of our departure, we joined forces with staff from Benin's Finance, Planning, Health, and Rural Development Ministries. These were the appropriate government stakeholders who had to work together to provide primary health care. Although some were a bit skeptical, our government colleagues agreed that, to learn more about the problems in the primary health care system, we had to begin with the local health centers and communities they serve.

We decided to visit three districts that were the focal point of some previous project preparation work to see to what extent we could build on what had already been done. Before arriving in a district, we requested that an open meeting be arranged. The purpose of the meeting, we said, was to find out what the people of the community expected from government by way of primary health care and what they were willing to do themselves to have the kind of health care they wanted. All told, we held eight meetings that were attended by representatives of some thirty-two villages. Sometimes, the entire village showed up.

PARTICIPATORY DISCUSSIONS

Long a Marxist state, Benin was just beginning to change. Needless to say, local people had some difficulty in participating in open discussions. Some said they were too "busy" doing other things to attend, and no women showed up at all. Nevertheless, we were able to get across that our objective was to learn from the people about their situation and what they felt they needed. We said we did not want a project that only represented the thinking of the World Bank and central officials. We asked the communities to appoint a committee of five or so local people who were wise about money, life, health, and how the community worked. We also stipulated that at least one or two mothers be included. These committees helped validate our analysis of systemic and operational problems that contributed to poor health care in Benin.

Before organizing the next phase of the work, we checked back to see if community representatives had been named. The communities had indeed done this and presented us with the names of five people from villages in each of the three districts we had visited.

PREPARING THE PROJECT

Now that we had identified a good set of village stakeholders, we set up a workshop to generate a diagnosis of the existing primary health care system. A member of the Bank team—the architect—had experience in running participatory workshops. He served as the workshop designer and facilitator. The minister of health issued invitations to representatives of communities in a sample of three districts in various regions of the country for a workshop in Cotonou, Benin's capital, and we reserved a hall in the ministry that was large enough to accommodate the eighty participants.

About fifty participants came from the various communities we had visited. They were ordinary citizens, including about twenty mothers, rather than the tribal chiefs who usually represent the villages. A few technical staff from local German and Swiss projects also attended.

In addition to the village stakeholders, we invited officials from the central ministries, regional and district health offices, and local health centers. We did this to be sure we would be working on the entire system of health care rather than just part.

Brainstorming

On the first day we brainstormed about health issues and problems. Each participant had the opportunity to cite a problem. We went around the room again and again until all problems were written up on sheets of flip chart paper, which we mounted on the walls. The participants then assigned the problems to several categories they established: buildings and facilities, medicine, staffing and skills, primary health care, and so on.

We then spent a significant amount of time discussing the diagnosis of Benin's current health care system, using the categorized list of problems as the basis for discussion. We did this to be sure that the different types of people attending the conference—from village mother to high-ranking government official to World Bank staff member—understood the problems in the same way.

Small Group Work

After attaining closure on the diagnosis, we devoted the second day to developing appropriate ways to solve the problems. To do this, we broke into small groups, each of which dealt with one of the major problem areas. We made sure that the officials responsible for the areas being addressed were part of the group. The villagers chose for themselves the groups they wanted to join. As might be expected, group size turned out unevenly and some balancing had to be done. On completing the work, the small groups reported their conclusions to a plenary session. A discussion of the recommendations took up the remainder of the day.

A small group of officials from the Ministries of Health, Finance, Planning, and Rural Development then wrote up the conclusions of the workshop and shared them with all participants. The proceedings subsequently served as health policy and guided the work of ministry officials in preparing the specifics of the project proposal.

Feedback

Before completing the mission, the joint Bank-ministry team again visited the original villages to discuss the results of the workshop and see if the recommendations were what people really wanted. The villagers supported the work of their representatives, giving the design team further confidence that it was on the right track.

PREAPPRAISAL

In April 1988 the Bank team returned to Benin for preappraisal. Again we held a workshop with representatives of the same four stakeholder groups (villagers and officials from the ministries, health offices, and local health centers) who had attended the first workshop. This time, participants reviewed the written project proposal to ensure that it was consistent with what was learned and understood several months back. About sixty-five people attended the second workshop. We again assigned small groups to work on the same categories identified at the first workshop.

The written proposal was a good reflection of what the participants wanted. Two new concerns appeared, however. The first had to do with who really represents and speaks for the villages. After considerable debate, the participants decided that village representatives should be elected democratically and that the village should enter into a legal contract with the Ministry of Health (MOH), defining the responsibilities of both parties for improving the health status of the local populations.

The second had to do with implementation priorities. The communities with which we were working were not necessarily those with the greatest need. Although they recognized that other communities were in really dire straits, the participants nevertheless felt that their communities deserved priority given their involvement. In the final analysis, all concluded that it would be best to continue working with the same set of stakeholders during initial implementation.

APPRAISAL

The Bank team returned in June 1988 to appraise a project that now looked like this:

- Improve the quality of primary health care delivery at all levels of the country
- Develop pilot hygiene and sanitation programs for disadvantaged urban communities
- Improve sector financial resource mobilization, allocation, and management capabilities
- Strengthen institutional capabilities of the MOH
- Improve human resource capabilities in the health sector.

For a third time, we organized a workshop with the same stakeholders to review the final version of the project. By that time, we had gone over it carefully and put it into Bank style and format. In so doing, we believed we had not strayed from what the stakeholders said they wanted and were willing to do. But the only way we could be sure was to subject it fully to the scrutiny of those stakeholders who had been working on this project since the beginning. As it turned out, our proposal did indeed reflect what they wanted and had been proposing all along.

ENCOUNTERING DELAYS

As we were reviewing the project in Washington and getting ready to invite government for negotiations, the Swiss Development Corporation indicated that it wanted to increase its cofinancing contribution by more than fourfold. Of course, we in the Bank welcomed cofinancing as a matter of policy, so we were pleased with the Swiss offer. It meant, however, returning to Benin for a joint reappraisal of the project during which time the Swiss became full partners in supporting and nurturing the participatory process. We then had to change the project to accommodate budget cuts mandated by the structural adjustment program. As a result, we didn't begin negotiations until March 1989. The Bank's Board approved the project in June 1989 and the credit became effective in January 1990.

COST

The Bank's applied time devoted to this project from February 1988 to appraisal in June 1988 was about forty-three staff weeks. Appraisal added another twenty-one staff weeks. Government paid the modest costs of the three workshops—around $6,000. Preparing this project in a participatory manner was neither expensive nor time-consuming.

IMPLEMENTATION EXPERIENCE

The project has just started its fifth year of implementation. After matters delaying loan effectiveness were cleared up, the first year went extremely well. In every respect, the pace of implementation that year was well above any reasonable expectation for a project like this. I attribute this to the high levels of commitment of all concerned and to the thorough understanding of objectives, strategies, and tactics all stakeholders developed in working together. This understanding and the commitment it generates are attributable, in my opinion, to the participatory project planning processes we used.

It is unfortunate that implementation ran into trouble during the second year. A new democratically elected government cleaned house at the center. An entirely new team of officials appeared on the scene, who not only knew nothing about the project but were also distrustful of anything done by the previous government; thus, every aspect of the project involving the MOH came to a halt. The dynamism at the local level, however, did not wane during this period. By the third year we were pretty much back on track, and the project is doing well in all important respects.

SECOND PROJECT

The design and development of a second project, presented to the Bank's Board in May 1995, closely followed the participatory process, which had proved so effective the first time around. Virtually all meetings with the government, which occurred during the series of World Bank missions concerning this project, were attended by representatives of *all* key stakeholder groups including local health committee members from all over the country. Preparation of this project was intimately linked with government efforts to prepare a revised national health strategy for the period 1995-99, which was the subject of a Health Sector Round Table held in January 1995. We were quite successful in encouraging the government to give stakeholder participation more prominence in the sector strategy, both by highlighting accomplishments to date and by outlining steps to consolidate and build on successes in this regard. To make an effective contribution to the strategy from a participation perspective, the Bank mission undertook numerous field visits with MOH staff and held town hall meetings to discuss the views of the various stakeholders on their participation experience thus far.

ACHIEVEMENTS

With only about 50 percent of the credit disbursed and a closing date scheduled for 1997, assistance under the first project has already resulted in a number of notable achievements, which have both expanded and clarified the role of various stakeholders (including the ministry) in the planning, financing, execution, and evaluation of sector activities. For me, the most notable among these achievements include the following:

- The creation of local health management committees—*comité de gestion de la commune* (COGEC) and *comité de gestion de la sous-préfecture* (COGES)—with real authority and autonomy, through which communities throughout Benin manage cost recovery funds and participate in the planning, implementation, and evaluation of sector activities carried out in health facilities. The members are elected democratically, and anyone may serve, provided that at least one member is a woman.

- The establishment of a central procurement agency (Centrale d'Achat), which assures the affordability and constant availability of essential generic drugs at all levels of the health system and is managed by an autonomous board, composed of various stakeholders and including representatives of local health management committees. Previously, drug procurement was done—poorly and corruptly—by the MOH itself. Given the fact that no drugs are produced in Benin for its small market, this wasn't a job that could

be handled well by the private sector. What was needed was a small cadre of people who could follow the international pharmaceutical industry and wisely buy the small quantities Benin needs. The agency is kept responsive to the communities through the villagers sitting on its board.

- The establishment of Comité National de suivi d'Execution et d'Évaluation des Programmes du Secteur de la Santé (CNEEP), an intersectoral committee at the national level, and Comité Departemental de suivi d'Execution et d'Évaluation des Programmes du Secteur de la Santé (CDEEP) at the departmental level. These interministerial committees undertake periodic assessments of the progress made in implementing the objectives set out in the national health strategy. They are composed of high-level representatives of central and line ministries and other key stakeholders.

- The reorganization of the MOH, which, following an organizational audit, encompasses the creation of three new directorates for *(a)* planning, coordination, and evaluation, *(b)* administration and finance, and *(c)* family health and the strengthening of departmental directorates for health to accommodate the government's intention to decentralize sector management and administration.

ISSUES

- *Local health committees:* After several years of operation, COGES and COGEC have demonstrated their potential. This experience has also highlighted issues that still need to be addressed. For example, some COGES/COGEC members lack motivation because of a number of factors, most notably a lack of *(a)* understanding of their roles and functions, *(b)* skills in community financial management and group animation techniques, *(c)* opportunity to exchange information and ideas at the departmental and national levels, and, for some, *(d)* financial remuneration. Although the bylaws of the local health management committees state that elections should be held every two years, elections have not been held that frequently or routinely. Some aspects of financial management of these committees are not fully explicit in the bylaws. Furthermore, accounting capacity is lacking. Also, although COGEC bylaws provide for one seat each for a woman and a youth, elected by their peers to represent their interests, COGES members are elected from among the COGEC officers (presidents, treasurers, and secretaries) leaving the possibility that women and youth may not be represented at the subprefecture level.

CASES

- *Intersectoral coordination.* The establishment in 1988 of CNEEP and CDEEP constituted an important step by the government to improve program coordination and to strengthen decisionmaking capacity in the MOH. Their creation was meant to correct weaknesses in the planning, coordination, monitoring, and evaluation of sector investments, which were largely donor-driven. Since their creation, these two organs of intersectoral coordination have not been sufficiently active, particularly at the departmental level; they must be revitalized to enable them to carry out their important functions. Furthermore, although their membership accommodates representatives from other line ministries and some NGOs, at present no permanent seat exists for representatives of the local health committees, whose perspectives on investment planning and monitoring would be valuable.

- *Policy and institutional reforms.* In addition to the Bank's success in strengthening and concretizing the language on participation in the draft national health strategy for the period 1995-99, we made two other important contributions to strengthening partnerships in health. First, we worked with government to prepare a revision to the administrative text that lays out the bylaws of COGEC and COGES. Major amendments were introduced to *(a)* expand membership to other partners working on related issues in the same commune or subprefecture (NGOs, indigenous social groups, school teachers, personnel working on relevant development projects such as water and sanitation, and so on), *(b)* clarify aspects of financial management and other operations, *(c)* establish two additional seats on the COGES and mandate that they be filled by one woman and one youth, and *(d)* specify procedures for hiring with COGEC/COGES' own funds, independent auditors to audit their own accounts annually.

We also worked with government on a draft decree amending the bylaws and internal regulations of CNEEP and CDEEP to replace the 1988 decree creating these committees. Amendments were introduced to *(a)* specify the functions and staff profiles for their respective secretariats, *(b)* provide for the representation of COGEC and COGES and other key nongovernmental partners in these entities, and *(c)* to streamline its operations. These two texts will be signed by the time this project is presented to the World Bank's Board of Executive Directors.

CAPACITY BUILDING

Second, direct project support will be given to COGES/ COGEC and CNEEP/CDEEP to strengthen their capaci-

ties. Considerable effort will be warranted under the project to ensure the following:

- Operations at these various levels are realistic in terms of the capability, availability, interests, and comparative advantages of the various partners.
- Health managers and other health personnel work effectively and in cooperation with partners.
- The need for conflict management is appreciated and effectively met.
- Partners will occasionally be given the opportunity to share experiences and exchange ideas and best practices with their counterparts at the various levels of the system.
- Information on the perspectives of the partners and the quality and extent of participation flows freely and expeditiously, both up and down the system.

As part of its annual review of sector performance, CNEEP and CDEEP will evaluate progress made in building and sustaining participation of key stakeholders in health and will revise plans for the coming year accordingly. Central MOH, in consultation with COGES/ COGEC members and decentralized MOH staff, has compiled a list of indicators for monitoring performance in this regard. The project will also support the costs of strengthening the capability of CNEEP and CDEEP to undertake participatory planning and evaluation of sector activities as well as the costs of their operations.

RESULTS

Although the Benin case is very much alive and ongoing, the participatory approach has already had positive impact on the lives of community members. Three years into the first project, an independent survey directed by a local sociologist was commissioned to obtain feedback from people who participated in preparing the project. Through interviews and focus groups involving elected village representatives and other villagers; local, regional, and central health officials; and the personnel of health facilities, the following was learned:

- Village people now know more about what health services are available.
- People are satisfied with the increased availability and decreased cost of drugs through health centers (and, as a result, increased utilization of health services).
- Funding for essential drugs is guaranteed, because local health committees, not the minister of health, manage the cost recovery funds.

- People appreciate the local control they now have over funds collected by the health facilities. (These funds now more than cover replenishment of drug stocks and, in some cases, even other essential nonsalary operating costs.)
- The involvement of women in the project is a strong factor in building community support and has raised the status of women as community leaders.

Perhaps the most significant of the findings of this beneficiary assessment is that local health staff are performing better. Roles and responsibilities of the different actors and stakeholders in the sector have been recast in a significant way, causing the system of accountabilities to be altered. Increasingly, MOH staff—particularly service providers—are accountable to those they serve (their clients) rather than exclusively to their superiors in the administration, which had been the case in Benin several years ago. This is due in large part to the fact that their clients are now involved in the planning of health sector interventions and in the evaluation of health sector performance.

Central MOH staff visiting and collaborating with communities is now becoming much more standard practice—even in the absence of World Bank missions. The participatory approach is evolving beyond the preparation and implementation of Bank-financed projects to becoming a permanent way of doing business for the health sector in Benin.

BRAZIL

MUNICIPALITIES AND LOW-INCOME SANITATION

Abel Mejia was the Task Manager for the Brazil Municipalities and Low-Income Sanitation Project.

In February 1992—just three months after joining the Bank—I went on mission to Brazil to decide the fate of a problem project, one that might quite possibly be canceled. The problem was clear: the portion of the project that would provide water and sanitation to slum communities wasn't moving. No disbursements had been made three years after effectiveness on this part of the loan (62 percent of the total) and no real prospects were foreseeable for disbursing them.

This project was intended to bring water and sewerage to some of the most congested and difficult slums in the world. The notorious *favelas*—or shantytowns—of Rio were among the intended beneficiaries. It seemed to me that this is exactly the kind of loan the Bank should be making. Cancellation would be unfortunate.

INCREASING FRUSTRATION

Canceling, however, would surprise no one. My colleagues in the World Bank who prepared and appraised the original project beginning in 1986, were quite discouraged about its prospects. They had tried time and time again to get Caixa Economica Federal (CEF), the Brazilian government's gigantic national development bank and the implementing agency, to move ahead—all to no avail.

Preparation of this project began in collaboration with Brazil's National Housing Bank—an institution well known to the World Bank and quite competent at water and sewerage work. But along the way, the National Housing Bank ceased to exist by the stroke of a political pen. CEF took over BNH's responsibilities.

From every appearance, CEF had the ability to make sound loans for water and sanitation systems. But, as it turned out, CEF management's heart just wasn't in dealing with slums and slum dwellers—perhaps understandably, because few successful precedents exist for providing water and sanitation to the *favelas* and their counterparts throughout the world. Bills aren't paid, illegal connections blossom, and care and maintenance are the exception rather than the rule. For lenders and water companies alike, serving the slums has been a losing proposition, and few advocates of doing so can be found in water companies.

COULD PARTICIPATION HELP?

As I prepared for the mission, I learned that staff from the Bank's Transportation, Water, and Urban Development Department's Water and Sewerage Division (TWUWS) had been visiting Brazil during the past year to help us get this loan moving. Their interest was the same as ours: to find ways to prevent the cancellation of this innovative project.

TWUWS believed that involving slum dwellers in the design, operation, and maintenance of a water and sewerage system was the only way it could be done well. TWUWS wanted to do "action research" in the area of community participation in water and sewerage systems, something they called "structured learning." My own previous experience in rural irrigation for poor farmers led me to the same conclusion about involving the people. Clearly we were *simpatico*.

My colleagues in TWUWS had been hard at work in Brazil identifying allies who wished to move ahead with this loan and its purpose. They had identified allies in CEF, in the state and municipal water companies, and in the nongovernmental sector. Although they hadn't yet succeeded in getting the loan moving, they told me that the new project manager in CEF, a veteran from the National Housing Bank's Water and Sewerage Department, was enthusiastic about the project.

PLANNING THE MISSION

We wanted to get this project moving and moving in the right direction. But, at the same time, we had to face reality. On the positive side, we knew that CEF had lending agreements with eight or so state water companies (SWCs) and that these companies wanted to borrow for capital investments. We also knew that we had an action-oriented person running the project in CEF, and allies in the SWCs.

We met with the SWCs, along with CEF, and laid our cards on the table. We said that we would have to recommend canceling the low-income part of the loan if the SWCs were unable to submit borrowing proposals to CEF within the next two months. We told them, if they submitted proposals, it would be possible to persuade our management that things were moving on this loan. But, it was up to them, we said, as only they knew what could be done.

Our strategy worked. Within two months we had proposals from six of the eight companies, and CEF knew others were on the way. Unfortunately, the proposals were wish lists, lacking practical ways to design water and sewerage systems in the *favelas*.

THE *FAVELA* CHALLENGE

Developing an efficient and effective water and sewerage system for any *favela*—and particularly a Rio *favela*—is a real challenge. Rio *favelas* climb the high hills surrounding the city. Houses appear to sit on top of one another and often do. Population density is extremely high. Their layout has no rhyme or reason. Virtually every bit of space is in use by someone somehow. The laying of pipes, even underground, would more than likely intrude on someone's sense of ownership. Adjudicating disputes from the outside can be next to impossible.

At the same time, the laws of hydraulics can't be changed, and engineers don't like to negotiate their designs with nonengineers. Setting the reservoir higher than the houses is much cheaper than pumping the water up to them. The number of users and the volumes to be delivered determine the size of the pipe, regardless of whether a convenient place can be located to lay the pipe. It's almost impossible to get to one house without going through or under someone else's. In addition, *favela* populations are not insignificant. We are now working with one, made up of 30,000 houses. There is simply no way to do anything without working closely with the people, yet there is no way for a water company to negotiate directly with 30,000 individual families.

A NEW IDEA

In the process of discussing how to proceed, we came upon an approach that had not been tried before in Brazil or, for all we know, in any other country. It struck us that the way to deal simultaneously with the "hard" and "soft" aspects of this problem was to get a different type of team to do the work. We decided that engineering companies bidding on the project must team up with community participation NGOs or individual specialists. We discussed this with our colleagues in the SWCs and found pretty ready acceptance of the idea. The engineering and community participation specialists indicated they were willing to give it a try.

The original project wisely established simple and straightforward criteria for subproject funding, which included:

- Cities with populations greater than 50,000
- Areas having per capita monthly incomes below $87
- Per capita, investment ceilings of $98 for water and $140 for sewerage
- Obligatory stakeholder participation and hygiene education parts of the subproject.

WHAT IS STAKEHOLDER PARTICIPATION?

We were now ready to move. The water companies started issuing bid solicitations. We then began to discuss the criteria we would use to approve projects. Most of the criteria were pretty objective: city size, income, investment limits, and so forth. But what about stakeholder participation? What exactly is it?

We knew that different people had different interpretations of participation. For some, simply interviewing potential beneficiaries to establish demand preferences is participatory. Some believe "informing and educating" constitutes participation. Others insist that the essence of participation is a negotiation between the engineers and the beneficiaries. Still others want to sit down with the beneficiaries and the engineers to build the system from scratch using facilitation techniques.

BEING PRAGMATIC

To be honest, we weren't sure ourselves what constituted participation and how to make *ex ante* judgments about it. So we decided to let the water companies define it and go with their definitions. Then we would use structured learning to keep abreast of what was happening so that we could systematically learn from this experience. We structured the learning to track the following:

- Methods of "revealing" specific, price-sensitive demand, instead of assuming that demand existed, as is normally done
- Hypotheses and assumptions on project design and community involvement and how these influenced speed, cost, and effectiveness
- How the project is managed, for example, directly

by the SWC or through hired firms
- Who pays for operation and maintenance—users, cross subsidies, capital subsidies, and so on
- If and to what extent institutional intermediation was used
- The nature, type, and ease with which collective choice decisions were reached
- Project outcomes
- Project impact.

It is now just over two years since my first mission on this project. Some sixty-odd subprojects are now underway that account for 65 percent of the original project cost estimate. None is complete, although some are in the advanced stages of construction. As expected, different interpretations of participation are being used and the subprojects are being designed using different techniques. The most commonly used approaches, however, involve two different versions of community negotiations. The first starts with the design and then negotiates it with the community. The second starts with community involvement from which the design emerges.

GETTING STARTED

Let me describe the latter approach, which was used in the *favela* called Morro do Estado. Morro is in a satellite city close to Rio. We chose Morro as a pilot because it looked somewhat easier than the other pilot possibilities. One factor in its favor was its small size, about 2,000 families.

Next we had to find someone who could and would work in Morro. Generally, engineers who design and build water and sewerage systems hold extremely negative attitudes about *favelas*. We had heard, however, of someone who had a reputation for understanding how slums work and for working in them.

This person is a sanitary engineer by training and work experience. He comes from Recife—one of Brazil's poorest regions—where he worked for the municipal water authority. He is now a consulting engineer in private practice. When we talked to him, he spoke of *favelas* and their inhabitants in a different way than most. He stressed that many were solid, permanent communities where people had lived for as long as forty years. He talked about how impressed he was by the energy and creativity of *favela* dwellers who have to—and do—take care of everything themselves, as they receive precious little help from government. He described to us how he had worked with some *favelas* to generate affordable and effective water and sewerage systems on a small scale. When we told him about our plans for this project, he became interested and excited over the possibilities.

After reflecting on and comparing his view of *favela* dwellers with what we heard from conventional engineers, we knew he would be a great asset to this project. We then had a starting point. We began what turned out to be the most arduous task of getting both the Bank and the Brazilians to agree to sole-sourcing a design contract to his firm. It took us four months or so to get all the agreements and begin the work. We got approval from the Bank's procurement adviser to hire the firm as an exception based on the highly specialized nature of the work.

IDENTIFYING STAKEHOLDERS

The first action we took was to learn about the community, how it was organized and operated. To do this, the designers had to be present in the community when the people themselves were present—often on weekends and late at night. The initial phase served to identify who were the key stakeholders and in particular who were the community leaders. They came from all walks of life and places, but mainly were associated with religious, sports, or other types of clubs that exist in communities everywhere.

THE IMPORTANCE OF WOMEN

It was the women's clubs, however, that proved the most effective instruments for working with the community, and the women themselves turned out to be the key to getting the subproject under way. In a *favela,* more often than not, a woman is the actual head of the household. She is the permanent feature. The men tend to come and go. The designers met the women first when they came into the community and worked with them on a daily basis to organize local involvement. In a real sense, women were the local community.

BUILDING TRUST

As the designers learned about the community, the community came to learn about them. The local people saw the respect the designers had for them. They saw the designers' admiration for people willing to take charge of their lives and do something about it. To enter the community and gain trust meant in part accepting what the official community calls *favela* illegality, including narco-traffic, violence, and the ubiquitous and illegal informal lottery.

In the process, the designers helped the community to learn about and understand the water company: how it operated, what it could and could not do, and the basic hydraulics of water and sewerage. At the same time, the community helped the designers learn about them. All the individuals involved learned together what was possible and not possible, what they really wanted, and how they had to behave to get what they wanted. So the actual engineering design of a functioning water and sewerage system run by a modern SWC, was a social, iterative process between experts and ordinary people.

EARLY PROCUREMENT ACTION

Once we were sure that local demand and a willingness to work things out existed, we started the procurement process—well before all the details were worked out. The first step in construction would be trunk line work—connecting the *favela* with the SWC's main trunk lines. The next step would be connecting the trunk lines to the houses.

Bidding trunk line construction work and pipes and fittings for house hook-ups and actually selecting the contractor made the whole thing real for the people of Morro. They realized that what we were doing was not another election year promise. In election years, *favelas* got some partial attention, but no serious effort was ever made to serve the entire community. We dissolved the election-year skepticism through our large-scale, early procurement. This in turn motivated the local people further to do what only they could do: organize themselves to work effectively with the water company.

CONDOMINIUM APPROACH

One of the key lessons for the people in the community was something called the condominium approach. At the bottom of it was the understanding that the water company could not deal directly with each family in a "helter-skelter" community like Morro. Instead, families had to band together to negotiate and commit to operate and maintain the service to a group of some twenty to fifty *barracos* (homes). This way of generating and supporting communal interdependence helped work out affordable solutions: people could afford what they wanted and the water company would recover its capital and operating costs—a "win-win" game for all concerned.

The designers made the initial suggestions for organizing a number of *barracos* into a condominium and then negotiated the details with those involved. There had to be and indeed was flexibility on the part of the designers to accommodate what the local people wanted in forming condominiums as well as other things. For instance, a water tank had to be placed at the highest point in the *favela* to service the community. Of course, the several possible locations for the tank were already occupied by a house, church, or other structure that was important to at least some or all.

Negotiation was required to work out the water tank siting problem. But perhaps the word "negotiation" misses the essence of what really went on. It wasn't just the designers negotiating with the community; more important, it was also the community working together to take care of both individual and communal needs.

The Morro do Estado pilot project took about six months to design at a cost of about $100,000. Since this was our first such opportunity, learning was the objective. A lot of people had to learn: the designers, the water company, CEF, the Bank, and the people living in the *favela*. While the pilot was going forward, initial work began on other larger and tougher *favelas*; the lessons from Morro flowed into the second and beyond. The design phase of any project, however, is never really finished; redesigning goes on with construction and implementation. What is surprising, perhaps, is that the adjustments appear to have gotten done with ease and good will. By the time of construction and implementation, all became a team committed to producing something of real value.

COST AND TIME

From time to time, I ask myself if this is a cost-effective approach. I must say I haven't got a satisfactory answer yet. The $100,000 design cost of Morro works out to $15 per capita—not a large amount. More important, we are not only seeing final costs within the investment parameters set by the original Bank-financed project but at amounts substantially below the subproject estimates prepared by the SWCs.

These final costs—not just in the pilot but in the subsequent subprojects—are generally 50 percent below (in one case 25 percent below) the SWC estimates. Of course, design and design costs are one thing. Whether the system will work well, be sustained, and generate payments that cover the investment and operating costs are the final tests. We have yet to get to that stage.

ON REFLECTION

This project is doing more than providing water and sewerage to a *favela*, in my opinion. It is a starting point for individual and community development. Person after person has told me how she is looking forward to receiving water bills at "her" condominium. People also say—without being asked—that they intend to pay their bills. It's as if the existence of a postal address and a water bill with one's own name on it confers a new, permanent identity in the society—no longer at the margin, no longer a faceless member of a *favela*, but a full-fledged citizen. Beyond that, people in the *favela* speak of the possibility of realizing a long-held dream: having their own telephone number, just like "other" people in the country.

If anything gives me confidence that these systems will be sustainable, it's an empowerment I have seen that is almost palpable. Of course, a lot of other things have to be right for the systems to be sustainable: governance, economic management, jobs for people, and more. Our project can't take care of these things. Only time will tell.

CHAD

EDUCATION V PROJECT

Makha Ndao is the Task Manager for the Chad Education V Project.

Photo by Curt Carnemark

Chadians value education highly, so local involvement and significant local contributions to the cost of education have been a long-standing tradition in Chad. During the 1979-82 war, Chad's education system deteriorated seriously. The slow recovery from the period of disturbances caused local communities to play an even greater role in financing and operating their schools. The Education V project, financed by the International Development Association (IDA), has been supporting rehabilitation in this sector.

During further disturbances in December 1990, looting and damage occurred in the building housing Chad's Ministry of Education, which lost a great deal of its records, files, and equipment. Schools throughout the country suffered various kinds of damage; books and other teaching materials were in short supply. To rebuild the education system, the government of Chad developed an Education-Training-Employment strategy for 1990-2000. Chadians from many backgrounds and sectors (mainly from the public sphere) and most major donors helped create this strategy. In 1991 the new minister of education asked the Bank to help the government implement its new strategy.

In our initial conversations with the minister, he asked that we prepare the new project in a manner that involved local people and responded to their real needs and concerns. We were delighted with the request and quickly responded in the affirmative. During our next mission, we visited local communities and held discussions with officials and citizens at the local, regional, and national levels. We then sat down with the officials at the central level to decide the specific actions and steps needed to plan the project.

It soon dawned on all of us that, although we were in full agreement with planning the project, none of us really knew how to do it. We decided to start by finding a tried and tested methodology with which we were comfortable. The Bank offered to find the methodology, and, as Task Manager for the project, I undertook the search myself.

CHOOSING A METHODOLOGY

In talking with my Bank colleagues, I learned about a methodology called Objectives-oriented project planning (ZOPP) (see Appendix I) that was originated by Gesellschaft für Technische Zusammenarbeit, a German aid agency. I found that a nearby company offered seminars on ZOPP, one of which I attended along with my Bank project team members.

ZOPP seemed to fill the bill nicely; the project team returned to Chad enthusiastic about sharing what we had learned with our Chadian partners in the project. At a meeting, we told our Chadian colleagues that we could use a methodology called ZOPP and proceeded to explain how it worked. As we described ZOPP, I noticed that people were giggling and laughing. I asked what was the matter. They good-naturedly explained that in Chad, the word "ZOPP" was a slang expression with sexual connotations, and we all had a good laugh about it. But they had a more serious concern. They said we were acting in a typical Bank manner by prescribing how to do things.

We got over both these problems in good fashion by recognizing that ZOPP was the only participatory methodology we knew. Besides, we explained, ZOPP is not the usual way of doing things in the Bank, and we might have to persuade Bank management that using it made good sense. Also, we simply dropped the ZOPP acronym and replaced it with its English equivalent "OOPP" or Objectives-oriented project planning.

IDENTIFYING THE STAKEHOLDERS

The first step in the ZOPP methodology is identifying the stakeholders of the projects and then beginning to understand what they want. It was a simple matter to recognize the official stakeholders in an education project. But we wondered who really spoke for the local community and if there were issues of gender, ethnicity, social class, religion, or other factors that we had to take into account.

The government organized four regional conferences attended by high ministry officials, school inspectors, school directors and teachers, members of local school associations, and representatives of NGOs and women's groups. At these meetings, we discussed local primary education problems and ways to correct them. We were pleased that two of the meetings were held in a traditional manner, under a tree—*sous l'arbre à palabre*—where passers-by joined in the discussion.

As a result of these meetings we learned that Chadians at the local level are seriously committed to and closely involved in educating their children. One unexpected benefit for us was learning local people's concerns about their ability to collect and account for educational funds and about dealing effectively with the well-educated people who ran the schools and taught in them. Clearly, local people needed education on how to run a school and would greatly welcome this as part of the project. We also noted how women came and spoke up at these meetings, often complaining that not enough girls were getting educated in the country.

DESIGNING THE PROJECT

All of this was helpful, but it still had not been translated into a project suitable for Bank financing. To get the contents of the project identified and to do the detailed preparation, government convened a six-day national "OOPP" conference for participatory project planning. The minister of education invited ministry staff, regional officials, NGOs, and several of us from the World Bank to a project planning conference. All told, about thirty people attended the conference.

Purposely, government set the date of the meeting to coincide with a planned Bank project mission to the country. In selecting the stakeholders, we thought that the NGOs would represent local people at a conference otherwise attended by government officials. As it turned out, the NGOs tended to represent their own interests, and it fell to others to represent the views and interests of local people based on what we heard at the regional conferences. We also learned, to our dismay, that no women were present at this meeting, because no one took any special action to ensure their presence. Nevertheless, the participatory planning process went rather well, in our opinion, even though it was the first time any of us used our so-called OOPP method.

THE NATIONAL OOPP CONFERENCE

We hired a consultant from a nearby country to plan and facilitate the conference. The consultant was experienced in the OOPP methodology and worked well with Chadians.

We devoted the first day to identifying stakeholder interests. We did this simply by asking and encouraging the participants to express their own interests, hopes, expectations, and fears related to Chad's education system and a possible Bank-financed project. At the end of the day, all of us at the conference could see pretty clearly how the potential project activities might affect each stakeholder.

We spent the second day delineating the specific problems that existed in providing sound primary education in Chad. We did this by means of a "problem tree" that clearly identified the causes of the problems the participants mentioned during the first day. We noted how well the participants worked together even though this was not their normal way of working. This is not to say that everything went smoothly. At one point, a Chadian participant said to one of us from the Bank, "I am telling you that I have a headache, and you keep telling me that I have a foot ache and you want to force me to take a medicine for that." Hearing that made us from the Bank think twice about our own feeling that we were really just part of the group.

On the third day, we developed the objectives of the project. As it turned out, this was pretty easily done by converting the problem tree into a "decision tree." One key objective was to reinforce a decentralized system in which local communities had more autonomy and responsibility for their schools, while central government provided part of the finance and technical guidance and assistance.

Day four was devoted to developing alternative ways of attaining the objectives we had decided on the previous day. We did this together listening to proposals, discussing them, and then choosing what we considered to be the best. We were pleased that the methodology facilitated a consensus among a group of people whose interests and views had so severely differed on the first day.

Days five and six were devoted to developing logical frameworks for the project and its various components. The logical framework employs a project-planning matrix that looks like this:

	Summary of Objectives/Activities	Verifiable Indicators	Means and Sources of Verification	Important Assumptions
Goal				
Purpose				
Activities				
Outputs				

Participants broke into small groups, each working on one or more goals in a detailed fashion. Bank staff became part of several small groups.

THE PROJECT

In Bank project terms, the last two days of work produced a project with these components:

- Classroom construction (800 primary school rooms) and rehabilitation (200 classrooms)
- Purchase and distribution of primary textbooks and teacher guides
- Restructuring and improvement of in-service and preservice teacher training
- Strengthening primary school management and inspection
- Development and implementation of a girls' education program
- Promoting pedagogic improvement projects in individual schools
- Strengthening the capacity of 100 parent associations
- Institution strengthening of the Ministry of Education.

COST AND TIME

The total project cost is $33.8 million. The Bank is providing an IDA credit of $19.3 million. Eighteen months elapsed from Initial Executive Project Summary to Bank Board approval in May 1993, well within the standard for education projects in Africa. Three fund sources paid for the preparation of this project. The Bank's budget contributed enough to pay for the seventy-eight staff weeks applied to the project by four Bank staff members and one consultant. We made six missions from identification to appraisal. I believe these preparation costs are significantly below average for education projects in our region. The previous IDA credit contributed about $8,000 for the out-of-pocket costs of the national conference, including the fees for the facilitator, who resided in the Central Africa Republic. The government's budget paid for the salaries and associated costs of the Chadian officials.

PROJECT QUALITY

Implementation is just beginning (the credit became effective on January 18, 1994), so I cannot say much about how the participatory approach has affected sustainability and ease of implementation. But I can share some immediate results of the participatory planning process. The project went through the peer and management review processes quickly and easily, which pleased us because the project was mainly prepared by the Chadians. During identification and preparation, a large number of people within Chad learned a great deal about what was wrong with their educational system and what could be done given the financial constraints of the country. The actual project was produced by many of the people who will have to work together to implement it. They really "own" it, and, more important, they really understand it. Finally, we have something in it that the local people really want—help for parent associations in interacting with the school directors and teachers. I doubt if we would be doing this if it hadn't been for the *sous l'arbre à palabre*.

Implementation has been delayed some because of the economic and political situation in Chad and the constant change of ministers and directors. In this difficult Chadian context, the broadly based preparation process and the resulting network of committed stakeholders has been keeping the project going through times of changing officialdom.

ON REFLECTION

I think the process of identifying objectives and building consensus brought stakeholders at all levels together and produced a project plan that the local schools, donors, and government could really "own." This project demonstrates, in my opinion, that a participatory approach can be employed within the time frame and procedures of the Bank, if the Bank and government are genuinely committed to the process. If I were to do it over again, I'd first have a consultant train four or five Chadians in the ZOPP methodology. Then, with those four or five trained national facilitators, I'd ask the Chadians to identify and prepare the project themselves as a basis for discussing with the Bank our financing *their* project.

COLOMBIA

ELECTRICITY SECTOR REFORM

Turid Sato, who was the Task Manager for the Colombia Electricity Sector Reform Project, is now codirector of Organizing for Development, an International Institute (ODII).

Photo by Curt Carnemark

In late 1984 I received a new assignment as the senior loan officer for Colombia in the Country Programs Division. Over the holidays, I acted for the division chief while he was on vacation. To my astonishment, a telegram arrived from the Colombian finance minister saying, in essence, that the electricity sector was bankrupt. Because the Bank had been supporting the sector for thirty years, could we help them solve this problem? At first, I thought the message was exaggerated, but after some investigation and a Bank workshop I organized in January to assess the situation, it was clear that the crisis was real.

BANK WORKSHOP

The workshop consisted of fifteen Bank staff familiar with Colombia, including the relevant division chiefs. One of the staff was a Colombian power engineer who had considerable experience in Colombia itself. The participants determined that one major problem was the overbuilding of hydroelectric power plants and a high debt load, which, because of a rapid devaluation of the peso, had suddenly mushroomed from $1.8 billion to $3.5 billion. What should be done? At about 5:00 P.M. the group's thinking gelled, thanks to an engineer who said "The Colombians need an institutional mechanism to provide oversight for the entire energy sector." Everyone agreed. A nationwide energy board was proposed as the solution. In addition, it was time to *(a)* stop new construction in the electricity sector, such as a planned $3 billion hydroelectric project called URRA, *(b)* make better use of installed capacity, and *(c)* increase tariffs.

The trouble was: we weren't the Colombians. The Colombian civil service is competent and doesn't welcome outside directives. Only the Colombians could decide what they were willing to change and to what extent.

FIRST MISSION

So on a mission in February 1985, my task was to find out if we could find a way of working together with the Colombians. From my graduate studies and work on institutional development at the Bank, I knew about a participatory process that I thought might be useful. It was called Appreciation-influence-control (AIC) (see Appendix I) and required all stakeholders in the electricity sector to participate in a search for solutions. The Colombians—including the minister of mines and energy, who was new and seeking priorities for a work program—were delighted with my proposal of this approach.

We agreed to schedule a three-day conference in April, but the Colombians didn't trust the Bank enough to include it as a participant. They thought the Bank was seeking the chance to put a new loan in place. After considerable negotiation, they were persuaded to change their minds and include Bank representatives in the conference. While I was back in Washington, the Bank's resident representative in Bogota assisted the government in drawing up a list of participants and handling the logistics. In the interim, the Bank sent comments on the URRA project, the major beneficiary of which was a huge utility called CORELCA. The Bank's view—that the project had no justification and that the electricity sector needed to diversify away from its heavy reliance on hydroelectric power—set off a firestorm.

CONFERENCE PREPARATION

The Bank's resident representative worked one-on-one with the Colombians to organize the conference and did a great job of pulling together the key stakeholders—that is, the people with the power, influence, and knowledge to change the electricity sector. These stakeholders included the ministers, permanent secretaries, heads of the utilities and their contractors, several mayors (because some of the utilities were municipal), congresspeople, several expert consultants, and members of the opposition party. The special interest groups who wanted to keep building more hydroelectric plants also wanted to attend and were invited. Although the Colombians were initially reluctant to do so, they accepted the Bank's suggestion to include six project department people from the Bank and the Inter-American Development Bank, because they too were stakeholders. All the above mentioned people accepted the invitation, so we had all the people who

collectively had the power to change the electricity sector—a bipartisan group that we hoped would carry forward any commitments they made, despite the fact that elections were only a year away. The invitations were signed by the ministers of finance, mines and energy, and development planning. I was pleased that everything was in order and that the Colombian stakeholders would have a chance to work together to find their own solutions. A few days before the conference, I arrived with two facilitators, one of whom had developed the AIC process, and another Bank consultant.

DEALING WITH OPPOSITION

But, when we got to Santa Marta, the small northern town where the conference was to be held, we encountered a major problem in the form of a new member of the local conference team chosen by the minister of planning. The new team member flatly vetoed the participatory approach already agreed on. She wanted a conventional "talking heads" conference and insisted that "the ministers want to make speeches, not participate in games." After many hours of exhausting arguments about the agenda, the AIC consultant and the other facilitator said, "We can't run this conference the way you want it. Our only choice is to pull out. We are leaving tomorrow morning." And they left the meeting.

After a final attempt to persuade the local team, I felt I had run out of options. "If you insist on a traditional conference, I'll announce tomorrow at the opening that we cannot guarantee any results with a traditional format, and therefore we will have to leave the management of the conference to you." With this, our local counterpart changed her mind, but she still insisted the ministers would never go along with the idea of working actively and equally with others in a search for solutions.

DAY 1: THE AIC CONFERENCE

We had willingly agreed that the four ministers would give introductory remarks. This went well and underscored that the conference was being held under their auspices.

Then the AIC consultant took the floor. He introduced the process we were about to use. The conference, he said, would help the participants find ways to understand and manage three levels of "environment":

- The internal or *controlled* environment (of the organizations that have the power and responsibility to carry out projects in the electricity sector)

- The relationship with others outside the electricity sector who *influence* or are influenced by the achievement of the sector's purpose (beneficiaries, contractors, credit companies, advisers, and so on)
- The relevant context that needs to be *appreciated* to understand the impact of economic, political, and cultural factors on the achievement of the electricity sector's purpose.

These three concepts—appreciation, influence, and control—he explained, form the core of the AIC method. "You will see how the "A," the "I," and the "C" play out in this workshop," he said. "This is a different approach to problem solving. It holds a lot of potential, and I need your commitment to stay with me for the next twenty-four hours. After that, if you don't like the format we are using, you can go back to a traditional conference. Here is the assignment: Imagine now that you are ordinary Colombian citizens. We have just received news that all the power plants in the country have been blown up. You are all out of jobs. Over the next twenty-four hours, you will act as ordinary citizens and devise a new electricity sector, an ideal one, that serves the interests of all Colombian people."

With this, the conference launched into the "appreciative" phase, designed to understand the economic, political, and cultural context of the Colombian electricity situation and to stimulate the group to come up with as many ideas as possible.

The participants were divided into heterogeneous groups of ten, structured to include people from across the spectrum of the energy sector and each with a group facilitator. They were told to come up with ideas and listen to each other without comment or judgment. Questions would be allowed but only to clarify, not to criticize. These guidelines would enable them to come "unstuck" from the present dilemma and unleash their creative energies, to invent without thinking about practicalities or all the reasons their ideas would never work. Role playing as ordinary citizens would also reduce the power differences among the group. The conferees agreed to accept the challenge and, within one hour, the small groups were buzzing with ideas.

The press and electronic media were another matter. Because the Colombians had almost doubled the participants previously agreed to, the conference room had proved too small. We had moved onto a verandah, where many reporters waiting outside a fence were able to hear the loudspeaker. They took the facilitator's announcement literally, and we had quite a time persuading them the World Bank hadn't blown up the electricity sector!

THE APPRECIATIVE PHASE

The first assignment to the conferees was to come up with an ideal future for Colombia. After ten minutes for individual reflection, they were to go around the group with each person contributing an idea. They were to keep going around until all ideas had been exhausted. One of the group members was to be chosen as a rapporteur. The facilitator would go around to ensure that everyone was heard and that they listened uncritically.

Working in this mode, the groups made lists on flip charts. They drew illustrations of their visions. They really had fun. The six ministers, past and current, participated as equals. The minister of mines and energy gracefully stepped up to the role of concerned citizen and was a model for everyone else.

The process enabled all the stakeholders, despite their relative power positions, to share information never previously brought together, to learn from each other and to build a common appreciation of the entire electricity sector and its relationship to the broader energy sector and the national economy. After about an hour, each group summarized its ideas for the plenary. Common themes emerged, but also many original ideas to which the plenary was receptive.

DAY 2: THE AIC CONFERENCE

The "appreciative" phase continued the next day, with another assignment for the same small groups. Using the same process, they were asked to examine present realities, both positive and negative. Again, the groups reported back to the plenary. With the help of the AIC consultant, the plenary was able to reduce all of the thinking into one overarching vision: a functioning system that provided electricity as a basic right of every Colombian citizen.

There was one major disagreement. The manager of CORELCA, the huge utility that had been involved in the URRA project, was furious. He stood up and said that he wanted to discuss URRA—*now*. He ignored the facilitators' attempts to calm him, so the minister of mines and energy stepped in, saying "We will get to this issue in proper order. I ask you to wait." The CORELCA official wouldn't take his seat. Finally, the minister took him aside and told him that, if he was not willing to participate in the process, he should leave. So the man did leave. The rest of the people there agreed that the minister had done the right thing.

This completed the "appreciative" phase or the "A" in AIC.

THE INFLUENCE PHASE

Next, we moved to the "influence" phase—the "I" in AIC—during which the themes and priorities for change and understanding the potential reaction in the political environment were discussed. The same groups formed again. They were to listen fully to each other first and then debate, pushing the limits of each idea.

In the middle of the "I" session, each group made a preliminary report to the plenary, indicating roughly their agreements and disagreements. Anticipating the need for synthesis, we had asked the budget director from the finance ministry to be both a facilitator and a synthesizer of the many ideas we expected would come forth. He was a quiet man whose leadership qualities were not therefore obvious, but we had observed that he had an intuitive grasp of how the electricity sector worked in its totality. He reviewed the flip charts and drew lines around the main themes and viewpoints. Then, with little preparation, fed back a concrete, twenty-minute synthesis of the issues and strategic options. The participants returned to their groups and continued with more focus and clarity.

The groups were given some schematics with which to work. First, they were given a stakeholder map to enable them to analyze the strategies they considered necessary to achieve their ideal outcome. This helped them consider all of the stakeholders associated with each strategy and whether each stakeholder would favor or oppose that strategy. They also produced an AIC table. For each of their strategic priorities, they could list all the stakeholders in the left-hand column and then indicate if, in relation to the strategy, the stakeholder had appreciative, influence, or control power. This gave some indicators of the relative power of the stakeholders.

At the end of the "I" phase, the groups reported again to the plenary for general discussion. Thanks to the synthesizing efforts of the budget director, various main themes had been identified and options and strategies had been proposed for each theme, along with an assessment of the political feasibility of the strategies. One option, proposed by the minister of planning, whose family happened to own one of the largest engineering firms, was to privatize the entire electricity sector. The plenary's reaction to the idea was chilly.

Aside from that issue, the plenary looked at the list of main themes that had emerged from the group discussions and voted on the top four: *(a)* a new direction for policy, *(b)* finance issues, *(c)* permanent improvement in the management of the entire sector, and *(d)* a new climate of collaboration among the different stakeholders. Participants recognized that investments had to be redirected and, more generally, that most of the problems could only be resolved with participation from a broad range of stakeholders. For instance, because the electricity sector was organized along regional lines, no mechanism existed for taking a national perspective into account. Colombia needed an institutional mechanism that could look at the issues and recommendations emerging from the conference—and also future issues—in the context of both the entire energy sector and the national economy. They debated whether a national board should be created for the electricity sector or for the overall energy sector but did not reach a conclusion during the "influence" phase.

DAY 3: THE CONTROL PHASE

The "control" phase, which took place on the third day, was structured so that clear outcomes and commitments emerged from the conference. We started by putting up flip charts around the room, each listing one of the main themes developed the day before. We asked people who had the power to implement recommendations to volunteer as "champions" of each theme and form groups. Then we asked the participants to select the issue they wanted to work on. They tended to choose the group in which they had power and/or a stake, or for which they had a strong desire to influence. The groups were instructed to prepare action plans specifying what would be done by whom, where, and when.

The next morning, the groups reported back to the plenary. Among the concrete recommendations were:

- *Institutional reform.* A "rector" or some kind of governing entity, for managing the electricity sector in the context of the whole: investment policy, financial reform, technology, and so on
- *New policy direction.* A freeze on new construction for five years; diversification from hydroelectric to other power sources via conversion of existing power plants (hydroelectric had gotten 90 percent of the investments in the sector over the previous thirty years); and geographic diversification (the majority of power generation was in one watershed)
- *Financial issues.* Change in the structure and levels of tariffs; external borrowing to buy time.

The groups reported these conclusions to the plenary, and they were accepted with little debate. They had arrived at a consensus by working together for the last three days.

During the final session of the conference, the group focused on next steps and designated a mid-level task force to prepare a report of the conclusions. The members were appointed by the minister of mines and energy and represented all the stakeholders in the sector. Finally, this minister took a microphone with a long cord and walked around the room giving it to whomever wanted to speak—and almost everyone did. The team spirit and commitment to action could be felt in the air. In one way or another, they said, "For the first time, we know what is happening. We came up with the answers, and we know what to do." As people were making their own commitments about the future, their voices were filled with emotion. They pleaded with the minister and said, "Please don't drop the ball." The minister responded, "The results of the conference have been brilliant. You have given me my work plan for the coming year."

OUTCOMES

The AIC conference had fundamentally changed the working climate. The key actors in the sector moved from a situation of inaction to a commitment to detailed proposals for change, seen in the many activities that were set in motion.

For instance, the task force completed the report, and the minister of mines and energy held a series of workshops to review and obtain commitments to implement the work plan. The report was used in the government's political negotiation process in the Parliament.

The minister of mines and energy began implementing some of the workshop recommendations before the final report was even completed. He immediately froze construction and set up an interim coordinating body called the Technical Energy Board. This board was the forerunner of the National Energy Board, whose creation required and eventually received the approval of Congress. The National Energy Board, which then replaced the Technical Energy Board, worked in cooperation with all the entities in the sector to carry out sectorwide planning responsibilities and formulate policies and investment programs for the sector.

Later, with broad support, the minister integrated the electricity and energy sectors and brought them under his aegis (previously, the electricity sector had gone around his ministry through its own contacts reporting directly to the ministers of finance and planning).

The minister personally reported the conference conclusions to the World Bank and the Inter-American Development Bank and got their support for financing an energy sector study to help formulate a detailed energy strategy grounded in the Santa Marta conference report along with two follow-up workshops to help design coordination mechanisms and implementation plans.

In 1986 the Bank provided a $400,000 Energy Sector Management Assistance Program (ESMAP) grant for work on the detailed strategy. This was carried out by Colombian energy experts under the guidance of the Technical Energy Board and the ESMAP division. Even though the elections brought a change in parties, the fact that the conference and the follow-up had been bipartisan led the new government to implement many of the recommendations detailed in the energy sector report.

The new policies set the stage for the Bank, the Inter-American Development Bank, and the Export-Import Bank of Japan to each make $300 million loans, temporarily alleviating the financial crisis.

By the time the Bank's loan went to the Bank's Board, in autumn 1987, the Colombians had already met most of the conditions—which they themselves had proposed in the first place.

The positions of some of the participants enabled them to use their influence at the right time in the policy process.

As for the AIC process, the Colombians continued to ask the Bank for help with other key issues, such as a transportation strategy, an information system for the country, and internal organization problems of the state petroleum company. We have conducted approximately ten workshops to deal with these and other matters using the AIC process.

The Colombians persisted with the commitment their participatory process had produced. In the 1987 Bank reorganization, however, the key people in the Country Programs Division moved on to other jobs. For this reason, the Bank's follow-up lacked consistency and did not support all the recommendations of the AIC workshop.

SUBSEQUENT EVENTS

The process that began at Santa Marta, however, did not stop. In 1987 the Bank's Operations Evaluation Department undertook an in-depth evaluation of the history of lending to the power sector in Colombia and in 1989 issued a report that described a "checkered" picture. The report suggested that the Colombians continue with an internal process to come up with their solutions. A second strategy session was held in Santa Marta in 1990. This strategy session led to the design of a three-year effort to restructure the power sector.

Unfortunately, Colombia encountered serious shortages of electricity in the early 1990s, and all major cities suffered frequent blackouts. A once-a-century drought—probably caused by "El Niño"— primarily caused the shortages, exacerbated by the country's overdependence on hydroelectric generation and the failure to maintain the actual availability of alternative electricity capacity in the country.

CASES

ESMAP then became involved again. Many workshops and seminars were held involving all stakeholders in the electricity sector and providing "appreciative" mechanisms for airing all views. These also became the "influence" mechanisms for debating many of the structural problems that had affected performance, such as the risk-laden strategy of too heavy a reliance on hydroelectric power, lack of a regulatory mechanism, the mixing of generation and transmission in the system, and low tariffs. New policies were adopted to address all these issues including privatization of electric utilities. The National Energy Board, which was originally designed as an "influence" mechanism to mediate and negotiate among the many conflicting parties in the energy sector, was replaced by the Ministry of Mines and Energy. The ministry's role was to work in cooperation with the national and sector stakeholders to formulate and negotiate annual investment programs for the energy sector as a whole. For the electricity sector, a new Regulatory Commission, resembling what was recommended at the first Santa Marta conference, has now been created, and the Bank has recently made a technical assistance loan to support implementation of the Colombian-bred reforms.

These activities are detailed in an ESMAP report entitled *Power Sector Restructuring Program Report.* It devotes a chapter to the design and implementation of the process and states that "the restructuring of the sector was made in Colombia, by Colombians, for Colombians.... The role of ESMAP, the Bank and foreign consultants was limited strictly to ancillary support."

The manager of the ESMAP program in Colombia believes that the process adopted by the Bank—not the Bank's technical advice—facilitated the change in attitude that led to the changes in policy. The Bank facilitated a process for problem solving, leaving country officials to do their own diagnostic work and thereby learn more fully about their own problems and set their own future directions.

An energy economist, who was one of the small group facilitators at Santa Marta and is now the minister of mines and energy, had this to say: "The participatory process in the power sector started in Santa Marta in 1985. It has continued with many, many seminars before arriving at a scheme that we are all pleased with. I believe the participatory approach was the only route to restructure this complicated sector. The challenge now is to implement it. This is my top priority."

COSTS AND TIME

The cost of the Santa Marta conference was about $25,000–$30,000 contributed by the Colombians and $5,000 by the Bank. In addition, six months of my staff time was devoted to investigating the electricity sector. ESMAP's subsequent work came at additional cost.

ON REFLECTION

Originally, I had thought of AIC as a good strategic planning tool. But, in Santa Marta, it turned out to be much more than that. It had empowered those who had to live with the results to take charge of their own problems and their own future. It had shown itself to be a self-organizing process, low-cost, and repeatable. I thought about what a change this had been from the development paradigm centered on the transfer of resources, technology, and skills, in which experts defined solutions.

In Colombia the AIC process continued to be popular; many requests emerged from the different ministries, state-owned enterprises, and even the private sector. All in all, I was able to support ten of these requests, mostly with money from different trust funds rather than from the Bank's own budget resources. The process achieved three major successes:

- First, the process proved effective as a means to pull together all the stakeholders for an entire sector, enabling them to understand the whole situation, discuss options, and make choices for action in a congenial atmosphere. Previous attempts for organizing problem-solving sessions had led to much acrimony among participants.

- Second, the process was empowering. When the Colombian stakeholders saw the totality of the situation, they realized that they themselves were responsible for the conditions of the sector, not the Bank, not the Inter-American Development Bank, nor any other external actors. They realized that they had to take charge of formulating policies and institutional reforms in the energy sector.

- Third, the workshop—short as it was—helped the Colombian stakeholders to strengthen their resolve. I mentioned how this process, much to our surprise, engaged people's emotions at a deeper level than most conferences. For example, the Colombians afterwards referred to the workshop as the "Spirit of Santa Marta." Over time, in many different settings, we have seen this team spirit emerge, often expressed as a feeling of elation and harmony among the participants, generating the energy to move forward. These feelings have proved to be an important foundation for the commitment, unity, and patience required during the frequently arduous implementation period.

On the downside, the participatory process was not fully understood in the Bank, and the two follow-up workshops that were organized to continue the "influence" phase of the process were stopped. The Colombians, however, did continue the participatory process for the energy sector. This led to major reforms in oil exploration policies, domestic oil price levels, and gas development strategies. The AIC workshop did fundamentally change directions in the electricity sector; for a long time to come, the Santa Marta participants were the initiators of reforms in Colombia. Leadership emerged as well. Several of the younger participants at that workshop later became ministers.

Although I would like to have seen many things done differently, what was started at Santa Marta in 1985 and continued in fits and starts by the Colombians illustrated for me what true development is: namely, to augment your ability to plan your own future and deal with the problems you are facing in a democratic, transparent way. The Colombians have set the pace and paved the way for doing sector work, policy formulation, and program implementation—all as one integrated, democratic process.

After leaving the Bank, I helped form Organizing for Development, an International Institute (ODII), which is devoted to action learning and democratic approaches to development. We have implemented the AIC self-organizing process in many countries for both public and private organizations at every level of society from village to global.

EGYPT

MATRUH RESOURCE MANAGEMENT PROJECT

Bachir Souhlal is the Task Manager for the Egypt Matruh Resource Management Project.

Photo by Bachir Souhlal

The Nile irrigates more than 90 percent of Egypt's agricultural land. Unfortunately, limited scope exists for expanding Nile-irrigated land, although some potential exists in the country's rainfed areas. Rainfed farm and grazing land are mainly worked by poor tribal farmers who sometimes distrust government and with whom government officials have thus far had little effective contact.

In late 1990 the government asked the Bank to help identify ways to improve agriculture in the Matruh Governorate, particularly for poor and remote farmers. The governorate is in Egypt's Western Desert bordering on Libya to the west, the Mediterranean Sea to the north, the Sahara Desert to the south, and the Nile Delta to the east.

Approximately 250,000 people inhabit this large area, 85 percent of which are Bedouins. These traditionally nomadic people have in the last decade switched to a more sedentary lifestyle. Although the government has attempted to integrate Bedouins into the mainstream of Egyptian society, they remain an isolated, tribal society whose leadership still performs many administrative and judicial functions. The Bedouin are among the poorest and most vulnerable of Egyptians.

STARTING THE WORK

In October 1990 I led an identification mission to comply with the government's request for a livestock project in the Matruh Governorate. The mission, including a Bank research specialist and a consultant, joined staff from Egypt's Agriculture Livestock and International Cooperation Departments for a field trip to the governorate. As we traveled the Matruh Governorate, we noted that the Bedouins are no longer nomadic. They had accepted incentives offered in a government program about a decade ago to settle into a more sedentary lifestyle. They now raise mostly sheep and goats, which seriously overgraze the sparse vegetation in the area. Figs, olives, and other crops grow throughout. Environmental degradation and poor resource management practices are evident everywhere. Fortunately, we also had the chance to talk to United Nations Food and Agriculture Organization volunteers, staff from the Agha Khan Foundation, and Gesellschaft für Technische Zusammenarbeit staff who were working in the area. They were excellent sources of information.

It became clear to the mission that a traditional livestock project was not the appropriate solution. Resource management, particularly the capability to catch and retain rain water, had declined severely through an endemic cycle of poverty, lack of viable production alternatives, and uncoordinated regional development. Intuition told us that if things were to change, all stakeholders would need to make an effort. Local people would have to change the way they behaved, individually and collectively. Government would have to learn how to work with the local people and develop their trust and confidence. Finally, the Bank would have to learn how to contribute its knowledge and resources to fit what the local people were capable of and willing to do.

GETTING TIME AND MONEY

On returning to the Bank, we reported that a regular livestock project would not suffice. Instead, the Bank should encourage the government to address the fundamentals of natural resource management in the area. Initially, our thought was to ask the United Nations Food and Agriculture Organization to prepare the project. After deliberation, however, the mission recommended something new—an approach that would have central and local government officials collaborate with Bedouins to identify and prepare the project.

This approach would, of course, require both money and time. Bank management agreed to the approach and time needed, but no money was readily available to support the special kind of preparation we felt necessary. I offered to search for funds and came across the Japanese Grant Facility and an old friend in the United Nations Development Programme who was interested in what we were suggesting. We quickly put together and submitted a Japanese Grant Facility application.

To our surprise, we quickly got a grant of 35 million yen, the equivalent of $250,000, with virtually no strings attached. It proved, however, much more difficult to get the government to formally accept the grant than it was

to get it from the Japanese. We faced a long delay, but, thanks to courage on the part of a government official, we were able to move relatively quickly. The United Nations Development Programme put up an additional $100,000. The Bank became the executing agent for both grants, which allowed us to be closely associated with project preparation. But the local people did the actual work of identification and preparation, instead of a team of external experts.

SETTING UP A LOCAL TASK FORCE

First, we established a local task force consisting of ten people from the central government, twenty from local government and local institutions, and ten from the Bedouin community. Local government authorities chose the Bedouin representatives on the basis of their judgment about whom the community trusted and respected. This task force stayed intact, working closely together, throughout preparation of the project. To help them with their work, we hired a British consulting firm. This firm had the experience and capability to help prepare the project using a participatory approach. It also helped the members of the task force prepare the types of data and documents needed by the Bank.

LEARNING ABOUT MATRUH

The task force—now about forty-six persons, including part-time assistance from the consulting firm—set out to learn everything it could about the governorate and its people. To start, the members combed texts of all sorts, some dating back to the nineteenth century. Early on I had asked the government to collect texts and prepare a local library that was put to great use by the task force. We learned a great deal from these texts about geography, topography, economics, history, and culture, but we weren't satisfied with that alone. We knew we had to go to the people, quickly but thoroughly. We decided to use a technique, called participatory rural assessment (see Appendix I), that appeared well suited to our needs. It would provide a good understanding of the people and what they needed through intensive and participatory contact with them.

PARTICIPATORY RURAL ASSESSMENT

The task force formed itself into about seven teams to learn more about the governorate and the Bedouins who inhabit it. We used the following elements over a three-month period to identify what should be included in the project and how to implement it. In each case we sought to have groups of informants participate with us in developing the information, policies, activities, and institutions that would constitute a project that would sustainably help the Bedouins as well as meet Bank quality standards:

Semistructured Interviewing

These guided interviews with Bedouin households were conducted by a subteam of the task force. Usually we interviewed a group of households together—an extended family or larger community. Only some topics were predetermined in our preliminary planning for the interviews, leaving room for local people to talk about their own interests in their own way. We always asked open-ended questions and probed into answers and new topics raised by those being interviewed. Typically, these interviews provided data about the household—how many were in the household, how they related to each other, how they related to neighboring households, the household's history, assets they owned, activities they engaged in, who did what, who made the decisions, who controlled income, who did the hard work, and so on.

But these interviews did more than just gather data. They also gave both sides a feeling for and understanding of the other, thereby generating vital insights. For instance, we learned—when they told us how they exported lambs directly to Saudi Arabia at prices much higher than they could get locally—that the Bedouins are quite entrepreneurial.

Participatory Mapping

Maps are especially important in rural development projects in which planning, implementation, monitoring, and evaluation are required. The best sources of information for such maps are the people who live and farm an area. The maps allow us to collect and position a lot of information and recognize spatial relationships. They reveal differences in farming practices and pinpoint constraints. The shared generation of a map creates consensus and facilitates communication among respondents. At the same time, it helped the team gain insights into the way people think, their priorities, and their reasons for wanting or not wanting to do something.

Transect Walks

This is a simple device to ensure that the team explores and understands fully the spatial differences in an area (catchment, village, or field, for example) under study. We walked to the periphery of the settlement, along with a select group of local people, observing differences in

land use, vegetation, soils, cultural practices, infrastructure, trees, livestock, water availability, and so forth. Actually, the local people did the observing, while the team recorded their observations because local people always see things outsiders are likely to miss. After the walk, we produced a transect diagram—a stylized representation of the area covered by the walk(s).

Seasonal Calendars

These calendars focus on local livelihood systems. They show month-by-month patterns of rainfall, crop sequencing, water use, livestock fodder, income, debt, migration, wild harvests, labor demand, labor availability, health, diseases, prices, and so on. We put them together from interviews with local people, using several different sources to create each calendar. Usually the calendars were created at a meeting of several households at which people decided among themselves what are the appropriate answers to the various questions asked. We always created our calendars and other records on the spot and in front of the group, so that data checking occurred immediately.

Social and Historical Profiles and Time Trends

We used these techniques to help understand key changes over the years in land use, erosion, rainfall, population, tree cover, income opportunities, common property resources, and so on. We also asked respondents to forecast how they expect things to be in the future and how they would like them to be. Again, we always did this with large groups of Bedouins to produce a lot of interaction between us and the Bedouins, and among the Bedouins themselves.

Matrix Ranking

We used this technique to learn from the people what they thought about particular matters in both absolute and relative terms. We began these sessions by listing measures about which we needed their judgment (for example, possible project activities). Then we asked a group of local people to state their negative and positive feelings about the measures. They were also encouraged to add their own measures and then rank order or assign scores to the various items on the list. We did this exercise a number of times with groups of people representing different tribes, areas, and wealth. This helped us better focus project activities on the poorer segments of Bedouin society. These exercises often turned into brainstorming sessions; team members became active participants, offering at times concepts and suggestions that were new to the Bedouins. These sessions produced the participatory, community-based implementation arrangements that form an important part of this project (see below for a description.)

FOCUSING ON WOMEN

As we went along, we noticed that only men showed up for meetings with the teams (not unusual for a Muslim community). But women were important for the project to succeed because they take care of small animals, produce crafts for sale, haul water, harvest wood, and perform many other tasks. We enlisted a female member of the British consulting firm and paired her with a female Bedouin veterinarian who was working on a Gesellschaft für Technische Zusammenarbeit project. These two held meetings with women to cover much of the same ground covered at the all-male meetings described above.

These vital meetings with women greatly contributed to the project. For instance, although women are publicly silent, we learned that all major decisions were taken by the men only after they spoke with the oldest woman in the household. When men say at tribal meetings "I have to think it over," what they often mean is they have to first discuss it with the women. But what we really learned here is that the contents of the project had to be socially acceptable and that women would have a strong voice in deciding when it was acceptable.

LOCAL OWNERSHIP

In this project description, I frequently say "we." Actually, my Bank colleagues and I were only involved in a small part of the actual work, that is, when we could visit on mission. The local team and the local community did much of the work. The consultants, like the Bank staff, were present only on certain occasions. Yet, all of us who were engaged in this project felt, and indeed were, part of a special community engaged in "inventing" a new future for the Bedouins of the Matruh Governorate.

THE FINAL RESULT

It took about one year to prepare the project. The proposed project contained the following components, each of which was thoroughly vetted within the large preparation team and within the constituencies the team members represented:

- *Natural resource management* was intended primarily to conserve the water, land, and vegetation of the Matruh Governorate. The project provides 800 underground cisterns, earth and stone contour dikes

on 6,200 feddans (1 feddan equals 1.037 acres), cemented stone or gabion dikes across wadis to intercept the water flow and create about 500 feddans of new fruit orchards, rangeland improvement and management of 14,000 feddans, and more.

- *Adaptive research and extension* focuses on dryland farming and livestock production systems, range management, sustainable agriculture development, and training directed at the local communities. Among other things, four subregional resource centers, built to bring services (research, extension, and credit) closer to the local communities, would be supported with adequate staffing, technical assistance, vehicles, equipment, and materials.
- *Rural finance,* in modest amounts, was provided for small farmers, the landless, and rural women for on- and off-farm income-producing activities.

The project as proposed in the locally produced feasibility study went through the Bank's project cycle fully intact and rather rapidly. Negotiations went particularly well; we started in April and the Bank's Board approved the project in May 1993. In my opinion, the ease of negotiations was due to the understanding and consensus developed in the country through the participatory preparation process. Further evidence is that effectiveness, scheduled for the first quarter of 1994, took place on February 2, 1994, fewer than six months after the signing of credit. Effectiveness usually takes much longer in Egypt, in part because Parliament must approve each credit. Parliament was closed due to elections for about half the time it took for the project to become effective.

MORE THAN COMPONENTS

The preceding project description leaves out the most important point about this project, which is special because of its thoroughly participatory and empowering community-based implementation arrangements. "Community groups," which build on traditional Bedouin lineage structures—the *bayt*—will prepare community action plans to tailor the objectives of the project to local circumstances and capabilities. Once the plan is prepared and approved, the community group will be involved in implementing it and monitoring results. A condition of credit effectiveness was the preparation of three such plans, which were ready on time.

The community groups will help monitor project outcomes by adding on-the-scene interpretations to make better sense of the numbers we usually collect. In addition to participatory monitoring, we will also be doing "hi-tech" monitoring using a geographic information system, whose satellite images will help focus attention on natural resources and the impact the project has on them.

In addition to community empowerment and action, trust and respect have been established between the Bedouins and the government. I certainly hope it will prove sustainable, and I'm encouraged by what some government officials have said to me about how much they have learned from the Bedouins in the process of preparing the project.

TIMING AND COSTS

Identification and preparation started in October 1990 and concluded in January 1992. About 3.25 years elapsed from the first identification mission to effectiveness. I hear this is relatively fast for the Bank, especially in Egypt and in our region. The project cost about $350,000 to prepare, not counting the cost of Bank staff time and travel on the project. This certainly compares well with projects prepared in a more traditional manner. The real test will be in implementation speed and the quality of the outcomes. We are already off to a good start with the speed of effectiveness.

ON REFLECTION

Not too long ago, someone asked me what value participation added to the Matruh Resource Management Project. I said that one was that the Bedouins realized we were not attempting to use them, as had been their previous experience with outside authorities. This opened the way for trust to build, and the trust became mutual before long. I cannot imagine that occurring when a group of external experts rush in and out gathering facts and making judgments and quick recommendations. Equally important, the Bedouins saw possibilities to take care of what counted for them, began to think about their situation, and made genuine commitments to do something about it.

Through participation, we lost "control" of the project and in so doing gained ownership and sustainability, precious things in our business. We also gained more influence with the local people, and they were more open to listening to our suggestions and to the experiences of other people in the world that we could provide. Although we learned a lot and developed understanding and empathy for Bedouin life, we could not know what would work for them in the future. Only they can know this.

If I had to do this project over again I'd do some things differently, but I would still have prepared it in a participatory manner. I got a great deal of support from colleagues in the Bank and the country while going about this work. But I also sometimes encountered what I consider to be a general lack of understanding about what participation can do to make the Bank's work more effective. It was a tough, stressful, time-consuming battle to prepare this project. At the same time, it is truly satisfying to be able to manage a project that generated so much mutual trust and respect where little had existed before. In so doing, possibilities opened up that did not previously appear to be present for the Bedouins or the Egyptian authorities or the Bank.

CASES

INDIA

ANDHRA PRADESH FORESTRY PROJECT

Ann Clark was the
Task Manager for the
Andhra Pradesh
Forestry Project from
1992 to 1993.
Ajit Banerjee is the
forester who helped
initiate the forest
protection committee
approach in West
Bengal.

Photo by Samar S. Jodha

I started work on the World Bank-supported project in the Indian state of Andhra Pradesh at its very beginning. I had just finished work on a forestry project in the state of West Bengal in which I had learned something important from the West Bengalis: poor people *can* protect the forests and earn income at the same time. In Andhra Pradesh, we helped disseminate the idea, but it took those of us from the Bank a long time to discover and value this simple but effective approach.

FOREST COPS

The idea of using what are now called forest protection committees (FPCs) began in 1972 in West Bengal. At that time, the role of the state Forestry Department was mainly to protect the forests from illegal use by unauthorized persons. Foresters spent most of their time on armed patrol, hunting forest product poachers and evicting people encroaching on forest lands, yet foresters behaving like police were losing the battle to conserve the forests. Even though the forests continued to degrade rapidly, local people became increasingly aggressive toward the foresters, whom they generally considered corrupt. In the Arabari Range of West Bengal, the local people had literally thrown the department out of its territory, threatening any forester who entered with bodily harm.

One forester, however, had a different idea on how to save the forests. He felt that people living in the forests were not thieves. If they could supplement their incomes through legal forest work and organized extraction of forest products, he believed they would not haphazardly destroy the forests. In fact, he wondered, would not the local people actually protect the forests if they had a real stake in them? So he went to Arabari to talk to the local people about a new way of managing the forests—largely by and for the people. On its part, the Forestry Department would provide real support to the local people, who would receive some of the economic benefits on behalf of the government.

AN ACT OF PERSONAL COURAGE

Although this forester—who now works with us in the Bank—modestly denies it, others say that he exhibited extraordinary courage in introducing this new approach. Simply going into Arabari put him into personal danger. Nevertheless, he eventually gained the trust of the local people. In a participatory manner, they crafted a way to halt forest degradation, begin reforestation, and enable poor people to earn a legitimate living while conserving the forest.

DIALOGUE AND NEGOTIATION

Developing the new forest management approach jointly with local people did not happen overnight, however. It took about nine months of dialogue and negotiation. The dialogue started with the foresters being frank about the mistakes they had made in forest management and in dealing with their conflicts with the people. It was not long before the local people reciprocated. They admitted breaking the rules and explained why they felt they had to do so. This led to joint exploration of future arrangements that would take care of the needs of the people while they in turn took care of the forests. By forming themselves into a unified, village-based organization—a FPC—villagers organized themselves to negotiate with one voice with the Forestry Department. By negotiating among themselves, the villagers also learned negotiating skills.

COMMON INTERESTS

Initially, the people of Arabari and the Forestry Department reached a verbal understanding about their respective rights and obligations. Among other things, the agreement provided equality of contributions and benefits for all members of the community. The members of the FPC took on the duty of keeping the forest free from poachers. FPC members also agreed to protect shoots thrown up by Sal stumps so that they would eventually become salable poles.

When the poles were harvested, FPC members got the culls, plus a percentage of the revenue from the sale of the good poles. But long before the first Sal harvest, members of the FPC were legitimately harvesting many nontimber

products from what became "their own forest." The foresters began playing a more socially useful role than that of "forest cop." Instead, they enabled the protection of existing forests against further degradation. With their own eyes, they could see reforestation beginning in areas that had earlier been all but written off by the department.

Faith in the local people and the new approach seemed to pay off. Over time, the news of good results for the local people spread to other communities. Things then began to change in this part of West Bengal. More and more people who lived on the edge of a forest and depended on it for firewood and other forms of subsistence banded together to form FPCs. The creation, however, of new FPCs proceeded slowly because people felt wary of the delay in getting formal government approval for benefit sharing.

FPC APPROACH SPREADS

The FPC approach began to spread throughout that state, mostly of its own accord but in some cases assisted by local foresters. By 1988 more than 500 FPCs had been formed covering an area of more than 70,000 hectares. A large number of FPCs had sprung up spontaneously following a West Bengal Government Order in 1989. This order fully recognized the verbal agreement between the foresters and the local people, which among other things entitled FPC members to 25 percent of the final Sal tree harvests. A year later, FPCs numbered 1,250 and covered an area of 120,000 hectares. The cost of regenerating the forests in this manner proved remarkably low, about 250 rupees per hectare or 5 percent of the cost of creating a hectare of plantation trees.

Following the West Bengal success story, the government of India urged all state governments to adopt the FPC model. So far, fourteen states have not only adopted but improved on this model of protecting and regenerating degraded lands. It appears, however, that governments in India and elsewhere have been generally unwilling to share control of remaining non-degraded forests with the local people. Instead, traditional government forestry practices are still being applied to these forests and are not working anywhere near as well as the FPC approach to conserve the forest, particularly in forests with good capacity for self-regeneration.

BANK SUPPORTS FPC IN WEST BENGAL

When we approved the first Bank forestry project in West Bengal in 1981, we seem to have entirely missed the piloting and demonstration of FPCs. The Bank's main objective at the time was to support increased fuelwood production in areas outside forests. This project, therefore, mainly supported creation of village woodlots, strip plantations, and farm forestry covering about 150,000 hectares at a project cost of almost $30 million.

By the time we got around to starting preparation for the next forestry project in West Bengal in 1989, it was clear to us that village woodlots and strip plantations were neither directly helping poor people to the extent envisaged nor halting degradation of natural forests.

I was also involved in preparing the second West Bengal Forestry project, which largely supports the extension and improvement of the FPC movement, as well as the farm forestry program. Implementation is not yet complete; the project is behind target in creating new FPCs in the northern part of the state. But the southern portion is going well. Some 2,350 FPCs (up from more than 1,700 when the project became effective) now cover more than 65 percent of the degraded forest in the state, including the entire southwest (about 335,000 hectares). From the air, you really notice the flourishing green areas that just a few years ago were largely barren. In 1994 the West Bengal Forestry Department began reorganizing itself to support FPCs.

INTRODUCING FPCs IN ANDHRA PRADESH

I was also part of the January 1991 identification mission for what was to become the Andhra Pradesh Forestry Project. After a while, I became its Task Manager. When we arrived, we found that Andhra Pradesh Forestry Department staff had done a lot of good work in preparing a proposal for what would be their first operation with the Bank. The FPC approach had not yet been introduced in this state; their experience had also been with village woodlots and strip plantations—supported by a bilateral donor who was not going to extend its support. The department was proposing a continuation of this approach for the new project. The proposal also contained requests for guns and ammunition, money to pay the salaries of more staff, subsidized distribution of seedlings for farm forestry, improving tree genetics, research, staff training, and the like.

On our part, we explained that the Bank simply does not finance such things as guns, ammunition, and operating salaries. We said we doubted that subsidized seedlings would be economically justifiable. In addition and more important, we shared the experience in West Bengal, both with village woodlots and strip plantations on the one hand and forest protection committees on the other. We said we understood that India's overall priority is to halt the continued degradation of existing forests and that the Bank is seeking lending operations in support of it.

OFF TO A GOOD START

We left Andhra Pradesh feeling that prospects were good for reworking the existing proposal into a strong project proposal. Our discussions with the department's leadership were frank and cordial. We felt that we had persuaded them to prepare a substantial component along the lines of the FPC approach and that they had agreed to take a close look at existing forestry policies and their effect on enlisting private support for sound forestry practices. They also agreed to do further work in advance of our first preparation mission that we had scheduled for May 1992.

We returned in May to continue the discussion and see how preparation was going. Not a great deal of progress had been made from our point of view. No policy change proposals had been prepared and, although the original proposal had been somewhat restructured along the lines we discussed, it was still mainly a "village woodlots and strip plantations" project. Nevertheless, officials had a strong desire to move ahead with preparation and what seemed to us to be an openness to a change in thinking and direction. The officials asked if they could get some help to prepare the project to Bank standards, and we agreed to see if we could arrange it.

On returning to Washington, we arranged for a consultant team to be supported through a donor country consultant trust fund. The terms of reference specified that local consultants also be engaged. The consultant team spent the summer of 1992 working on preparation of the project. Looking back, I recognize that I was not really thinking about having the project prepared in a participatory manner. Nevertheless, I suggested that the consultant team consider engaging the local consultants we used on the West Bengal project. In my opinion, they did excellent work in West Bengal. The foreign consultants agreed to do so.

MORE LEARNING NEEDED

In retrospect, I am glad this happened. If this project was to be done, much learning by different stakeholders had to take place both within the Forestry Department and within other organizations working in the target areas. At least five government agencies would be involved plus a number of NGOs. They had little experience working together as a team. Moreover, the institutional competence in the forestry area was pretty much limited to policing and tree farming. Of course, the consultants worked collaboratively with various officials on the many technical matters that needed to be covered in the comprehensive forestry project we had underway, but a key activity carried out toward the end of preparation proved invaluable for the future of this effort. The local consultants organized and facilitated a three-day ZOPP (see Appendix I) workshop that brought together officials from the Forestry Department and other agencies. The lead foreign consultants and central government representatives also attended as participants.

ZOPP WORKSHOP

Prior to the workshop, the consultants interviewed some forty officers at various levels and locations in the involved agencies. The interviews revealed that important institutional issues needed to be dealt with, such as coordination among the several independent departments and agencies that would have to work together, inadequate institutional capacity to protect existing forests, the quality and productivity of forest work, personnel management and the highly centralized operating format of the Forest Department. The workshop's stated purpose, therefore, became "examining the institutional framework for the project to identify any gaps that needed to be filled." For most participants, this would be the first time they got to see the whole project and had a chance to think about their ability to carry it out.

Although the consultants could have prescribed policy, structural, and procedural "solutions" to these problems, they knew that such prescriptions would not produce the needed changes. Their experience told them

that when those whose institutional and individual behavior needs to change grapple with such problems in a well-designed, intensive, participatory learning experience, the prospects for real change increase greatly.

The workshop started with a presentation of the project as it stood after the joint work of the consultants, Forestry Department officials, and the local people with whom the consultants and officials interacted during field trips. The head of the Forestry Department opened the session (and then participated for the full three days); one of the foreign consultants described the preparation process, and one of the Forestry Department deputy heads outlined the proposed project. About twenty-five people attended.

STAKEHOLDER ANALYSIS

The first order of business for the attendees was a stakeholder analysis. It identified the interests, expectations, and potentials of all the important groups, organizations, and institutions that would be affected, one way or another, by the proposed project. Almost sixty different groups were identified, including villagers from adjoining forests, rural women, cattle owners, tribes, the World Bank, and so on. A judgment was made about the project's positive and negative effects on each group, and an institution was designated to deal with the matter. For example, a positive result was villagers' involvement in

Figure 2.1. Problem Tree for Forest Protection

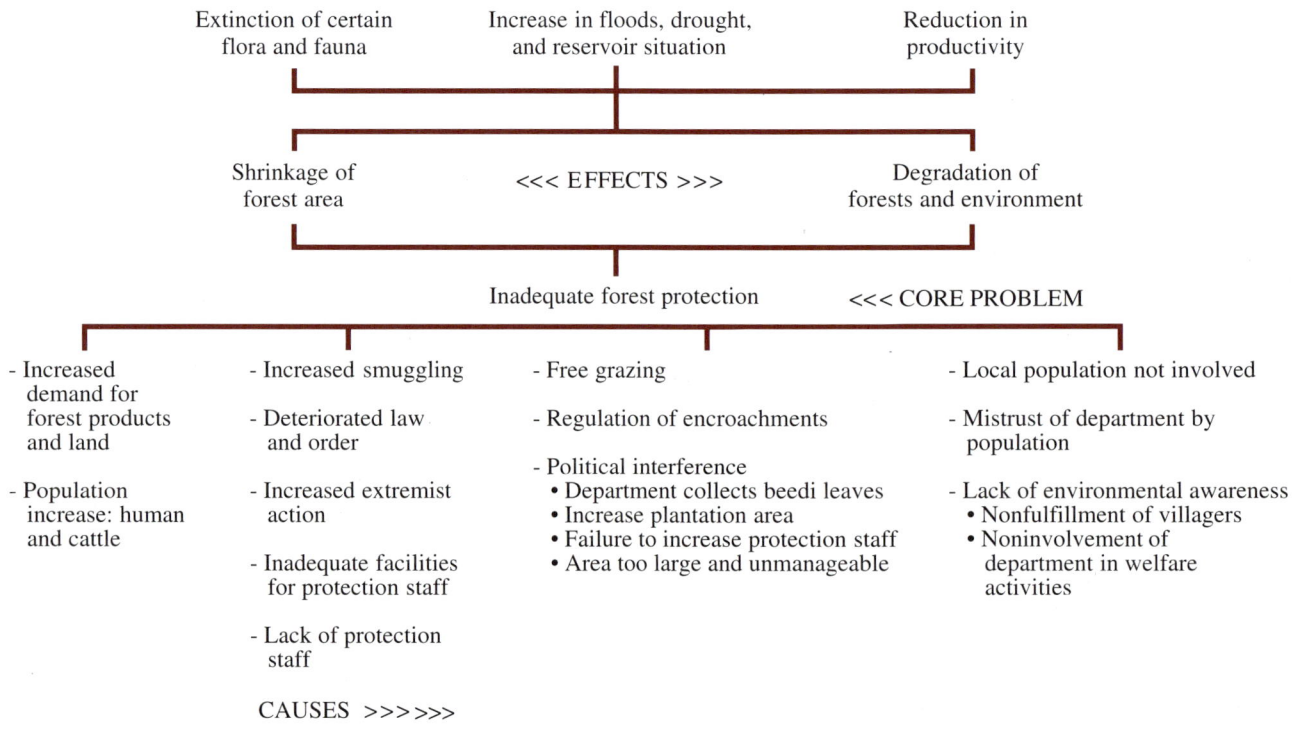

Figure 2.2. Objectives Tree for Forest Protection

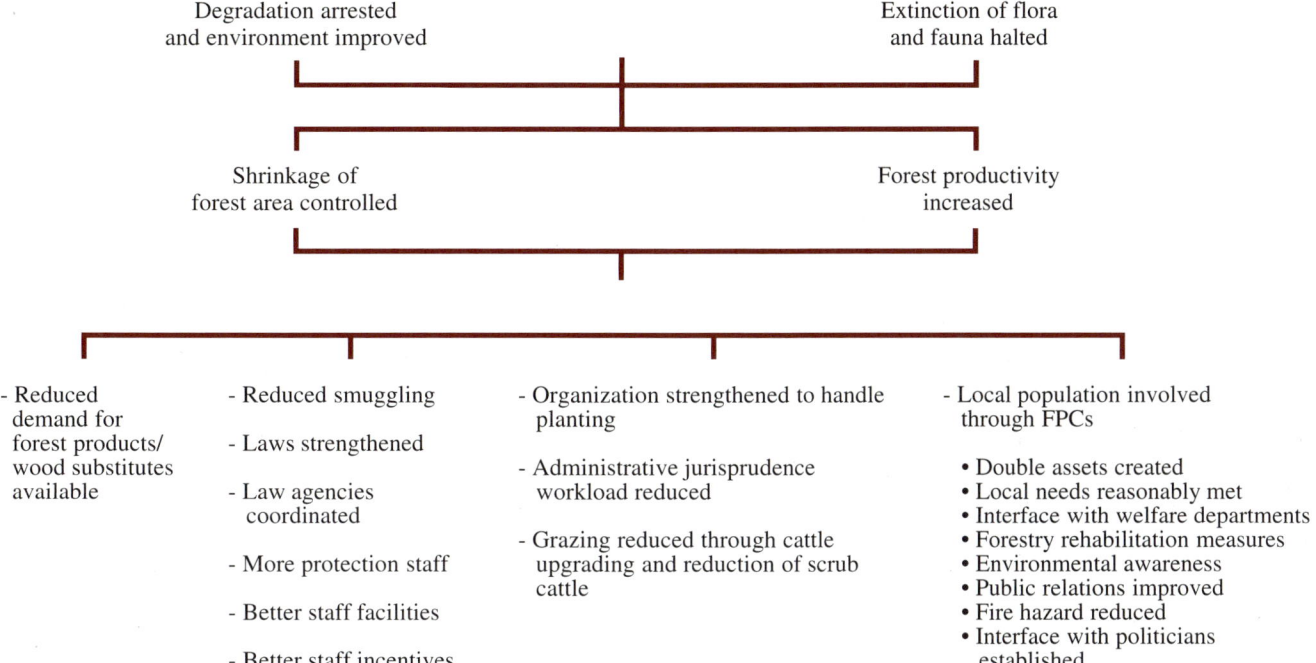

protection and generation of the forests, assisted by the Forest Department and NGOs through the establishment of FPCs. A negative result for cattle owners was the reduction of the number of cattle; the animal husbandry unit was designated to handle the matter.

PROBLEM TREE

The next step was a problem analysis and construction of a "problem tree." This involved the following:

- "Brainstorming" in which each attendee contributed one or more problems drawn from personal experience
- Clustering the problems identified during the brainstorming
- Identifying the cause of each problem
- Identifying the consequences if the problem was not solved.

The portion of the tree dealing with the forest protection problem cluster is shown in figure 2.1.

OBJECTIVES TREE

Having completed the problem tree, the next step in the ZOPP methodology is to create an "objectives tree." The objectives tree is really a mirror image of the problem tree and indicates what the future will look like by solving each problem. This is done by converting the negative conditions in the problem tree to positive conditions in the objectives tree, with the criterion that an objective must be both desirable and attainable. Figure 2.2 is the resulting objectives tree for forest protection.

ACTION PROGRAM

The next session converted objectives into the specific actions needed to attain each objective. Alternative sets were created when possible. For each set, the group reviewed such matters as policy, probability of success, timing, resource requirements, cost-benefit ratio, and so on. Box 2.1 shows several of the detailed actions selected for forest protection.

NGO WORKSHOP

A separate two-day workshop was held with Forestry Department staff and representatives of a wide range of NGOs. Central government staff chaired this workshop, which lent a lot of credibility to the effort. The first session explained the proposed project to the NGOs and invited their suggestions and participation. The discussion then focused on formation of FPCs based on a recently issued enabling Government Order. It also cov-

Box 2.1. Forest Protection Actions Excerpted from ZOPP Problem Tree

**Involvement of Local
Population in Forest Protection**

I. Rehabilitation of headloaders (firewood poachers) into plantation activities

II. Participatory management by the villagers

III. Reforestation of encroached areas under the concept of FPC by actively involving the encroachers themselves

IV. Training of villagers and farmers in the development of protected forests

Meeting Local Needs Reasonably

I. Opening up local fuelwood depots, bamboo depots, and small timber depots

II. Supply of bamboo to local artisans at subsidized rates

III. Raising fodder plots in the forest adjoining the villages

**Interface with Welfare
Departments in Welfare Activities**

I. Participation in implementation of welfare in tribal areas

---

ered how NGOs could contribute to FPC development. The workshop was fruitful. The NGOs made many valuable suggestions for how to modify the proposals and agreed to future collaboration. The foresters also became less suspicious of the NGOs.

SECOND PREPARATION MISSION

When we arrived for the second preparation mission at the end of September 1992, we found a great deal of enthusiasm on the part of all concerned—the officials from the various agencies, the consultants, the NGOs, and others. The project scope, size, and components struck us as sensible and acceptable to the Bank. The FPC approach had become a major part of the project.

The results of the workshop gave me confidence that there was now a quite widespread buy-in to try the Forest Protection Committee approach. I cannot say that the ZOPP workshop alone did this. All the collaboration among multiagency staff and foreign and local consultants provided an environment for thought, learning, and judgment. In addition, a team of officials visited the West Bengal project sites during the fall. The team was carefully selected to include staff who opposed the FPC approach or were skepti-

cal about it along with those who indicated openness or outright support. All members of the team came back convinced that the FPC approach was viable. The question was not *if* but *how* to go about establishing FPCs.

After returning to Washington, we began planning the preappraisal mission, set for early December 1992. To ensure ownership of and agreement with the project report prepared by the consultants, I decided to invite the head of the Forest Department and the head of the consultant team to Washington for detailed discussions of the proposal before preappraisal. It went well. The two were quite uniform in what they advocated, which made sense to us. The fact that the head of the Forest Department mentioned to me on leaving that he was considering a few small changes in the proposed forestry treatments did not worry me.

FACING A MAJOR BREAKDOWN

Preappraisal began in early December as planned, but we were in for a big surprise. The Forestry Department head disavowed the previous work and presented us with a new proposal. It was essentially the same as the original proposal—funding for additional Forestry Department staff and a huge component of subsidized seedlings for distribution had crept back into the project.

It felt like we were back to square one. I was disappointed. The consultants and Forestry Department staff who had been working together were perplexed. When we went to the field, we found staff well informed about the project and keen to start implementation. The proposals that the Forestry Department staff had seen, however, were the later version issued by the Forestry Department head, not the ones prepared jointly with the consultants. The problem with the Forestry Department head's new proposal was mostly related to general forestry management and the organizational aspects of the project. Also, despite earlier enthusiasm about trying the FPC approach, no further contacts had been made with NGOs by the Forestry Department. Except for the preparation of guidelines for establishing FPCs, little else had been accomplished.

Through patient discussion, however, the situation turned around. By the time we left, we thought we had reached agreement on what would and would not be covered by the project and the steps that had to be carried out before appraisal could begin. One of these steps was to contract the Tribal Cultural Research Institute to carry out participatory rural assessments (PRA) (see Appendix I) to obtain feedback from the direct beneficiaries on the proposed project.

During the May 1993 appraisal mission we found ourselves back on the roller coaster. The Forestry Department head kept returning to the essence of the original proposal. On his priority list were more staff, strip plantations, and seedlings for distribution. It was also difficult to persuade his team of the need to adopt effective, low-cost technologies for forest land treatments.

On the positive side, some movement in the direction of FPCs was apparent. The feedback from pilot PRAs in the tribal areas was encouraging and included many specific suggestions for improving the FPC approach. Training of Forestry Department staff in PRA had started. Furthermore, an order had been issued to set up at least two FPCs in each range as soon as possible; a few had already been created. Some of the new FPCs existed only on paper, but others (for which staff had been trained) were solidly prepared in the participatory manner that is fundamental to the success of the FPC approach.

FORCING THE ISSUE

During the mission, our team concluded that we had a weak basis for a successful appraisal. What we really had were two projects—one prepared collaboratively by senior members of the Forestry Department, other agencies, and the consultant team and the other belonging to the head of the Forestry Department. Not that they were mutually exclusive, but the latter still included a number of proposals that the mission could not support. This was a difficult situation.

Before departing, I went to the state forest secretary, the person to whom the Forestry Department head reports and put the problems on the table. The secretary indicated both serious concern about the issues and personal commitment to the FPC approach. He said he would assess the situation immediately. As it turned out, he became convinced of the jointly prepared proposal and confirmed support for it. I later heard that senior Forestry Department officials also went to the secretary on their own to express their support for the proposal they had helped create during the ZOPP workshop. That is rather extraordinary behavior for Forestry Department civil servants. Perhaps the network of publicly stated conviction and support created during the project preparation phase and the ZOPP workshop prompted people to behave differently.

RESOLUTION

We left again satisfied but still not sure the issues were finally settled. We knew they were, however, when we learned not too long after our return from appraisal that a new head of the Forestry Department had been appointed. We were told that the previous head had been transferred to another post, allegedly because of earlier problems and changing state priorities. Negotiations took place in November 1993 and the Bank's Board approved the project in February 1994. The project became effective in July 1994. I am no longer the Task Manager for this project but I understand from my successor that the project is still on course and widely supported by those involved.

PREPARATION COST AND TIME

The timing and costs for this project were fairly standard for a forestry project in this part of the world. Preparation took about twenty months. The Bank logged 110 staff weeks during this time. The consultant contract cost approximately $300,000.

ON REFLECTION

The next time I do a project like this, I will build more participation into the early preparation phase and the consultants' terms of reference. I highly recommend holding a participatory workshop for any project requiring important institutional change, which includes, I suspect, the vast majority of Bank-financed projects. It would have been better to have the ZOPP workshop right at the beginning of project preparation rather than three-quarters of the way through.

It would also have been helpful to allow the Forestry Department more time to internalize the project and conduct pilot PRAs with villagers, NGOs, and other constituents before proceeding to preappraisal. Because this sort of project requires a long lead time, we need to be able to get project resources at an earlier stage than is now possible.

Some disappointing events occurred during this otherwise rewarding experience. I am not sure I fully understand why. At times I wonder if the participatory, collaborative approach used in preparing this project failed us somehow. After all, it makes little sense to do a project that lacks the support of the top person. But in the end, I am convinced that the participatory approach served us well. It built a large network of support for what in every respect is the best way we now know of to protect forests and help poor, fringe forest dwellers at the same time.

LAO PEOPLE'S DEMOCRATIC REPUBLIC

HEALTH SYSTEM REFORM AND MALARIA CONTROL

Willy De Geyndt is the Task Manager for the Lao Health System Reform and Malaria Control Project.

Photo by Willy de Gendt

The Lao People's Democratic Republic (LPDR) is the tenth poorest nation in the world. Its people have suffered through decades of war and wrenching poverty. About 4 million live in this sparsely populated, agricultural economy. About sixty ethnic groups, many with their own distinct cultural practices, share the nation's limited resources. The vast majority live in rural areas, usually engaging in subsistence farming. Government institutions are fragile, and few modern practices have been adopted. Many donor agencies and foreign NGOs are assisting the country.

I began working in the LPDR in 1989. It was my first experience in a truly poor country, having spent the previous seven years in the Bank working in Latin America and the Middle East, mainly in middle-income countries. I had a lot to learn about this kind of country and culture, which has rhythms distinctly different from the Latino and Arabic ones I knew so well.

JUST ANOTHER HEALTH SECTOR REPORT?

When I transferred from Latin America and the Caribbean region to the Asia Technical Department I became the Task Manager for a health sector study. A team of us worked diligently on this study, including the "in-depth policy dialogue" with the country's sectoral leadership, for about eighteen months. Actually the dialogue was quite brief and successful. For the Lao, we were merely another international agency with a report containing an outsider's view of what they should do. So they gracefully obliged according to their culture by agreeing to the recommendations.

The government had agreed to the development strategy we recommended, including identification of the first health investment project. But I was uneasy. Agreement came too readily. I invited the then vice minister (now minister) of health and his assistant—my in-country counterpart—to a meeting at my hotel in Vientiane so we could talk in an informal setting. Their medical schooling in France and the informal venue fortuitously influenced the tone of the conversation and the behavioral expectations. We had a long talk about the health needs of the country as they saw them. From this talk emerged the elements of what became the Health System Reform and Malaria Control Project, now under implementation.

We readily agreed that controlling malaria—endemic in the LPDR—is an obvious high priority. Controlling this disease in a country like the LPDR takes a lot of effort and money; the Bank is the obvious donor to finance it. Because the task is formidable, a phased approach seemed to make the most sense. Health care delivery, especially for infants, children, and mothers, needed major improvement. The LPDR had scarce capacity in this area. Much had to be learned about what to do and how to do it. Ethnic diversity and low population density made the problem more complex. In addition to improving the delivery and financing of health care, we also agreed that improving health awareness through education could provide a big payoff. Finally, we agreed that strengthening the institutional capabilities at the central, provincial, and district levels was essential.

On returning to Washington, our project team discussed the various approaches for getting the project properly prepared for Bank financing. It was clear that government had neither the human resources nor the money to prepare this kind of project. We would have to assemble a team of experts to do the job and find the funds to pay for it. We applied for and got grants from the Japanese Special Fund for Policy and Human Resources Development for a total of $800,000. The government of Belgium contributed about $25,000 and the government of France $24,000 from their consultant trust funds. The Bank put about 145 staff weeks into preparation.

FIRST PREPARATION MISSION

We mounted our first preparation mission in October 1990. I brought along with me an architect, a health economist, and specialists in public health, management, and malaria control. We did the preparation work essentially the same way we had done the earlier sector work—in the expert mode.

Again we talked to numerous people in the country: officials at the central and provincial levels, health practitioners of all types, other donors, and NGOs. Preparation went along smoothly. Government supported us, albeit in a passive way that allowed us to go about our work as if we were one more agency that had knocked at its door. We were able to compile the basic data we needed for analysis and report preparation. What we suggested, proposed, and wrote was fully and readily accepted by the minister, the vice minister, and the other officials with whom we were working in a close and amicable fashion.

SECOND AND THIRD PREPARATION MISSIONS

Our second preparation mission went as well as the first. In November 1992 we launched what we hoped would be the final preparation mission. By that time, we were well enough along to make final commitments for preappraisal in March 1993 and appraisal in September of the same year.

We all felt we had come to understand this new (to us) country quite well. We believed our local colleagues had also come to know and understand us and the institution we represented. Although ours was the first Bank health operation in the LPDR, the Bank had been doing business in this country for some time in other sectors, including two fully disbursed structural adjustment credits. More important, it seemed to us that our in-country counterparts now had started to trust us. Indeed, they were quite frank and open in their interactions with us.

A LIGHT WENT ON

In one of the continuing conversations I was having with the vice minister, however, he started to ask questions about the Bank, saying he wanted to understand it better. He went on to say that, in his opinion, the Bank was just another NGO but perhaps one that was more thorough and cautious before beginning its work and that obviously had more money. When he said this, a light went on. I recognized for the first time why things were going so well. The health officials expected us to do what the NGOs do—that is, design and execute our own program in some part of the country. For some reason, it never really got across to our in-country counterparts that they would have to implement, run, and sustain the project we were helping them design.

ENGAGING LAO COUNTERPARTS

I returned to Washington in a state of depression. We had what looked like a great project—on paper. My colleagues and I were certain this project made sense for the LPDR. We also knew from countless briefings and discussions that our Lao counterparts agreed with it. But now I realized, their agreement was only limited, constituting mainly a nonobjection to what we were proposing.

I saw then that our Lao counterparts never really got involved in the learning and invention that we were engaged in and committed to. It was *our* project. We, a team of "external experts," had:

- Wrestled with the facts of Lao health care to construct the diagnosis
- Created a vision of how the future might be after many iterations, debates, and arguments among ourselves
- Crafted a strategy to take the country from its dismal present to a better future
- Were preparing the tactical blueprints, plans, and budgets to make things happen.

I also recognized that there was simply no way we could turn over our learning, excitement, and commitment to our Lao counterparts by briefing them, talking at them, or giving them reports to read. They hadn't learned much when we listened to and consulted with them. If they were to learn—to grasp and internalize the action possibilities—they had to do the creating, arguing, debating, and anguishing that we had done. Only in that way could they internalize this and translate it into action.

SHIFTING TO A PARTICIPATORY STANCE

Even though it was late in the process, I had to shift to a participatory stance and get the help of people who knew how to prepare a project in a participatory manner. I disliked changing course and mission team composition in midstream. We were a good team. We had worked well and hard together, and we had done a very good, "ex-

pert-mode," project preparation. In my back-to-office reports I expressed my concerns about the lack of country involvement in project design and preparation and received full support from my managers to make the necessary changes.

Fortunately, I received an offer from a colleague at the Bank's central Population, Health, and Nutrition Department who wanted to do some operational work. He became our new public health specialist. He had vast experience working at the district level in African countries with poverty levels comparable to the LPDR. He knew from practical experience as a district medical director how to get users and decisionmakers to participate in planning and executing their own health programs. He confirmed my instinct that shifting to the participatory mode made sense. In addition, I hired a health planning consultant who also turned out to have talent in the area of computers. He had many ideas about using computers to design projects in a participatory manner.

Over the winter we designed a Health Care Planning Workbook for use with our Lao counterparts. This workbook provided a way for them to plan a provincial health program themselves. It contained a series of matrices. Each was set up to record expected incidence of Lao health problems for a typical district in the most populous Lao Province, the one we intended to include in the project. The incidence data would then indicate the caseload that health care personnel would have if they were to take care of all the health needs of the population they served. Using data the Bank team had assembled, we completed sample matrices for all possible elements of a basic health care services delivery system, as illustrated in the table below.

The finished workbook—which we had translated into Lao—consisted of matrices with sample data insertions and an equal number of pages without data insertions. We also used Dbase to develop a program that would convert workbook data into such categories as civil works, equipment, supplies, drugs, and staffing. It would then calculate the corresponding costs and print the results as investment and operating costs.

TABLE 2.2 EXAMPLE OF CALCULATING COSTS FROM CASELOAD DATA

Target Population	Incident	Frequency (percent)	Caseload	Action
Women	Pregnancy	4	1,880	Immunize against tetanus
Women	Child spacing	4	1,880	Family planning
Children	< Age 1	4	1,880	Fully immunize
All	Cough > 2 weeks	3	1,410	Ziehl test
All	Positive Ziehl test	0.3	141	TB treatment

COMPUTER-AIDED PARTICIPATORY DESIGN

With these two tools in hand, we designed a strategy to involve Lao health officials and personnel in the preparation of the project. Indeed, we intended to have them do it entirely on their own. Our plan was to return in March for preappraisal as scheduled. At that time we would present the workbook to the counterpart officials in the ministry, go over it with them, and train two of their staff in the use of the workbook. The blank sheets would have to be filled in—working with their provincial and district colleagues—with accurate local data in time for a second preappraisal in June.

For the June preappraisal, we proposed holding a five-day participatory workshop involving national level staff and key officials at the provincial and district levels. These were, it seemed to us, the main stakeholders in the LPDR health care system. No doubt it would have been useful to involve some patients in the workshop. But we decided against it on the ground that the first priority was to involve the political and sectoral decisionmakers to generate political commitment and ownership at those levels.

The ministry officials accepted our request to complete the workbook by June and hold a participatory workshop at that time. We decided to use some of the Japanese Special Fund for Policy and Human Resources Development grant to do quick surveys and collect data in certain specific areas (HIV incidence, private sector pharmacies, and user fees) to help the effort along. Central and provincial staff would manage the studies and hire local people to do them.

Satisfied that we had the basic health services component on track, I turned with some apprehension to the other components. Fortunately, the health education component was being prepared in a collaborative process with the staff of the Lao Health Education Institute. I had seen the write-ups of this component and they looked solid, but I hadn't paid attention to the process being used.

ALREADY USING PARTICIPATION

To help prepare the health education component we had hired a Thai consultant who spoke Lao. She did her work by holding intensive workshops with the staff responsible for health education. The staff themselves diagnosed the country's health education problems, generated a vision of what it should be, developed strategies to realize the desired future, and then prepared the blueprints. They then went to the provinces to work with the provincial staff, thereby giving the central staff the opportunity to apply what they had learned by doing participatory project preparation with their provincial colleagues.

She had been doing all along what we just recently decided to do in the basic health services component. She was also running training workshops to build institutional capacity before project implementation began. It was clear to me that what was being proposed in this component had a sufficient amount of learning and commitment behind it to make the implementation and sustainability risks acceptable.

I can't say the same thing for the malaria control component. It was prepared using the "expert" stance. The experts had done almost all the work and almost all the learning; their national counterparts had only "agreed" to the proposed activities. Although it was an excellent piece of work, somehow we would have to find a way to shift the stance to participation for this component so the Lao would decide for themselves and learn in the process what should be done and how to do it.

SECOND PREAPPRAISAL

On our return in June, we concentrated on the Basic Health Services Component and the participatory workshop. We held this five-day workshop in one of the two provinces (Savannakhet) covered by the project. About forty people attended, drawn from national, provincial, and district health care cadres. Two staff from the central level had been trained by us previously and acted as facilitators. A Thai consultant—fluent in Lao—was able to understand the discussions and reported back to us on the flow of the proceedings. The provincial health authorities made the necessary arrangements and decided whom to invite at each level, taking care to ensure that the people at the workshop were representative of the whole.

The three of us from the Bank stayed in the background, available to participate as resource persons if asked but primarily observing the process. But we also added value in the form of a portable computer, loaded with the Dbase program our consultant had designed for that purpose, and a printer. At the end of each morning and afternoon, we entered the workshop's consensus numbers, providing instantaneous feedback on changes in the workload and cost variables.

BASIC HEALTH SERVICES WORKSHOP

On the first day, the facilitators formed the participants into two heterogeneous groups. For the entire five days, these groups, after discussing and debating matters among themselves, inserted data into the blank section of the workbook. The facilitators ensured that everyone spoke, regardless of level, rank, or function. After both groups had completed their work, they compared results and negotiated a consensus position.

During lunch and dinner, the consultant inserted the data into the Dbase program. From it, we printed out the human and financial resources required to carry out the kind of basic health services program implicit in the choices made by the workshop participants. The first run generated a $35 million program, an amount totally out of the question for a province of 600,000 people. The participants concluded that they had been too ambitious and went back to the drawing board to reshape the program by spreading actions over a longer time period. Iteration two produced a $20 million program, more realistic but still too big for the human resources the LPDR could assemble and train. After further discussion, further modifications, arguing, debating, reshaping, and computer runs, a program of just less than $10 million was developed and agreed to by the participants.

Although I couldn't understand what was being said, the excitement running through the room was impossible to miss. This kind of conceptual planning was unusual for the Lao, but they picked it up quickly and used it well. Many said that they had never worked so hard in their lives, but it was well worth it. We knew that a great deal of "embodied" learning took place with the participants. They learned what they themselves would have to do to implement and sustain "their project," which they learned as the group of people who would have to work together to implement and sustain the project.

PROJECT OWNERSHIP

Clearly, this is what constitutes country ownership of a Bank-financed project. The vice minister with whom we worked was pleased with the workshop. He promised to do exactly the same thing in the other province in July, before we returned for appraisal in September. The vice minister kept his promise. The September appraisal went off without complications.

After returning from appraisal we began preparation of the loan package for internal Bank review. A difficulty at this point in the project cycle was to write the staff appraisal report and memorandum and recommendations of the president in language that suitably expressed the spirit of the participation mode and conveyed the essence of the participatory process used. I kept falling back into old habits and had to struggle to bridge the gap between participatory language—with less precision and more flexibility—and Bank standards, which demanded a higher degree of certainty and precise, hard numbers.

Negotiations with the country, originally scheduled for April 1994, didn't take place until August. While the lengthy, time-consuming process of clearing the staff appraisal report, memorandum and recommendations of the president, and legal documents went on, the Laotians grew increasingly eager to start implementing *their* project. I was able to obtain and apply the resources of a second Japanese Special Fund for Policy and Human Resources Development grant ($600,000) to start in-country capacity building and begin pre-effectiveness activities. This was a crucial step because it allowed us to keep up the momentum, to do additional learning through piloting and demonstrating before mainstreaming the project, and especially to fill the financial void and the lack of on-the-ground action between appraisal and credit effectiveness.

During that lengthy Bank-processing period (it will likely be more than one year in this case), the basic health services component organized a workshop to define their 1994 preproject action program, organized a study tour to Thailand, started two pilot health centers, and organized English language and computer literacy courses. The health education component ran a five-week intensive information-education-communication training course for thirty participants and organized surveys in three provinces of people's health knowledge, practices, and beliefs as an essential condition for designing health messages and deciding on the most effective message media. The national leaders of the malaria control component called together the eight participating provinces to explain the objectives and the suggested approach.

Given the LPDR's fragile institutional infrastructure, it was clear that a large infusion of hands-on expatriate technical assistance would be needed to assist the country in implementing the project. Client participation and project ownership are necessary but may not be sufficient conditions to have a successfully executed project. Expert advice and assistance is still needed in this country. As for many countries, the LPDR is reluctant to use their borrowed money to pay for outside technical assistance. I therefore continued to approach bilateral donors and was successful in securing cofinancing from Belgium for a $2 million technical assistance grant-in-kind for project implementation. We plan to use part of this to generate ownership through participation for the malaria component.

PREPARATION COST AND TIME

Interestingly enough, shifting the stance in the middle of preparation neither added more time nor cost to preparation. The time and money we spend (or cause to be spent) on preparation are mainly for data collection and report preparation to meet the Bank's internal loan-processing requirements. Workshops, participation,

CASES

collaboration, and the like are not very costly. The real choice is whether external experts do it by themselves or collaborate with the local stakeholders. If behavioral change is the objective, the only way to do it is with the local stakeholders.

ON REFLECTION

I certainly learned a lot from this experience—which is far from over. Fortunately, the Lao have also learned a lot in the process. This learning has led to a level of involvement, ownership, and commitment that otherwise could not have been attained. My Lao counterparts say this *used to be* the Bank's project but *now it's ours*.

I'm not yet willing to place bets on implementation success or failure. I'm not sure that the several months of thinking about the workbook approach and the two five-day workshops are enough to generate the kind of embodied learning necessary for effective implementation and sustainability. We will need to keep at it through implementation.

I'm going to supervise the basic health services component by repeating the kinds of workshops we arranged during implementation. The Laotians have already set up the health management teams at the provincial and district levels to oversee and guide implementation. Supervision missions and expatriate technical assistance staff will work closely with these teams. In this way, I believe the Bank can effectively participate with the local people in making the adjustments and changes always necessary during implementation.

I'm comfortable with the health education component, because those who will have to implement it have been working on the design for about two years, including lots of training.

The use of computers has made a great difference. I've always considered computers good for linear thinking: spreadsheets, calculating, and word processing, for instance. I had previously used "timeline" management software to prepare and monitor a project, but it had never dawned on me that a computer could be used to facilitate collaboration. By running the choices the workshop participants made through the Dbase program, officials from different levels and areas and with different skills had a new, common language to unite them. As one or another argued for their functional or geographic area, the effect on the whole could easily be seen in the "bottom line" the data base produced. I must say that this has helped me see more clearly how we are imprisoned in our sectoral and functional views of life. I also see how this gets in the way of collaborating with each other to serve the poor people of developing countries.

MEXICO

HYDROELECTRIC PROJECT

Scott Guggenheim was one of the social scientists working on the Mexico Hydroelectric Project.

I looked over the dark, smoky, adobe hall and wondered how I'd gotten into this situation in the first place. Our mission was supposed to complete the social and environmental appraisal of two large hydroelectric dams. Instead, we were cringing behind a large table, watching a raging argument develop between company officials and three or four hundred angry peasants. This was not the way to begin a participatory project.

WHY DOESN'T RESETTLEMENT WORK?

Involuntary resettlement in Mexico differs little from large-scale resettlement elsewhere in the world. Large institutions, in this case, the national power company (CFE), acquire land through eminent domain so they can build hydroelectric dams, irrigation systems, highways, and so on. But people *live* on that land.

Four built-in characteristics of most resettlement situations make them inherently difficult. Perhaps the most significant factor is that it is *involuntary*. People do not have the option of *not* relinquishing their land. At the same time, although all legal systems require governments to pay compensation for expropriated property, in practice, most compensation systems are determined through administrative rather than market mechanisms. They usually fall short of providing enough money to replace what's been lost, and few opportunities exist to negotiate better rates. Resettlement situations typically pit large, powerful institutions against poor, weak, and often (though not always) isolated communities. Information, political and economic resources, and organization are not equally balanced.

Unlike most other examples described in the *Sourcebook*, the affected communities are not central to the achievement of project objectives. It doesn't matter, for example, if local communities are committed to developing national energy sources or not. The people who build a hydroelectric dam normally don't want their involvement, only their departure. Managers of irrigation projects, who might organize the most participatory water user associations downstream, don't think of the displaced people as project participants. Construction companies that must work against tight budgets and strict deadlines rarely want to take extra time to plan and consult with people whose major contribution to a project will be to get out of its way.

Finally, an often underappreciated feature of the resettlement environment is that the people who will be displaced are frightened. Most have heard stories of displacement elsewhere and know that the rosy visions of new homes and farms often don't turn out to be true. For most, losing their land is tantamount to losing their source of livelihood in an environment in which there are few ways to replace it. For them, a failed resettlement program isn't a "lesson learned" or a lowered rate of return. It's a leap into poverty.

Because it lies on the extreme margin of the project landscape, resettlement provides a test case for development alternatives based on participation. With such unfavorable preconditions, examples of successful, participatory resettlement provide a special kind of evidence for claims about the scope and potential of participation to improve development.

RESETTLEMENT IN MEXICO

The Mexico Hydroelectric Project was going to be the first Bank investment project in Mexico's energy sector in seventeen years. The country was in dire need of electricity. Bank involvement was a new opportunity to support long overdue production, efficiency, and management reforms in the sector. The project, conceived to be the first of four large loans that would be made over the next two years, consisted of the Aguamilpa and Zimapan hydroelectric dam projects and a variety of policy and institutional reforms; hence, it provided an important opportunity to piggyback social and environmental reforms onto a major development program.

The resettlement plans developed for the 3,000 people who would be displaced by the Mexico Hydroelectric Project were neither better nor worse than the typical resettlement component. At the point when the Bank became involved, project technical planning (dams, powerhouses, roads, and so on) had advanced well beyond the resettlement plans, which were little more than skeletal copies of a standard (and unsuccessful) resettlement package that had been tried elsewhere in the country. They included unrealistic proposals for long-distance relay irrigation to sites that subsequent research showed were unsuitable for agriculture or for breeding new, dwarf fruit tree varieties that could adapt to the harsh mountain environment where the people were expected to move. Heavily influenced by the engineering strengths of CFE, the resettlement plans showed few signs of having been developed or modified through discussions with those whose lives they would profoundly change.

But why should resettlement be treated like this? Wasn't there a better way? The Task Manager, project lawyer, and I thought there was. I'd already worked on enough projects to know that few technical agencies have as full control over resettlement situations as they think they do. Diversifying skills and increasing participation are not just philosophically good principles; they're necessities. In addition, Mexico has some of the finest social scientists, community development experts, and participation specialists in the developed or developing world; although CFE didn't know it, Mexican social scientists have generated one of the world's richest literatures on resettlement and its solutions. The skills and knowledge were there; now we, CFE, and the Bank had to learn how to work with them.

Although the project was already in negotiation, our team introduced tight conditions to require the company to develop an organizational structure and obtain professionals skills that would be conducive to participatory planning.

The Mexican delegation balked, but the Bank held firm. The resolution of the situation was helped, I have to admit, by an equally intractable procurement problem. Negotiations broke down; for the next seven months the project sponsors tried to raise money privately.

Many things had changed when they returned to the Bank seven months later. A national election had triggered a national political crisis, followed by a nationwide campaign to improve local participation in development. Our in-country counterparts were now much more receptive to our ideas about what needed to be done. Helped by late night beers, we spent long hours in discussion about a new approach to resettlement—an approach based on creating an institutional capacity for consultation and participation.

DEVELOPING OR HARNESSING CAPACITY

We began by asking three basic questions that we thought lay at the root of the resettlement problem. The first was if the company knew enough about the people being displaced and their needs to prepare a good resettlement plan. The second was if the company had the skills and experience to manage a participatory resettlement program. The third was what channels were available for the people being resettled to make sure that agreements were respected and information flowed to decisionmakers when construction schedules began tightening.

Field-level information was strikingly incomplete. But more important than the lack of good planning information was the conspicuous lack of contact with the villagers being resettled. The company's planning teams had been set up to *plan* the resettlement programs and *explain* them to the villagers. They weren't equipped to *learn* from them or to collaboratively decide how they might want resettlement to proceed.

New teams were recruited. This time they came with different skills and experiences. Mixed groups of young professionals—from university, NGOs, and social work and applied science backgrounds—were sent into remote villages with terms of reference that required them to stay there for three weeks out of every four. The problem changed from one of getting the staff to listen to the people, to one of getting them to stop listening long enough to write something down.

If giving villagers a "voice" proved surprisingly easy, developing an institutional framework to act on the information proved surprisingly difficult. Yet there would be little point in having highly participatory fieldwork if the information were lost in some office building. Virtually all of our involvement in the project was about revising the institutional design for participation, rather than "doing" participation ourselves. CFE's organizational shakeup created a new, high-level Social Development Office that reported directly to the company management. Similarly, each project had its own, on-site high-level office that reported to the engineer in charge of construction.

Why was the company receptive to these changes? Undoubtedly the size of the Bank loan helped. It was believed that this would be the first of four projected $500 million lending operations to the Mexican energy sector in seventeen years. But other factors were equally important. The new company president came from a political background and had already introduced several organizational reforms. Other changes taking place in the country's own development dialogue were leading to more requirements for environmental and social impact analysis. Given the virtual nonexistence of such units within CFE, the plan we'd developed during negotiations was as good a start as any.

Filling in the organizational boxes with qualified staff was the next step. In my experience, companies that are generally well run, such as utilities and parastatals, can attract and direct good staff once they understand what is required. After some discussion over which qualifications were relevant for the new position, CFE assembled a good group of experienced planners, economists, and social scientists to staff the new unit.

Making sure that the company included units with enough incentives and weight to do resettlement right was part of the solution to the problem of power imbalances. We wanted, however, to make sure that there were independent sources of information and appeal as well. Each state government formed a "comité de concertacion" involving different line agencies and headed by the governor to review and assist with the resettlement plans. The National Indian Institute—a branch of the Education Ministry—provided field monitoring. The company also appointed a senior, independent resettlement adviser (an internationally famous Mexican social scientist) to the company president to conduct intermittent field reviews of the project.

MAKING THE STRATEGY INTO A PROGRAM

The two projects took different approaches to turning the general resettlement strategy into on-the-ground programs. Most of the people affected by the Aguamilpa project were Huichol Indians, a group known for their wonderful artistry and symbolically rich rituals but also among the most desperately poor people in the country. Aguamilpa's first attempt to organize group meetings and discussions about resettlement among the Huichol met with nearly complete failure. Villagers had no tradition of group meetings with outsiders; virtually the only such experience they'd ever had was when they were summoned by local governments to learn that their houses would be sprayed for malaria and yellow fever.

The project's independent adviser quickly recognized that a more culturally appropriate approach was needed. The company increased the number of small field teams and began house-to-house visits to the remote settlements dispersed in the high Sierra Madre Occidental. Local community leaders were offering to help. The project gradually built a series of basic service programs such as health, cultural recreation, and basic needs that developed trust *before* they moved into the resettlement discussion. After years of "top-down" planning, the Huicholes for the first time began contributing their ideas about good locations, proper housing designs, and where to find the right priests (*mara'kames*) for a proper inauguration. The video we made of the project ends with a small group of beautifully costumed old men, some of the Huicholes' most respected *mara'kames*, blessing the large dam and new villages.

Zimapan was a different kettle of fish. Lying in Mexico's central plateau, these communities have marched across the pages of Mexican history for hundreds of years. The irrigated orchards that would soon be flooded, for example, were expropriated from large *haciendas* and given by a grateful government to its revolutionary supporters during Mexico's great agrarian reform of the 1930s. For centuries they'd lived in a hostile symbiosis with the outside world: they depended on employment in the large grain *haciendas* of the rich, yet internally they'd had to repress dissension to avoid losing their lands to hungry outsiders. Unlike the Huichol, they were used to collective action. The *ejido* assembly hall, where we had first met the villagers, was the forum for all secular decisionmaking.

More recent developments had led to some deep cracks in the social structure. Seasonal migration to Mexico City and the United States reduced many people's ties to the land. The poor harvests and shared poverty of former years was giving way to a new crop of parabolic antennas on adobe huts. Dissatisfaction with the religious hierarchy had plowed the way for extensive evangelization by Protestant missionaries, further dividing the communities.

The participation strategy in Zimapan was more sophisticated than in Aguamilpa because the strategy itself was negotiated locally. Community antagonism toward the first resettlement proposals had been so intense that people had repudiated their official leaders, who had acceded to the company's plan, and formed their own leadership. This evolved into a "negotiating committee" that developed a protocol for all resettlement discussions with CFE: full disclosure of information, joint financial audits, no individual deal making, and so on. Although the new resettlement unit was allowed to field social workers, the only binding arrangements were those signed jointly in the monthly meetings in the assembly halls. Saul Alinsky would have been proud.

THE RESETTLEMENT SUMMIT

The company as well as the villagers liked the new arrangements. Field tensions quickly diminished. Particularly in Aguamilpa, the farmers came to trust the new teams and even started coming to them for advice. As the new social development staff started to think about long-term social impacts caused by CFE's development program, the company decided to hold a national resettlement conference to discuss the approach being developed for Aguamilpa and Zimapan in light of resettlement

elsewhere. The conference brought together engineers, researchers, activist groups, and academics.

The more open, more participatory approach drew favorable reviews from unexpected quarters. Articles in national and international newspapers compared progress in Aguamilpa and Zimapan favorably with resettlement elsewhere. Visitors from as far away as the United States and South America were also struck by the high degree of local involvement in the initial program.

INSTITUTIONAL RESISTANCE

The first sign that implementation would not be all milk and honey came when a new head of the social development unit was appointed. Concurrently serving as political adviser to the company president, he removed many of the most competent staff. Field morale plummeted. The company also decided that it did not like reporting to independent monitors, whose analyses couldn't easily be discarded when they reported bad performance. Antagonisms with Zimapan villagers flared up again when villagers were excluded from the company's replacement land selection committee. The company, unused to so much outside scrutiny, was reasserting itself.

Relations with the Bank also became more brittle. Reports by the independent monitors showed that several of the agreements reached with the communities (and us) were not being fully implemented. At times, Bank pressure seemed to be the only way to induce a response.

PROBLEMS WITH PARTICIPATION

It wasn't just the power company's intransigence that made for difficulties. Village-level problems also made the participatory strategy hard to implement. Two problems stood out. First, despite their small size, the communities themselves were highly factionalized. Participation was defined as much by who didn't want to work together as by who wanted to make joint agreements. Second, the communities were highly stratified. One group of farmers was desperately dependent on land, particularly on the irrigated fruit orchards that would be destroyed by the reservoir. The second, more diverse group consisted largely of land-poor or even landless laborers who had left the communities to work as *braceros* in the United States. Although most of these people had started off poor, many had become relatively wealthy once they received green cards that gave them access to regular seasonal employment.

As long as the issues confronting the communities were general ones that applied to everybody, community leadership could negotiate fair deals on behalf of everyone. But once the big issues were resolved, private deal making and special arrangements guided by the interests of the rich became an increasing problem. Poor people were increasingly excluded from resettlement decisionmaking, and over time a new, small elite developed within the community that jealously guarded its monopoly of power, sometimes through force.

WOMEN'S VOICES

Rich and poor weren't the only fracture lines in Zimapan. When CFE began its first community consultations, many of the participants were women, because their husbands were off in the United States or other parts of Mexico for the agricultural harvest. Initially too shy to speak up in public meetings, they became more assertive over time. Even some of the resettlement demands changed. Once the women had a chance to say what they wanted, negotiations had to include not just requests for land but also some credit to open sewing shops or a small bakery.

This didn't last long, however. As the consultations began to produce tangible actions, the men attended meetings and women were increasingly scarce in the monthly meetings. The social workers, who were mostly young women, continued to visit their homes and transmit their requests for schooling, health, and other services that rarely occurred to the men who now dominated the meetings. Women never again had the same voice in the big negotiations with CFE.

SO WHAT HAPPENED?

I left the project about two years after the first villages were moved to make way for the coffer dams, although I've tried to maintain some contact with the Bank staff and consultants who have taken over.

Aguamilpa supervision reports that resettlement is working well, a particularly encouraging outcome because the Huicholes were especially vulnerable to the debilitating effects of mishandled resettlement. During my last mission there, not only had all of the resettled families remained in their new sites, but relatives had started to move into the area.

Resettlement in Zimapan's main villages got off to a bad start when people from the largest town discovered that one of the ranches bought by the project's land selection team lacked the promised irrigation water. Furthermore, as the villagers studied their new, irrigated, highly capitalized ranches, on which they'd formerly been low-paid workers, they realized that they didn't have the

skills or experience to run them. Coming at the same time as Mexico's dissolution of common property *ejido*, the villagers opted to sell the replacement farms negotiated with the company rather than move there, despite their original agreements. It seemed less risky to combine rainfed farming back in their home villages with seasonal emigration. In other villages, in which the approach evolved to the point that farmers could select their own land, it appears that resettlement went smoothly.

Compensation payments provided another flash point. Initial underassessments by the company were suddenly matched by an equally absurd overassessment by the community's negotiating committee. Company threats were matched by community visits to legislators and on-site work stoppages. For the first time, compensation rates were renegotiated and assessments raised to reflect the real costs of replacing them.

DOLLARS AND SENSE

No easy way exists to measure accurately the costs of our more participatory approach to resettlement. On the Bank's side, the costs consisted of little more than taking me along on regular missions. Our role wasn't to *do* the participation, only to help the company form and implement a more participatory program. Incremental costs for the Bank, therefore, came to about twelve weeks of staff time over the two years that I was with the project.

The cost issue is less clear when it comes to the borrower. The two projects have been the most expensive resettlement operations they've ever financed, costing at least double the most expensive previous program. There's no question that the higher resettlement costs are caused by greater participation; negotiation forced compensation rates up considerably—at least to market rates and probably somewhat beyond them. The company also had to form social and environmental impact units at a time when the Bank was otherwise recommending substantial staff slimming.

Project costs must be weighed against the benefits gained from the new approach. Aguamilpa and Zimapan are among the few large dams ever completed on time in Mexico. Although not every delay in the other projects can be attributed to fractious resettlement, many can be. During roughly the same period that Aguamilpa and Zimapan were being built, two other large dams—not financed by the Bank—were canceled entirely because of resettlement protests that blossomed into armed confrontations and marches into Mexico City. Because of the enormous costs of dam construction—nearly a billion dollars for the two projects—each year's delay in project commissioning would have implied foregone benefits that exceeded the total cost of our entire participatory resettlement package by orders of magnitude.

I think that the program's social benefits exceeded the economic savings. The project's "participatory stance" led to happier people, not just among the resettlers but among the technical staff as well. During supervision we repeatedly met field engineers and supervisors who commented how relieved they were to be working on a project in which they didn't feel surrounded by hostile, bitter people.

Finally, I think that the nation as a whole benefited. There isn't any real way to capture the true costs of using state power to force resettlement, but they're high. Resettlement colonies in other projects we visited were often squalid places, mired in poverty and unhappiness. The children of Aguamilpa and Zimapan are already back in newly built schools, on their way to becoming the country's next generation of engineers, economists, and perhaps even anthropologists.

ON REFLECTION

This is not a case in which hindsight produces a much clearer vision of what could have been done differently. Certainly it would have been better to begin the participatory approach earlier instead of having to rebuild from a fragile and already confrontational base. Yet many of the project's problems were not really related to planning.

My experiences in Aguamilpa and Zimapan taught me a lot about participation and development. More than ever before, I'm convinced that people make the projects. Yet, good people trapped in powerless positions can achieve little. Resettlement in Aguamilpa and Zimapan worked because the power company hired good people and gave them a mandate and sufficient resources to do what they already knew how to do. Once the field teams were in place, many of the ideas they came up with were much different from what I would have suggested, but usually they were better.

Resettlement also worked because community consultation and dissemination of information was so much better than in any previous resettlement program. People may not always have agreed with what happened, but they were rarely surprised by it. Furthermore, because there was so much more openness about what was supposed to happen, NGOs and other state and national agencies were able to pressure Mexico's civil institutions. Peasant resistance committees visiting state capitals may have been troublesome to project managers, but they returned resettlement to the national political system in which it belongs.

Not all the lessons are positive ones. Pressed by time and swept up in the enthusiasm and camaraderie of a new idea, we didn't operate with a clear understanding of the limits of our participatory approach, nor with an objective assessment of our role in making it happen. Field visits by Bank staff led to local beliefs that the Bank was on "their side." Such sentiments led to strong resentments in government agencies and raised legitimate questions about the Bank's proper role.

How important to the overall outcome was, in fact, the Bank's work in introducing a more participatory approach to the project? It's difficult to step back enough to provide a fully objective evaluation, but I think the Bank made a limited number of critical interventions that paved the way for new ideas. The Bank's big comparative advantage comes from its focus on policies and institutions, not in "doing" participation per se. We helped create the enabling environment that provided incentives and opportunities for CFE staff to work with the communities, insisted that the company assign qualified staff, and introduced cleaner lines for decisionmaking. We played almost no role in developing the specific participatory methodologies and activities.

That said, there's no question that the Bank's signals were heard throughout the power company. Details of the long discussion of resettlement at the Bank's Board were known by every engineer we met. As the project advanced, the Bank's Mexico Department director and the energy division chief gave the project a big boost by visiting the communities and meeting spontaneously with some surprised resettlers. These visits were as important for the impression they made on CFE management as for any facts they found in the field. Perhaps most important of all was that the Task Manager made a strong point of visiting the field sites on virtually every supervision mission, no matter how brief it was. Knowing that the Bank would come led to flurries of activity before and after our missions, during which some of the annoying problems that had been lingering on through bureaucratic inertia were magically solved on the spot.

The other big mistake we and CFE made in the project was in not thinking carefully enough about the implications of community stratification. Particularly in Zimapan, most of our assumptions about communities' abilities to make satisfactory collective choices turned out to be wrong. "Letting them decide" often turned into a way for unequal village social systems to become even more unequal.

Could we or CFE have done much more about it than we did? I'm not sure. In their few, short years of life, development projects cannot undo social systems that have developed over centuries; this applies as much to the big bureaucracies with which we work as it does to the small communities affected by projects such as this one. I'm not convinced that we have the analytical and operational tools we need to deal with the local-level problems of conflict and inequality that we face once we get through the higher-level problems.

Several years after I left the project, I asked my in-country counterparts in the different Mexican agencies what they thought we'd done well and where they felt we made big mistakes. Somewhat to my chagrin, nobody singled out the Bank's use of a field anthropologist with years of experience working in central Mexico as being especially important. Instead, they focused on the Bank's "weight," the fact that such clear signals about participation came down to their own management. More than anything else, they said, the consistency of our overall message opened up space for them to try new ideas, often despite strong internal opposition to changing the status quo. One senior engineer, who strongly supported the changes, told me that he believed that the Bank has a lot more power to introduce changes than it thinks it does and a lot less than the government thinks the Bank does. The question was if the Bank had a clear enough strategy and resolve to make institutions like his more open to a participatory approach.

They also liked some of our technical exchanges. Early into the project, I helped organize a visit to the Hopi-Navajo relocation program in the United States so our Mexican team could see how industrial countries also mess up resettlement. They used that trip well, commenting self-consciously about the differences among the levels of community participation in the program and adapting that program's creative approach to participatory monitoring of housing construction. We also mailed down a huge amount of literature on participation and resettlement that was copied and circulated.

What they liked least was the Bank's lack of self-awareness during field visits. They thought we were fair game for anybody who wanted to manipulate the missions—from project heads who warned staff not to relay bad news, to wily farmers who saw a chance to get a new round of concessions. Some of the more thoughtful people noted that because of the project's size, CFE and, by extension, the Bank, transformed and often in effect replaced traditional conduits and mechanisms for local decisionmaking. Neither the Bank nor the company, they said, had ever understood the ramifications of these changes on a regional environment. These are good points that I return to often.

Finally, I have to say that introducing a participatory approach was not all fun and games. Old ways fight back. We had our share of good times, and many of my in-country counterparts who developed the project remain not only close friends but also people who have gone on to reform projects elsewhere in Mexico. Still, it would be naive in the extreme to claim that all it took was a launch workshop and participatory training to get the new approach adopted. "Buy-in" and "ownership" are part of the story, but so are Bank pressure and willingness to stand firm on agreements.

MOROCCO

ENHANCING THE PARTICIPATION OF WOMEN IN DEVELOPMENT

Sunita Gandhi is the Task Manager for the Economic and Sector Work: Enhancing the Participation of Women in Development.

Photo by Sunita Gandhi

"Why not ask the women themselves?" This was the question that kept running through my mind as I sat around the table one afternoon with members of my division. We had been called together to discuss an issues paper that had been prepared as a forerunner to the Morocco Women in Development sector study. Here we were, sitting in Washington, talking about the different things that could be done to help the women of Morocco, yet no one had thought to ask the women what they wanted. So when it came my turn to comment, I expressed this thought. My division chief immediately endorsed it. Both he and our director were receptive to the idea of a "bottom-up" approach. Shortly after our discussion, I was asked to manage the Morocco Women in Development Sector Study.

STARTING IN A "COLD CLIMATE"

Because participatory sector studies were not customary in Morocco, I realized we would have to start by bringing together key Moroccan stakeholders from government, academia, and the NGO community to share their experiences in working with women and get their ideas on how we should proceed with the study. To do this, we organized a one-day workshop in July 1993 in Rabat. This event marked the beginning of the preparation process for the study. It was also the start of a long and involved effort to build consensus for participation at all levels in the country and within the Bank.

Now, you must understand that we were starting all this in a "cold climate." The Moroccan government finds the question of women's economic independence to be controversial and up until this point had been reluctant to even *discuss* it with the Bank. Direct participation of the local population in development strategies is also a sensitive issue. As a result, getting the ministries to attend a workshop on women's development turned out to be much more complicated than first envisioned.

IDENTIFYING STAKEHOLDERS

The first step was figuring out whom to invite. We knew we wanted to involve all those working with or interested in the affairs of women. With regard to government stakeholders, we invited all relevant ministries, which totaled nine. We also had local consultants compile lists of all NGOs and academic institutions that were doing work in this area. By the end of this process, we had identified all potentially interested parties—or so we thought.

Our government counterpart for the study was the Ministry of Agriculture. Due to the nature of the topic, however, we were faced with a prevailing reluctance on the part of the other ministries to participate in such an event. Nevertheless, I persisted in organizing this meeting because I believed that without a consensus at the ministry level, we would never achieve the support and legitimacy needed to move the process forward. I soon realized that I would have to change tactics to bring the different ministries to the table. So, instead of billing this as a high profile workshop, I decided to present it in a much less threatening way, as a "joint discussion" with those involved in women's activities. I visited each ministry personally and asked them to attend an informal gathering to discuss the issues. On the day of the workshop more than sixty people attended when we had expected only twenty-two. Not only was every ministry we visited represented, but participants from women's NGOs and other groups we hadn't known even *existed* heard about the meeting and turned up. I think those who attended were a combination of people who were genuinely interested as well as those who were just curious to see what the Bank was doing.

THE FIRST WORKSHOP

The objectives of this first workshop were to determine priority areas for the sector study and discuss a participatory approach that would enable us to identify women's perceptions of their own development. I should mention that this was the first time that government officials and NGOs had sat down together at the same table to discuss

women's issues. I think the neutral banner of the World Bank helped facilitate dialogue between the two sides. Through the course of the afternoon, I could see that people were gradually shedding much of their initial skepticism and were beginning to think more about cooperating toward a common goal.

By the end of the workshop, the group had endorsed the use of a participatory approach. With regard to priorities, different views emerged during the debate, which were integrated with those of Bank consultants who were preparing the background document based on a review of existing literature. Out of this emerged four principal areas of concentration in order of their importance: (*a*) literacy and education, (*b*) labor-saving technologies, (*c*) maternal health and preventive health care, and (*d*) access to credit.

This list represented *our* collective view of *their* priorities. Now the big question was if the women would come up with the same priorities. If not, *whose view counts?* In addition, how would we reconcile these differences in views not only between *us* and *them*, but also between various parts of the country, because it was also quite possible that views would differ among regions.

CHOOSING A TECHNIQUE

When I returned to Washington, I was cautiously happy about the general consensus on using a participatory approach for the strategy development. The next step was choosing the right technique. I believed that local women are probably the best experts around when it comes to knowing what they need and what they are (or are not) willing to do to bring about the desired changes in their communities. I knew I needed an approach that would not only allow us to talk with women about what was important to them but go beyond this to involve them actively in the policy formulation process. This was my shopping list, but I didn't know where to look.

I mentioned this to a Bank colleague one afternoon over a cup of tea. He suggested that I consider using participatory rural appraisal (PRA) methodologies (see Appendix I). This was completely new to me, but I decided to look into it. The first thing I did was call Dr. Robert Chambers at the Institute for Development Studies in Sussex. After an encouraging conversation, he graciously sent me all sorts of materials on PRA. I immersed myself in them, drawn by the seeming dynamism of the process and the way it allowed people to modify their views as their contexts and priorities changed. PRA seemed well suited for our purposes, but I still had many questions. How could we correlate qualitative responses with "scientific" data?

Is it worth the extra time, money, and effort? Will the Moroccans want it? Where will the money come from? Could this be done on a large scale? Although I still remained a bit skeptical, it seemed worth a try—particularly after a comparison with other approaches. A few weeks later, I hired two PRA experts and took them with me to Morocco for the second workshop.

THE SECOND WORKSHOP

We held the second workshop in November 1993 with approximately the same set of stakeholders. This time around, the purpose was to discuss the specifics of undertaking participatory fieldwork and the possibility of using PRA. One of the PRA consultants introduced the participants to the basic principles of PRA and explained how it could be used to contribute to the study. A great deal of debate followed her presentation. Many questions were raised about how the regions would be selected for PRA and who would conduct it. One prevailing concern expressed was that the results would be qualitative and not "scientific." How would this kind of information be incorporated into the rest of the study?

The consultants and I did our best to respond to the questions and concerns. During this discussion, we made a point not to try to influence the participants in any one direction. I certainly didn't have all the answers, as this was new to me as well. I simply presented the pros and cons of using the methodology and why I thought it made sense within the context of Morocco. Then I asked them what they thought.

As I look back, I see that detachment is an important principle when presenting options, particularly on the part of the Bank. The Moroccans are particularly sensitive about anything "assumed" about or forced on them. So I made it clear that they could take it or leave it—the choice was theirs. This approach put the Moroccans immediately at ease. It let them know that they were in control and that nothing would happen without their approval. This really set the "learning" mood. From this point on, we were flooded with questions and ideas. Everyone was interested and eager to know more. We received many suggestions regarding regional site selections for the PRA.

A NEW DILEMMA

The main outcome of the one-day workshop was a general consensus on giving PRA a try. Participants, especially government representatives, held the strong view that Moroccans should be the ones to carry out the PRA, *not* foreign consultants. First, it was felt that talking to local people is a sensitive matter and should be done by Moroccans. Second, it was an issue of capacity building within the country. This left me in a difficult position. I knew that there weren't many PRA experts worldwide, let alone within Morocco. How was I going to find twenty or so Moroccans experienced in this area?

In the end, there was really only one option. We would have to train local people to do this. As you probably know, training programs—let alone PRAs—are not commonly a part of Bank-financed economic and sector work exercises. As such, this issue was debated quite vigorously at the departmental and regional level at the Bank. My managers were not as concerned about the methodology per se but more about the cost effectiveness of incorporating local-level participation in a sector study. I would have to do some convincing to get the funds to do this work.

PRESENTING THE PROS AND CONS

At a seminar on gender hosted by the regional vice president, I was given the opportunity to talk about the sector study. At this time, I mentioned the problems of finding funds for participatory work. I ran through the benefits compared with the costs of using a participatory approach, which in my view were that it would (a) lead to a greater dialogue between government and nongovernment institutions (something that was currently lacking in the country), (b) lead to greater ownership of the strategy by Moroccans at every level, (c) contribute to empowering people in rural and poor urban communities by giving them an opportunity to assess their own needs and propose solutions, and (d) likely lead to better implementation and sustainability of follow-on projects.

Then, of course, I stated the cons of using a participatory approach, that is, (a) participation may be time and resource intensive, (b) it raises expectations among local populations that may not be fulfilled if projects are not forthcoming, (c) it is organizationally and logistically troublesome, and (d) because methodologies used are not "scientific," the legitimacy of the results may be questioned by various experts. Fortunately, the conclusion drawn from all this was that the benefits of participation were likely to exceed its costs in terms of extra time and resources required. The regional vice president's special gender fund provided the critical funding we needed to move ahead.

TESTING OUR HYPOTHESIS

In February 1994 we decided to run a pilot PRA session. I had heard that Gesellschaft für Technische Zusammenarbeit (GTZ) was running a program in the

Zagora area and had established a relationship with the local population there. I contacted the head of the program who offered his staff to carry out the pilot. We hired a PRA consultant from Singapore who joined two local women from GTZ and one from the local university to carry out the four-day exercise in the rural village of Tinfu. In this way, we were able to "piggyback" on the work of GTZ. All this, however, was done in conjunction with the Ministry of Agriculture, our in-country counterpart for the study. From the pilot, we learned that men's and women's views were different. Whereas men wanted to build bridges and roads, women's top priorities were clinics, ambulances, electricity, running water, and collective ovens. This showed us that women's time horizons are short and their greatest concerns lie in meeting their immediate needs and removing the burdens of their daily drudgery. Although rural women valued girls' education, they viewed it as a long-term need, achievable only after their most pressing basic needs had been met. This was a significant finding given that *we*—that is government, NGOs, academics, and Bank experts—as well as quantitative studies had all identified education as the first priority above all else. These results confirmed my belief that we were moving in the right direction and that we would learn a great deal by conducting PRA on a wider scale. The central problem, however, of how we would integrate this information with the formal quantitative sector analysis remained to be seen.

DOUBTS START CREEPING IN

Task Managers who have supported participatory processes will tell you that it's hard to do when you are only in the country for a few weeks at a time. I quickly found out that these sorts of undertakings are dynamic and require continuous interaction with the different stakeholders. Participatory economic and sector work is a completely new concept in Morocco, particularly when it attempts to bring local stakeholders into the policy dialogue. Anything new is bound to raise a lot of questions. So when new personnel in certain ministries began to ask questions—and I was not there to answer them—they started making assumptions. Unknown to me or my Bank colleagues, these misunderstandings and lack of in-country presence would lead to difficulties down the road.

GENERAL ORIENTATION WORKSHOP

Meanwhile, I was back in Washington busily preparing for the two PRA training workshops. The first was a three-day general orientation workshop held for government staff, NGOs, academics, and a few members of the bilateral donor community. Its theme was "Using Participatory Methods." We intentionally held it in the South of Morocco away from Rabat, in a town called Ouarzazate, so that fewer people would attend. The interest was so great, however, that despite the inconvenience of travel and expense—which had to be borne by the participants—more than 100 people showed up. Sixty participants were from government (it is interesting to note that this was a significant increase from the ten who had attended the first workshop and twenty who had attended the second).

The workshop began with an overview of the government of Morocco's Strategy for Integrating Women in Development and the role of the economic and sector study. This was followed by a presentation on the importance of participatory methods in preparation of the sector study and the strengths and weaknesses of PRA compared with conventional survey research methods. Next came the fun part—the interactive and practical exercises.

GUESS WHO KNOWS?

Much of PRA training is based on the concept of "embodied learning" through social interactions, game-playing, group dynamics, and so on. We wanted to get people to shed their preconceptions and start thinking in new ways about whose knowledge counts. To set the right mood, we began with a warm-up exercise that I have since named "Guess Who Knows?"

With the exception of two people, the group was asked to gather in a circle and join hands. They were instructed not to let go or change the positions of their grip during the exercise. Next the facilitator asked them to entangle themselves any which way. They found this to be quite a lot of fun and came up with all sorts of contortions! The two outsiders were then asked to help untangle the mess. They were not allowed to touch—only give instructions as to who should do what. We started timing the process: six minutes to sort out the confusion.

Next, the group was asked to repeat the exercise and entangle themselves once again. This time it was the facilitator's turn to give instruction, but she simply said to them, "Untangle yourselves!" Again we timed it. "Just over 10 seconds!" the facilitator announced. "What do you think of this?" The group was surprised and excited. They broke up into small groups to discuss. One conclusion was that "local people know better how to get out of their own mess because they live in it." Another conclusion was that it took more time for outsiders to sort things out, despite their good intentions. Others, however, questioned if this really represents what occurs in reality. This led the group to ask, "What is our role as outsiders?"

The facilitators began a discussion around the role played by external experts in the development process. Through discussion, participants concluded that outsiders have another, more effective role to play as "catalysts" or "facilitators" as opposed to leaders of the development process. The exercise helped them to understand that when people are given the opportunity and encouragement to help themselves, they *learn* how to do it in the process.

The remainder of the seminar consisted of many such activities, which the participants enjoyed and ranked highly during the evaluation as preferable to the lecture format. The participants felt that learning about PRA by doing some of the actual group exercises such as mapping, ranking, and drawing matrices helped them better appreciate the value of participatory methods. I am certain that these interactions contributed toward a level of understanding and commitment on the part of the participants that no amount of lectures or book reading could have achieved. The flood of interest in the upcoming, intensive PRA training workshop came as no surprise.

AN EMBARRASSMENT OF RICHES

Everyone wanted to attend, yet we had spots for only twenty to thirty people. I was amazed that so many would go voluntarily into a village setting and endure such rough conditions. This was a bare-bones village with no electricity or running water. We had asked each ministry to restrict their nominations to two people and each NGO to one person. Even then we ended up with thirty-four (thirty-three women and one man) and a long waiting list. Many people came up to me personally that afternoon and expressed their disappointment in not being chosen for the training. None of us could have predicted such a level of demand for training in participatory techniques. In providing this training, the Bank is helping to build capacity within the country to undertake participatory work.

TRAINING IN A VILLAGE SETTING

For the ten-day intensive PRA training, we wanted the participants to live in a rural setting. We decided to hold the training in Sidi-Filah, a village two hours east of Ouarzazate, which was accessible only by dirt road. All the participants, trainers, and Bank staffers (a total of some fifty people) were to stay with village families to see if trainees could endure such living conditions for extended periods of time. We felt it would also give them

an opportunity to test some of the methods they were learning. It was agreed that at the end of the ten days, twenty people would be selected to go out and do the field PRA.

Preparations for the training were going smoothly, but on the other side—the bureaucratic side—we were experiencing lots of problems. We discovered that going into the field and talking to local people required a "visa" from the government. It took yet another round of personal phone calls and letters to get most ministries to agree. The Ministry of Economic Affairs and Statistics—the key ministry when it came to fieldwork and research—however, did not respond. We were not sure until the last minute if the field mission would go through.

A SUDDEN BREAKDOWN

When I arrived in Ouarzazate for the training mission, I was informed that a new person had just taken over as government liaison with the Bank. Apparently, he was under the impression that the Bank was trying to circumvent the government and go directly to the people. These misunderstandings had in turn been passed on to the director of statistics—the man in charge of granting our clearance. He was angry and wary of our motives. He felt that we were trying to carry out the fieldwork without his knowledge, despite the fact that a representative from the Department of Statistics had agreed to the PRA at the November workshop. I decided to fly to Rabat to request permission to proceed.

In the meantime, the governor of Ouarzazate, who had attended the opening of the training workshop, had become interested in the program. His presence at the opening session had given our project national television and media coverage. Ironically, all this attention served only to fuel the suspicion of central authorities and made things worse for us back in Rabat. To add to the difficulty of my situation, the governor himself asked me to proceed with the PRA activities in Ouarzazate, regardless of whether we received permission to do so from the central government. I thanked him for his support, but knew instinctively that I was better off not making any promises. We had been working in an environment of uncertainty from the beginning. There was no telling what would happen next.

BACK TO SQUARE ONE

"Final clearance has been denied." This was the message I received on arrival in Rabat. I was in a state of disbelief as the new government liaison with the Bank and director of statistics started raising the same old issues and questions that we had been answering for the past year. It was as if I was starting all over. What were we doing in Ouarzazate? Why was the Bank siding with regional governments? Furthermore, the director didn't understand our methodology and did not agree with some of the selection criteria and the regions we had chosen for the study. He was angry because he perceived us as flouting the authority of the central government. Again, I did not try to debate the issues with him or defend my position. I simply presented the pros and cons of the PRA methodology and the rationale for wanting to involve local women in formulating the sector strategy. After this I said, "If you don't think we should proceed with this, I don't either. This entire effort has been based on consensus. Your support of this is important. We will do what we can to persuade you, but if you do not agree, we are willing to withdraw the team."

With that, the attitude of the director changed dramatically. He had been afraid that the Bank was trying to run the show and was visibly relieved to realize that the Moroccans were in the driver's seat. From this point on, he was much more receptive to everything I said. At first, he asked us to hold off while the government undertook their national census. This would mean a delay of more than four months and possibly much longer. I decided to present to him the risks of delaying as opposed to the benefits of doing. First, I explained, the newly trained Moroccans might forget what they had learned if the PRA was postponed; second, the outside trainers were already in the country, and I was not sure they would be available if we did this later; third, too much delay might lead the Bank to decide to withdraw its support for the study because of a perceived lack of government interest; and fourth, several critical projects were coming down the pipeline that would need a strategy for integrating women.

Little by little, I could sense his reluctance dissipating. The last obstacle to overcome was the selection of regions. At this point I realized how worthwhile it had been to spend the extra time and energy developing the elaborate (thirty-point) selection criteria and site designation through a process of consensus. The broadly based support we had garnered by involving the various ministries from the start gave legitimacy to the site selection process. In the end, the director made only one change to our regional lists. We received our "visa" for PRA the following day.

CARRYING OUT PARTICIPATORY RURAL APPRAISAL

Now that the director of statistics had given his final approval, we were ready to begin. The PRA was conducted over a four-month period and covered five rural and two urban regions. The trainees were divided into teams of three. We sent five teams to rural areas and the remaining five people to urban areas. Within each region, the teams covered four or five *douars* or villages, often in isolated regions and desert communities. The first step was to meet with the local authorities and bring them on board. We explained what we had come to do and asked for their assistance in selecting which villages within their region would be most suitable for the PRA. We found that gaining their support from the beginning ultimately ensured that our work in the *douars* progressed smoothly.

Most *douars* contained anywhere from fifty to one hundred families. In doing the PRA, our objective was to bring together members of the community—both men and women—in an open dialogue to generate learning and spark innovative thinking on a wide variety of issues. The team used a number of techniques, including open-ended interviewing, focus group discussions, matrix ranking, mapping, and seasonal and historical diagramming to bring out the rich experiences and local knowledge of the villagers.

This was a highly interactive process in which the participants were able to modify their views as the PRA went along—adding to their previous models or maps, shifting priorities, rethinking their strategies, and inventing new options—as they began to view and discuss their problems, constraints, and opportunities in new ways. The process was iterative and continuous. Each exercise built on the information and ideas generated in the previous one. For example, during a focus group discussion, women identified certain top priorities but were undecided on which of these was most important. The matrix ranking exercise helped them clarify their priorities and think through the choices they were making by giving each a fixed number of points (representing money) and asking them to allocate these among a list of needs that they had identified earlier. When asked to look at the same issue in a different way, some women found that they valued one item more than another and as a group began to articulate and understand the reasons why. It was a learning experience for the team as well as the participants to see how their responses changed and evolved during the course of the PRA.

EMPOWERING WOMEN

In our efforts to discuss problems and find solutions to the constraints facing local women, we were always careful to include the men and work with them as well. We realized the importance of their participation in this effort and the need to sensitize them to the hardships women face. These group interactions helped them to understand how constraints on women affect the family and village as a whole. In this way, they became part of any collective solutions. So, although women remained the focus of our study, we knew it was essential that those who held the power—the village men—were involved in the process. It was clear that without their support, change would be impossible.

Having said this, we noted that organizing women into focus groups for discussion and decisionmaking had empowering effects on them; in at least one instance, it gave them confidence to take the initiative to improve their circumstances. Shortly after the PRA was completed in one village, local authorities visited the community. As was customary at such meetings, the men were seated at the front of the room and the women gathered at the rear. On this occasion, the representative of the local people was quite vocal in expressing the community's desire for installation of tube wells (in locations situated conveniently near his own home).

Suddenly, a woman at the rear stood up and voiced her objection to this request. As a result of the information generated during the PRA, she was much more aware of what was good for the village as a whole. Along with other women, she had worked through a cost-benefit analysis type of exercise that showed that a tube well would only benefit a few. She then put forth her own suggestion for a collective oven, which she argued would benefit many more of the families in the village. She received support in this from many of the other village women, who then also felt encouraged to speak. These women had gained strength from having done their own analysis and examining the pros and cons of various options. The consensus they had built around these priorities during group discussions and focus groups gave them the power to speak and the knowledge to defend their choices. We heard many similar stories from team members returning from their different regions following the completion of the PRA.

NEXT STEPS

The next step will be to bring representatives of the women who participated in the PRA together with senior ministry officials to present the priorities and strategies for their own betterment that they themselves have devised. Although we have taken our PRA results and

synthesized them, we will be presenting the information in a language and format that has been filtered and formalized through *our* lens. But, I believe it's equally important (and more powerful) for local women to present their own findings using their own locally constructed floor diagrams and models. I think lots of people assume that local people can't solve their own problems. My guess is that it will be quite a revelation for many to see that village women not only have the ability to identify constraints and invent solutions but that they can be quite good at quantitative analysis as well.

The locally derived strategies that will be presented to Moroccan policymakers will constitute a fresh source of information. With regard to the sector study, we will use these findings to enrich the strategy document and refine some of our assumptions. Not only will this input influence sector recommendations, but it will be available to help guide the future work of the participating ministries.

ON REFLECTION

We are not at the finish line yet—the months ahead may still bring further uncertainties—but I can say that introducing participatory economic and sector work in Morocco has not been easy. We have made many mistakes along the way, but I know that's part of the learning process. We hope that, by the end, we will have insights to share with those who are interested in undertaking similar participatory sector studies.

Already, I can see the impact that this consensus-building process has had on everyone involved: government ministries that only last year showed marginal interest in this initiative are now eager to be the main conductors and sponsors of this study; a broad range of government officials and NGO personnel have been exposed to a variety of participatory methods and techniques; a smaller group of their representatives have received PRA training and field experience that they will be able to pass on to others in the country; and the director of statistics is now in favor of utilizing PRA on a larger scale in Morocco—perhaps within the context of the nationwide census.

Participation in the context of economic and sector work has not only generated interest, ownership, and collaboration among different government agencies, NGOs, and research institutions, but, more important, it has opened up a realm of possibilities for involving local people in their own development.

MOZAMBIQUE

COUNTRY IMPLEMENTATION REVIEW

Jacomina de Regt
was the Task Manager for the Country Implementation Review in Mozambique.

Photo by Jacomina de Regt

Mozambique has been at war since 1964, first to gain independence from Portugal in 1974 and then again for some fifteen years in a civil war. This means that anyone under the age of 20—about half the population—does not know what it means to live in peace. My first exposure to this country at war was in December 1988 while on a Bank mission to Maputo. Maputo was then a desolate city. Shops and houses had been boarded up and abandoned by their owners. Few cars were in sight. People got around on foot. Telephone service was erratic, and electricity and water were only occasionally available. Food and other amenities were scarce.

Two years later, I was assigned to the Bank's new resident mission in Maputo. By then, things had improved somewhat. But it was still a difficult place to live. More than anything else, however, the difficulties and frustrations I faced revolved around getting things done at work. I did not realize just how difficult it was in Mozambique until I actually lived there. Previously, I had come as a member of a Bank mission, well looked after by Mozambique officials. I know now that the attention we received was at great sacrifice to an official's governmental and personal responsibilities, which had to be set aside when Bank (and other donor) missions arrived.

EXTRAORDINARY EFFORTS REQUIRED

But we in the resident mission had to work with the government day by day. Without extraordinary efforts, even simple things could not get done. Picking up the telephone seldom resulted in reaching the right person or even any person. If I wanted to get something to someone, I had it sent by messenger. And if I wanted to see someone, setting up a meeting could take a lot of time. Living and working in Maputo allowed me to understand in a different way why the Mozambique portfolio had so many implementation problems. A generation of war simply does not produce the kind of policy and administrative environment needed to implement, much less sustain, good development projects.

Although the war was a handy scapegoat on which to blame problems, I also realized it was more than just the war that was causing the problems. Clearly, too little communication took place among the various parts of the government, a situation that was not really a consequence of the war.

RECOGNIZING THE PROBLEM

Donor-financed projects almost always have project implementation or coordination units staffed with well-paid, competent people. The fact that these people often come from government service weakens that service and demotivates those left behind. No two donors follow the same procedures, thereby immensely complicating administrative actions in government. No wonder implementation problems occur. Maybe we are part of the problem also, and maybe we can do something about it.

In addition, the administrative system was hierarchical, operating on archaic rules and regulations often based on old Portuguese codes. Virtually all the decisions were made at the top.

Then, in January 1991, I returned to Washington to attend the Mozambique Country Team retreat. The retreat's purpose was team building. We chose to "build" our team by working on a real piece of work, designing the format for the next Mozambique country implementation review (CIR), scheduled for February 1991 in Maputo. We also sought to clarify the roles, functions, and decisionmaking powers of the country team compared with the divisional team. The seminar was facilitated in a way that had some Mozambique Country Team members playing the roles of various government officials while others played normal Bank roles.

INSIGHTS AND POSSIBILITIES EMERGE

Something important happened at this unusual retreat. By identifying and playing the roles of the various stakeholders in government, the entire country team together realized the lack of unity in the government of Mozambique. We began to see that we might be able to use the upcoming CIR to bring together the various parts of government. We hoped to get the core ministries, line

ministries and the project implementation units of Bank-financed projects talking to each other about the real implementation problems they faced. In doing so, we thought it might be possible to develop a network of support for implementing Bank-financed projects.

Having been placed in the field to improve implementation, I had responsibility for designing and organizing the CIR. I thought to myself that perhaps this would be the real start in Mozambique of what the region is calling an "implementation culture." The more I think about it, "culture" is a good word, because it includes everyone. And clearly, everyone must work together and learn to understand each other's constraints to implement a project in Mozambique.

DESIGNING A PARTICIPATORY CIR

The facilitator of the Mozambique Country Team team-building retreat did a great job. I asked him if he could help me design and facilitate a participatory CIR for Mozambique on short notice. We would use a workshop format in which all participants—government and Bank—would work together intensively on the problems hindering project implementation. Fortunately, this facilitator had become interested in what we were doing and reshuffled his workload to be with us.

I hurriedly put together some materials about the Bank's Mozambique portfolio, a draft schedule for the CIR and two process and outcome scenarios. One scenario was of Bank and government staff learning together how to correct implementation problems and committing themselves to doing so. The other scenario was that the Bank would study the problems, report them to government, and recommend the solutions. I gave them to our facilitator for reading on the plane. I also shared them with my country team colleagues to get everyone thinking about it and to see the differences between the "participatory" scenario and the "Bank-mainly-does-it" scenario. To push the participatory scenario, I asked the Central Bank to invite all the coordinators of Bank-financed projects to a meeting to find out what topics they wanted on the agenda. The four agenda points identified during that meeting were maintained throughout the process.

IDENTIFYING THE STAKEHOLDERS

The first step was to determine who should be invited and find a way to get them there. At the Mozambique Country Team retreat we had already identified the Bank participants, about fifteen in all. We wanted a large Bank contingent to ensure that we talked not only to the government officials but also to each other. On the country side, we targeted the core ministries and the agencies implementing Bank-supported projects. Our target was to get, at a minimum, all the Central Bank and Finance Ministry staff handling World Bank-supported projects, plus the project director or coordinator or both of each Bank-supported project from the implementing agencies.

All told, the minimum workshop would have about sixty participants. We decided to limit it only to the Bank's work because we believed we had a lot to do to develop a better working relationship with our in-country counterparts. Once a sounder relationship was established, we could then invite other donors.

CONVENING THE CIR WORKSHOP

Once the facilitator arrived, we quickly got to work. We went over our invitation list with the governor of the Central Bank and discussed the way we wanted to run the CIR. We asked the governor to issue the invitations and stress the importance of attending.

We set the CIR for February 26 through March 1—four full days. A seminary just outside Maputo afforded adequate space and isolation from day-to-day work pressures. The resident mission provided the supplies, mainly flip charts, magic markers, and the like. The seminary provided simple but adequate food. Buses brought the participants in the morning and returned them to the city in the evening.

The vice governor of Banco Mozambique (the Central Bank) and the World Bank resident representative opened the session. Both made short, appropriate speeches welcoming the participants and stating the objectives of the workshop:

- Identifying obstacles to project implementation
- Finding ways to overcome the obstacles
- Incorporating what we learned into ongoing and future projects
- Creating a spirit of teamwork and constructive dialogue among all concerned.

WARM-UP EXERCISE

We used a "white card" exercise to get people acquainted with each other and accustomed to the openness and informality of the session. The purpose was to break the old mold of extreme formalism in working together. We gave each person four blank cards and asked each to write one important implementation problem on each card. Next we shuffled the cards and displayed them on the floor. We asked the participants to choose any four cards that interested them—except their own—and begin a discussion with another participant not known to them.

After the discussions, the participants "brainstormed" and categorized a list of major problems. The following list then became the agenda for the CIR:

- Role of project implementation agencies
- Procurement
- Disbursements
- Planning and monitoring (budget, accounting, audit, and evaluation).

A NEW WAY OF WORKING TOGETHER

The opening session worked. People's moods had changed by the end of the session. I could see this clearly in the way people spoke to each other and to the group, paying less attention to rank or organizational location. More important, the participants set the agenda for the CIR instead of having it set for them by the organizers of the event. Perhaps this may seem unexceptional to some, but for many, perhaps most of the participants, this is the first time they attended a meeting or seminar in which the agenda was theirs to create.

We set up small groups to work on the various parts of the agenda. We—the organizers—assigned the participants to the various work groups. We had multiple groups working on each issue. At the end of the session, each group made a report of its findings, conclusions, and recommendations to a plenary session. The plenary then discussed the validity of the findings and the utility of the recommendations.

We repeated this format until we completed each of the four agenda items. We, as the organizers, maintained control over the assignment of participants to the various groups. We did this to give as many participants as possible the opportunity and experience of working with different people. I must say we received a lot of opposition on this. The small groups wanted to stay together after they had gone through the difficult process of establishing a way of working together and had worked out their "internal" hierarchy. Nevertheless, we stuck to our guns.

On the afternoon of the third day, representatives of the small groups began to work on preparing an annex to the CIR final report summarizing the discussions about each agenda item. While this was going on, an executive committee consisting of the operations adviser and resident representative on the Bank's side and senior Central Bank and project officials for the government, was formed to prepare a summary report. We set up each group with a balanced representation of government and Bank officials as well as both core and line ministry government representatives. The flip charts from the previous small group presentations were available as input, as well as the charts prepared by the facilitator during the plenary discussions.

LOCAL PARTICIPANTS TAKE THE INITIATIVE

At the initiative of several local people, we established two new agenda items and set up groups to deal with these neglected matters. As one of these focused on "information needs," we asked the director of planning to work with them. The second dealt with "pay and remuneration" issues, so a Ministry of Finance representative joined the group to present government's latest thinking on this matter.

The work of report preparation and the new agenda items started on the afternoon of the third day and continued during the morning of the fourth day. The "pay and remuneration" group decided to split itself in two, with working-level staff of the central bank constituting the second group. By lunch, each of the groups had completed its work of preparing annexes and the summary report. After lunch we conducted an evaluation session, again using the "white card" approach. We distributed the final report at the end of the evaluation session.

TOUGH TALK FROM A MINISTER

The ministers of health and education, the vice minister of agriculture, and the vice governor of the Central Bank came to the closing session. Each working group made a brief presentation of what the annexes and the summary report concluded. The minister of health closed the session and took a tough stance on the need for change in the way the Bank organized and sent missions to Mozambique. The minister urged the Bank to ensure that its mission members know about the country before arrival and also know the whole development plan. This would, he said, reduce the burden on government officials to "educate" Bank mission members.

The minister's tough talk took some of the participants by surprise as it is normal for such sessions to end with platitudes. I felt good about it, as it signaled to me that we had accomplished our objective of creating a new atmosphere of openness and frankness with one another.

RESULTS

We all learned a lot at this session. The recommendations constituted a long list. Some of the important ones included the following:

- A unit should always be responsible for project implementation. Such a unit can be placed inside the ministry if the project deals with only one agency or outside if the project deals with several ministries and agencies.
- Project implementation unit functions should be harmonized with those of the ministry, which implies that at times project implementation will be slower with only gradual improvement in the capability of existing ministries.
- The dilemma between capacity building and project implementation needs to be addressed explicitly. Project implementation units should only coordinate implementation. They should not be implementing bodies. This needs to be addressed in all new projects. The question of salary and remuneration also needs to be looked into seriously as this issue is causing distortions within the government.
- The World Bank needs to standardize its criteria and eliminate delays in responding to "no objections" to procurement. It should continue to offer training courses, develop standard contracts for technical assistance, create a procurement library in Mozambique, and establish a system to back up Task Managers so someone is always present at headquarters to handle procurement requests.
- The Central Bank's ability to handle disbursement and payment requests should be decentralized. Project implementation units should be trained to handle the disbursement and payment requests themselves. Central Bank staff working with the public will be instructed to be more polite.
- The Ministry of Finance and the National Planning Commission should be actively involved in project preparation to enable sectors to propose realistic investment programs that will receive an adequate recurrent budget. The Ministry of Finance and the World Bank should harmonize the accounting requirements. To solve the huge backlog of audits, the Central Bank will recruit one audit agency to carry out audits for all projects.

I think that some of these recommendations would have been much less frank if we had done a CIR in the regular way. On the other hand, the project implementation units had so much anger and frustration with the centralized decisionmaking system that it would have been hard to restrain them even if we wanted to.

With four years' hindsight and three CIRs under my belt, it is clear to me that "power" was the real issue at these meetings. The Central Bank and foreign exchange control department resisted any attempt to devolve responsibility or delegate decisionmaking to the line agencies.

EVALUATION

My immediate evaluation of this participatory CIR was positive. In my opinion, the CIR achieved its three, albeit modest, objectives to *(a)* identify obstacles to project implementation, *(b)* find ways to overcome the obstacles, and *(c)* create a spirit of teamwork, openness, and constructive dialogue among all concerned.

We would, of course, have to wait to see what effect the CIR would have on the design of new projects, but we all knew what we had to do.

The participants evaluated the experience positively as measured by the fact that twice as many positive comments were written than negative comments on the white cards prepared for the evaluation discussion. In my opinion, the following techniques enabled real participation to occur in an otherwise formal, hierarchical society:

- The "white card" exercises, because they broke the formal meeting customary in Mozambique
- Assigning people to groups in a way that provided the opportunity for everyone to work seriously with every other person at some point
- Asking the participants to set the CIR agenda
- Having everyone participate in writing the final report
- Using a skilled, experienced facilitator (even though the facilitator did not speak Portuguese).

One of the local participants captured the essence of what I believe the seminar produced by saying: "It will be years before the public administration will work efficiently in our country. For the foreseeable future, work will be accomplished based on who you know, and now we have created a network of personal contacts that will facilitate project implementation in the future."

COSTS

As I calculate it, this CIR cost approximately 50 percent more than if we had sent just a few key Bank staff. Most of this cost came from the unusually large number of Bank participants we sent to the CIR and the additional two days we spent on it. In my opinion, this was time and money well spent.

ON REFLECTION

Some people seem to think that we have a choice in our business between participatory and nonparticipatory approaches in going about our work. I do not see it that way. We have no choice but to practice participation because development is a social process. It occurs when people come together and choose new behaviors that they have learned about by working together. There is simply no other way to build ownership and a productive network of relationships other than by involving the relevant stakeholders in participatory sessions such as this. In the final analysis, it is the process of collaboration that creates ownership and lasting relationships.

We did the next CIR in October 1992, in essentially the same manner as in 1991; in my opinion, it worked well. Quite a bit of opposition, however, came from the Central Bank on the "informality" of the process. They clearly let us know that they preferred formal and well-rehearsed meetings. Although we dropped the "games" to accommodate the Central Bank, we went further in the second CIR with the flexible agenda. In part this was forced on us by events. The Mozambique peace accord was ratified on the first day of the CIR and the second was declared a public holiday. We therefore concentrated on the "essence" of the process: a series of negotiations among stakeholders to enter into "contracts" to remove the implementation bottlenecks identified during the CIR. For instance, a group of project coordinators would walk into the small room in which the Ministry of Finance staff was located and try to get them to commit themselves to a period for contract clearing, whereas the project coordinators would commit themselves to sending in the whole dossier for a contract.

Unquestionably, what we started in 1991 still permeates the way Bank and government officials interact in Mozambique. Compared with other country teams or other CIRs that I have attended in neighboring countries, hierarchical formalism is now much less present in both the formal and informal interactions between the Bank and government officials.

The overall record of implementation progress, however, has not improved dramatically. Implementation breakdowns still occur much too often. We now resolve breakdowns faster through the network established during the CIRs. But systemic administrative problems still exist. Maybe the participant at the first CIR sized up the future well in saying it will be years before the system is efficient.

But I feel that the main reason we have not made more progress is our failure to engage the political level—the ministers—in the participatory process and network. They are willing to come to the start and finish but are apparently unwilling to engage in the social learning and invention that goes on during the participatory process.

Officials at the lower levels are not able to make major changes without the support of the political level. Involving the political level in the participatory process is, as I see, a major challenge that we must learn to overcome.

The reason the political level was not engaged successfully also has to do with the fact that until quite recently, the implementation culture had not really permeated the Bank. If we only raise implementation issues every eighteen months and spend the rest of the time on lending and economic policy, the message is clear: implementation is really not so important.

The third and most recent CIR (July 1994), now renamed the "country portfolio progress review," was a good example of how one can get the message across that implementation is important. The Bank sent one single message: until you get implementation moving (defined as getting disbursements up), there will be no new lending. This review *did* have the continuing participation of political officials; the coordination and implementation staff considered their participation a positive sign.

I think even more could be done to develop an implementation culture. This probably includes broadening the dialogue by including other stakeholders who can affect action on the ground such as donors, NGOs, and beneficiary representatives.

NIGERIA

WOMEN IN AGRICULTURE

Katrine Saito is the Task Manager for the Bank's Women in Agriculture Project in Nigeria.
Esther Gadzama works in the resident mission (Lagos) as the Bank liaison for the WIA program.

Photo by Katrine Saito

In Nigeria, women play a dominant role in agricultural production. This was confirmed by the findings of a study financed by the United Nations Development Programme (UNDP) in which I became involved when I joined the Women in Development Division of the Bank's Population and Human Resources Department in 1987. The study revealed that women make up 60–80 percent of the agricultural labor force in Nigeria, depending on the region, and produce two-thirds of the food crops. Yet, despite the facts, widespread assumptions that men—and not women—make the key farm management decisions have prevailed. As a result, agricultural extension services in Nigeria (as in other African countries) have traditionally been focused on men and their farm production needs, while neglecting the female half of the production force. Most extension messages targeted at women emphasized their domestic role with topics on child care and family nutrition.

It became clear that despite a decade of Bank assistance in building up Nigeria's agricultural extension service, women were receiving minimal assistance and information from extension agents. The study caught the eye of the head of the Nigeria's Federal Agriculture Coordinating Unit (FACU) and the Bank division chief on agriculture in the West Africa department who were both committed to finding a solution. In 1988 their support led to the creation of Women in Agriculture (WIA) programs within the existing state agricultural development projects (ADPs) in an attempt to address the gender-related deficiencies within the existing extension program. The ADPs were created in the 1970s with funding assistance from the Bank. Their overarching objective was and continues to be increasing the production of both food and industrial crops by stimulating agricultural production at the small farmer level.

Up until this point, the ADPs had contained only a home economics wing responsible for home-related women's activities. The WIA program, which was launched as a pilot (again with UNDP funds), sought to improve agricultural extension services for women. Existing home economics agents were retrained in agriculture and extension methodologies, placing special emphasis on women's activities. Pilot efforts were begun in different areas that were intended to supplement our ongoing sector studies as well as provide practical insights on how to change extension services to meet the needs of women. As Task Manager of this research project, I worked with Bank project staff and with FACU in developing program guidelines for assisting women farmers.

BRINGING STAKEHOLDERS TOGETHER

From the beginning I knew this was going to be a process of learning by doing. We had many questions but few ready answers. Through the pilot programs, we worked with local ADP staff to test out different approaches. About a year into our action research, it was clear to us that local people had better ideas than we did about what could work. We had been hearing accounts about different WIA initiatives in each state that seemed to be occurring in a sporadic, ad hoc way; some ADPs were making tremendous progress and others were doing nothing at all. We decided to bring everyone together in a National Planning Workshop to take stock of various WIA initiatives around the country, share lessons and experiences among regions, and develop three-year action plans for each state. We approached FACU with the idea of inviting local-level stakeholders to join national and state agriculture development officials and Bank agricultural staff at the workshop. Again, the director of FACU was supportive. He felt strongly that those at the policy level (himself included) should better understand women's constraints at the local level before any recommendations for policy reform were made. He believed that this was best achieved by broadening the policy dialogue and bringing a range of different stakeholders into the learning and decisionmaking process. It was his enthusiasm and keen support for this initiative that made the workshop a reality.

GIVING VOICE TO WOMEN FARMERS

In Nigeria, female farmers are often among the voiceless—particularly when it comes to influencing agricultural policies and projects. We were determined to give them voice in the WIA policy reform process but were uncertain about the best way to achieve this. We considered bringing women farmers from across the country to participate directly in the workshop, but this was problematic for a number of reasons. The political situation in Nigeria at the time was extremely volatile and made in-country travel difficult. Strikes and riots had broken out in many parts of the country, and military troops were everywhere. There were no reliable means of public transport, particularly in the rural areas. Moreover, the majority of these women had never traveled outside their villages, and many would have to travel with their babies. Getting the permission of their husbands to come to the capital posed yet another obstacle.

In addition to logistical difficulties, we had to take into consideration other factors related to the effectiveness of women farmers as participants in this high-level forum. This would be an entirely new and potentially overwhelming situation for them in which they would have to interact with powerful stakeholders such as ministers and senior government officials. We were also uncertain of their ability to articulate their problems and needs effectively in this sort of context.

For all these reasons, the solution appeared to lie with the female extension agents who interacted with women farmers on a regular basis. These women were accustomed to working with male bureaucrats, traveling alone, and were better able to articulate constraints faced by women farmers and propose solutions on their behalf. We felt confident that these women extension agents were well qualified to represent the interests of women farmers because they were from the same areas and often were farmers themselves. They had firsthand knowledge of the situation and good working relations with the women farmers. Although it should never be *assumed* that certain groups will accurately represent the interests of others, in this case, we had every reason to believe that female extension agents would serve as reliable proxies.

FIRST NATIONAL PLANNING WORKSHOP

In the days preceding the July 1989 workshop, demonstrations against the government had broken out in many cities, making travel to the capital even more difficult. On the day it was to begin, a coup was attempted in Lagos. I wondered if anyone was going to show up. But to our surprise, some sixty-four participants—mostly women—from all over Nigeria made their way to the workshop. Sixteen ADPs were represented in total. The delegates were primarily the female heads of the WIA units, chief extension officers, and ADP project managers (mostly men). Senior ministers and officials from the sponsoring government departments of FACU and the Federal Department of Agricultural and Rural Development were also present. The Bank was represented by project division and resident mission staff.

The three-day event started with opening remarks and greetings from the head of FACU, the resident mission representative, and myself. We devoted the first day to defining problems. Each WIA representative presented her assessment of the types of problems encountered by women farmers in her respective ADP, explaining how extension services were currently meeting local needs and how they could be improved. Believe me when I tell you that these women were impressive! They were well-informed, dedicated, dynamic, and articulate. They all came with prepared presentations and blew us away! The head of FACU was visibly impressed. He had originally told us he could only attend for the first hour but ended up staying the entire three days. The excitement and energy in the room was almost tangible. It was a great learning experience for everyone and a real eye-opener to see the innovative things that local women were doing to meet their needs. This sharing of ideas and practices opened up a realm of new possibilities, providing participants with a range of options they may have not previously considered. The presentations were followed by a plenary session, during which the common problems and constraints that had been expressed throughout the day were discussed.

STRATEGIC AND TACTICAL PLANNING

On the second day, the participants broke up into teams to undertake strategic and tactical planning. They were asked to come up with three-year action plans for integrating women into the mainstream of ADP activities for their respective areas. Each team was made up of three or four state ADPs, which we grouped into FACU regions: northeast (Jos), northwest (Kaduna) southeast (Enugu), and southwest (Benin). Each state ADP was represented—at a minimum—by a WIA person and a senior ADP manager. We felt it was critical to have ADP managers involved to build ownership of the plans by management. Once participants had devised their strategies, we asked them to be as specific as possible, detailing activities, training, logistics, staffing, timetables, and, of course, budgets. The teams worked throughout the day and into the night. As technical specialists, those of us from the Bank, FACU, the Federal Department of Agricultural and Rural Development, and the resident mission served as resource people. We went around from group to group, listening, offering suggestions, and giving technical advice when needed in shaping the tactical plans. The whole process was informal. We all huddled around tables and worked out the three-year plans with little more than pencils and paper.

COLLABORATIVE DECISIONMAKING

Participants were actively brainstorming, discussing, and exchanging all sorts of ideas. They were sharing experiences with other team members and getting ideas for their own programs by learning what others were doing to address similar problems in their states. Appropriate technology and innovations were constantly being exchanged among the women. Extension agents from one state presented a new gadget that they had developed with women farmers for feeding chickens and channeling their droppings into fish ponds. Others had invented different types of weeders or had other sorts of farming inventions and tips to share. Another group, through their own initiative, had started a cooperative woodlot and was charging a fee for fuelwood. Yet another had organized a nursery and was selling tree seedlings to earn income. It was obvious that a lot of knowledge was floating around at this workshop—it was just a matter of pulling it together. We found that combining this local knowledge and creativity with the technical expertise of the government and Bank worked extremely well in producing plans that were locally tailored, financially viable, and technically sound.

GROUP DYNAMICS

The interesting thing about these small group arrangements was that it broke the formal office hierarchy that existed between the female extension agents and their ADP managers, who were male. I think this was largely attributable to the pressure situation this was. The stakes were high. Each team had to make a presentation in front of everyone the next day, and they obviously wanted to do a good job. This forced them to cooperate and work together to come up with a detailed plan of activities, a way to pay for them, and indicators to measure how their objectives were being met. The direct interaction between extension agents and managers was key. For one thing, it helped the men recognize that the women were experts too and had valuable knowledge to contribute about the situation of women farmers. Both realized that they needed each other's experience and knowledge to get the job done. Although the women could put forth their perspectives based on firsthand experiences in the field, managers could put a budgetary perspective on solutions being proposed, while gaining an understanding of the impact their decisions would have on women farmers.

This iterative process of learning and negotiation sensitized all sides to the potential advantages and disadvantages of proposed reforms. I noticed that, at first, many managers felt uneasy about making commitments to budget items. They protested that they did not have the authority. This was another instance in which the presence of the head of FACU came in handy. He was able to assure them that making tentative commitments was, in fact, all right and that budgetary decisions would be formalized later.

BUILDING OWNERSHIP

On the final day of the workshop, each ADP presented its action plan, covering staffing and training needs, organizational structure, logistical support, and proposed income-earning activities for women farmers. This time, presentations were made by the program managers rather than the extension agents, as we felt it was critical for management to gain ownership of the plan. We knew without the personal involvement and commitment of the ADP managers to the reforms being proposed, the likelihood of changes being implemented was minimal. Bringing about change in favor of women farmers required ownership by *both men and women* at all levels. We knew from past experience that sensitizing or empowering one set of stakeholders to take action while leaving other key players out of the process could lead to problems down the road or, worse, no action at all. Therefore, by publicly presenting action plans—in the presence of other stakeholders at the plenary—each state ADP was demonstrating their commitment to take action in improving services for women farmers. The head of FACU was so enthusiastic after hearing the innovative action proposals that he too made a public commitment to move forward with the WIA program. He emphasized the need to set up an institutional framework to capture and maintain the momentum generated at the workshop and to help implement and track the progress of these programs.

ORGANIZATIONAL CHANGES

Fortunately, the ADP structure within which the WIA program was to be housed was decentralized and, in this sense, already conducive to supporting localized, participatory activities. Each state ADP has field offices staffed by local extension agents with FACU playing a coordinating role from the capital. Establishment of the WIA program ensured that extension services in every state in Nigeria have female extension workers at every level of operation from state headquarters in the capital down to the villages. The

structure of the WIA program itself is also decentralized and integrated into the extension service.

At headquarters, the WIA head holds the rank of deputy director within the state ADP and is responsible for the overall planning and implementation of the WIA program. She is assisted by subject matter specialists who work for WIA at the zonal level, supervising and monitoring the implementation of the WIA programs in their zone. These specialists interact with research and technology institutions, participate in problem identification and field training, and provide support to WIA block extension agents. At the block level, these agents work directly with women farmers, identifying and organizing women into groups in the eight-cell blocks and registering groups into cooperative societies. The formation of WIA farmers' groups facilitates the dissemination of agricultural innovations and provides women farmers with better access to farm inputs and credit than they would have as individuals.

STAFFING AND TRAINING

One outcome of the workshop was that it resulted in a large-scale administrative "switchover" taken with the cooperation of the key government ministry and the state ADPs. Although it was envisioned that all WIA agents have—at minimum—a diploma in general agriculture, in practice, too few women had these qualifications. To resolve this, a large cadre of existing home economic agents were redirected into the agriculture wing of the ADPs and retrained to become WIA agents. Building on this existing cadre meant that a huge number of women agents were mainstreamed into the agricultural department with no net addition to the ranks of civil service.

Women's extension services received a higher profile; resources were devoted to training the new WIA agents in agriculture and extension methodologies. In states that have a shortage of qualified female staff, male agents try to work with women in groups (although it is generally found that women agents are better conduits for technology dissemination for a variety of reasons).

Following the national planning workshop, a female extension agent who had demonstrated strong leadership skills and dynamism at the workshop was hired to be the Bank liaison for the WIA program. She was charged with tracking the activities and progress of implementation in each state. Her firsthand knowledge of the situation, technical expertise, and personal drive proved critical to the success of the program. As WIA coordinator, she divides her time between the resident mission and the field and has proved extremely helpful in facilitating Bank supervision missions.

PROVIDING INCENTIVES

All staff assigned to the ADPs come from state ministries of agriculture, other relevant departments, or parastatals. Because they are existing government staff, the project does not have to pay their salaries. To attract and motivate WIA staff, however, they receive a salary that is one grade level higher than their ministry counterparts as well as transportation and medical allowances. In general, ADP staff enjoy better conditions of service than their ministry counterparts.

BUILDING ON EXISTING PARTICIPATORY STRUCTURES

About one-third of Nigerian women belong to cooperative societies or other locally organized associations. Members may be united by common age, religion, trade, or economic activity. Some groups are informal and temporary, while others have well-established principles and operating procedures. The functions of such groups in rural areas include rotating credit and savings, sharing labor, borrowing money through cooperatives, and group farming. The institutionalization of such women's groups started with the ADP system. Under the auspices of the newly established state WIA programs, these groups were targeted by state ADP field staff to initiate and execute project activities. The WIA program helps to build the capability of these local groups by assisting them to register as cooperative societies to qualify for credit and farm inputs and be recognized by other institutions and NGOs.

The WIA program has three different ways of targeting women's groups and building their capacity. It works with pre-existing organizations in which members are already pursuing a specific goal such as credit or communal work. Second, WIA agents help organize women into blocks or cells so that they can receive ADP assistance. Third, the ADP system uses NGOs to identify women's beneficiary groups. There are currently more than 5,000 of such groups in Nigeria, and more are being organized.

PARTICIPATION IN SUBPROJECTS

The WIA program that emerged from the workshop envisions a system in which WIA agents work with groups of women in their area of operation. Each women's group elects four key leaders: a president, secretary, treasurer, and adviser. Decisionmaking authority rests with the group although at certain times, the elected officers can make decisions on the group's behalf. The women participate in all aspects of the project, from identification to planning and implementation. WIA agents assist them in selecting the type of project they want to engage in, such as cassava processing, groundnut oil production, ram fattening, and so on, depending on which enterprise will be most successful in their locality. A multidisciplinary approach is taken during planning and implementation. Block extension supervisors, technical specialists, and other resource persons from ADP field offices advise the women's group on a regular basis, providing technical inputs when necessary and monitoring their progress. Local women's groups are not required to obtain official status to participate in WIA activities or receive assistance from ADP officials. In fact, the majority of women reached by this program are members of informal groups.

FOLLOW-UP AND REPLANNING

Eighteen months after the first workshop, a Second National Workshop of the WIA program was convened to take stock of the action plans' implementation. The same groups of stakeholders were brought together to share their experiences, successes, and problems. By this time, all states had ongoing WIA programs, although some had started more recently than others. Objectives of the follow-up workshop included problem identification, replanning, and making mid-course modifications for the following year based on what had been learned. New annual targets for the WIA program, including the number of female farmer groups were collectively set.

The preliminary findings of a mid-term rural household survey, which had been conducted between workshops to monitor progress and measure achievements of the WIA program, were disseminated and discussed at the conference. The survey was carried out in three different parts of the country and revealed that WIA frontline agents were an effective channel of communication and feedback on the needs of women farmers. The increased demands from the women for information and technology had been stimulating the supply from the WIA units and FACU.

Recommendations and action plans emanating from the first participatory planning workshop had led to several positive results:

- The number of female extension agents doubled between the two workshops.
- The number of female farmers in contact with the extension services tripled.
- Better diagnosis of information and technology needs by gender was being undertaken.

CASES

- Male extension workers were being trained in women's activities.
- Female extension agents had been successful in introducing male agents to women farmers.
- A concerted effort to register women's groups as cooperatives with legal status had facilitated their access to bank credit and inputs.

Workshop participants also identified mobility problems and a lack of appropriate technologies among the main constraints that needed to be addressed in the coming year. Although many states had an increased number of women agents, they were still not reaching their targets due to different levels of access to transportation. Men tended to monopolize the available vehicles; whenever there was a shortage of fuel for mopeds, male extension agents were given preference. In addition, not enough progress had been made in developing appropriate tools and equipment to relieve women farmers of some of their most basic labor and energy constraints. Provisions to correct and address these problems were designed into the following year's action plans along with any other activities that had not been achieved in the previous year. Both the Bank and the government found this participatory approach to project planning and replanning to be an effective way of translating field knowledge into specific action for improving women's productivity in agriculture.

Costs

The initial study by the Bank's Population and Human Resources Department, Women in Development Division, that revealed the ineffectiveness of the extension program in reaching women farmers and the pilot projects that were launched to test various approaches were funded by the UNDP at an approximate cost of $40,000, which included hiring two Bank consultants and conducting two missions. The first National Planning Workshop and the follow-up workshop held eighteen months later were paid for by FACU at an estimated cost of $10,000 each. The UNDP funded the mid-term rural household survey undertaken between workshops at an approximate cost of $65,000.

On Reflection

Frankly, the program developed better than we'd expected; this is due primarily to the dynamism and resourcefulness of the Nigerian women. Also important was the support of Bank project staff and Nigerian government officials. We did, however, encounter some difficulties along the way. Some staff both in the Bank and the government were less than enthusiastic and constantly questioned the need for such an "emphasis on women." But the momentum generated by the workshop was difficult to stop. It created a much greater awareness among policymakers about the needs of women farmers, led to a rise in the number of women extension agents, and resulted in a significant increase in the percentage of women reached by the extension system. I have no doubt that the program has benefited both the agricultural sector and the activities of rural women considerably. Women farmers have increased their standard of living through improved production, which is a direct result of the new technologies now within their grasp. It is also heartening to see that women farmers now regularly visit the ADP headquarters to express their grievances and dissatisfaction about such things as the method of fertilizer distribution, for example. Until recently, women were rarely heard—only seen—and in this sense the WIA program has dramatically increased their voice and participation.

The program, however, has not been without its problems. Although the workshop generated financial support for the WIA program through annually budgeted activities, the reality has been that many of these activities are not being fully implemented. Priority is often given to other activities of the Extension or Technical Services Department; WIA comes last in the allocation of resources. Some states are also experiencing difficulty hiring and keeping adequate numbers of qualified female agents.

Staff relocation poses a significant problem as many married women are unwilling to move from city centers to the more remote rural areas. Employing married women from "local government areas" is being considered as a possible way of reducing this problem. Currently, both FACU and the Bank are working with the ADPs to develop strategies that will address these deficiencies and allow the WIA program to realize its full potential.

PAKISTAN

SINDH SPECIAL DEVELOPMENT PROJECT

Neil Boyle is the Task Manager of the Sindh Special Development Project.

At the time of the 1987 reorganization, I'd been with the Bank about ten years. The reorganization produced a lot of problems for Bank staff. But it also provided me a useful opportunity.

By that time, I had come to the conclusion that we couldn't help our clients produce sustainable development through episodic missions, dedicated to producing yet another project as quickly as possible. In many cases, our borrowers lacked the governance and institutional capacity to implement development investments properly, much less sustain them. Tacking technical assistance onto large investment loans didn't do the job; indeed, as fragile institutions attempted to implement the loans we typically make in the urban sector, their institutional capacity often diminished.

So, when my time came to be "rehired" in 1987, I said that I would really like to make a long-term commitment to one country, in fact, to one part of one country—the Sindh, in Pakistan. I hoped to be able to penetrate the system in which we did our work, get to know the people well, and find a way to help build needed governance and institutional capacity before we started lending. That's how what became known as the Sindh Special Development Project (SSDP) got started.

I knew then—and even more so on looking back, that the people of the Sindh—elected officials, bureaucrats, and citizens—would have to collaborate to devise answers on how to build this capacity. We would have to learn together while doing.

STARTING WORK IN THE SINDH

Pakistan, where I had worked a number of times, began to change in the late 1980s. In 1988 the first democratic national elections occurred after decades of authoritarian rule. By the early 1990s, the government had begun the process of privatizing, reforming currency controls, improving taxation, reducing trade barriers, and promoting exports. These changes had accelerated a mass movement to the cities and a strain on infrastructure, with accompanying shortages in water supply, sanitation, energy, transport, and communications.

I was pleased about the opportunity to work in the Sindh Province, which includes Karachi as its capital. Karachi, is less traditional than some other Pakistani cities, full of people from elsewhere and bursting with energy and opportunities. With an estimated population of 10 million, it is also the country's largest industrial, commercial, and financial center with the worst urban problems.

Although the government of the Sindh (GOS) needed large infusions of capital to deal with these problems, it had a reputation for poor management and, by all accounts, was not in a good position to handle major infrastructure projects. Although I am trained in engineering and finance, my interest in the Sindh was in figuring out how we could help put institutional capacity in place so that the provincial governance system and the policymaking machinery would be able to sustain the Bank's investments. That was the challenge.

THE KARACHI WATER BOARD

In 1987 we were preparing a new water project with the Karachi Water and Sewerage Board (KWSB). Like the GOS, KWSB also had a reputation for poor management. Without considerable change, it was in a weak position to absorb major Bank loans, which it was going to need to meet the demand for water and sewerage. Fortunately, our discussions with KWSB's senior management team led to an agreement to undertake an institutional reform program. To support the reform, KWSB applied for a British Overseas Development Administration grant.

We needed to find a way to help KWSB understand its problems and develop a transparent, effective organizational style. Instead of doing an expert study, I was interested in using an organization development approach to the transformation. But, of course, this approach would not work unless the KWSB managers were willing to change both the organization and themselves. And these changes could only be effective after they had gained fresh insight into the organization's deficiencies and why they needed to change their own behaviors.

CREATING A LEARNING MOOD

On my second mission, I brought along an organizational development consultant I believed could give KWSB the help it needed. Early on, an opportunity presented itself. I was attending a rather sensitive meeting with the senior staff and a sanitary engineer from the Bank. The chief engineers from two separate departments of KWSB were reporting about their projects to senior management. These projects had run into delays and mistakes, which came out into the open during the meeting. My questioning brought out the fact that these delays and mistakes were due primarily to institutional and organizational problems. Given that the two separate and unrelated departments had similar difficulties, I pointed out that KWSB's problems appeared to be systemic. Staffed mostly by engineers, KWSB did not have the practice of looking at the way it managed itself. It didn't take long for the entire room to erupt into a heated argument in which everyone started blaming something on someone else.

I had previously asked the consultant to wait outside, because the meeting was sensitive and he was new and unknown to the KWSB. At the point that things got really out of hand, I slipped into the hall and invited him to come in. At first, the presence of a stranger dampened the conflict, but it soon flared up again as people attacked each other and made excuses for themselves. I took the opportunity to introduce the consultant as someone who might be able to help. The group gave him the floor. He asked everyone to take a blank sheet of paper and anonymously write a list of KWSB's organizational problems. He shuffled the papers, summarized the lists on a chalk board, fed back what the managers were saying, pointed out that considerable agreement appeared to exist about the problems, and made some suggestions about what might be done.

The senior management team calmed down and began to discuss KWSB's internal organization and managerial behavior—its real problems—probably for the first time. They indicated strong interest in working with the consultant. We went back to the hotel excited, because the group that had the power to make decisions and change the organization was now ready to take action. We asked ourselves if a similar process could be undertaken with the Provincial Cabinet and administrative departments in which even broader institutional problems existed.

GROUND RULES

Using the Overseas Development Administration grant, KWSB hired the consultant on a long-term contract. His mandate was to take the role of a facilitator, always helping KWSB understand itself and search for ways to change; help the senior management team see what was going on and reflect back to them what had happened in their recent meetings or events; and help them internalize important learnings, although the decisions would always be theirs.

During the first months, however, distrust of the consultant kept bubbling up. We had expected this and dealt with it through open communication, reflecting back any veiled suspicion and reiterating the consultant's purpose: he was there to help the organization understand its own functioning and the problems this was causing them. Along the way, he would help them learn ways to correct the problems. We stressed he was also there to help the Bank team learn so that we could be of assistance. Yes, he would be a liaison for the Bank—but not a spy.

Working for both the Bank Task Manager and KWSB's managing director remained a delicate matter for the consultant. He had to be clear which information could be relayed to whom. Over time, a high level of trust developed among the three of us. To keep it that way, both the managing director and I grew to understand that this meant the consultant had to be discreet. The consultant, I must say, did not let either of us down.

ACTION RESEARCH

The process the consultant brought to KWSB was "action research." He and I had learned about this technique at the National Training Laboratory, where we had both separately spent several years studying organizational, group, and individual behavior change. Action research is a process that helps people change their organizations and solve their problems by carrying out their own data collection, diagnosis, planning, and evaluation—learning while doing. The role of the outsider is that of facilitator rather than expert.

REALITIES OF THE INFORMAL ORGANIZATION

At KWSB, the senior management team and the consultant began by using action research to map strategic pathways of power and influence to understand how the managers actually got things done. When I was there on mission, I participated.

The senior management team discussed the findings in group meetings and one-on-one sessions with the consultant. Gradually, the recognition spread that, for the last four years, they had been running KWSB as an amalgam of three organizations—which is how KWSB came into existence—with three different service rules, medical insurance plans, and pension plans. There were no staff meetings. The managing director would hold six meetings at once, with anyone permitted to enter his office. All this resulted in gridlock. For example, to authorize payment to contractors took 174 clerical steps. Customers didn't pay their water bills; government agencies, not individuals and businesses, were the worst offenders. The agencies played a ping pong game: the electric power agency didn't pay for its water; the water agency didn't pay its power bills; the telephone company didn't pay for its electricity or its water; and so forth.

DEEPENING THE CHANGE PROCESS

We had started at the top of the organization, working with the managing director and the department heads, because we had access there. As these leaders became more committed, the collaborative probe went deeper into the organization, drawing in division managers, section chiefs, and supervisory and executing engineers and their assistants.

We didn't work exclusively with each tier. At any given meeting, we tried to model openness by including several levels and constantly encouraging those lower down to give feedback and participate in decisions. We also saw to it that documents that we gave out were widely distributed and not withheld by any manager from his staff. One outcome was that lower-level people took more and more responsibility in meetings, sharing more, assuming leadership roles more assertively, and so forth. It was truly inspiring to see this develop over time.

The consultant kept feeding back to the senior management team what everyone was learning, thereby stimulating discussion and helping the managers at all levels recognize that they were empowered to make changes.

In addition, the consultant and I conducted many informal discussions with the senior management team, helping them see, without being threatened, how their behaviors worked and didn't work, recommending new management techniques and helping them internalize learning and invent collaborative ways of getting things done.

ORGANIZATION STUDY

Throughout this process, the organization was articulating its own issues and finding much more commonality than anyone had expected. After about a year, the senior management team and top staff were ready to assume responsibility for KWSB's problems and move to goal setting and action plans. After discussion with staff, the senior management team hired a local consulting firm in 1990 to undertake an organization study.

The organization study became the principal tool for driving the reform/modernization effort forward. It provided a comprehensive organizational diagnosis and recommendations to the KWSB Board of Directors. The Board of Directors and the senior management team committed themselves to almost all of the recommendations in the organization study and set out to implement them. The steps taken over the next two years either came out of the organization study or evolved as the KWSB managers reflected about them together and with those lower down in the hierarchy, making adjustments based on what they had learned.

WATER PROJECT RESULTS

The most dramatic result of the new organizational style, transparency, and collaborative processes has been solvency. The KWSB increased water tariffs fivefold between 1987 and 1993 and improved collections by 40 percent. The most recent tariff increase, two years ago, enabled the authority for the first time to cover all of its operating costs except depreciation. Most of these tariff increases occurred in the absence of additional water supply. Until new supply is commissioned in 1997, the emphasis will be on reducing current expenditures.

THE SINDH SPECIAL DEVELOPMENT PROJECT

As word got around of the improved performance of the Water Authority, other government institutions began asking the Bank to help them improve their performance. The time was ripe for major change. The federal government was experiencing great fiscal imbalances and had to tighten up on discretionary grants and bailouts to the provinces. In 1988 an urban-based political party with strong interests in improving the conditions of urban Sindh became the majority party in the GOS assembly and took over the Cabinet. These factors came together to focus serious attention on urban development and, as the Sindh Special Development Project progressed, the Sindh Cabinet naturally took an active interest.

Preparation

I should be able to give the date when we began to prepare the SSDP, but the learning approach we used makes that a bit difficult. Again, we had to obtain funding. In 1990 we got a grant from the Bank's Japanese Grant Facility (the precursor of the Special Fund for Policy and Human Resources Development). But we couldn't spend the money until the GOS and the government of Pakistan had formally accepted the grant. The GOS took three months to approve the legal agreement, and there was a seven-month delay with the government of Pakistan.

While we were waiting for the approvals, we kept preparation going with bailing wire and trust. The KWSB consultant and several Pakistanis at times had to wait quite a few months for their pay. To cover other expenses, we were able to hold things together by using technical assistance money from other projects.

We began to lay the groundwork for the provincial fiscal and administrative reform program, which we expected would be the cornerstone of the SSDP. This experience gave us insight into the ad hoc, arbitrary way the GOS developed policies—similar to KWSB several years earlier. No institutionalized means existed for collaborative policy formulation within the bureaucracy, much less among the bureaucrats, politicians, and public. In effect, policy was formulated in "stovepipes" consisting of each department and its minister. Little, if any, lateral consultation took place and certainly none with the public at large.

Working with the Entire GOS

In January 1991 the final grant approval came through, and work intensified on preparation of the policy reform program, thanks to the leadership of the minister for planning and development, who saw the reforms as contributing to the administration's platform of improving urban infrastructure and services.

During that year, we used the same participatory techniques we had used in the KWSB project. Working with the whole government rather than just one agency, however, was more complex. To help GOS come to terms with this complexity, we conceived of policy as being formulated at three levels—technical, administrative (including legal and regulatory), and political—and then helped create the institutional apparatus to make it work. We started with ad hoc working groups at the department level. These groups each made recommendations to their minister. After discussion and modification, the minister then negotiated the recommendations via meetings and informal discussions with other members of the Cabinet.

The recommendations amounted to a broad and detailed reform program, covering five urban subsectors: land management, urban transport, urban environment, water and sanitation, and municipal development. In addition, the GOS would focus on strengthening its taxation and financial management. Although the details were to be spelled out during implementation, the ad hoc working committees proposed some far-reaching strategies, such as property tax reform based on market value, an across-the-board labor redundancy program, the privatization of the Karachi Transit Corporation, and a provincial urban environment program. The Cabinet members supported these proposals. The GOS expected the program would take about two decades to implement.

REFORM PACKAGE AND MEMORANDUM OF AGREEMENT

The Bank team was happy with the effective work of the ad hoc committees and the support the ministers were able to generate. The process and the resulting learning represented significant strides in both the reform and collaborative decisionmaking process. But all of this was too informal. Despite the consultations, we were worried that the Cabinet was still not adequately involved. A lasting process and structure for turning the recommendations from the departments into official policy still needed to be created. Much more work needed to be done to institutionalize the decisionmaking process so that the politicians and bureaucrats could collaborate with each other.

Given that the Bank team often was the only constant in the picture, moving ahead was not easy. The GOS itself experienced almost perpetual turmoil. New ministers were appointed all the time and, except for 1991 and early 1992, their involvement was sporadic. Nevertheless, as early as mid-1991, key Cabinet members were telling the Bank team that they needed a formal policymaking structure and process to link the various government entities to each other and to the public—a structure and process that would survive the GOS's perennial political changes.

In June 1991 I went on a mission to Karachi to appraise the project. As I pondered the problems, I thought about a three-tier institutional arrangement that would bring bureaucrats from different levels and politicians together in the policymaking process. The good working relationship that was now in place between the senior officials and the Bank gave me the courage to suggest my idea. The people we were meeting with—the chief secretary, the minister of planning and development, and the chief minister—were interested.

We agreed to incorporate this three-tier arrangement and the basic content of the policy reform program into a memorandum of agreement between the mission and the GOS.

NEW CABINET

But by June 1992 all the ministers I had been working with were gone—the entire Cabinet resigned to protest a military intervention in the Sindh. So we had a new Cabinet and a new chief minister. In September 1992 the new chief minister signed the memorandum of agreement. I know the GOS well enough to say that, thanks to the broad participation of the chief secretaries, assistant chief secretaries, and other levels of the bureaucracy in the departmental ad hoc working committees, the ideas in the memorandum of agreement had support that survived the government leadership changes. Without that, the new chief minister would never have signed. Eleven months later, we negotiated the project, including the policy reform program, without a hitch.

A THREE-TIER ARRANGEMENT

The institutional arrangement agreed to by the GOS consists of three tiers. Each tier has a particular function and makes recommendations to the next tier up in the chain:

- *Ad hoc interdepartmental working groups* to look at the core functions of government. Composed of middle-level civil servants, these groups develop and assess the technical feasibility of policy proposals and work toward harmonizing departmental viewpoints. Their recommendations go to the Secretaries Committee.
- *Secretaries Committee.* This includes concerned secretaries (the highest ranking civil servants and heads of the provincial administrative core and line departments) and is chaired by the chief secretary. Its purpose is to examine the policy measures presented by the working groups and assess their administrative and legal-regulatory feasibility and consistency with accepted public administrative standards. Its recommendations go to the Cabinet Committee.
- *Cabinet Committee.* This top-level tier is a committee of concerned ministers from the Cabinet of the GOS and is chaired by the chief minister. Its purpose is to examine the policy measures for political feasibility.

At the top, to provide overall coordination of the SSDP, the group agreed to establish the Executive Planning and Action Coordination Organization (EXPACO). This organization serves as the secretariat to the Cabinet Committee. EXPACO's work is carried out through the following directorates:

- *Policy Action Coordination Unit* for policy formulation and implementation
- *Institution Strengthening Coordination Unit* for institution strengthening
- *Project Planning Unit* for planning, monitoring, and supervision of major works.

EXPACO is headed by a director general with civil service rank equivalent to a secretary. EXPACO reports to the chief secretary of GOS. Four high-level GOS staff people make up EXPACO, with all other support functions provided by a private contractor. The views of the public are brought into the policymaking process through advisory and steering committees composed of public and private NGO representatives.

How the Arrangement Works

The GOS approach to formulating land management policy provides an illustration of how the three-tier structure works.

The land management reform package was developed by an ad hoc working group made up of experienced senior officials from several administrative departments of GOS, land registration offices of both GOS and municipal government, and the Board of Revenue.

To provide input to the working group from many stakeholders, the GOS also established an Urban Land Advisory Council. To take into account the views of "shiftees," the people who are often forced to relocate because of government development policies, the council included a spokesperson representing the highly organized squatters and encroachers. The concerns of the shiftees were also voiced by the Bank, based on numerous consultations with the shiftees over the years.

After several months of work and debate, in 1991 and 1992 the working group sent a policy reform package to the Secretaries' Committee to be reviewed for legal, administrative, and regulatory adequacy as well as for the trade-offs that might have to be made. The package passed this test and was then sent to the Cabinet Committee, which gave it final approval.

Using the Three-Tier Process: The SSDP Credit

Since then, the GOS has used the three-tier decision-making process to prepare detailed policy action programs for the first five years, finalized with the Bank in September 1992. An important part of the negotiations was the agreement that future financial support would depend on how well the GOS implements the policy reform program.

SSDP Approved by Bank

The SSDP project, $46.8 million, was approved by the Bank Board in December 1993 and signed by the government of Pakistan on March 10, 1994, four years after the first mission. The project was declared effective in September 1994.

To help Karachi and to a lesser extent six interior cities, the credit will support the following:

- Immediate actions on alleviating environmental degradation and traffic congestion
- GOS's newly created policy planning arrangement and institution strengthening
- Fiscal and administrative reforms in GOS
- Engineering studies for infrastructure improvements.

Other loans or credits or both will be prepared while the SSDP is being implemented, but these will be approved only when GOS has demonstrated the success of its reforms and the ability to sustain the Bank's investments.

NEW ACCOUNTABILITY

More important than the credit was the shift from individual to group responsibility and the improved accountability of the entire government. The open meetings of the committees and EXPACO dramatically undermined closed-door dealings revolving around cliques, ethnic relations, and patronage. Once people make commitments in public, it is risky and potentially embarrassing to renege, because they will have to contend with the other stakeholders. The new transparency also led to a clear, public picture of how the government was operating—one that was not in the annual budget reports. Contrary to these reports, the GOS was running a deficit, as everyone unofficially knew.

A critical event that showed how far the process had moved took place as early as 1991, when I mentioned the deficit in a high-level meeting. One official became furious. But the secretary of finance wanted the truth to come out. He said, "I'd like to correct Mr. Boyle's numbers. The deficit is not Rs.3.5 billion. It is Rs.4 billion."

In June 1993 the Cabinet presented the fiscal 1994 budget to the Assembly. For the first time in five years, the chief minister, with the agreement of the Cabinet, chose to present the real picture.

COSTS AND TIME

From 1990 to 1993 approximately 830 staff weeks (572 by the GOS and 258 by the Bank) went into preparing SSDP. By Bank standards, 258 staff weeks is high. The institutional changes we have supported, however, require a long-term commitment and the kind of staff time that we devoted. Much of the time should be viewed as research and development in the form of action learning on the ground.

ON REFLECTION

As I think about our experience in the Sindh, I am pleased that we decided to work on institution strengthening before lending and that we have retained leverage by linking future loans to the pace and quality of reforms. It would have been difficult to carry out investments successfully, I think, if we hadn't supported the GOS in building sound capacity to make policies and investment decisions.

The Triad

I think the politicians, bureaucrats, and citizens could be seen as forming a *triad*. Initially, in the Sindh, the characteristics and relationships of the three groups added up largely to a closed system, impoverished of ideas and imagination and not able to manage long-term development. This *triad* concept has given us an important framework for the Sindh Special Development Project.

The gradually improving health and energy of the *triad* is, I think, more important than the physical development plans the Sindhis have made. I am pleased that in so many important areas the three legs of the *triad* are collaborating regularly and directly for the first time. At many levels, politicians and bureaucrats comprising the GOS and the representatives of ordinary citizens have diagnosed their problems, decided what issues they are going to own, and developed the solutions; the participatory policymaking machinery is also embedded enough to be used for new purposes. It will be used, for example, for problem solving in connection with the proposed Karachi Urban Transport Project. GOS will work through EXPACO to help reach a much-needed public consensus on mass transit investments, develop a transit authority, and lay the foundation of a legal-regulatory system for the transport sector. EXPACO will facilitate the work of the ministries, agencies, and consultative groups representing the population as a whole and present policy recommendations to the Secretaries Committee and the Cabinet Committee. This structure for involving the entire *triad* is neither "top-down" nor "bottom-up." We came to view it as "middle-out."

Navigating Bank Requirements

Participation activities in the Sindh were made possible by the grants from the Japanese Grant Facility and the British Overseas Development Administration. The Japanese grant paid for the KWSB participant-observer, the goal setting process, the organization study, process consultation, extensive coaching of KWSB leadership, project costing, and the restructuring of KWSB, including setting up decisionmaking procedures and steering committees. Other costs were covered by using language in the credit legal document, which was amenable to interpretation. It would be nice if we could draw on the Bank's budget for all this work; it would simplify matters and reduce preparation time. Another hurdle was the project cycle. The Bank's problem identification process requires standard research, analysis, and quantitative data. The participatory tools we used in the Sindh, on the other hand, were catalysts for plans based on the self-discovery, common sense, and collective experience of the people themselves. Translating these plans into a traditional Bank appraisal document was quite a task!

A third hurdle lay in formulating a long-term policy and institutional reform program—in SSDP, of maybe two decades—and linking future lending operations of the Bank to progress made on the reform program. We did this by grouping the program into five-year sections, but this was not easy because Bank processes don't work this way.

Intervention and Participation

I can't claim that everything we did was participatory. The Bank team's leverage lay in having the knowledge to be catalysts for "jump starting" change and in making suggestions based on our experience around the world. The three-tier structure and EXPACO are examples of ideas we proposed (although they were adopted only after extensive discussion among the bureaucrats and politicians who would have to change their behaviors to make the new structure successful).

Looking at the whole, some of the ad hoc working groups and advisory committees representing the civil society have functioned in a participatory manner and others have not. But the Sindh is a large social system in which capacity is unevenly distributed; gradual change seems to me to be a realistic expectation. As time passes, I think the more participatory working groups and committees will demonstrate their success and others will follow their example. Through EXPACO, GOS is already building its ability to prepare future projects collaboratively. Each time I visit the Sindh, I find progress. The Karachi Urban Transport Project I just mentioned is an example. There is much public debate (and sometimes criticism) of this project, but I believe the participatory process will give the debate not only an outlet but a policymaking function and ultimately a resolution.

The Future

Until now, we have given highest priority to the systemic problems within the government, because these problems were at the heart of the policy gridlock. As the SSDP progresses, the next step is to further involve the public in the policymaking process. We will explore ways of including beneficiaries and adversely affected people themselves in the deliberations, because the NGOs may not be truly representative. I think we should encourage the GOS to strengthen the advisory committees and, in time, introduce public hearings, although this is a sophisticated concept. The East Asian model of deliberative councils may be another mechanism of giving voice to civil society. We are also considering how we can help the GOS Provincial Assembly be a more effective force.

Impact

A strong signal that the participatory approach is working lies in the fact that ownership of the SSDP project has survived eight successive national and provincial governments, military intervention, and mass resignation from the provincial assembly in protest of the military. In March 1994 the government of Pakistan requested that the Sindh project model be replicated in other provinces. Disbursements of the International Development Association credit have begun, and bids have been called for the two largest physical components in the project.

PHILIPPINES

INTEGRATED PROTECTED AREAS PROJECT

Thomas Wiens was the Task Manager of the Philippines Integrated Protected Areas Project.

Photo by Thomas Wiens

It was on the eve of the appraisal mission that I realized we had a potential problem on our hands. We had been working with the Philippine government for a number of years to devise a policy framework that would help preserve the few good stretches of forest that were left in the country. Out of this was born the Philippines Integrated Protected Areas System (IPAS) project. It envisioned a shift toward a decentralized management system to resolve the resource conflicts among various user groups at the ground level.

But despite the original intent to give equal attention in project design to biodiversity preservation and the needs of directly affected groups, the project had been prepared in an expert, "top-down" manner, with minimal local participation at the onset. A local expert had drafted the new protected areas legislation, which had subsequently been passed by Congress. Teams of NGO consultants had been hired by the government to identify priority areas to include in the project. They were then charged with developing management plans for ten of these based on scientific criteria. These same NGOs were also given responsibility for holding public meetings in these areas to disseminate information and obtain community feedback on the new legislation.

Up to this point, I had been focusing most of my energy on the draft legislation and hadn't paid much attention to the participatory aspect of the project. I assumed that, because it was being done by local NGOs, participation would take care of itself. I was soon to learn that this was not the case.

WARNING SIGNALS

By the time we arrived in Manila for the appraisal mission, I had received many signals from the NGO community that the public consultations had not been done satisfactorily. Apparently, many stakeholders who expected to be included in the earlier discussions had been left out. From what we were hearing, we knew potential issues with indigenous peoples would arise that would have to be addressed. A number of Indigenous Cultural Communities (or ICCs, an acronym used in the Philippines to refer to tribal peoples) currently inhabited a good portion of the proposed park lands. It was clear that we would need their participation and support to implement the project. But somehow, we hadn't managed to achieve this. What had gone wrong?

PREPARATION BY EXPERTS

When I delved into the matter, I discovered that the NGOs hired to help the Department of Environment and Natural Resources (DENR) to prepare the project were essentially technical in orientation—a collection of scientists, academics, and forestry specialists brought in for their expertise in biodiversity preservation. No one on the team had any experience working with indigenous peoples or using participatory approaches. Although they were the right kind of NGOs to design the technical framework for the program, they were the wrong kind to undertake collaborative decisionmaking with local people. This reflected the fact that our thinking up until this point had been more focused on getting the "system" right and identifying what was worth protecting. Although we knew that people constituted the main threat to the effectiveness of such a system, their needs had not been in the forefront in designing the legislation.

CONSULTING THE PEOPLE

We realized we would need to get the local people involved to remedy the situation. One of our tasks during appraisal was to redraft the implementation guidelines, which would spell out in detail how the legislation was to be implemented and clarify any ambiguities. We decided to take this opportunity to consult the people about the new legislation. We wanted to identify any critical problems related to the IPAS design and ask them if they were willing to join the proposed park system. To do this, we suggested that the mission be set up as a joint consultative appraisal between the government and the Bank. This was readily accepted by the DENR.

Participatory NGO Enlisted

PANLIPI, a national legal services NGO, was contracted to identify the relevant stakeholder groups and organize the meeting agenda for the mission. This was a rather unique situation as PANLIPI was brought into the process personally by the secretary of the DENR, who was a former human rights lawyer. In addition to being trusted by the government, PANLIPI had a good reputation among indigenous communities and had built a relationship of trust by providing them with pro bono legal services. Because of their good relationship with both sides, PANLIPI was able to organize the necessary meetings between the mission and the communities in each of the four areas that had been selected. They identified the stakeholder groups that would be met by the appraisal team based on their knowledge of the groups in the area and used their connections with the local NGOs to arrange open meetings with the various indigenous groups. In my view, PANLIPI did a pretty good job of staying neutral and ensuring that all relevant stakeholder groups were brought into the dialogue. By this, I mean both groups that supported the project and those that strongly opposed it.

Information Sharing

The four sites chosen for appraisal by the joint mission were selected because they presented the greatest challenge for implementation of the IPAS program and had the most complex human and sociological problems. The appraisal team spent between two and three days in each of the four areas. We met with local NGOs and indigenous communities as well as with the local authorities and church groups that interacted with them. Some meetings were chaired by PANLIPI, but most were hosted by the local NGOs in the area. As far as the meetings went, I don't think enough information was provided in advance to the participants, so a fair portion of the time was spent explaining to them what the project was all about. The proposed new system called for active local management and possible restrictions on resource use; therefore, we wanted to ensure that those who were going to be affected by the project (or could affect its outcome) clearly understood the rights and responsibilities the IPAS would bring.

Negative Feedback

The DENR officials took a lead role in explaining the objectives and benefits of the new legislation, whereas we (the Bank staff) mainly just listened, observed, and spoke only if there was a specific question directed to us. Then it was the people's turn to tell us what they thought. In Mindoro, the Mangyan leaders along with representatives of Mangyan community organizations from across the island began almost immediately by pointing out serious flaws in the system that the expert design team had overlooked. For example, the Mangyan people had looked at the IPAS maps for Mindoro and discovered that a portion of the park had been classified as a "strict protected zone" in which virtually all human activity was to be banned. They subsequently informed us that a number of Mangyans lived within this zone and depended on hunting, fishing, and gathering of forest products for their livelihood. Not surprisingly, they found these regulations to be unacceptable and incompatible with the traditional lifestyle of their people. Like other ICCs, the Mangyans have close attachments to their ancestral lands and possess customary laws for regulating the use and transfer of these lands and their natural resources. They made it clear that the recognition of these "ancestral domain rights" and the actual demarcation of the boundaries of this domain were preconditions for considering their participation in the protected areas system.

In Palanan, we discovered that livelihood concerns were the central issue for the residents. The town was in the middle of the proposed national park. Most of the men made their living from illegal logging, and some asked us quite matter-of-factly if we could cut a road through the virgin forest to facilitate their trading and give them some contact with the outside world! This startling request helped us to understand an important reality: if we didn't change the project and place a greater emphasis on livelihood issues, we would not have any hope of sustaining it or getting the local people to stop relying on logging as a source of income. Similar concerns were raised during consultations at the remaining two sites.

A SHIFT IN OUR THINKING

These consultations clearly demonstrated weaknesses in the IPAS management plans designed by the consultants. Although we knew the plans were stronger in their technical descriptions than in their social analysis, we hadn't realized how far removed they were from human realities. Because of the difficulties involved in demographically surveying certain areas, basic information on how many people inhabited the region and which areas were most densely populated was often lacking.

Now I've heard it said many times before that consultation with local stakeholders is not the same as participation. After all, we—the team of outside experts—still had ultimate control over the decisions that were being made. Talking directly to the people, however, was certainly better than making those decisions in isolation from Manila or Washington, D.C. We learned a great deal from these consultations; the things people told us influenced our way of thinking dramatically. On our return to

Manila, there was no doubt in any of our minds (Bank and DENR staff included) that the project would have to be redesigned to respond to the expressed needs and priorities of those whose lives were going to be directly affected. We were now much more focused on "people's problems" and realized that the project plans, as they stood, were not centered on people.

For one thing, we realized that the protected areas legislation was inadequate to deal with the interests and concerns of indigenous peoples as they had been conveyed to us. It was obvious that if we did not change the project to correspond with these realities, we would not win the cooperation of the ICCs and their support groups. We therefore set about redrafting the implementation guidelines based on what we had been told. Now, implementation guidelines for any legislation can modify its impact to a greater or lesser extent, depending on how flexible the legislation was in the first place. The changes we made following the consultative appraisal mission were designed to skew the implementation of the law in favor of ICC rights to traditional means of livelihood and occupancy, decentralized park management, and community managerial boards that gave a strong voice to indigenous peoples.

Another persistent complaint we had heard from ICCs in Mindoro was that the process of delineation and recognition of their ancestral domains was incomplete. They were understandably frustrated and wanted to know why. Recognizing this issue as a potential obstacle to ICC acceptance of the IPAS, we followed their suggestion and requested DENR to show good faith by completing its stalled delineation work prior to project implementation. In addition, we revised the implementation guidelines to emphasize ancestral domain rights (including precedence over IPAS laws in the event of conflict) far more. We also earmarked project funds to continue the delineation work in this and other areas.

INSERTING PARTICIPATORY ARRANGEMENTS

With regard to project design, we got the message loud and clear that the existing project allocated too little money toward livelihood purposes. From the wide array of ideas, suggestions, and requests that were put forth by communities during the different meetings, it was apparent that the only way to reflect community desires in project design was *not* to specify potential livelihood projects in detail prior to implementation. Rather, we decided to more than double the funds for such activities, develop some general criteria, and design a community-based mechanism for identification and selection of such projects "on-the-fly."

And that is exactly how we ended up proceeding, by tossing out many of the other activities budgeted during preparation, while increasing the range of permissible activities and enlarging the funds available from 20 percent to 50 percent of the total project budget. In short, we felt that the "social fund" approach was the only practical way of responding to so many different needs and priorities. This was a critical step in ensuring *real* participation by local people in the project, because it gave them control over financial resources and how they would be spent in their communities. By devolving resources to the local level and responding to the demands of the ICCs for ancestral domain rights, we were betting on taking much of the "heat" out of the opposition. Would inserting participatory arrangements at this late stage work? We decided to put it to the test.

FOLLOWING UP

Once we had translated the local input into a new set of participatory arrangements, we suggested that the DENR organize a series of follow-up meetings with the same communities. We recommended that NGOs be hired to conduct the follow-up. DENR readily agreed.

Four NGOs were sent back to the four areas we had visited. Of these, PANLIPI was sent to Mindoro—the island that had voiced the most opposition to the IPAS during the previous consultations. All four NGOs returned with the revised implementation guidelines that had been influenced by indigenous peoples' input. They also took back the new terms of the project, which were also much improved by giving real control to local people over decisions that would affect them. The objective of these follow-up meetings was to provide an opportunity for local stakeholders to review the revised arrangements, provide feedback, and propose any further modifications. They were also intended to begin the process of self-selection of representatives for the Protected Areas Management Boards (PAMBs).

In Mindoro, for example, follow-up meetings with the various stakeholder groups were held in a workshop format. PANLIPI greatly emphasized the voice of the ICCs because they are the most affected by the IPAS. The views of support groups such as community workers, the Church, NGOs, and local government units, however, were also given due consideration. In the initial workshops, the different stakeholder groups were mixed together. It was observed, however, that in these instances, the NGOs and local authorities tended to dominate the

sessions; therefore, during subsequent meetings in other areas, workshops for tribal people were kept exclusive to avoid the influence of other groups on their perceptions and feedback regarding the IPAS legislation. In these cases, the DENR, local government unit officials, the Church, and NGOs were allowed in as "observers."

The workshops began with a presentation by PANLIPI on the terms, conditions, and implications of the IPAS law and revised implementation guidelines. Participants were then divided into small groups to review the maps and documents and discuss the items that affected them. PANLIPI primarily played an observer role in these discussions, responding only to questions of clarification regarding implementation of the IPAS law. Through this interaction with each other and with PANLIPI, local people carefully considered the implications of the legislation and weighed their options with the understanding that they were free to refuse membership in the parks system. In the process they learned what their rights and responsibilities would be under the IPAS and what tasks they would undertake as members of the community management boards. Once they understood the overall framework and assessed their own means and ability to participate, they collectively adopted resolutions concerning topics such as ancestral domain, livelihood, IPAS restrictions, resource use, management boards, and tourism. In doing this, they were making promises in the presence of other stakeholders about the actions they were or were not willing to undertake.

AN UNEXPECTED OUTCOME

The results of the follow-up meetings were that three of the NGOs came back from the field reporting strong community support for the revised project with no significant problems or objections. After weighing the costs and benefits of the newly revised terms of implementation, the affected groups concluded that participation in the IPAS was in their best interests. They agreed to join the national parks system.

But the events that transpired in the Mindoro workshops were dramatically different. To begin with, participants rejected the basic premise of the follow-up meetings. This had been expressed to them by PANLIPI as "discussing arrangements for community representation on the Protected Areas Management Boards." The participants argued that they could not talk about the terms of their participation in the project when the legislation itself was not acceptable to them. By being adamant on this point, they succeeded in shifting the focus of the workshop from "representation" (which implied voice) to "acceptability" of the IPAS program itself (which implied an "exit" option). This question, they felt, had not been adequately addressed during previous consultations.

The proceedings of the tribal workshops in Mindoro were dominated by objections and protests over the perceived primacy of environmental concerns over the human needs of the Mangyan people as reflected by the IPAS legislation. The overwhelming opinion of the ICCs as well as the Church and NGO groups was that the revised terms of the project did not go far enough in meeting the demands of the Mangyan people for self-determination and ancestral domain. The ICCs felt that *their* indigenous land-use systems were more appropriate than what the IPAS had to offer.

During the workshop, the ICCs also rejected membership on the management board, which they felt would be controlled by the politicians and bureaucrats. They viewed tribal representation on such a board as a "token" that could be manipulated as an instrument for justifying government programs. The local groups, therefore, refused PANLIPI's invitation on behalf of the government to choose tribal representatives to the PAMBs because they rejected the *concept* of the IPAS as a whole. Other points of contention included, the permit system, provisions for mining resources in ancestral lands, and tourism projects that could convert tribal lands into a "Mindoro zoo"! The principal message from all of this was that the local people had been left out of the process and no changes we could make at this stage would suffice. The opposition to the IPAS legislation had solidified. The indigenous people had reached an overwhelming consensus: "We don't want to be a national park!"

SETTING A PRECEDENT

This was the message that PANLIPI carried back to Manila from the ICCs of Mindoro. It was an outright rejection that ultimately resulted in Mindoro being dropped from the protected areas park system. In this instance, participation had meant giving local stakeholders the option of saying "no" to a project because consensus and commitment to it were lacking. The long political struggle between the Mangyans and the government over the scope of ancestral domain claims proved unresolvable within the context of the IPAS legislation; although I regretted the loss of Mindoro, I believed it was better than having the government and the Bank invest resources in a project doomed to failure. I also felt that "allowing" local communities to opt out of a project set a good precedent by discouraging future expert project preparation efforts and pointing out the benefits of building local consensus and

ownership in the early stages of project design. The lesson of Mindoro also helped us create a *better* project by forcing us to pay more attention to participation when putting implementation arrangements into place.

COMMUNITY MANAGEMENT BOARDS

For those areas that agreed to join the parks system, the IPAS legislation sought to institutionalize local participation by decentralizing the management of protected areas and giving greater control and representation to local people. We built provisions for a multistakeholder PAMB in each region into the implementation guidelines. The next step was for communities to select their representation on the management board. During the follow-up consultations, the NGOs contracted by DENR began to work with the communities to develop a process to select their representatives to sit on the board. Stakeholder groups were free to choose their board representatives in any way they wished. The ICCs learned about the different rights and responsibilities they were committing to in accepting board membership. These tasks included approving management and zoning plans, setting rules and licensing resource use within the park, and collecting fees and fines. Perhaps, most important from the standpoint of the ICCs, representation on the PAMB meant that they would have a say in the sort of livelihood activities to be funded by the project. Moreover, local NGOs would be hired to assist them in preparing and implementing these projects.

In several cases, the ICCs expressed concern that their power on the PAMBs would be diluted by other, potentially more powerful, stakeholders. They rightly predicted that pressure for representation from a growing number of user groups in the area would expand membership on the management board from the initial limit of fifteen members. In view of this, DENR decided to establish an executive committee for each PAMB. This three-member committee—consisting of one representative from the DENR, ICC, and NGO communities—would have the decisionmaking authority for the board. The new terms of this power-sharing arrangement were welcomed by the ICCs.

COSTS

The funds for all the preparation work, including the participatory components, came from a Japanese Technical Assistance Grant. The joint appraisal meetings were relatively inexpensive, costing somewhere in the range of $5,000 to $10,000. The follow-up consultations, however, were more extensive. They totaled about $30,000 to $40,000. Each of the NGOs was given approximately one-fourth of this amount. With regard to time costs, the participatory interaction did not delay the project in anyway. In fact, the follow-up sessions were intended to fill in some of the time between appraisal and effectiveness, lest the expectations and enthusiasm raised during appraisal diminish by the time project implementation began.

ON REFLECTION

The project went through many changes between identification and approval. This evolution took time and certainly would have been much easier and faster if we had known at the beginning what we know now. We started out with an expert-designed, technical preparation that then shifted to an NGO-driven consultative process during appraisal. From this it evolved into a highly participatory project in which one community walked away and the others acquired resources through the livelihood fund and representation on the managing board.

If I had to do it over again, I'd start at the point at which we ended up this time around—by introducing participation as early as possible into the process. One of the benefits participation brings is that it allows everyone to see clearly what different stakeholders are and are not willing to commit themselves to. The participatory stance that was taken during follow-up with the communities allowed indigenous groups to decide what was in their best interests. I think this fact, combined with the participatory implementation arrangements that were added, will go a long way to ensure that this project is one that the people living within the protected parks system are willing to maintain and support.

The change in our stance over the course of preparation and appraisal was a gradual process of getting deeper and deeper into the project and developing an understanding of the inextricable link between participation and project success. Once we made a concerted effort to seek out the different stakeholders and bring them into the decisionmaking process, the project began to change—for the better—in innumerable ways. We may have been slow in starting, but this only goes to prove that it's never too late to get it right!

PHILIPPINES

COMMUNAL IRRIGATION PROJECTS

Charles Gunasekara *was the Task Manager for the Philippines Communal Irrigation Projects.*

CASES

In 1982 I went on my first Bank mission to the Philippines, where we'd been working with the National Irrigation Administration (NIA). I was supervising completion of several previous loans and finishing preparation of a new loan. I arrived at a time when NIA was adjusting to some important changes. Created to help develop greater food self-sufficiency in the Philippines, NIA began by investing mainly in large irrigation systems. But by the beginning of the 1970s, it began to place more emphasis on communal irrigation systems that would benefit remote poverty-afflicted areas.

In learning about my new assignment, I kept hearing about NIA's work with farmers. My NIA counterparts told me that the agency had consciously set out to collaborate with farmers and to build on centuries of farmer-run irrigation schemes. To do this, NIA was fielding community organizers to work hand-in-hand with the farmers to provide training and team support building. Their goals were to increase the ability of farmers to work together, negotiate effectively with the government, operate and maintain the system, and manage it financially.

The tone at the agency was energetic; many people there spoke respectfully about the farmers' collaboration. Although NIA was a traditional engineering agency, the engineers I met told me that the participatory experiments had persuaded them of the value of working with the farmers.

SEEING FOR MYSELF

Having arrived in Manila, I wanted to get out into the field and see what was working and what wasn't. On my first mission, I visited a community in the north of Luzon. The community organizer—I'll call her Rosa—had arrived there about a month before. She had been getting to know the farmers, working with them in the fields, participating in their social life, and meeting with the local irrigation association (IA). I could see how she appreciated and sensed the needs of the farm families, especially of the women. I found this attitude of respect and caring among the community workers almost everywhere I went.

For centuries in the Philippines, farmers have gotten together to build and maintain simple communal irrigation schemes. Rosa's community was no exception. The farmers already managed their own canals, using temporary dams made of logs and stones to divert water from a stream nearby. Rosa and one of the village elders, Tio, took me to see one of the dams. Tio was about seventy years old. He could remember long ago chancing on the stream we were looking at and dreaming of directing these waters to the rather arid lands cultivated by his father and those of the other villagers. Some years later, he had been able to obtain the support of his friends and relatives and built a diversion, which gave them a small amount of water.

Although still crude, the system had matured to include a main dam and canal and many small ditches, constructed by the farmers of several communities and serving about 400 hectares. During the annual floods, the dam and many other works would be washed away. Every year, the farmers would rebuild the damaged structures and repair the main canal, contributing as many as 10,000 person-days of voluntary labor. The work was organized informally.

NIA RESPONDS

Over many years, Tio and his co-villagers also tried to get outside help to improve their system. Finally, NIA responded. During the 1970s, drawing on its 1974 charter, which authorized it to delegate management to the farmers and collect payments from them, NIA had been experimenting with participation in small, communal irrigation pilot projects. NIA had obtained grant funding from the Ford Foundation to support the development of processes for farmer participation. This flexible funding enabled NIA to undertake action research that could not be funded through the usual government budgets.

A multidisciplinary learning group composed of NIA officials, some of the newly hired community organizers, and people from social science, management, and agricultural engineering institutions provided advice to the NIA assistant administrator who managed the pilot projects. The learning group examined the implications of NIA's experience in these pilot operations for determining changes in NIA's policies, procedures, and training programs.

The group found that cost recovery was an important aspect of the participatory approach. As they helped pay for the systems, the farmers developed a financial stake in the projects. But, more important, repayment helped motivate NIA personnel to treat the farmers as clients and to be interested in promoting strong IAs that would be capable of repayment.

By 1980 NIA had shifted away from its strictly engineering approach to a sociotechnical approach. NIA involved irrigation staff who were to implement the new approach to develop detailed processes for farmers' participation. NIA undertook a large training program. With assistance from experienced community organizers and social science and management institutions, it trained newly hired community organizers in farmer mobilization and action research; it taught the engineers how to work with the farmers and guide the irrigation associations in operations and maintenance; and it trained farmer leaders in meeting techniques, leadership, and management.

COMMUNITY ORGANIZERS

By the end of the 1980s, NIA had almost 750 community organizers. The organizers are carefully chosen for their ability to relate with delicacy to the farmers and to speak the local language. Typically, they take about ten months to lay the groundwork for construction of new irrigation schemes. They work behind the scenes, encouraging the farmers to organize formally their IAs and to take the lead. The IAs help to secure the rights-of-way, contribute to the design work, and enter into an agreement with NIA, which covers cost issues and defines their respective roles in implementation and subsequent operations and maintenance. During construction, the IAs contribute about 10 percent of the costs in cash or in kind.

When construction is completed, the IA evaluates the work and formally takes over the system, accepting full responsibility for the operations and maintenance and repayment of NIA's chargeable cost at no interest (this excludes overhead, roads, and such). To ensure financial transparency, NIA and the IAs hold monthly reconciliation of costs chargeable to each IA. This encourages the IA to meet their financial obligations. Once an IA is well under way, the community organizer visits only periodically and shifts attention to a new area.

SETTING UP AN IRRIGATION ASSOCIATION

Rosa had already been talking with the farmers about NIA's proposal. During these meetings, the farmers had been able to deal with various reservations they had. For example, their concerns about accountability for village funds were allayed when they developed clearly stated and understandable procedures, including the organization of monthly reconciliation meetings, the training and support NIA would give to the villager designated to handle finances, and the public display of financial statements.

Rosa invited me to a general assembly where she hoped to obtain the farmers' agreement to proceed. The villagers agreed to NIA's proposition that, with their participation, NIA would improve and expand the irrigation system and that the farmers would set up a formal IA to handle operations and maintenance and over time pay for the construction. By assuming these responsibilities, the IA would clearly demonstrate its commitment to the project.

Over the next several months, Rosa helped the farmers develop their local group into a more formal IA. They set up a three-tiered structure, with an elected president, a board, and sector-level groups. The board, composed of the heads of the sector groups, determined how the rebuilding and maintenance responsibilities would be divided among the different sectors and how water would be rotated during periods of scarcity.

Although the board helped with communication and coordination, each sector had its own structure, leadership style, and organization. Each was responsible for mobilizing and managing the needed labor and materials. As it did for other IAs across the Philippines, NIA provided training to the farmers so they could manage their organization and helped the IA register as a corporation with the National Securities and Exchange Commission. This meant that they could own property, make contracts, collect fees, and impose sanctions.

With Rosa's help, the sector committees developed by-laws (specifying the number of board members, for instance) and divided the responsibilities for such matters as water rights, monitoring of materials and costs, and matching of farmers with the paid irrigation construction jobs. Rosa later told me that the IA had done a good job of reviewing all of the rules and decisions with the members and ensuring that both water distribution and maintenance were handled equitably.

GAINING BANK SUPPORT

Until the early 1980s, Bank support had mainly focused on NIA's large- and mid-sized national irrigation schemes. These had been built by NIA engineers without farmer involvement. In 1981 a Bank team reviewed NIA's participatory work and endorsed the agency's intention to expand participation to all local and some national irrigation schemes. This led to the first Communal Irrigation Development Project (CIDP) loan of $121.9 million.

CIDP I was the first foreign-assisted project to focus entirely on communal irrigation development and farmer participation. It became effective in late 1982, just after I had come on the scene. The loan was to cover 33,500 hectares, about two-thirds to be new irrigation and one-third to be rehabilitation of existing communal systems. About $3.5 million of this was dedicated to institutional development (farmer and staff training, community organizers and supervisors, meetings, and technical assistance).

PARTICIPATORY DECISIONMAKING

CIDP I was added to my supervision responsibilities. On one of my missions, I heard that the farmers' committees in the village I had initially visited had "walked through" the NIA plan with the NIA engineers. The plan laid out a new water course for the main canal and some of the smaller canals and provided for a new dam. During the walk through, the farmers had requested some modifications because they knew certain landowners would resist giving rights-of-way unless they were paid a high price. After several meetings to discuss jointly various issues, the farmers' suggestions were incorporated into the plan and the layout was presented to the IA general assembly for further modification and approval; thus, the NIA engineers and the farmers learned and innovated together.

With Rosa's help, the IA had then secured the water rights and obtained the rights-of-way. Given that everyone stood to benefit from the new main canal, all but one of the farmers along the route had agreed to give right-of-way without charge. The exception was a man who would lose a considerable number of fruit trees; the IA agreed to compensate him. Because the farmers had worked out a clear plan and dealt thoroughly with all the rights involved, the construction went smoothly and was completed on time.

TURNOVER CELEBRATION

Six months after the irrigation system was completed, I was on another supervision mission and had the opportunity to visit the village again on the day management was officially turned over to the IA. The officers of the IA signed documents approving the construction costs (which, in turn, would determine the annual amortization payments due) and assumed responsibility for the management of the system. The signing was followed by a party and speeches. Rosa congratulated the farmers, saying she was confident that the success of the IA and the new experience the farmers had gained in their committees had prepared them for this moment.

By this time, the association had set up various management positions, such as operations manager and gatekeeper, and had selected a water tender and fee collector for each sector. The fees were to be paid in kilograms of paddy per hectare: 130 kilograms of paddy per hectare during the wet season and 95 kilograms per hectare for the dry season. For each sector, the water tender would deliver the bills to each farmer and, after the harvest, a fee collector would pick up the paddy from each farmer and provide him a receipt. The collector would then sell the paddy and turn the revenues over to the association.

I learned that the farmers had already brought 250 hectares of previously arid land under irrigation. In addition, they had increased their yields from an average of 2 tons to about 3.5 tons per hectare. This was a very poor community and, from the new clothing worn by families at the meeting, I could see that the people had already benefited from the big boost in their crops.

Shortly after the turnover event, I heard that the sector groups of the IA had elected new board members. New leaders had emerged during the work with NIA; as Rosa had hoped, many of them were elected, including two women whose contributions were widely recognized. The leadership during the operations and maintenance phase would thus be strong.

FARMER MAINTENANCE

Participatory projects are not completely smooth. Four years after the Luzon villagers had assumed responsibility for their irrigation system, I visited Tio's community again. NIA had moved Rosa to another community and, left to their own devices, the farmers had permitted the main canal to become overgrown. When I sat with the farmers, they were pretty embarrassed. They said, "We were just going to clean the canal. This is the only one we haven't got to. But our yields are as high as ever, and we have been able to keep all the new land under cultivation."

Looking around the area, I could see that the irrigation system, although not in perfect condition, was providing a steady supply of water. Farming was going well. The new prosperity had led someone to construct a mill, and many people had made significant improvements in the size and quality of their houses. I concluded that, although I might have preferred a higher standard, the farmers had stabilized system maintenance to a norm with which they were comfortable—one that was doable and

sustainable. I also concluded that, thanks to NIA's participatory process, this irrigation system now truly belonged to the farmers.

EXPANDING THE SYSTEM

The Luzon village is just one example. I visited many communities all over the Philippines. As NIA expanded the participatory approach, it was finding much greater satisfaction among the farmers with the irrigation schemes, dramatic increases in the acreage irrigated during the dry season, and increased conscientiousness among the IAs regarding pay-down of the debt to NIA and maintenance of the canals. Because of local funding constraints, design changes, and law and order difficulties, delays were the norm for many, if not most, of NIA projects (and most of the Bank's projects in the Philippines as well). In some cases, the IAs ran into difficulties with major repairs, and NIA had to step back in. Nevertheless, in the participatory projects, thanks to the involvement of the farmers in the planning, many problems were avoided. As a result, the delays were shorter and less frequent.

FIELD OFFICES

NIA's support for the farmers grew during the course of the pilot projects and continued during full-scale implementation. As an example, to stay close to the IAs, NIA established a widely dispersed network of sixty-seven provincial irrigation offices, which were strengthened with Bank assistance. The goal of these offices was to help develop communal IAs. Among other things, they foster information sharing among IAs. Through this visitation and peer training, the farmers learned a great deal from each other.

NIA provides bonuses to these offices and their employees based on their cost effectiveness. This encourages them to treat the farmers as valued customers whose satisfaction is indispensable to NIA. From my many visits to communal projects, I can say that, in general, NIA staff are respectful of the farmers' wishes.

CIDP II

In the late 1980s, as we completed supervision of CIDP I, we began preparing the second communal loan. As we considered how the new loan might build on the old, which had ultimately resulted in the irrigation of about 50,000 hectares, we had much to review.

We wanted to be sure the Bank continued its long-term, program approach to supporting NIA and that lessons learned from one operation could be built into the next one. During our preparation missions, NIA set up a series of meetings with selected IAs to conduct comprehensive discussions of the experiences to date. A number of these meetings were in the northern Luzon region. Since the time I first visited there, the number of IAs had almost doubled.

During the course of these meetings, we developed an understanding of two major sets of needs. The first set had to do with record keeping about the projects and their impact. The second had to do with the opportunities created by the greater availability of water.

RECORD KEEPING

The Bank team had been reviewing the IAs' books throughout the 1980s and recognized the integrity and thoroughness demonstrated by virtually all of the IAs. Although they started off with little knowledge of modern accounting and bookkeeping, most of them could show their membership what funds were coming in, and how they were being spent.

Nevertheless, as the communal systems expanded, both the IAs and NIA needed more systematic accounting and national reporting. They also needed to improve their tracking of water distribution, cropping, rainfall, flow statistics, operations and maintenance, crop performance, and agricultural incomes.

In CIDP II, we agreed to support the further development of performance monitoring and training at all levels. The training programs helped the associations develop needed skills in decisionmaking, resource mobilization, conflict resolution, and performance monitoring.

MORE SOPHISTICATED NEEDS

The improved irrigation services at the communal level and the greater availability of water have led to a higher and more varied set of agricultural needs. During preparation of CIDP II, the Bank team attended a series of meetings organized by NIA with the farmers around the country. These meetings dramatized the farmers' needs and desires. In some areas, the more successful IAs had already developed their own solutions, investing in threshing floors, bulk procurement, storage facilities, and marketing and providing credit to other groups of farmers.

This stimulated the less successful IAs to do the same—and more. Some of the farmers thought they needed to form cooperatives to get group credit, crop insurance, and marketing services and to build drying floors. As one of the farmers put it, "We have the water.

We have enough food for ourselves. We can really improve our incomes now if we get the right kind of assistance." They wanted better weed control in their canals and paddy lands. They wanted to diversify their crops, particularly in the dry season. They wanted to understand more about fertilizers and pest management and to procure the needed seed, fertilizers and agrochemicals.

Both NIA and the farmers said they were committed to meeting these needs through participatory processes. For these purposes, NIA devised a novel grassroots approach. For all communal irrigation systems rehabilitated or established under CIDP II, NIA collaborated with the IAs to prepare and implement agricultural development plans. These plans cover most of the needs raised by the farmers, including cropping patterns, equitable water distribution in the case of shortages, reforestation, soil and water conservation, nurseries, and other support services. They also include farmer training, extension visits, demonstration programs for crop production methodologies, and pest management and mechanization, as well as cooperatives and other means for bringing greater credit and marketing schemes to each IA.

CIDP II was appraised and approved in 1990. It became effective in January 1991. The loan is for $46.2 million. Although supporting the activities just described, it covers new irrigation works on about 10,000 hectares and the rehabilitation and improvement of about 15,000 hectares. CIDP II was deliberately kept small because of the somewhat tight fiscal situation in the country. We expect the irrigation schemes built under CIDP II to help about 20,000 farm families directly. In addition, these families and the many other small irrigators in the nearly 3,000 NIA-assisted communal schemes, will benefit from the institution strengthening and improved agricultural support services that CIDP II supports.

SUPERVISION

Things are going fairly smoothly in spite of financial difficulties that have slowed the pace of implementation. Supervision missions about twice a year for CIDP II appear to be adequate, particularly because we make a point each time of visiting the farming communities.

By 1994 we could already see improvements. The Bank receives quarterly progress reports from NIA, and the IAs have improved the pay-down of their loan obligations as well. We also get a comprehensive report on the status of the communal schemes. Our review indicates a substantial increase in average family incomes. My friends in the IAs tell me that their improved records on water allocation and cropping are helping to ensure a more equitable distribution of water and to ease the resolution of disputes.

To participate with NIA in the implementation of the Agricultural Development Plans, each IA has formed an Agricultural Production Subcommittee. The subcommittees meet often, after obtaining suggestions and complaints from the IA members, to arrange water scheduling, review accomplishments to date, establish annual objectives for the next stage of implementation, and provide input into the annual work plans of the community organizers and extension workers.

RESULTS

Farmers' participation in irrigation seems to have paid off. My visits around the country tell me that the results of a study conducted in 1985 by the Institute of Philippine Culture of the Ateneo de Manila University continue to hold true:

- In participatory systems, production yields averaged more than 3 tons per hectare in both the wet and dry seasons, whereas, in nonparticipatory systems, yields were a little more than 2.5 tons per hectare.
- In the dry season, the participatory systems expanded their irrigated area by 35 percent, whereas the nonparticipatory systems expanded by only 18 percent.
- Farmers' degree of satisfaction with the resulting canals and structures also differed between participatory and nonparticipatory projects. In the nonparticipatory systems, farmers abandoned 18 percent of the canals constructed with NIA assistance and judged an additional 20 percent of the new structures to be defective. In contrast, in the participatory systems, only 9 percent of the canals were abandoned and 13 percent seen as defective.
- One of the ways farmers were required to contribute to the costs of construction was through "equity"—labor, materials, and land. They were required to contribute 10 percent of the construction costs or 300 per hectare (whichever was less). The non-participatory systems fell short, raising only 54 per hectare, whereas NIA's participatory systems generated 357 per hectare on average, thereby exceeding the minimum. This represents an immediate 60 percent recovery of costs for the institutional development activities related to participation.
- With regard to organizational structure, irrigation associations developed through participatory approaches were found to be more "rooted" in their communities. Organizational leadership in participatory systems included more tenants and small farmers, whereas in nonparticipatory systems the leaders tended to be wealthier. These differences indicated that in participatory IAs, the socioeconomic status of the leadership was closer to that of ordinary members than was the case for nonparticipatory IAs. This may have contributed to the more equitable water distribution noted below.
- With regard to equitable water distribution among members during times of scarcity, the participatory systems were more likely to (a) rotate water according to a schedule, (b) allow each group in turn to make use of all available water for an allotted period of time, and (c) employ personnel to supervise water distribution to ensure equity.
- Significant differences were also discovered between participatory and nonparticipatory systems when it came to the financial practices of associations. Up to 50 percent of participatory systems employed practices such as conducting annual audits of their accounts, preparing financial statements, using vouchers for expenditures and monitoring payments on each member's card. Fewer than one-fifth of nonparticipatory systems are engaged in such practices.

THE BANK'S ROLE

The Bank has been lending to a relatively successful agency that was client-oriented and supported participation. This was due, in part, to the support NIA received from the Ford Foundation and from other aid organizations. The Bank team as well as NIA benefited from the experience and expertise of these organizations. Our contribution over time could be described as follows.

- *Flexibility.* It proved unrealistic to try to predict rigidly the time needed to develop the associations and ensure their ability to participate. Also, targets that were too rigid tended to undermine the farmers' authority over the systems and, in turn, their commitment. In CIDP II, the desired flexibility was achieved by committing to work programs only one year at a time. Each year's work program took into account the performance of the preceding year.
- *Coordinating between NIA and other agencies.* Although other government agencies were charged with providing the necessary support services, they seldom functioned in a coordinated manner. To a great extent, the Bank team provided a liaison function. For example, NIA had trouble getting the budgetary agency to release funds appropriated for NIA, and

the IAs had trouble getting credits in a timely manner from the Land Bank. We were able to use the Land Bank's good offices to facilitate timely action by these agencies.

- *Applying appropriate technology.* Sometimes traditional engineering approaches lead to work that is not the most appropriate to the situation. So, in the communals, we supported NIA in using the simplest techniques possible. For instance, we encouraged them to adopt drainage crossings, using check gates and spillways where appropriate instead of siphons and diversion weirs. Through many efforts such as these, we were able to reduce costs and limit the need for higher levels of skill and supervision. Most important, because these systems were simple, the farmers could understand and manage them.

- *Helping resolve problems.* This was an important area for the Bank. For example, a private firm was discharging effluent into one of the irrigation systems. We asked the president of the firm if something could be done. After a lot of resistance, he finally said, "Well, I do have an idea, but I don't think you will accept it." As a matter of fact, we thought his idea was pretty clever and agreed to it. So he constructed a series of ponds, ran the effluent through them and relied on the natural anaerobic action to render them harmless. This worked satisfactorily. When I went back a few months later, the last pond had fish and frogs and aquatic vegetation, and a goat was drinking from it.

- *Preserving NIA's autonomy.* In another instance, someone wanted to turn NIA into a regular line agency receiving most of its revenues from government coffers. This step would have potentially destroyed the linkage between NIA's services and its revenues, which helped keep NIA oriented toward meeting the farmers' needs. I can't say the Bank team single-handedly prevented this move, but I hope that our influence helped.

ON REFLECTION

In hindsight, I am happy that my initial instinct was to support and build on what was already working wherever possible. I had observed in the past that when we introduced new approaches—rather than building on indigenous capabilities—the process was tedious and the results were often suboptimal or unsatisfactory.

I also felt that because our country counterparts sometimes lacked commitment or ability, we tended to seize the initiative and, with the borrower inadequately involved, we sometimes made most of the decisions and provided most of the expertise. The result was that the people in the country were not learning much and thus tended to have a lower commitment and to become more dependent on the Bank. By giving the farmers control of their own systems and making them partners of NIA, the Philippines approach appeared valuable to me in avoiding a lot of these problems.

For these reasons, we did our best to use the available human skills and physical resources and to see to it that, wherever possible, system design was based primarily on NIA's approaches and standards, making changes only where essential. For example, I've mentioned the simple drainage crossings, check gates, and spillways that were used. We also helped NIA reduce the costs of headworks by eliminating unimportant aspects of the design.

Working in the Philippines over a long period of time has made it possible to take a process approach to supporting NIA. We avoided the tendency to plan things to death. Implementation was used to modify and adjust plans based on new developments and information. NIA and the IAs had as much flexibility as possible to go at the pace most appropriate for them. Wherever we could, we adopted a work plan approach to be developed each year rather than rigidly scheduling the work for the entire loan period. This meant NIA could operate "in synch" with the dynamics of the IAs and other events in the country. I think the Philippines experience shows that such flexibility is valuable for the Bank.

As for the future, the Philippines communal irrigation program is at another crossroads. Based on the strength of past participatory efforts, the existing IAs and irrigation systems continue to function fairly well. But institutional support for the existing systems and development of new systems is at a standstill. Because of a new local government code, the authority for the communals had evolved from NIA to local government units. This has taken place without full appreciation for the need to adjust all of the aspects of the program—such as financial authority, supervision, cost repayment procedure, and other policies. People in both the Bank and the Philippines are attempting to arrange for NIA to have a role in assisting the local governments. I hope this will be possible.

REPUBLIC OF YEMEN

EDUCATION SECTOR ADJUSTMENT PROGRAM

Yogendra Saran is the Task Manager of the Yemen Education Sector Adjustment Program.

Because of its rapid expansion, the quality of secondary education in Yemen had been deteriorating steadily for many years. The Bank's 1992 Education Sector Report pointed this out clearly and emphatically. When the minister of education arrived at the Bank to negotiate the Basic Education Project for Yemen, we discussed the next project in his country. We agreed that it should focus on the development of human resources to meet the emerging needs of the economy and should target secondary and post-secondary nondegree education. We also agreed that the quality of secondary education was the crucial issue and should be addressed in the next project. Finally, we agreed on adopting a participatory approach at this stage and that two working groups, each chaired by a deputy minister, would deal with secondary education community colleges.

DEFINING THE APPROACH

While in Washington conducting our pre-mission planning, we proposed through correspondence the idea of convening a national workshop of professional educators and other parties to address the quality issue. The members of the working groups and the minister of education accepted our proposal, and planning of the workshop began. In further discussions, the Bank team offered to facilitate the workshop in a participatory manner.

Our first decision was that Bank members—staff as well as consultants—would act as facilitators rather than experts. Our objective was to put the planning of the project, including objectives, strategies, components, costs, and plans, firmly in the hands of the Yemenis. We agreed among ourselves that two things would be vital for improved educational quality in the country. First, the whole system had to be addressed, not just a part of it as we had in past education projects. Second, those in the system had to do the learning about what was wrong at present and how—in a Yemeni way—improvements could be made.

CHOOSING A METHODOLOGY

As a long time trainer, I knew of a number of techniques to foster participation during the workshop. So we decided that in my opening statement, I would suggest that the task of the participants was to develop a planned change program to improve the quality of education at the secondary and postsecondary levels. I would also say that the role of Bank staff would be to facilitate the work of the participants using some techniques with which we were familiar. But the agenda of work and the substance of work would belong entirely to the participants. We planned my final opening remark as an offer for the participants to accept the proposal just made or to reject it and create their own task assignment.

IDENTIFYING THE STAKEHOLDERS

We were able to identify the stakeholders in the education system with ease. We decided that what we needed were people working on education in both the private and public sectors, because the former is an important element of postsecondary education in the country. Unfortunately, we could not identify any NGOs, women's groups, or parents associations that might be able to contribute significantly to this work on secondary education and beyond. NGOs and women's groups exist, of course, in Yemen but none deal with secondary or postsecondary education.

We sent a set of objectives, a plan of action, and criteria for the composition of the workshop as a proposal to the Yemenis. Our objectives were first to identify priority areas and barriers to change and then to add input to the terms of reference of the working groups developing the planned change reform program. We proposed that the workshop include thirty people, one-third of whom should be women, with a wide distribution of professionals in the education system. Two days of working sessions were planned.

I had been working in Yemen for about five years and considerable trust had developed among all of us involved in this effort. I was pretty sure that the Yemenis would be favorably disposed to our suggestions. They wrote back agreeing to the program, setting the workshop date to coincide with our next mission to Yemen (a project identification mission) in July 1992. The Ministry of Education would convene the workshop, chaired by the deputy minister of education.

THE FIRST WORKSHOP

When we arrived in Sana'a in July 1992, we held discussions with the working groups that had been set up by the minister. Working group members for secondary education, consisting of high Ministry of Education officials, had concluded that Yemen needed more classrooms, equipment, and textbooks to avoid overcrowding and really nothing else to improve the quality of secondary education. They did not see the need to hold a workshop or to identify other priority areas of change. Accordingly they had not sent out any invitations or made the logistical arrangements we had been expecting.

We didn't challenge the conclusion of the working group but instead engaged the members in a discussion of just how they believed more investment in improved facilities alone would increase the quality of education. In this long meeting it became obvious to the members of the secondary education working group that they really could not answer the "quality" question or develop a comprehensive strategy without involving professionals, researchers, administrators, and teachers in the dialogue. The invitations were then sent, arrangements made, and we started work.

The Community College Group, consisting of private sector representatives from the Sana'a Chambers of Commerce and Ministry of Education officials, desired a broader dialogue with employers. We agreed that the mission would conduct seminars for the private sector and then explore the modality and scope of cooperation with industry.

SMALL GROUPS/PLENARY SESSIONS

The workshop included three of us from the Bank and about forty participants, although we had only expected thirty. We decided to set up three working groups of about thirteen participants each. The workshop would have four stages, each ending in a plenary session in which the small groups would make reports. The stages would handle the following tasks:

- Define the quality problem
- Determine what to do about it
- Identify the barriers and decide how to overcome them
- Develop the methodology for measuring and ensuring that quality would be produced by the actions taken.

We gave each participant three blank cards at the start of each stage. The first job of each individual was noting down three major problems or issues he or she believed crucial on the cards. Next, individuals would explain what they wrote on the cards to the group. Then the group prepared a consensus report for presentation at the plenary session. We Bank facilitators worked with the group, making sure all got an opportunity to contribute and help develop a consensus.

PRIORITIZATION BY BID ALLOCATION

During the plenary reporting sessions, we recorded all points made on large flip charts so everyone could see them during the next stage. We then had the participants prioritize their conclusions by using a bidding system. Each participant had to allocate a total of 100 points to the various problems or issues developed by the group as a whole.

The workshop unleashed a tremendous amount of energy and creativity. We were pleased and a bit surprised by the way the participating women made themselves heard and served as a real force for ideas and consensus. The participants liked it from the start. At the first break, several told us that they had come expecting yet another Bank-run session in which they'd be lectured; instead they were actually doing the work themselves to their surprise and delight. Another surprise was that the original notion that all that was needed was more schools and textbooks had vanished. Indeed, after the bidding, another objective turned out to be the first priority by a large measure, that is, teacher performance.

WORKSHOP RESULTS

This workshop produced the diagnosis of the quality problem in the Yemeni education system. It also set objectives that would constitute a Bank sector operation, that is, a planned change program to improve significantly the quality of secondary education in Yemen. Seven key areas were named for secondary education: teacher performance, physical facilities, curriculum development, evaluation, school management, learning resources, female access to education, and community colleges. Community college workshops would also be held in two cities outside the capitol with broad private sector participation to identify the needs for mid-level personnel in the emerging modern sector of the economy.

THE SECOND WORKSHOP

We believed that quality education would show up—or not show up—in the local schools themselves rather than in the types of central programs that government would

run. We therefore asked the minister to invite school headmasters to attend a workshop in Sana'a. In certain respects, the headmasters were really the voiceless members of the education system. At the bottom of the rung, they were expected to do what the ministry directed. But some of us had the intuition that what the local headmasters had to say might indeed be the most important contribution to the change program. Indeed, headmasters were underrepresented in the national workshop, and little focus was given to what the local schools themselves might contribute.

All told, forty headmasters joined us at the regional workshops along with some people from the ministry and the working groups. The participants first reviewed and discussed the output of the national workshop, that is, the Planned Change Program, and discussed how the local schools could participate. They then broke into small groups to prepare detailed proposals.

SCHOOL-BASED SUBPROJECTS

Again the workshop unleashed an immense amount of creative energy. The headmasters (three were headmistresses) had a great deal to say about what could be done well locally and with local community involvement. What came out of these workshops was a decision to include a school-based subproject component of the project in which local schools could get funding for their own proposals to produce higher quality in education. As a practical matter, relatively small amounts of money could empower up to 100 local schools to innovate and become an integral part of the national program to improve the quality of education.

To be frank, we from the Bank liked this part of the project best. It confirmed what we had come to believe: the closer you get to the people, the more practical and useful are the actions that can be taken. Although this component was small, we saw it as the opening wedge to bring local people in communities into the process of school development and management.

DETAILED PLANNING

Following the second round of workshops, which had included the Sana'a and Aden Community Colleges as well as headmasters' workshops, the detailed work of preparation began. Here the experts began to take on a larger role in developing strategies, timetables, specifications, detailed action plans, and resource needs. Indeed, we had something unusual as we went into negotiations for the project. We already had three volumes of detailed, well-done implementation plans that flowed from and were fully consistent with what the large number of participants—almost 200 all told—themselves invented. We expect that the implementation specifics will come as no surprise to the stakeholders, who will be ready to act swiftly and surely once the credit becomes effective.

GOVERNMENT CHANGES

Lest anyone thinks all this went perfectly, let me share a little about a real scare we had. When the preparation was well advanced with subproject development, cost estimates, and resource allocations nearly complete, the government changed. We went on the preappraisal mission just after a new government took over with a new education minister. Of course, we feared that the new minister might want to start from scratch. We called a one-day meeting, however, with his new education officials and others in the system to go over the project. After that one-day session, the minister said let's go ahead as planned. One important, positive lesson from this experience is that when a project is prepared in a participatory manner by a large network of stakeholders in the country, its chances of surviving a personnel change at the top are greatly improved.

COSTS

We started this project with the identification mission. Sixteen months later (about standard cycle time for an education project in our region) we began negotiations. The total preparation cost involved a Japanese preparation grant of close to $1 million. Bank staff input was about ninety staff weeks, much fewer than the normal 130-150 staff weeks in our division. We had done, however, a great deal of detailed implementation planning by this time, which is unusual and will most certainly facilitate a more rapid and easy implementation of the project.

RESULTS

No concrete results, of course, have yet been achieved. But if the Bank's emphasis is right about the need for country ownership and commitment, it is present in this project. Also, the educational content is appropriate. Finally, the local strategy and priorities fit well with the local culture and realistic possibilities in the country. After all, the local people did it, not outsiders. Indeed, they've decided to make organizational and structural changes in the ministry itself. In our judgment, these are sound changes. It will be interesting to see how these changes are accepted by the affected staff and how fast and well they are introduced. I believe that real institution strengthening will occur in the ministry and at the local school level because the affected stakeholders decided what *they* wanted to change and how.

ON REFLECTION

From time to time, my colleagues and I have asked ourselves if we would have done anything differently if we were to do this same project again in Yemen. Our answer is, "No, not really." We would have liked to have more local community involvement than we had, but to get that we would have needed more leaders within the system with an understanding and practice of participation. Such leaders did not exist at the start of this project, but they do now, and we will work with them in future projects.

CHAPTER III

PRACTICE POINTERS IN PARTICIPATORY PLANNING AND DECISIONMAKING

Photo by Ron Sawyer

In chapter I, we shared our understanding of participatory development. In chapter II, we shared the experiences of a few selected Task Managers who have carried out the Bank's work using participatory approaches. In this chapter, we provide answers to questions Task Managers have about using participatory planning and decisionmaking processes in Bank-supported activities. We draw largely on chapter II examples to help readers identify how their colleagues have used participatory processes in their work. We also cite additional projects and World Bank activities that may not be described elsewhere in this document.

GETTING STARTED

This section is about the first important step in starting participation: getting government support. In most of the *Sourcebook* examples, this was not a problem. In others, Task Managers used various means of persuasion, from initiating pilots and field visits to sustained dialogue, orientation workshops and building alliances with those who support participatory approaches. Sometimes Task Managers faced outright opposition. In these cases, some held firm to Bank policies supporting participation, others proceeded without participation. This section answers the questions of *when* and *how* you start participation.

121

When to Start

Start participation as soon as possible, remembering that it is never too early or too late to start, as indicated in the following examples:

Starting at Identification

In the **Chad Education** example, Chad's government developed an Education-Training-Employment Strategy for the next decade, in order to rebuild an education sector destroyed by war and disturbances during the 1980s. Chadians from many backgrounds and sectors and most major donors participated in creating the strategy. In 1991 the government decided to implement this strategy with the Bank's help. The minister of education requested that preparation of the new education project involve local stakeholders and respond to their needs and concerns from the beginning.

Starting in the Middle of Preparation

In the **Lao People's Democratic Republic (LPDR) Health** example, the designers and sponsors shifted from the external expert stance to the participatory stance mid-way through preparation. Although this was not the first Bank-supported project in the country, discussions with the vice minister of health revealed that he and his colleagues expected the Bank to implement the project. The Task Manager immediately shifted out of the external expert stance and into the participatory stance. He did this so that the appropriate stakeholders in Laos (who would have to implement the project) would help create, learn about, and take ownership of the project well before implementation began.

Starting during Implementation

In the **Brazil Municipalities** example, a Bank loan to a financial intermediary was on the verge of being canceled. The problem was clear—the component that was to provide water and sanitation to slum communities was not disbursing. The new Task Manager assigned to this project had previous experience working with poor farmers in the irrigation sector. He believed that the only way to save the loan was to take a participatory stance, involving the slum dwellers in the design and management of water systems. Working with like-minded allies in the Bank and Brazil, the Task Manager helped develop a new approach that enabled engineers, social organizers, and slum dwellers to collaborate in designing effective, affordable water and sanitation services for some of the worst slums in the world. Three years into implementation, the Bank loan was resuscitated by initiating participatory planning and decisionmaking in subproject design.

Never Too Early, Never Too Late

These examples clearly indicate that it's never too early or too late to start participation. They also help us recognize that participation often begins in a nonparticipatory manner. A sponsor (the central government is usually the sponsor for Bank activities) decides to pay attention to a particular geographic area within a country or to a particular development concern. So in a sense, whenever participation begins it is *always a bit late* and always preceded by prior opinions, attitudes, and judgments of its sponsors.

Getting Government Support

Governments' stand on stakeholder participation is critical. Without government support, the Bank can do little to initiate, broaden, and sustain participation. This does not imply that Bank Task Managers remain passive. It does mean, however, that Bank Task Managers must obtain government consent to work in a participatory manner. We now share some of the experiences that

Task Managers have encountered in getting government support for the participatory stance.

When the Government Is Supportive

In most of the *Sourcebook* examples, using the participatory stance instead of the traditional external expert stance was not a problem for government. Either Task Managers proposed the idea to a receptive government or vice versa. In the **Chad Education** example, the minister of education specifically asked that the project be prepared in a participatory manner. The problem for the joint country-Bank design team then became finding a participatory methodology. None had planned a project in a participatory manner, and now had to learn how.

Dealing with Skeptics

Sometimes government counterparts working on an activity with the Bank Task Manager are skeptical about participation and need convincing.

Encouraging Field Visits

In the **Benin Health** example, the Task Manager asked his government counterparts to keep an open mind until they met with the villagers. Participating in face-to-face interactions served to persuade the government officials that involving the local people in project preparation made good sense.

During preparation of the **India Forestry** example, officials from the Andhra Pradesh Forestry Department went on a field visit to review West Bengal's experience with participatory Forest Protection Committees. The head of the Forestry Department helped ensure that the team included skeptics as well as supporters of participatory approaches. All returned from the trip convinced of the value of participatory approaches to forestry. Not only had they seen local people earning income while conserving and helping regenerate the forest, but their West Bengal forestry peers told them the participatory approach made their work professionally rewarding and personally more satisfying. Whereas the West Bengal foresters once had an antagonistic relationship with the local people, they now work cooperatively with them and are welcomed and valued for their services. On returning home, the team shared what they had seen with their colleagues, thereby helping to sway other skeptics in Andhra Pradesh.

During the identification of the **Pakistan Privatization of Groundwater Development** project, the Task Manager organized a field trip to the Dominican Republic and Mexico for irrigation officials from the central and provincial government in Pakistan. The trip focused on one theme: the transfer of the management of irrigation systems to water user associations. The report of the group concluded, "In the Dominican Republic and Mexico, the process of transfer has been rather quick, and tangible results have surfaced even earlier than expected. The major reasons appear to be the will of the government, the highly committed efforts of the organizations assigned the job of transfer, the mental receptivity of the farmers, and other sociological factors. The successful programs of transferring the responsibility of irrigation management to the farmers' organizations in these two countries, along with the accruing benefits, are a source of encouragement for Pakistan to embark on a similar program."

Educating and Persuading

In the **Morocco Women in Development** example, officials wanted to restrict the dialogue to government circles instead of involving nongovernmental organizations (NGOs) and rural women. They believed participation would neither work nor add much to what they already knew. The Task Manager decided

POINTERS 1

to avoid a hard sell for participatory processes. She visited all the concerned ministries personally and asked them to attend an informal gathering to discuss the issues. At the gathering, she laid out the pros and cons in a balanced manner for government to decide. At their request, she held a follow-up workshop to explain the specifics of the proposed participatory technique. Once the officials recognized that the decision was theirs to make, they decided to give participation a try, provided Moroccans did the work instead of foreign consultants.

Building Alliances   Although Task Managers initiated participation in many of our examples, none of them did it alone. Allies within the country were always needed. In the **Egypt Resource Management** example, a government official took personal responsibility for cutting through the red tape involved in making the project preparation grant effective. In the **Brazil Municipalities** example, disbursement rates were so poor three years into implementation that the loan was slated for cancellation. Implementation began in earnest only when the Task Manager and staff from the Bank's central Water and Sanitation Division collaboratively built a strong, personal relationship with the national project manager and his team in Brasilia. Together they sought out other Brazilian allies in the state water companies, consulting firms, and NGOs. All shared the common goal of providing sustainable services to slum communities. One lesson that can be drawn from the way alliances were built is that governments and societies are not monolithic. Almost always, someone in the country—sometimes many—support participation because it produces sustainable results.

Piloting   Piloting can be used to demonstrate the effectiveness of participatory planning in situations in which uncertainties exist and borrowers are accustomed to external expert means of project preparation. Pilots can be useful in convincing government skeptics that involving stakeholders in project planning is beneficial, that risks are manageable, and that potential exists for delivering a positive development impact.

The Task Manager in the **Albania Rural Poverty Alleviation** example decided to collaborate with rural farmers to test what would work in providing credit and rehabilitating infrastructure in their communities. Some of their government counterparts, however, believed that involving the local people in designing the project was a waste of time because villagers "knew nothing" about complex issues such as credit delivery mechanisms. Nevertheless, the Task Manager managed to build an alliance with a few like-minded government officials and obtain funding from the United Nations Development Programme and a French NGO to carry out a pre-pilot to experiment with ideas formulated in collaboration with local people. The Bank team, along with Albanian private consultants, worked with the villagers to design the pre-pilot, set criteria, and create implementation arrangements. The resulting social fund mechanism, which incorporated village credit committees and community-generated proposals for infrastructure funding, proved effective in reaching communities and building local ability for participatory decisionmaking. As a result, more and more officials in the government started to take notice. They became so interested in both the pre-pilot and its use of participatory approaches that they considered the pre-pilot as "appraisal" and pushed for approval of a larger Bank pilot project. The ensuing Bank-financed project was designed based on lessons learned from the participatory pilot.

Dealing with Opposition

Holding Firm In the **Mexico Hydroelectric** example, negotiations between the government and the Bank broke off—at least in part—over the government's unwillingness to prepare resettlement plans that met the requirements of Bank policy. Technical studies had not been completed, and levels of local participation had been insufficient in preparing the resettlement plans. The government withdrew the loan request and sought money elsewhere. The government, however, returned to the Bank seven months later to reinitiate the request and develop resettlement plans that were in keeping with the Bank's resettlement requirements, including participatory planning.

Waiting for the Right Moment There may not always be a "happy ending." Government may adamantly oppose the use of participatory processes. In that case, the choice is either to withdraw or proceed in the external expert stance and wait for the right moment. In the **Brazil Municipalities** example, participatory planning began in the third year of implementation, reminding us that it's never too late to begin.

IDENTIFYING STAKEHOLDERS

Once the government and the Bank jointly agree to work in a participatory stance, they can begin the process of identifying the appropriate stakeholders. Typically, Bank Task Managers have collaborated with government to identify relevant stakeholders by asking questions and seeking answers from both in-country and Bank sources. Often, the objective itself has defined the relevant actors. Sometimes, firsthand observation was used to identify appropriate stakeholders. In other cases, disseminating information about the proposed activity enabled interested stakeholders to show up by themselves.

Who Is a Stakeholder?

In the context of Bank-supported activities, stakeholders are those affected by the outcome—negatively or positively—or those who can affect the outcome of a proposed intervention. The examples in the *Sourcebook* reveal that determining the relevant stakeholders for any given concern depends on the situation and type of activity to be supported. Task Managers generally take the pragmatic position that the development concern being addressed identifies the stakeholders. Once a participatory stance is taken, getting the right stakeholders becomes essential to producing good results. Not all parties, however, can automatically be assumed relevant; in addition, for every development concern being addressed, a broad spectrum of stakeholders exists ranging from directly affected parties to individuals or institutions with indirect interests.

Government For the Bank, government is always a key stakeholder. In every case, central government officials were the obvious and first stakeholders that Bank Task Managers worked with. This is because the government is a Bank shareholder, the primary decisionmaker and implementer of policies and projects, and the one who repays the Bank loan or credit. Usually more than one central government institution has a stake in a Bank activity. A core ministry is always involved—finance, planning, the central bank, or a similar ministry. Depending on the activity, officials from other core and line ministries may have a stake in the activity as well. Officials from other levels of government, including state

POINTERS 1

or provincial authorities and local- or municipal-level officials, virtually always have a stake. Indeed, the Bank and the government must enter into a close partnership in which shared development objectives keep the partnership together. In general, Task Managers in the chapter II examples experienced little difficulty in identifying the relevant government stakeholders in preparation of Bank-supported operations.

Directly Affected Groups

Those directly affected by a proposed intervention are clearly among the key stakeholders. They are the ones who stand to benefit or lose from Bank-supported operations or who warrant redress from any negative effects of such operations. The poor and marginalized are often among this group. It is these directly affected stakeholders, Task Managers tell us, who are the most difficult to identify and involve in participatory efforts.

Indirectly Affected Groups

Many individuals or institutions may be indirectly involved or affected because of their technical expertise or public and private interest in Bank-supported policies or programs, or they may be linked in some way to those who are directly affected.

Such stakeholders may include NGOs, various intermediary or representative organizations, private sector businesses, and technical and professional bodies. Identifying and enlisting the right intermediary groups has proved tricky at times for Task Managers and in some situations turned out to be a process of trial and error.

In the **Philippines Integrated Protected Areas** example, a group of NGO consultants were hired to design a technical framework for biodiversity preservation as well as attend to the public participation component of the program. Although this group of scientists, academics, and forestry specialists were ideally suited to address technical issues, they had no experience with or linkages to directly affected groups. At appraisal, the Task Manager discovered that the real concerns of the people had been missed. To remedy this, a national legal services NGO, PANLIPI, was brought in to identify key local stakeholders and facilitate meetings between them and the government-Bank appraisal team. PANLIPI was respected by the head of the key government agency involved, who was a former human rights lawyer. PANLIPI had provided pro bono legal services to indigenous communities so they were known and trusted by the indigenous groups. PANLIPI also had links to other local NGOs, which were able to arrange meetings with local communities.

How to Identify Stakeholders

Trusting Your Judgment

Much still needs to be learned about how to identify and involve stakeholders. No hard or fast rules exist to tell us whom to involve and how. What we do know is that stakeholder involvement is context-specific; what works in one situation may not be appropriate in another. Trusting and using one's judgment, therefore, may be the best advice Task Managers can give each other at this point in time.

In both the **LPDR Health** and **Yemen Education** examples, the in-country stakeholders in participatory events were limited to government employees, including low-level staff stationed away from headquarters. The Task Managers believed that involving field-level staff—who are among the "voiceless" within the bureaucracy—was the furthest down they could go at the time. Although a preference often exists for including directly affected stakeholders in participatory events, this may not always be appropriate or possible. If design is proceeding from the participatory stance, then it is probably wisest to trust the judgment of those closest to the action—from the Bank's perspective, the Task Manager. After all, many of the participatory activities in the *Sourcebook* are first-time events for all concerned; some caution in not going too far or too fast may have been prudent.

A good way to identify appropriate stakeholders is to start by asking questions. Task Managers have shared with us the types of questions they ask themselves and then others. These questions are not an exhaustive list but rather a preliminary road map to guide Task Managers:

- Who might be affected (positively or negatively) by the development concern to be addressed?
- Who are the "voiceless" for whom special efforts may have to be made?
- Who are the representatives of those likely to be affected?
- Who is responsible for what is intended?
- Who is likely to mobilize for or against what is intended?
- Who can make what is intended more effective through their participation or less effective by their nonparticipation or outright opposition?
- Who can contribute financial and technical resources?
- Whose behavior has to change for the effort to succeed?

Observing Stakeholders

No substitute exists for firsthand observation, even though it is rarely done in practice. In the **Brazil Municipalities** example, Bank and government sponsors were convinced that the only way to provide water and sewerage facilities to slum dwellers was to involve them in subproject design and implementation. Once in the participatory stance, the next question for the sponsors to address was how to identify the appropriate slum dwellers to involve? To answer this question, the first action taken by the design team was to learn about the slum dwellers: how they were organized and how they operated. To do this, the designers had to be present in the community when the people themselves were present—often on weekends and late at night. This helped them understand that the slum dwellers were associated with religious, sports, and other types of clubs. They discovered, however, that it was the women's clubs that were key. In a *favela*, more often than not, a woman is the actual head of the household. She is the permanent feature. The men tend to come and go. In a real sense, women were the local community and were the appropriate stakeholders for involvement in subproject design and implementation.

In-country resources

Seeking Help

Many of the Bank's borrowers have national institutes or centers with information on the demography, cultural practices, and socioeconomic situation of the countries' stakeholder groups. Local social scientists, academics, NGOs, government officials, and resident mission staff can also help identify appropriate stakeholders.

In the **Egypt Resource Management** example, the designers created a small library of basic reference material about the Matruh Governorate and the Bedouins who live in it. A consulting team provided social scientists and other skilled people to work with the project design team to identify the local stakeholders and their relationships to one another and the government. Local authorities assisted the Task Manager in identifying Bedouin representatives to serve on a joint task force. In the **Morocco Women in Development** example, local con-

POINTERS I

sultants from the university drew up lists of potential stakeholders from the NGO and academic communities to invite to an initial planning workshop.

Bank resources

Social assessment and other types of social science data can help Task Managers get answers to the questions noted above. For example, in several recent Global Environment Facility projects, stakeholder profiles have been prepared to help determine who should be involved in biodiversity conservation projects and how. A document showing how stakeholder profiles can be prepared is available from the Environment Department's Social Policy Division (ENVSP).

The Bank's regional technical departments and ENVSP include social scientists who can help design social assessments or help identify consultants to do so. Such consultants generally possess specific regional, country, and ethnic group knowledge.

The Bank's libraries also contain a wealth of information that may be helpful in identifying different stakeholder groups, determining their relationship to one another and understanding the social, cultural, and institutional factors (for example: gender, ethnicity, income level, social organization, and power relations) that affect the ability of stakeholders to participate. For example, one of the best sources of information on indigenous peoples is *The Encyclopedia of World Cultures*, edited by David Levinson (1993) and available in the Bank's library.

Sourcebook resources

The best way to learn about participation is to experience it directly. The second best way is vicariously, by seeing what others have done in the name of participation and then seeking their guidance. We encourage you to get in touch with the Task Managers and staff who have shared their experiences in chapter II and find out how they identified appropriate stakeholders for their operations.

Disseminating Information

The design team undertaking the **Sri Lanka National Environment Action Plan** convened an open public meeting, as is standard under environmental procedures. They developed a list of relevant stakeholders by seeking help from in-country and Bank resources but also advertised the meeting in the local newspapers. By making sure that information about the proposed activity was widely disseminated, the design team enabled interested stakeholders to show up on their own accord.

Photo by Debra Sequeira

INVOLVING STAKEHOLDERS

Once stakeholders have been identified, the next step is to enlist their participation. After this, sponsors and designers have sought to work with affected stakeholders through a variety of approaches. But "special" measures are needed to ensure that groups that are normally excluded from the decisionmaking process have a voice. To achieve this, designers and sponsors have first organized the "voiceless," mandated their representation, held exclusive participatory sessions with them, employed "leveling" techniques that allow stakeholders at all levels to be heard, and used surrogates—intermediaries with close links to the affected stakeholders. But what happens when opposition exists? This section concludes with examples of this type of situation.

Building Trust

To many of the identified stakeholders, an outsider bringing offers of "participatory development" may seem suspect. Prior experience with public agencies, public servants, and donor projects has, in many places, created negative impressions that need to be rectified. In the chapter II examples, improving communication, engaging stakeholders in repeated interactions, and working through intermediaries who have ongoing relationships of trust with poor and vulnerable groups helped gain the participation of affected stakeholders.

Sharing Information In the **Benin Health** example, trust was built by sharing information about what was intended by the proposed project. The Bank Task Manager and a number of (then still skeptical) central government officials held a series of "town meetings" with groups of skeptical villagers. During these meetings, the villagers came to learn about the *hows* and *whys* of the possible project, while having the opportunity to express their expectations from government for primary health care. In so doing, wariness about outsiders faded as the villagers became convinced that they would not be giving up more than they might get in return. Once trust was established, village members were invited to form their own village committees and participate in project planning.

Interacting Repeatedly In the **Egypt Resource Management** example, intensive and repeated interaction between design teams and Bedouins during project preparation helped the Bedouins realize that the outsiders were not attempting, as in the past, to use them. As both sides developed a feel for and understanding of one another through iterative planning sessions, suspicion of each other began to dissipate and the basis for trust, respect, and cooperation was established.

In the **Brazil Municipalities** example, slum dwellers had learned from experience that the water companies were not interested in dealing with slums. They, in turn, did not pay their water bills and constructed illegal water connections. The sponsors of this project realized that building trust between the water companies and slum dwellers was going to take time and effort. The design teams spent weekends and nights in the slums learning about the community. The local people saw that the designers were making an effort and that they admired the local people's initiative and creativity in taking charge of their lives. In the process, the designers helped the community learn about and understand the water company: how it operated, what it could and could not do, and the basic hydraulics of water and sewerage. Joining the local stakeholders and learning together with them what was possible, what they

POINTERS I

really wanted, and how much they were willing to change their behavior to get it, helped create mutual trust and cooperation between the designers and the slum dwellers.

Working through Intermediaries

In some instances distrust is so great that intermediaries may be required to bridge the gap. In the **Philippines Integrated Protected Areas** example a national NGO, which was respected by government, indigenous peoples, and local NGOs alike, was able to use its unique position to bring the different parties together. In one instance, PANLIPI used its influence to persuade two rival NGO groups to cosponsor a public meeting. They also persuaded a church mission group not to boycott the meeting but instead attend and participate. All these small steps led to the beginnings of a dialogue on the terms and conditions for future collaboration between the designers and local stakeholders.

Involving Directly Affected Stakeholders

A great deal can still be learned about how to work with directly affected stakeholders in Bank-supported operations once they have been identified and enlisted. The lessons of the chapter II examples point to several approaches for enabling intended beneficiaries—as well as those likely to be adversely affected—to participate in planning and decisionmaking.

Working with the Community

In the **Brazil Municipalities** example, it became apparent that the only way to save the Bank loan from cancellation was by the direct involvement of slum dwellers in the design of the subprojects. Consequently, several approaches were used to work with them. The most commonly used approaches were two different types of community negotiations. One started with the water company deciding the engineering design first and then negotiating it with the entire community along with issues of billing, operational responsibilities, and user contributions. The second started with community involvement from which the design emerged. Perhaps the word "negotiation" misses the essence of what really went on. It wasn't just the designers negotiating with the community but, more important, the community working together to take care of individual and communal needs and making commitments about what they were and were not willing to do.

Working with the Representatives

In the **Benin Health** example, town meetings with the entire community were followed by local communities being invited to form their own village health committees to represent them at future planning events. The rules of the game set for selecting committee members specified including at least one mother, someone good at handling money, another good at getting things done, and a person wise in the ways of village life. This ensured that the important functions that had to be undertaken at the village level to address health care needs were represented on the committee. Members of the village health committees collaboratively designed the project along with government officials and other stakeholders during three planning workshops. Through their representatives, each community was able to have input into the project.

Working with Surrogates

Another approach to involving directly affected stakeholders is through intermediaries or surrogates. Surrogates may be any group or individual who has close links to the affected population and is capable of representing their views

POINTERS I

and interests during participatory planning. In the **Nigeria Women in Agriculture** example, female extension agents served as surrogates for farm women at a national planning workshop on women in agriculture. The objective of the workshop was to create three-year action plans for improving extension services for women. The transportation and time constraints involved in traveling to the capital combined with the fact that rural women needed the permission of their husbands to attend made direct involvement of women farmers difficult. The credibility of these female extension agents to speak on behalf of farm women was based on their daily interaction with them and the fact that these agents were from the same areas and many were farmers themselves. But the **Chad Education** experience warns us to exercise caution in selecting surrogates to speak for the directly affected. In this case, the Task Manager was surprised to find that NGOs invited to a planning session on behalf of the poor represented their own interests instead.

Photo by Gloria Davis

Seeking Feedback

In cases in which stakeholders participate through their representatives or surrogates, Task Managers often follow the rule of thumb that one should trust those who speak for the ultimate clients but from time to time verify directly with those whose opinion really counts. The chapter II examples offer a number of approaches for follow-up and feedback. Apart from serving the cross-checking function, these approaches also facilitate broader ownership and commitment among those affected by the proposed intervention.

Making On-Site Visits In the **Egypt Resource Management** example, a local task force that included Bedouin representation prepared the Bank project report. During preparation missions, the Bank team—which could not attend all participatory rural assessment sessions (see Appendix I)—interacted directly with communities to ensure that their interests were being accurately represented in the project document. These exchanges occurred in both a formal and informal way. Formal sessions were arranged and facilitated by Bedouin representatives on the task force. Members of the task force reported to the community on the progress of project preparation. Open discussion followed in which local people expressed their opinions and asked questions. Their feedback, duly noted by the Bank team, was later incorporated in the final project document. In addition to these formal meetings, the mission members went unannounced into random villages (usually prior to the scheduled meetings). They introduced themselves and asked farmers if they had heard about the project and what they thought of it. This informal feedback was compared with what the mission was hearing at the more formal meetings and at the task force sessions. It served as a way of verifying consistency and checking for biases. The Bank team always included a female member who was paired with a female Bedouin veterinarian to carry out the same formal and informal interactions with the Bedouin women.

Stakeholder Review of Documents

Another way Task Managers obtained feedback was by providing the opportunity for stakeholders to review and revise draft documents prepared by the design team. The **Egypt Resource Management, Morocco Women in Development,** and **Philippines Integrated Protected Areas** examples are all cases in which directly affected stakeholders provided information, ideas, solutions, and recommendations that were later incorporated into reports and project documents by the designers. In each instance, a follow-up was done during which the wider membership of the directly affected groups were able to review what was being said and proposed and make changes if necessary. Task Managers found this follow-up to be crucial in fostering broader ownership and commitment beyond just those who were present at the participatory planning events.

Photo by Curt Carnemark

Involving the Voiceless

Some groups—especially the very poor, women, indigenous people, or others who may not be fully mobilized—may not have the organizational or financial wherewithal to participate effectively. These are often the exact stakeholders whose interests are critical to the implementation success and sustainability of Bank-supported programs. Special efforts need to be made to level the disequilibrium of power, prestige, wealth, and knowledge when stronger and more established stakeholders are meant to collaborate with weaker, less organized groups.

Building Capacity

For instance, in the **India Forestry** example, the sponsors and designers helped local people form and strengthen their own organizations. During the lengthy organizing process—as much as nine months in West Bengal—the local people learned how to work together to take care of their individual and communal needs. Once organized and having clarified their own interests, their willingness and ability to use the new power and skill of speaking with one, unified voice increased significantly.

In West Bengal, capacity was built by supporting a process through which forest dwellers could come up with their own decisionmaking structures. Rather than taking a rigid position about the right design for the local forestry protection committee, sufficient flexibility was allowed so that local forest dwellers could come up with their own processes for planning and negotiating.

Mandating Representation

In the **Benin Health** example, the sponsors and designers foresaw the possibility of women being left out. So they made participation of at least one mother on each village health committee a "rule of the game." In the **Chad Education** example, no special measures were taken in advance to mobilize and invite women. The result? None showed up at the national participatory planning workshop; by then it was too late in the process to do anything about it.

Organizing Separate Events

In designing the **Togo Urban Development** project, initial studies revealed that women had almost exclusive responsibility at the household level for the sanitary environment, providing water, managing waste, and family health. Yet, during the preappraisal mission, the first two meetings included no women. So the Bank team suggested holding a separate meeting at which the women could articulate their priorities and concerns. Their main concerns—which differed from those of the men—were men's unemployment, the need for standpipes and latrines in markets, providing central play space for children, access to drinking water, access to finance and credit, and training in management, hygiene, health, and literacy. The women's agenda was fully incorporated in the final project design, which included employment generation through labor-intensive public works and a training program in environmental management geared to the needs of a largely illiterate and mostly female population.

Similarly, in the **Philippines Integrated Protected Areas** example, PANLIPI, the NGO hired to conduct follow-up workshops with local stakeholder groups, discovered that the sessions were being dominated by local authorities and NGOs at the expense of indigenous communities. To let the voice of tribal people be heard, PANLIPI decided to hold exclusive workshops for the tribal groups and admit other parties as "observers" only.

Leveling Techniques

Power differences among stakeholders can be diminished through the use of participatory techniques. Skilled design and facilitation of participatory processes can promote "level" interactions. Small working groups, governed by facilitator-monitored "behavioral rules" that ensure that all participants speak and receive respect for their contributions, is one way of doing it. "Leveling" is facilitated when people listen to or observe quietly what others say without criticism or opposition. In the **Egypt Resource Management** example, outsiders watched respectfully as the Bedouins drew maps on the ground. Quiet observation encouraged the "voiceless" to express themselves through nonverbal representations. Similarly, role reversal, when the Bedouins led outsiders on transect walks instead of the other way around, helped level the playing field. Role-playing exercises, such as used in the **Colombia Energy** example, which helped sensitize powerful stakeholders to the lives others lead, are another means of leveling.

POINTERS 1

Using Surrogates   The **Nigeria Women in Agriculture** example demonstrates the use of extension agents as surrogates for women farmers at a national planning workshop. The Task Manager wanted to ensure that farm women had a voice in formulating policies and programs targeted at them. Not only did it prove logistically infeasible to bring them to the capital, however, but power differences also had to be considered. It was thought that in making presentations to the minister and other senior government officials, women farmers might feel intimidated and overwhelmed and might not be able to articulate their needs effectively. Bringing in female extension workers provided a reasonable substitute. Although they were familiar with the situation of women farmers, they also had experience working with male bureaucrats and local government officials. It was therefore easier for them to speak to more powerful stakeholders and participate more equally in preparing action plans on behalf of farm women.

In the **Mexico Hydroelectric** example, community meetings in Zimapan between the national power company, CFE, and the communities included mostly women because their husbands were migrant laborers, working in the United States or other parts of Mexico for the agricultural harvests. This gave the women an opportunity to participate in the resettlement negotiations and express their needs, which included credit to start up sewing shops, bakeries, and other sorts of microenterprise activities. As the men began to return and reassert themselves in the meetings, however, women's participation began to drop off. Their voice in the process, however, was maintained by female social workers who continued to visit their homes and transmit the women's requests for schooling, health, and other services.

Involving the Opposition

Chapter II contains no examples in which the designers encountered sustained "opposition" when the participatory process started early and began with consideration of a broad development concern. This was so even when it was clear that harmony did not exist among the stakeholders before the project began. Sometimes collaboration among different stakeholders may not be possible, however. In these cases, either resources should not be committed to the proposed activity or a group of stakeholders may have to be left out, generally by modifying the concern being addressed.

Stakeholder conflict is often produced by the external expert stance. When external experts formulate a complete, fully developed proposal and present it to the people it affects, immense room exists for misunderstanding on the part of those who were not involved in preparing the proposal. In the **India Health and Family Welfare Sector Study,** NGOs invited to a forum with government unanimously rejected a preset agenda and action plan. They perceived the plan as a *fait accompli* and their participation in the workshop as a token gesture of collaboration. Instead, they wanted to start from scratch and come up with their *own* workshop agenda and action plan. The sponsors agreed to this request, and both NGOs and government broke up into small, mixed groups to devise a new action plan. This plan was adopted during a plenary session and was incorporated into the final report.

Starting Early   In most instances, fully developed proposals are really "take-it-or-leave-it"
and Broadly   propositions, no matter how much lip service is paid afterward to collaborative decisionmaking. After sponsors and designers spend millions of dollars and many years preparing a complete plan, they are not likely to be open to

significant changes. For those who perceive a loss for themselves in the proposal, outright opposition may appear to be the only possible stance; the greater the loss, the stronger the opposition is likely to be. As we know from sometimes bitter experience, once opposition mobilizes, it is difficult—if not impossible—to resolve the matter. The **Philippines Integrated Protected Areas** example illustrates well the mobilization of opposition that could not be overcome in one of the intended project areas. In the other three areas, however, initial opposition gave way when participatory implementation arrangements were used to give local stakeholders decisionmaking power in a formerly "top-down" project.

When all stakeholders collaborate in designing their collective future, it increases the chances of former differences being resolved and a new consensus emerging around issues everyone can agree on. This is probably so because people who have to live and work together can often find ways to agree if given the chance. Unfortunately, people do not often get the chance to work together to determine their collective future. Development projects prepared in the external expert stance do not provide that chance. The participatory process, however, facilitates working together. So participation can be a "conflict avoidance" process to the degree that it helps stakeholders with different interests explore and potentially find common interests.

Finding Common Ground

In the **India Forestry** example, the foresters were shooting at the local people who were starting to shoot back before the participatory planning began. By focusing on common interests—how to protect the forests while ensuring economic survival for local people—the **West Bengal Forestry Project** eventually resulted in sustainable collaborative action. Through nine months of repeated dialogue and negotiations between the foresters and the local people, the forest dwellers agreed to take care of the shoots thrown up by Sal stumps so that they would become salable poles. When the poles were harvested, the forest dwellers got the culls, plus 25 percent of the revenues from the sale of good poles. The Sal stump growth subsequently became the main agent of reforestation, leading the foresters to proudly show off "their" forests.

Despite the success stories, consensus will sometimes be unattainable and no basis will exist for future action, especially in situations with a long history of entrenched conflict and divisiveness among the parties. In such cases, the result is no action, which is probably better than action that will fall apart during implementation for want of consensus. Although this strategy may not always lead to a Bank loan, it will, we believe, lead to making those loans that have a reasonably high probability of producing what they promise, that is, being implementable and sustainable. This point applies equally to the government and the Bank.

Dealing with Deadlock

Alternatively, when strong opposition exists to a project from one set of stakeholders, a Task Manager may, in certain circumstances, proceed by leaving out that set of opposition stakeholders and working with the others. Employing this approach has many potential dangers, but it does happen from time to time and has worked. In the **Philippines Integrated Protected Areas** example, the decision to drop the entire island of Mindoro from the proposed national parks system was taken once it was clear that the local residents were unwilling to support such an initiative. Nevertheless, the project as a whole proceeded. The Task Manager felt that this outcome—however unexpected—was ultimately in the best interests of both the government and the Bank. The lack of commit-

POINTERS 1

ment from the people of Mindoro would have made implementation difficult and sustainability improbable. In this case, the participatory process saved the sponsors from committing scarce resources to a project component that would have performed poorly.

Photo by Kathryn Funk

PARTICIPATORY PLANNING AND DECISIONMAKING

Once appropriate stakeholders have been identified and measures taken to ensure their involvement, the next question to answer is how do stakeholders engage in participatory planning and decisionmaking? This section documents approaches that sponsors and designers have used to collaborate with other stakeholders in this process. Participatory planning and decisionmaking should start by creating a mood for learning rather than plunging directly into problem solving. The learning phase then sets the stage for strategic and tactical planning. The strategic planning stage in turn generates broad directions and priorities, which are operationalized into detailed implementation actions during tactical planning.

What Do Participatory Techniques Achieve?

The essential steps of project planning and replanning—setting objectives, creating strategies, and formulating tactics—can be carried out in both the external expert and participatory stances. The essential difference between the two is that, in the expert stance, undertaking these steps is the primary responsibility of the sponsors and designers; in the participatory stance, these steps are undertaken collaboratively with relevant stakeholders.

Participatory techniques (or methods or approaches) generate constructive collaboration among stakeholders who may not be used to working together, often come from different backgrounds, and may have different values and interests. This section documents approaches that designers and sponsors use to undertake participatory planning and decisionmaking with appropriate stakeholders collaboratively. To learn more about individual techniques, please turn to Appendix 1.

Creating a Learning Mood

In designing a participatory event, it is reasonable to assume that participants will arrive prepared to take action based on what they already know, or to take no action because they believe that change is impossible. Participatory planning and decisionmaking should start by changing this mood. Although techniques described may initially seem overly simple to Bank staff, Task Managers who have used them report that they have found them extremely useful.

Interrupting the Normal Mood

The **Mozambique Country Implementation Review** example used a "white card" exercise to enable participants to get acquainted with each other and break the normal mood of extreme formalism in work relationships. Each participant was given four blank cards and asked to write one important implementation problem on each card. The cards were shuffled and displayed on the floor. The participants picked up any four cards, except their own, and began a discussion with another participant they did not know. As a result the participants had to "engage a stranger" to get something done, an unusual way for a business meeting to take place in that country. Interaction among people who did not normally interact with one another broke the ice and resulted in establishing openness and informality for the participatory workshop.

In the **Egypt Resource Management** example, it was necessary to interrupt the distrustful, "no-action-possible" mood of the Bedouins toward outsiders. The designers achieved this through repeated sessions between themselves and Bedouin clients in which the clients did most of the talking and suggesting. A typical participatory session started with the Bedouins drawing maps on the ground with sticks and stones, while the outsiders respectfully watched the process. The outsiders noted what was drawn first, what was drawn disproportionately large, and so on. Maps usually led to transect walks, in which the Bedouins who had drawn the map led the outsiders in exploring spatial differences in the area. The reversal of roles put Bedouins in a leadership position in which their knowledge was valued and sought after.

Creating Common Purpose

In the **Colombia Energy** example, one-third of the time in the stakeholder workshop was devoted to creating a learning mood. Although the social and power differences among the participating stakeholders were not significant in this example, the potential for conflict among the competing interests in the energy sector was great. So the facilitator designed this phase to bring forth consensus among different stakeholders. He asked participants to envision and design an ideal future for the energy sector without thinking about constraints or setting any timelines for achieving this vision. Some participants expressed their visions orally whereas others chose to portray theirs visually through drawings. Participants were requested by the facilitator to appreciate everyone's contribution without criticism or opposition. It was during this stage that people began to realize that they weren't so far apart in their thinking after all and that nearly everyone wanted the same things for the energy sector in the long run. This unity of vision succeeded in creating a new—albeit temporary—community of people with shared understandings and goals. Motivated by the sense of a common mission, the group was temporarily able to form an effective planning community.

Opening up New Possibilities

Sometimes closed-circle brainstorming sessions can be preceded and improved by exposing individuals or groups to practices of groups elsewhere. The opportunity for the Andhra Pradesh Forestry Department officials in the **India Forestry** example to visit and see for themselves how forestry projects were being organized in West Bengal opened up a range of possibilities that were not seriously considered earlier. Bank staff and their colleagues possess a great deal of cross-cultural knowledge about what people in other countries or regions are doing to address similar concerns. Sharing this cross-national experience can open up possibilities for future action. The emphasis in the learning phase should be to expose stakeholders to a menu of options instead of limiting the horizon to any single way of doing things.

What Does the Learning Mood Produce?

When participatory techniques shift the normal mood and facilitate new, common learning they succeed in the following:

- Sharing information freely and broadly
- Drawing on the inherent possibilities of collaboration among stakeholders
- Bringing forth consensus (or making it clear that none exists)
- Setting the stage for action planning and collaboration that may be able to resolve former conflicts that previously paralyzed common action.

Strategic Planning

In this stage, decisions are made in pragmatic terms about the directions and priorities for action needed to change the current situation and reach the envisioned future. Effective strategic planning sessions are not free-for-alls or "gab fests." The use of participatory techniques during strategic planning serves to facilitate the formulation of group consensus in prioritizing objectives and inventing action possibilities for the future.

Prioritizing In the **Benin Health** example, stakeholders made a list of all the problems they could think of related to the state of the health care system. Listing everyone's concerns produced such a lengthy list that problems had to be clustered under broader headings such as buildings and facilities, medicine, staffing and skills, and so on. The categorization of problems helped develop a common view of health problems among such disparate stakeholders as village representatives and central ministry staff. Categorization also helped the different stakeholders see more clearly who owned a particular problem and who would have to change individual and institutional behavior to fix it.

In the **Yemen Education** example, about forty-five participants were each given three cards and asked to write down what they felt were the three biggest problems with the quality of education. During the plenary session, all these problems were noted on large flip charts. The facilitator helped narrow down the list of problems through a "bid allocation" scheme in which each participant had 100 points with which to bid. The participants were free to allocate the 100 points as they wished—to a single problem or any number of the problems that had been written on the flip-charts around the room. The problems that received the most points became the priorities for strategic and tactical planning.

Inventing Action Possibilities The ZOPP technique (see Appendix I) used in the **Chad Education** and **India Forestry** examples illustrates a strategic planning approach in which a problem tree is first created followed by a mirror-image objective tree. The very process of creating these diagrams, if well facilitated, can also promote information sharing and learning.

In the **Colombia Energy** example, the second phase of the AIC technique (see Appendix I) is called the "influence" stage. Here small work groups follow a stylized, "looking-backward" technique to create strategies that would move the country toward an ideal situation. In this exercise, participants work back from their ideal future vision to the current realities of today, listing the key events that have to occur in terms of both personal and institutional changes along the way. These key events, in effect, represent priorities for change. In this way, it becomes clear to all participants what needs to change to reach future goals. The facilitator invites each person to share their important key events with other members and record them on a circle on a flip chart. Others are invited to discuss and debate the importance of these events. What happens is that the key events tend to build on one another and concentrate on a particular segment on the circle rather than getting randomly dispersed. This then becomes the basis of the group's strategic plan.

Tactical Planning

Tactics are the detailed implementation and operational steps that permit action in the short and medium term. These steps have to be modified and adjusted during implementation based on information and new developments. Deviations from tactical plans will always and inevitably occur. When these occur, some degree of replanning will be required. This is the time to regather the stakeholders and replan tactics based on what was learned by all during implementation.

Budgets, staffing, recruitment plans, organizational design, blueprints, other specifications for physical construction, social marketing programs, accounting system design, capacity-building mechanisms, benchmarks for success, and so forth fall under tactical planning. These are the specific arrangements that produce action on the ground during the implementation phase. Tactical planning, our chapter II examples indicate, is largely the domain of experts. Although experts should be given time and space to design plans, it should be made certain that all stakeholders review and approve tactical plans.

Using Government Expertise Often, the government officials who participate as stakeholders in participatory planning take on the job of tactical planning. The **Benin Health** example indicates that a group of government officials (health experts) did the detailed tactical planning and report writing. Following this, the full body of stakeholders—including village representatives—reconvened to review and endorse (or modify) the plans.

Using Local Expertise In the **Egypt Resource Management** example, the sponsors engaged a social development-oriented consulting firm to help design the project. The firm was familiar with the way the Bank operates and knowledgeable about participatory planning. They worked with the joint government-Bedouin project design team to devise the tactics for implementation. Interestingly and quite appropriately, the specific tactics for environmentally sound natural resource management were created by committees of people from each local Bedouin community. Not only was doing this consistent with local cultural practices, but it also relied on the best available experts on Bedouin behavior—the Bedouins themselves.

Using Bank Expertise In the **India Watershed Development** project, the Bank Task Manager helped his Indian counterparts find technical solutions to operationalize their strategic plans. Once the local stakeholders decided to use vegetative conservation methods as opposed to mechanical methods, the Bank Task Manager brought the

POINTERS I

highly drought-resistant vettier grass to their attention. Not only did it prevent erosion, it helped feed hungry cattle. Bank staff can provide other types of expertise, including sharing their cross-national experience about implementation arrangements that have been used to enable poor people to influence development decisions and resources that affect them. We have highlighted such arrangements, based on a review of Bank experience to date, in chapter IV.

Using Existing Power

In the **Colombia Energy** example, the tactical planning phase was structured so that clear outcomes and commitments would emerge. Subgroups were formed around the strategic options agreed on during the preceding phases. Individuals with the real power to implement recommendations headed the subgroups. Workshop participants joined each subgroup depending on their technical competence and ability to influence the outcome. Each subgroup negotiated their recommendations with every other subgroup to prepare their part of a nationwide plan. During the final session, the participants selected individuals from among the group to form a National Power Board that coordinated the different plans and drafted a report summarizing the tactical plan. A series of follow-up stakeholder workshops reviewed the plans, which were then presented to the Colombian Parliament. In between these workshops, participating stakeholders shared the draft document with their constituencies for feedback and approval. This resulted in wider ownership of and commitment to the tactical plans.

TASK MANAGER ROLES

Task managers new to participation ask what role they should play in an activity being planned and decided in a participatory way. Another—and perhaps more straightforward—way of asking this might be, "Isn't it true that I have no role to play in participatory processes? Don't I just have to go along with what the in-country stakeholders want?" The answer is a clear and resounding "No!" Just as Task Managers play multiple roles when working in the external expert stance, they also play multiple roles in the participatory stance. The chapter II examples indicate that Task Managers have played the role of initiating, facilitating, participating, sharing expertise, observing, navigating, and nurturing.

Initiating

In theory, the government sponsor of an activity should choose the design stance. In the majority of the chapter II examples, however, the Task Manager decided to work in the participatory stance. In addition, Task Managers often took on the job of finding allies, arranging financing, convincing skeptics in the country and the Bank, identifying and involving stakeholders, inventing techniques, and building in-country participatory capacity. In the future, the participatory stance may be standard practice in borrowing countries, as in the **Philippines Irrigation** example, or government sponsors could always ask that the participatory stance be taken, as in the **Chad Education** example. But until this time, Task Managers will have to continue to initiate participation in many situations. The Task Managers to whom we have spoken see this role as a welcomed and satisfying one.

Facilitating

Only in one instance—the **Yemen Education** example—did the Task Manager take on the facilitator role, because he happened to be a skilled, experienced trainer. In several instances, Bank staff with facilitation skills served as facilitators, while the Task Manager and other Bank staff were participant-observers. In other cases, local consultants or government staff played this role, sometimes after being specifically trained for it through programs organized by the Task Manager. In the **Egypt Resource Management** and **Morocco Women in Development** examples special training was provided to government officials and others in the country to play this role with resources organized by the Task Manager.

Participating

The job of the facilitator is to design and carefully manage a process that ensures that all those involved can and do become fully engaged with the substantive matters under consideration. Facilitators need to remain "substance-neutral" to do their job. They have to concentrate on processes that ensure that the "voiceless" are heard, that other norms of collaboration are followed, that learning occurs, and that practical results are produced. Task Managers, however, are not—and should not try to be—"substance-neutral."

Task Managers represent the Bank's stake in each and every activity. They may have to take an advocacy stance from time to time—within the rules of the game enforced by the facilitator—in keeping with the Bank's mission, policy, and objectives. They bring expertise to the process that may not exist among the local stakeholders. By participating, rather than facilitating, these experts share what they know with the other stakeholders (as the other stakeholders share their expert knowledge with them) through the social interaction of participation. Experts cannot teach other participants all they know during the participatory process. Instead what they can do—and do more effectively than with written reports—is open possibilities for action that may not otherwise be imagined by other stakeholders.

Bank staff and their external colleagues can share with local stakeholders their worldwide knowledge about what other people are doing to handle similar concerns. Sometimes, as indicated in the **India Forestry** example, experts may be sharing what they learned elsewhere in the same country. Although Bank staff have had much experience in operating in the external expert stance, more and more firsthand experience in supporting participatory planning processes is being amassed. Similarly, learning and other information is being generated about arrangements that build local capacity through participation (see Chapter IV). Bank staff can share this cross-national experience with local stakeholders to open up possibilities for future action.

Sharing Expertise

Participation does not eliminate the role of experts in the field of development. It just changes the way experts communicate their expertise to the other stakeholders. It also increases their effectiveness. Local stakeholders do not know everything. Experts of all types—engineers, social scientists, economists, sector specialists, institutional specialists, and more—need to contribute what they know. In a participatory stance, what development experts have to offer has a much better chance of being accepted and used than when they rely on reports and briefings to share their expertise. Chapter II examples show no signs that experts or their expertise will soon be extinct in the field of development. In fact, biases favoring expert knowledge show up in several of our examples.

POINTERS I

Participation allows local people to speak for themselves. After all, they are the "experts" on what they want and need. Through participation, experts may open up other possibilities for local people for incorporation into their own expertise. Local people are also uniquely expert on what they are willing to change, to what extent, and how. The challenge for Task Managers is to find ways to bring this local expertise into Bank-supported activities.

Observing

In addition to sharing expertise and helping get the balance right between technical and local expertise, Task Managers also have to play an "observer" role in participatory processes. One result to look for, or "observation target," is a rather straightforward matter: "Are the technologies and methods the stakeholders intend to use sufficiently effective and efficient to make the project a worthwhile investment?" In other words, will the internal and economic rates of return support the investment? A related observation target is if the stakeholder's decisions are acceptable to the Bank with regard to its objectives and policies.

A relatively new observation target—one of immense importance for poverty alleviation—is if project implementation arrangements build local capacity so that the poor can sustain and build on the benefits of the development activity. Traditional engineering, economics, and sector expertise do not include everything needed to build local capacity. Social scientists have much to contribute in this area, as indicated in the **Mexico Hydroelectric** example.

Other observation targets are consensus and commitment. Put simply, the consensus target is when a sufficient number of key stakeholders freely agree on the content, strategy, and tactics of the proposed project. This is, of course, a matter of judgment. But observers of participatory processes are in an especially good position to make well-grounded judgments of the degree and breadth of freely reached consensus.

The final observation target is commitment. Bank staff and others tend to understand commitment as something that can only be seen clearly after the fact from what people actually have done. The participatory stance offers a different but practical interpretation of commitment. This interpretation moves commitment into the domain of observable human action and enables Bank and government staff to make assessments on the ground about the presence or absence of commitment before approving a project and beginning implementation. When in the participatory stance, Task Managers can observe "commitment" as action taken by speaking (or writing) a promise to do something in the future. Commitments can be trusted as reasonable indicators of future action when they are made under the following conditions:

- People are free to make whatever commitments they choose, including the decision to take no new action at all.
- People make their commitments publicly in the presence of other stakeholders.
- People understand what it will take to fulfill the commitment.
- People have or believe they can get the means and competence to fulfill the commitment.

Commitments—including contracts and formal agreements—cannot be trusted when made under duress or in secret in the absence of full information and understanding or resources and the ability to act.

Navigating

Another important role that needs to be played in many but not all circumstances is that of navigator. Many obstacles to participation currently exist in the way governments and bureaucracies—including the Bank—operate in the field of development. In almost all our Chapter II examples, Task Managers have exerted considerable effort to adapt external expert rules, principles, and practices when working in the participatory stance.

In the **Philippines Irrigation** example, after verifying that participation was a standard practice of the National Irrigation Administration (NIA), the Task Manager spent most of his time helping NIA work in partnership with the central government and the Bank. For instance, NIA had trouble getting the core budgetary agency of the central government to release funds in a timely manner. The Task Manager liaised between this agency and NIA to ensure timely disbursement of funds. The Task Manager also persuaded Bank colleagues to avoid setting specific, long-term targets for creating new irrigation associations. The Task Manager argued that it was unrealistic for NIA to try to predict the time needed to create and build the capacity of new associations. Also, targets set and imposed from the outside tended to undermine the farmers' authority and control over their irrigation systems. The desired flexibility was achieved by NIA committing its work program one year at a time, depending on progress in the previous year. This change in Bank requirements permitted NIA to build on existing irrigation associations instead of rushing to meet predetermined targets for creating new ones.

Nurturing

Nurturing may sound like an especially soft and passive role for Bank Task Managers and others to play in the field of development, which has such pressing and urgent needs. It may also be a difficult role for Bank staff to learn how to do with ease, skill, and comfort, given their education and experience and working in a culture of power and control. Nevertheless, it may be the role that produces the greatest results. Nurturers build on existing participatory capacity and help strengthen it. The Bank's in-country counterparts ought to be the ones who are participating with their clients and the other stakeholders. After all they—not the Bank Task Managers—have the responsibility to serve the ultimate clients. While in this role, Task Managers can nurture the collaborative possibilities that arise naturally in the culture. In so doing, they should be careful to avoid snuffing out the start of potentially healthy and desirable possibilities for social change. This role was played by the Bank Task Manager in the **Philippines Irrigation** example. The Task Manager first ascertained for himself that NIA was indeed working collaboratively with the farmer-run irrigation systems. Then he helped provide a way the Bank could support and strengthen NIA's existing participatory approach.

CHAPTER IV

PRACTICE POINTERS IN ENABLING THE POOR TO PARTICIPATE

Photo by Asem Ansari

Why devote a chapter of the *Sourcebook* to participation by just one group of stakeholders—the poor? The reason is a practical one. Participatory methods that have been used successfully to involve government officials and other relatively powerful stakeholders in development initiatives may be inappropriate or inadequate for reaching the poor.

Many cultural, economic, and political barriers effectively prevent the poor from having any real stake in development activities. Without special efforts by the designers and sponsors of projects and without appropriate policies to address and overcome these obstacles, the voices of the poor will not be heard and their participation will at best be token. Reaching the poor, therefore, requires working with them to learn about their needs, understanding how development decisions are made in their communities, and identifying institutions and mechanisms that can get opportunities and resources into their hands.

Involving the poor in decisionmaking and getting resources to them requires strengthening their ability to act for themselves. This occurs through investments in human capital such as education and health, investments in social capital such as local-level institutions and participatory processes, and support for community-based development efforts planned and implemented from the bottom up. These efforts require responsive institutions and legal and regulatory policies that enable, not hinder, local participation. We recognize, however, that crafting responsive institutions and creating an enabling environment facilitates the participation of all stakeholders, not just poor people.

This chapter shares the experiences of Bank Task Managers in this respect, highlighting some of the ways in which they have worked with in-country counterparts to increase the poor's ability to participate in development activities.

LEARNING FROM THE POOR

The first step in any effort to enable the poor to participate involves learning from them firsthand about the problems they face, how they have tackled them, and their proposals for gaining more control and influence over development initiatives. Task Managers gain an understanding of these issues in a variety of ways, including rapid participatory needs assessments as part of project design, broadly based participatory poverty assessments (PPAs) in the context of country economic and sector work (ESW), or more formal, large-scale, census-type surveys. Here we focus on some of the participatory methods that have proved useful in poverty assessments and ESW and that could be equally applicable during project preparation.

Learning What Poverty Means to the Poor
Several methods are available to explore how the poor perceive poverty. These techniques should be used by local people (or by a team of researchers that includes local men and women) who know appropriate ways to approach the topic. They should be used after researchers have spent some time in the local communities, clarifying the reason for their interest in learning about poverty there.

Defining Poverty The Bank's **Zambia PPA** used wealth-ranking techniques to learn how local people characterize poverty. Villagers were asked to sort a stack of cards, each labeled with the name of a head of household, into piles according to the relative wealth of the households, using any criteria of wealth they wished. Wealthy households were identified as those, for example, with the biggest fields or enough money to dress well and give to the poor. Those identified as poorest were commonly female-headed households or people living by themselves, dependent on relatives or neighbors for their daily needs. Ranking exercises such as these can lead to frank group discussions on poverty—often a sensitive and difficult topic.

In the **Burkina Faso PPA** simple "point-and-shoot" cameras were lent to various members of three representative communities, who were then asked to take pictures of what they thought constituted poverty in their communities. The cameras were handed out to men, women, and children, none of whom had ever used a camera before. The films were then developed locally and the prints shown and distributed for discussion by the community. They were subsequently shared with some of the country's senior policymakers.

Learning about the Poor's Priorities The design of community-level, poverty-focused initiatives always requires some kind of direct consultation with the poor to learn about what they consider to be the development priorities in their communities. Care needs to be taken when asking about their priority needs, because people's expectations may be raised even though the project may not be able to fulfill them. Researchers need to be honest about the likelihood that the communities consulted will benefit from the upcoming project and about the start-up time required before they will see any results.

Box 4.1. Organizing a Participatory Poverty Assessment

Task Managers who have been responsible for organizing complete PPAs highlight the following steps in the process:

- *Selecting technical support.* In practice, most Task Managers in charge of PPAs have started by locating a senior social scientist either in the Bank or outside to take responsibility for carrying the exercise through to completion.
- *Identifying objectives, methodology, and a research agenda.* The PPAs conducted so far have varied a great deal in the methodologies used, the scope of the research, and the duration of the fieldwork, which has taken from days to months.
- *Identifying in-country institutions and researchers.* Some combination of academic researchers, nongovernmental organization (NGO) staff, and government agency staff has been involved in most PPAs. An experienced local social scientist is generally needed to oversee the exercise and make a substantial input to synthesizing the conclusions. A competent local institution is also needed to deal with the logistics of mounting a large-scale field research exercise.
- *Identifying sources of funding.* Many PPAs have been funded from trust funds such as those provided by the Overseas Development Administration, the Dutch Poverty Trust Fund, the Swedish International Development Authority, the German Gesellschaft für Technische Zusammenarbeit, the United Nations Children's Fund, and the Canadian International Development Agency.
- *Designing a training input.* A significant training input may be necessary to familiarize the researchers with the participatory methods and systematic recording and reporting of fieldwork results.
- *Support to implementation.* No matter how well designed the research activities may be, a certain amount of support and supervision is usually needed while the teams are in the field.
- *Analysis and formulation of policy recommendations.* Task Managers stress that fieldwork results must be well documented and a certain amount of analysis must be done while still in the field—something the researchers may not be used to doing. Task Managers also recommend finding social scientists experienced in policy formulation in development agencies, such as the Bank, to assist the local researchers in their analyses.

Source: Andrew Norton and Tom Stephens. 1995. *Participation in Poverty Assessments.* Participation Series, Environment Department Paper, World Bank, Washington, D.C.

POINTERS II

Formal beneficiary assessments can offer insights into what poverty means for the poor and their priorities. A beneficiary assessment (see Appendix I) is a tool to gather information to assess the value of an activity as it is perceived by its principal users, the beneficiaries or clients. Formal beneficiary assessments with systematically selected populations can take four to six months, so early preparation is needed and can cost $30,000–$50,000.

In some of the communities visited in the **Zambia PPA,** focus group discussions were held with men and women to investigate what people saw as the main issues facing their community and potential ways of resolving them. Focus groups ranked problems in order of severity and identified potential solutions actionable at the level of individuals or households, the community, and outside agencies.

Providing Incentives for the Poor to Participate

People will not participate unless they believe it is in their interest to do so. All too often participation is seen as a way of getting poor people to carry out activities or share in their costs, when the benefits are not clear to those expected to participate. When these projects fail, it is often the participatory approach that is blamed. Some forestry projects, for example, have expected forest dwellers to plant and maintain community wood lots or engage in forest regeneration even though participants cannot be certain who will get the benefits when the trees mature. It is no surprise that poor people only support these projects as long as they are paid. Successful participatory projects, on the other hand, illustrate many incentives identified through participatory processes that support and encourage participation at the local level. A few examples of appropriate incentives follow:

Clear Benefits A key factor in the success of the **Fundasal Low-Income Housing** project was the incentive to own a home. This was so attractive to the beneficiaries that they were highly motivated to participate. No other incentives were required.

In the **India Forestry** example, forest protection committee members (who were local people) reached an agreement with the West Bengal Forestry Department that entitled them to a share of intermediate forest products plus 25 percent of the revenues from the sale of final harvest poles. This served as an incentive for them to cooperate with the government in protecting and regenerating the forests.

The legislation being presented to indigenous communities in the **Philippines Integrated Protected Areas** example restricted resource use and public access to forests. Designers restructured the project to fund alternative livelihood opportunities that would be proposed and implemented by indigenous communities themselves with assistance from local nongovernmental organizations (NGOs). It is expected that including funds for alternative livelihoods will provide an incentive for residents to stop logging. Indigenous communities also insisted on recognition of their ancestral domain rights and legitimization of land claims as preconditions of participation.

In the **Tamil Nadu Integrated Nutrition** project, women's working groups were developed to support community nutrition workers. An important factor in explaining the existence and strength of women's working groups in a given community was how the villagers' perceived the value of the services offered by the community nutrition workers. When a village did not consider the worker's services to be a priority, they were not inclined to form a support group around her; therefore, the provision of quality services meeting the needs of the beneficiaries was the first step in creating an environment conducive to community participation.

Prompt Action and Visible Results In the **Brazil Municipalities** example, the process of selecting contractors motivated the local community of Morro to organize and collaborate with the water company. They realized that this was not just another election-year promise and their election-year skepticism was dissolved by prompt and visible action.

In the **Rajasthan Watershed Development** project, encouraging field results generated considerable enthusiasm among staff and local residents. Village common and private lands experienced up to tenfold increases in fodder yields in almost all locations. These early, visible results demonstrated that the new program was producing significant gains and motivated people to participate more fully.

FACILITATING WOMEN'S PARTICIPATION

Among the poor, women are overrepresented; therefore, in our efforts to reach and engage the poor, we must recognize that some issues and constraints related to participation are *gender-specific* and stem from the fact that men and women play different *roles*, have different *needs*, and face different *constraints* on a number of different levels.

Because of such differences, we cannot assume that women will automatically benefit from efforts to involve poor people in project design and implementation. On the contrary, experience has made clear that, unless specific steps are taken to ensure that women participate and benefit, they usually do not. A World Bank evaluation of 121 rural water supply projects found that even in a sector in which women carried the greater share of responsibility, they benefited primarily from the 17 percent of water projects that had been specifically designed to involve them.

Photo by Deepa Narayan

POINTERS II

Barriers to Women's Participation

Systemic gender biases may exist in the form of *(a)* customs, beliefs, and attitudes that confine women mostly to the domestic sphere, *(b)* women's economic and domestic workloads that impose severe time burdens on them, and *(c)* laws and customs that impede women's access to credit, productive inputs, employment, education, information, or medical care. These differences affect men's and women's ability and incentives to participate in economic and social development activities.

Sociocultural Constraints

In seeking the participation of women in development activities, sensitivity is needed on the social and cultural barriers that may inhibit women's participation. In the Balochistan Province of Pakistan, the acute shortage of female teachers has been due, in part, to cultural constraints against girls going away to attend residential teacher training colleges. The lack of female teachers is, in turn, an important factor in the low enrollment (15 percent) of girls in primary schools. Most parents find it culturally unacceptable to send their daughters to boys' schools or to have them taught by male teachers brought in from the city and unknown to the community.

By adapting to these constraints, the new **Balochistan Primary Education Program** has succeeded both in increasing the supply of female teachers and in raising girls' enrollment rates to 80–100 percent in villages with new schools. Under the this program, potential teachers are recruited from *within* the village by parents on the newly formed village education committees; the program also provides mobile teacher training *in* the girl's village. After graduating, the teacher becomes a government employee, assigned to teach in the school established by her sponsoring village education committee.

Time and Mobility Constraints

In addition to cultural constraints, women's work often denies them the time to participate in meetings. As women's domestic responsibilities often require them to stay close to the home, lack of mobility may also be a constraint. Various practical measures—from providing child-care facilities to installing standpipes that reduce time spent fetching water—can make it easier for women to attend meetings or training sessions. In particular, the choice of time and place for meetings must take account of women's schedules and the availability of safe transport.

In the **Nigeria Women in Agriculture** example, specific steps were taken to reduce the conflicts in women's schedules and guarantee regular attendance: each group meets on the same day at the same time and place; reminders about the meetings are posted at highly visible and accessible locations; and, if the scheduled day conflicts with a market day, the women are consulted in advance and an alternative time found. Consequently, women rarely face the problem of not knowing where and when the meetings are held.

Legal Regulatory Constraints

Legal restrictions in some countries prevent women from participating in formal labor markets or holding certain occupations. They may also prohibit women from entering into contracts under their own name, inheriting property, or holding legal title to land.

The **Honduras Agricultural Sector Adjustment Credit** includes support for implementing changes in the law to allow women to have title to land. Before the new law, land tenure rules and regulations made land adjudication and titling cumbersome. The law also specifically forbade women from holding title to agricultural land unless they were widowed with dependent children under 16 years of age. Women relinquished even this limited title when their eldest son reached 16 years. This and other provisions not only excluded women from independent agricultural production but also prevented them from holding the collateral necessary to obtain credit for agricultural or other productive ventures. In 1992 the law on land tenure was modified to provide women with equal rights of access to land. Tranche-release conditions under the Agriculture Sector Adjustment Credit include satisfactory implementation of the new Land Tenure Action Plan.

In some cases, conditions are such that special legal or regulatory provisions may be needed to permit the equal participation of both men and women. In Pakistan, for example, several reforms were undertaken to facilitate girls' participation in the **Balochistan Primary Education Program.** Changes in the regulations governing recruitment, training, and support of *female* teachers were made so that women could be recruited to teach in their own village. This included lowering the minimum age to 14 years and raising the maximum age to 40 years; lowering the minimum qualification for matriculation; legalizing a mobile teacher-training program for women; and officially sanctioning new community-sponsored village schools and teacher posts. Without such changes, the demand for community-managed girls' schools would have far outstripped the number of qualified, available women teachers.

Using Appropriate Methodologies

Seeking Women's Views

Often the first step toward determining appropriate measures for supporting women's participation is to obtain good information—about gender roles, needs, activities, access to and control over resources, existing institutions, and the constraints operating against women's participation. This can be done through gender analysis, which, if effective, elicits the views of women and often involves gender awareness training for facilitators or interviewers.

Gender analysis leads to the formulation of a gender strategy that addresses *practical* gender needs (roles and responsibilities) and *strategic* gender needs (systemic issues of equity and empowerment). Effective gender strategies pay particular attention to resource allocation at both household and community levels.

Because gender planning is part of the overall planning process, it is critical that the integration of gender concerns occurs early in policy formulation, analytical work, and project preparation.

Gender-Responsive Poverty Assessments

Some recent poverty assessments have been designed explicitly to solicit women's views on a wide range of questions. In the **Cameroon PPA**, 50 percent of the interviewers and 50 percent of those interviewed were women. The resulting information on gender issues was fully integrated in the subsequent analysis and recommendations with strong policy implications. For example, women in Cameroon were found to be shouldering most of the burden of producing and marketing food. Their average labor hours per week were estimated to be more than double those of men. As a result, urgent action was recommended to give women access to time- and labor-saving transport and technology to allow them the opportunity to develop their own skills and participate in community projects.

Involving Women in Policy Work

In the **Morocco Women in Development** example, poor rural and urban women were given the opportunity to articulate their needs and priorities through a participatory rural appraisal process (see Appendix I) that provoked discussion among community members about development and gender issues and sought women's views in formulating national policy objectives. It was discovered that women's concerns and priorities differed from those of the men and other stakeholder groups. The findings of this qualitative exercise were used effectively to complement conventional survey methods, and the new perspectives gained were applied in defining the recommended program of action.

Working with Women's Groups

Making an effort to engage and involve women can bring significant returns. Over and over in our examples, we find that women's groups have proved to be one of the most effective entry points for initiating activities and reaching poor households.

In the **Brazil Municipalities** example, women's clubs proved to be the most effective instruments for working with the community. Within the *favelas*, the women themselves turned out to be the key to getting the subprojects under way. The designers met with the women first when they came into a community and worked with them on a daily basis in designing and implementing the water and sanitation subprojects.

In the **Nigeria Women in Agriculture** example, government field staff, recognizing that more than one-third of Nigerian women belong to cooperative societies and other locally organized formal and informal associations, built on these indigenous women's groups to expand the newly established state Women in Agriculture (WIA) programs. The WIA program used NGOs to help identify women beneficiary groups and then WIA field staff targeted them to initiate and execute project activities.

Under the **Gambia Women in Development** program, women's groups or *kafos* are the entry point for the skills development component of the project. *Kafos*, usually with about 100 voluntary members, traditionally provide mutual member support, sharing labor and making loans to those in need. More recently their roles have expanded to include income generation and basic education. Members of *kafos* have access to skill training provided by community development workers in business management and productivity enhancement. Some *kafo* members are being trained by community development workers to tutor in basic literacy and arithmetic.

POINTERS II

Photo by Katrine Saito

BUILDING COMMUNITY CAPACITY

When designing poverty-focused initiatives, Task Managers have found it necessary to learn about the characteristics of poor *communities* and the local organizational structure within which decisions are taken. As the examples from the previous section suggest, women's groups are often found to be among the most effective local-level institutions. Many other structures, however, exist at the local level that represent valuable organizational resources and provide potential ability for undertaking development activities.

Understanding Community Organizations

Seeing Invisible Groups

In a typical poor community, a whole range of organizations are operating: formal or informal, traditional or modern, indigenous or externally established. All these have different functions, be they productive, social, religious, or otherwise. It is often through these organizations that demand is expressed, participatory processes organized, and development services delivered.

Some of the most active community organizations are informal. They are not listed in any documents, and they may be unknown even to people familiar with the communities (extension agents, local development agency staff, and so forth). Learning about these groups entails visiting the communities and talking with inhabitants about the decisionmaking units present.

A simple "institutional mapping" exercise has been used successfully in several PPAs. Local people were asked to identify the community groups by drawing circles of differing sizes—the bigger the circle the more important and influential the institution it represents. The extent of shared decisionmaking among groups can be represented by how circles are placed in relation to one another: the closer together and the more overlapping, the greater the degree of interaction between the represented groups. These graphics, sometimes called "*chapati* diagrams," have proved effective in identifying informal groupings that are important "safety nets" for the poorer members of the community and revealing that some of the more obvious organizations are actually quite weak.

Building on Traditional Structures

Many of the projects described in Chapter II worked through *existing* community organizations and are built on the already established, collaborative experience of these groups.

POINTERS II

The **Nicaragua Municipal Development** project, not described in this report, used existing local grassroots organizations—the Sandinista Defense Committees—formed during the Nicaragua Revolution. Because of their structure, motivation, and the cohesion of their members, they proved an extremely effective instrument for reaching and involving the local population. Their participation in civil works construction improved the rate of return, increased the quality of construction, and enhanced efficiency. The planned five-year project was completed in three and a half years.

Even where *new* institutions are formed, they may be most successful if based on pre-existing relationships:

In the **Senegal Small Rural Operations** project, groups of farmers organized around a shared economic interest registered as a *groupment d'intérêt économique* (GIE) to identify and prepare subprojects, open accounts in the local banking system, and contribute funds for renewal of equipment and infrastructure. A mid-term review of the project found that the most functional GIEs generally evolved out of old informal groups characterized by social cohesion, mutual trust, and a history of joint action. Newly created GIEs that had been mobilized around a temporary, shared economic activity were the least efficient and most fragile.

The **Egypt Resource Management** example built on a traditional Bedouin lineage structure, the *bayt*, to create community groups that became involved in preparing community action plans and implementing and monitoring subprojects.

Catalyst Organizers

Establishing new groups and building on existing structures requires a good deal of groundwork to increase community awareness about the benefits of organizing to participate in project design and implementation. This preparation is often done by providing facilitators or "catalyst-organizers." These facilitators may be from the implementing agency or from an intermediary organization such as an NGO.

In the **Balochistan Primary Education Program,** collective action was induced with the formation of village education committees. Community workers went door-to-door to organize parents' groups, encouraging all parents to form an association. No parental involvement existed in schools at all, in fact many parents were not even aware that their children had a right to public education. Parents joined village education committees, which had clear mandates to perform specific tasks, such as identifying teachers and monitoring teacher and student attendance.

In the **Nepal Irrigation Sector** program, an association officer was sent out to each district to meet with farmers, inform them about the objectives of the project, and encourage them to organize themselves into an irrigation association (IA). In many villages, unofficial farmers' organizations were already functioning around the irrigation system. Association officers encouraged irrigation associations to form around pre-existing village societal organization, and villagers were asked to elect an executive committee for the IA through their own selection process.

Federated Structures

Effective community action is rooted in local-level systems and is relatively small in scale, often averaging some fifteen to thirty households that are engaged in collective action. To keep authority and responsibility anchored at the local level while providing integration and learning among similar groups, a pattern of "bottom-up" integration emerges in many of the examples we reviewed.

POINTERS II

In **Colombia's Community Child Care and Nutrition** project, home-based institutes are administered through a three-tiered community structure. First, parents of children enrolled in ten to fifteen centers form a parents' association. Second, parents at each center elect three representatives to join a local assembly with thirty to forty-five members. Third, the assembly elects five parent representatives to serve as its board of directors. The parents' associations, through the board, manage the project funds and the local contributions from parents.

Deep tube wells provide large areas with irrigation water under **Nepal's Bhairawa Lumbini Groundwater II** project. About 150 farm families are served by each tube well, but such a size proved too large for members to work together effectively. To remedy this, tube well users' groups have been subdivided into units of approximately thirty families each. Seven or so of these units are confederated into a water user group; four to five such groups form a water user association, which has an elected chairman. The subunits and water user groups control water distribution at the local level, whereas the water user association has decisionmaking authority over issues that affect the system as a whole.

Potential Pitfalls   A common failure in working with local groups is to create the institutional structure without paying adequate attention to the capability, knowledge, and technical skills the groups will require. Newly established groups have failed because too much was expected of them too soon. Likewise, attempts to modify the form or function of existing groups to serve project needs does not always work.

Building the Capacity of Community Organizations

Community groups, in addition to lacking sufficient funds to begin their own development efforts, frequently lack adequate organizational, administrative, and technical skills to design and implement such activities. Task Managers and their government counterparts have sought to assess and build this capability within Bank-financed projects. Most of the examples come from social funds, because these operations are currently at the forefront of the Bank's capacity-building efforts.

Assessing Capacity   Several social funds have included institutional assessments of community organizations during subproject appraisal or even earlier to determine the degree to which these organizations are operating in a participatory manner.

In the **Peru National Fund for Social Compensation and Development (FONCODES),** community organizations are assessed during subproject appraisal through a beneficiary assessment (see Appendix I). At the time of appraisal, FONCODES staff talk with villagers during site visits to verify that general assemblies were held in which members of the subproject management committee were selected by the community.

Indicators of Capacity   The **Social Investment Fund in Ecuador** used a set of indicators to determine the institutional strength of community organizations, including:

- Internal process and regular leadership renewal
- Degree to which members control and audit the use of funds
- Degree of physical participation of members in the communal activity
- Degree to which members participate in organizational decisions

- Administrative capabilities of the organization
- Technical capacity of the organization (education level, special courses, and training of leadership and members)
- Degree to which members are able to handle required technology by themselves.

Providing Training Training community organizations can empower them to better identify and prioritize their needs and develop strategies to meet them, begin microprojects, and sustain their development efforts once outside assistance is withdrawn. Training can be provided by project staff or subcontracted to NGOs or other local firms experienced in community-level programs.

The **Ethiopian Social and Rehabilitation Development Fund** project includes plans for an extensive training program for local community leaders and subproject management committee leaders, with special emphasis on the participation of women. Training is to be provided in local planning, needs prioritization, subproject preparation and supervision, and management of microproject funds and accounting. Local government officials and local NGO staff are in turn being trained to help communities prepare and implement subprojects.

Community participation training has been built into the **Benin Health** example. Each year at their annual training session, all members of Benin's health care profession receive specific training on how to work with and in local communities. They learn skills in listening, facilitation, and satisfying the needs of local communities. Through this kind of training, government employees are taught customer service and the value of being responsive to clients.

Branching Out Once groups have become skilled in tasks required for their participation in the project activities, they can go on to undertake other development activities on their own.

Many of the women's working groups that sprang up during the course of the **Tamil Nadu Integrated Nutrition** project to promote better health and nutrition practices in the villages later began food processing to supply the feeding supplement under the project. This had the advantage of contributing to income and employment opportunities. Women's groups that first mobilized around health, were the predecessors of the women's cooperatives and societies that later formed around larger-scale and diverse activities. Apparently their organizational capacities were strengthened to the point that they could begin activities outside the project.

Once local farmer irrigation associations in the **Philippines Irrigation** example had learned to work together in designing and improving irrigation systems, the more successful irrigation associations used this experience to collectively invest in threshing floors, undertake bulk procurement, manage storage facilities, and provide credit to other groups of farmers. This stimulated the less successful irrigation associations to do the same. IAs also collaborated with National Irrigation Administration in preparing agricultural development plans, which cover cropping patterns, water distribution, reforestation, soil and water conservation, farmer training, extension, demonstration programs for crop production methodologies, pest management and mechanization, as well as cooperatives and other credit and marketing schemes.

INTERMEDIARY NGOS

We have presented Bank experience in working with *community-based organizations* to reach the poor and facilitate their participation. We now look at the

Box 4.2. What Makes Community Organizations Work?

Task Managers may find the following list of five common characteristics of well-functioning community groups useful whether they are planning to work with existing groups or establish new organizations.

- *The group addresses a felt need and a common interest.* When people share a *common* problem that can be addressed by *group* action (such as a lack of water supply, a security problem, or a degraded natural resource), they are more likely to mobilize themselves and work with support agencies to change the situation than if the problem applies to only a few members. Social cohesion tends to break down as groups grow or spread over large areas and monitoring the behavior of individuals becomes more difficult. For this reason, as groups expand, they either create subgroups or formalize regulations and delegate decisionmaking to smaller working groups.
- *The benefits of working together outweigh the costs.* Benefits may be economic (cash savings, increased production, income, and time savings), social capital formation (increased ability to collectively solve problems), increased individual capacity (knowledge and skills), psychological (sense of belonging and confidence), or political (greater access to authority, greater authority, and reduced conflict).
- *The group is embedded in the local social organization.* Community organizations are most successful when based on existing relationships and groupings or when members share a common identity such as kinship, gender, age, caste, or livelihood.
- *The group has the capability, leadership, knowledge, and skills to manage the tasks.* As noted above, special attention needs to be given to ensuring groups have the necessary capacities for the tasks at hand. Those in leadership positions need to be respected and honest in their dealings. In some cases, safeguards may need to be put in place to ensure that these leaders are accountable to the group's members.
- *The group owns and enforces its rules and regulations.* All successful groups and associations are characterized by internalized rules and regulations that are known by its members. Group members should be able to participate in determining the rules and the enforcement mechanisms.

Source: Deepa Narayan. 1995. *Designing Community-Based Development.* Participation Series, Environment Department Paper No. 7, World Bank, Washington, D.C.

bridging institutions that can provide links among the poor (and their community organizations), their governments, and the World Bank. We focus here on one particular sort of intermediary institution—nationally or internationally based NGOs—although we recognize that this intermediation role may also be filled by different institutions, such as line agencies, local government units, or private firms.

NGOs as Intermediaries

Strengths Many national and international NGOs serve an intermediary function whether it be channeling development resources to community-based organizations, providing them with services or technical assistance, or helping to strengthen their capacity. Although NGOs vary in their ability and commitment to work with the poor, in many cases they have advantages as intermediaries in reaching people—including women, ethnic minorities, and the very poor—who are not represented equitably by formal institutions. For example, NGOs may have more field presence in a given area and employ local people familiar with local conditions. They may have better rapport with the poor and a clearer understanding of poor people's survival strategies and perceived needs than other kinds of intermediaries. They may be familiar with low-cost techniques and innovations relevant to poverty alleviation. They also usually have greater flexibility than the staff of official agencies. Many intermediary NGOs have experience in participatory project design and skills in participatory research, community mobilization, facilitation techniques, and group dynamics.

Limitations Several limitations of NGOs as intermediaries have also been identified, although it is difficult to generalize about the sector as a whole. Some NGOs have limited financial and management expertise and institutional capacity. Others work in isolation, communicating or coordinating little with other organizations (including government agencies). Many may be confined to small-scale interventions. They may also not fully understand the broader social and economic context in which they are working. Not all kinds of activities, therefore, are suited to the operational systems of NGOs, nor do NGOs always reach the poorest of the poor.

Intermediary Roles
The following are some examples of intermediary roles that NGOs have played in Bank-supported projects:

Identifying Community Needs The **Mali National Environment Action Plan** is giving communities an opportunity to identify and explore environmental problems and solutions. Because of their history of working in communities, NGOs in Mali are in a strong position to carry out assessments of environmental conditions in target communities. For this reason, the government engaged a Malian consortium of NGOs to identify, screen, subcontract, train, and supervise its member NGOs in carrying out the assessments.

Giving Voice to the Poor In the **Philippines Integrated Protected Areas** example, the objective of the joint Bank-government appraisal mission was to consult the indigenous cultural communities about the policy framework that would help preserve stretches of forest in which they live and ask them if they were willing to join the proposed protected parks system. Because of its close links to local communities, PANLIPI, a national legal services NGO, was contracted to identify the relevant tribal groups and organize consultative meetings between them and the joint appraisal mission. PANLIPI was also hired to conduct follow-up consultations with the indigenous cultural communities. The NGO discovered that the sessions were being dominated by local authorities and local NGOs at the expense of indigenous communities. To let the voice of tribal people be heard, PANLIPI decided to hold exclusive consultations for the tribal groups and admit other parties as "observers" only.

Organizing Community Groups In the **Shrimp Culture Project in Bangladesh,** NGO personnel and the government implementation agency's extension staff each perform their essential missions in cooperation with one another. The extension service has good technical skills, whereas the NGO personnel concentrate on mobilizing, organizing, and motivating farmers. Each group is performing those tasks for which they have a comparative advantage, and the two are coordinating their activities to good effect.

Channeling Resources During the **Guatemala Earthquake Reconstruction** project, FENACOAC, an NGO federation of sixty-nine rural savings and loan cooperatives, channeled more than $3.7 million to villagers in the form of microenterprise loans. Because of its extensive network of rural members, FENACOAC was able to reach large numbers of dispersed communities much more effectively than government or private sector banks. The federation took responsibility for informing beneficiaries (in this case cooperatives) of the microenterprise component of the project, identifying cooperatives that were eligible to receive funds, assisting them in preparing proposals, and disbursing the funds accord-

POINTERS II

ingly. The recovery rate from the entrepreneur participants has been almost 100 percent.

Understanding the NGO Sector

The term "NGO" encompasses a broad array of different organizations, varying enormously according to their purpose, philosophy, sectoral expertise, and scope of activities. In the development field, NGOs range from the large charities based in developed countries to community-based self-help groups in developing countries; they also include research institutes, churches, professional associations, and lobby groups. Task Managers need to understand this diversity to identify which organizations have the appropriate abilities, skills, and orientation to fill a particular intermediary role.

Community-based NGOs provide the institutional framework for beneficiary participation and are more likely to receive project goods and services than intermediaries. Among the *intermediary NGOs* with whom the Bank collaborates, the following distinctions are important:

Geographical Base — *National organizations* operate in individual countries, whereas *international NGOs* are typically headquartered in industrial countries and carry out operations in more than one developing country. Working through locally based NGOs has the important advantage of contributing to the development of the local NGO sector and is usually more cost effective. When local NGO capacity is weak, however, international NGOs can be good intermediaries, particularly when working in partnership with national NGOs.

In the **Benin Food Security** project, partnerships were encouraged between stronger, larger NGOs and weaker, newer NGOs to stimulate the transfer of methodologies and technology. This project began as a pilot that involved international NGOs and a few Beninese NGOs. After two years of the pilot experience, NGOs were brought together with government and donors at a workshop to design a new project based on the pilot phase. One of the findings at the workshop was that geographic concentration in the capital isolated many large NGOs from target communities. International NGOs had the human and financial resources to submit competitive proposals to include in project activities. They often, however, had the least recent or direct experience with potential client communities. When local NGOs lacked transport to access project areas, international NGOs had the necessary equipment and staff but lacked the local contacts. At the workshop, agreement was reached to modify the project in several ways, including creating incentives for NGOs to establish field offices in the project area, giving regional offices the authority to approve microprojects and disburse funds, and requiring international NGOs to partner with local NGOs to facilitate technology transfer and information sharing.

Primary Activities — *Operational NGOs* are engaged primarily in designing and implementing projects, whereas the main purpose of *advocacy NGOs* is to defend or promote a specific cause. Some NGOs engage in both sorts of activities. Advocacy NGOs, such as those defending the rights of indigenous peoples, may perform an important intermediary role in supplying information and facilitating communication and consultation.

PANLIPI, a legal rights NGO, helped gain the trust of indigenous communities at the appraisal stage of the **Philippines Integrated Protected Areas** example. PANLIPI's involvement also resulted in several changes in the project, including increased attention to indigenous land tenure, resource access, and livelihood issues and to greater participation by indigenous communities in managing protected areas. Generally, however, Bank-NGO collaboration on specific projects is more likely to involve operational intermediaries.

Orientation and Area of Competence

Not all NGOs are effective in ensuring beneficiary participation within their own programs. At one extreme are NGOs whose orientation and competence are similar to the private sector firms with whom they compete for contracts in project implementation or service delivery. Such NGOs may be efficient (and in strong demand) as *service deliverers* but are oriented to meeting the requirements of bureaucratic funding agencies; they may be less likely to use participatory processes. At the other extreme are participatory NGOs that see themselves exclusively as *enablers and capacity builders* and refuse to compromise their objectives or independence by collaborating in official programs.

A small number of exceptionally effective NGOs combine a high level of competence in service delivery and in community capacity building. The **Aga Khan Rural Development Program** in Pakistan provides an example of what can be achieved by such organizations, committed to "bottom-up" planning and combining strong technical expertise with effective institution building at the village level. Using infrastructure projects as the catalyst for institution building, this program reached 38,000 households and created 110 women's groups within four years.

Accountability

An organization serves the interests of those to whom it is accountable. In this respect, national- or regional-level *membership* NGOs, including federations of grassroots organizations or cooperatives, trade unions, peasant unions, or ethnic groups can be valuable partners in projects requiring broad participation (although women and marginalized groups are not always well represented). One difficulty, however, can be that they are often more politically embroiled and subject to state regulation.

The Indigenous People's Component of the **Eastern Lowlands Natural Resource Management and Agricultural Development Project in Bolivia** was prepared in a participatory manner by a regional Indian federation in collaboration with a technical assistance NGO. Following a major political confrontation, however, between the federation and the regional development corporation over control of the component, the component was redesigned, greatly reducing the power of the federation in project implementation.

Among NGOs that are not membership based, accountability to *client communities*, for example, through community contributions of cash, labor, materials, or facilities, is an important indicator of an NGO's participatory effectiveness. Nonparticipatory NGOs may regard community members purely as beneficiaries and the *funding agencies* as their clients.

Identifying Appropriate NGOs

Specific criteria—in terms of technical and operational capacity, outreach potential, skills in community capacity building, and knowledge of conditions in target communities—need to be matched to the specific task at hand. In general, the most effective NGOs are those that have already established participatory processes with their clients. The following list of indicators has been drawn up to guide Task Managers and their in-country counterparts to those NGOs that are likely to employ participatory practices effectively. Assessments should be based on the track record of the NGO rather than on its stated objectives.

Source of Information

A useful starting point for Task Managers unfamiliar with the NGO sector is the data base maintained by the Bank's NGO group in the Poverty and Social Policy Unit, which contains information on more than 8,000 NGOs worldwide. The NGO group also maintains a library of NGO directories and sector studies from a large number of developing countries. Within borrowing countries, information is frequently available from NGO umbrella organizations, local offices of donors (for example, the United Nations Children's Fund, United Nations Development Programme, and Ford Foundation), or from the government ministry responsible for NGO liaison. Some resident missions also keep NGO directories on file.

If an NGO is needed simply to provide informal advice on Bank-supported operations, sufficient information may be obtainable from local contacts, such as resident donor representatives or leaders of NGO consortia. If the goal is to identify an NGO for partnership in project design and implementation, a more active search is required, including field visits by consultants and interviews with a sample of community leaders and members in the areas of the NGO's activities. When NGOs are themselves to screen other NGOs in operations—as is often the case with social funds—formal eligibility criteria and case-by-case institutional appraisal methods are called for.

Selection Criteria

The **Bangladesh Second Road Rehabilitation and Maintenance** project sought an NGO to share information with affected groups, represent their interests, and consult with them to formulate a resettlement action plan. The selection process set out in the staff appraisal report considered three criteria. First, appropriate NGOs had to have a track record showing experience and ability to mediate and work with people at the grassroots level. Second, the skill mix, field experience, availability, and mobility of staff of each NGO was factored into the selection process. Third, the selection process focused on the proposed work plan and approach put forth by each NGO for this particular project.

NGO Assessments

When NGOs will be involved in a wide variety of activities or when little or no information is available, it may be helpful to conduct an NGO assessment. The Bank has undertaken NGO assessments on a national basis (in Uganda), in a specific sector (**India Health and Family Welfare Sector Study**) and in connection with specific projects (the **Nepal Rural Water Supply and Sanitation** project). Drawing from this experience, box 4.4 represents the factors that have proved useful in NGO assessments, par-

---

Box 4.3. Indicators of Participatory Effectiveness in Intermediary NGOs

- A flat management structure with decentralized authority
- Organizational structures at the community level to which funding and/or other decisions are delegated
- Use of iterative planning, involving consultation with local communities
- Contributions of cash, labor, raw materials, or local facilities by community members and organizations, making them clients rather than beneficiaries of the NGO
- Staff recruitment criteria, incentives, and training that support participation
- Strong field presence outside metropolitan areas with a high proportion of staff of local origin
- Community leaders and members have a positive perception of the NGO.
- Turnover of client groups as they "graduate" over time and intensive field attention is transferred to new groups.

Source: Thomas Carroll, Mary Schmidt, and Tony Bebbington. *Intermediary NGOs and Participation.* Participation Series, Environment Department Paper (forthcoming), World Bank, Washington, D.C.

Box 4.4. Tips for NGO Assessments

- The most useful NGO assessments are done on a sectoral or subsectoral basis. This allows the NGO universe to be divided functionally and geographically and permits systematic interviews and sample surveys.
- When evaluating newly formed NGOs or other NGOs that are new to a specific region or sector and therefore lack a track record, focus on the individuals who lead the NGO and what they have done in the past.
- Select an assessor who has a previous working relationship with government as well as NGOs to build trust.
- Build participatory elements into all NGO assessments on a systematic basis. Both terms of reference and survey methodologies should include indicators of NGO quality in community development as well as technical and managerial dimensions.
- An NGO assessment should include information about the technologies used by NGOs to communicate with members and to network with each other. Also, the analysis should cover the constraints limiting communication in remote areas.
- Whenever NGO consortia or apex organizations exist they should be given a role in NGO assessments. Nonmembers of consortia, however, should be informed of the federation's role.
- Bank resident mission staff should be involved in NGO assessments and, wherever sufficient capacity exists, resident staff members should be responsible for supervising and updating NGO assessments.

Source: Thomas Carroll, Mary Schmidt, and Tony Bebbington. *Intermediary NGOs and Participation.* Participation Series, Environment Department Paper (forthcoming), World Bank, Washington, D.C.

ticularly in NGO assessments that identify the participatory qualities of NGOs.

Obtaining Referrals In some cases, Bank Task Managers have approached a consortium of NGOs for referrals on partners in project design or implementation. Such federations can direct Task Managers to member NGOs and in some cases select and supervise them. A limitation of this approach is that not all NGOs are represented by such an apex body. This can create rivalry and isolate potentially suitable NGOs.

Soliciting Proposals When many NGOs are interested and qualified, Task Managers and their government counterparts may choose to select NGOs as they would consultants by soliciting proposals and selecting the best of these. A danger exists, however, that this could rule out qualified organizations that have strong expertise in community development but do not have skills in preparing proposals.

Bridging the Gap

Supporting Participatory Processes A paradox confronting the Task Manager is that the qualities that make NGOs participatory—and therefore attractive as intermediaries—may be inconsistent with many government, donor, and Bank requirements. One of the major constraints to group formation and capacity building is donor or government pressure to disburse and deliver services quickly. Unless procedures are made more flexible and both the Bank and the government are committed to supporting participatory processes, the NGO may be pressed into a service-delivery rather than capacity-building role.

This has happened in a number of Bank-funded projects, including **Liberia's Second Education** project. Under this project, schools were constructed rapidly and at low cost. No attention was given, however, to supporting the intermediary NGO in building community ownership of schools and planning for maintenance. As a result, many schools deteriorated or went unused. Similarly, in the **Zambia Squatter Upgrading** project, it was agreed in principle to pursue long-term community development goals by promoting active beneficiary participation. A stipulation was included, however, in the final agreement that, if the collective self-help approach used by the two intermediary NGOs interfered with the predetermined project schedule, contractors would be employed to carry out the work.

Ensuring Flexibility

Task Managers have found ways to ensure that they support rather than undermine the participatory strengths of NGO partners by introducing mechanisms that permit revisions in project priorities, greater flexibility in the timing and scale of implementation, and alternative procurement procedures. Sometimes, introducing mechanisms that allow NGOs to design and implement their own programs can also be effective.

Encouraging Partnership in Project Design

Collaborative decisionmaking from the outset concerning development objectives can help resolve the tension between the short-term project objective of the Bank or government and the long-term community development goals of NGOs. The most successful cases of Bank-NGO collaboration have involved mutual transparency and shared decisionmaking from early in the project cycle. If NGOs are to participate in a Bank-financed project in a significant way, it is important that they have a say as early as possible in the design of the project and in defining the terms of their involvement.

In examples such as the **Philippines Health Development** project, which aimed to reach the poorest members of society by building partnerships among the many health-oriented NGOs, local governments, and the Department of Health, involvement in project design was considered essential in defining effective operational partnerships, contributing to "quality at entry" and achieving successful implementation. Many of the NGOs were initially skeptical of involvement with the government. Giving them a stake in the decisionmaking process—in creating the terms of the partnerships—made it possible for NGOs to be the lead agencies at the local level and helped to overcome their skepticism.

NGO Liaison Units

A number of Bank-supported projects have created NGO liaison units. Under the **West Bengal Fourth Population** project, the government of West Bengal created a voluntary agency cell (headed by the additional director of health services), which is responsible for facilitating, supporting, and coordinating voluntary agency activities in the state. With the establishment of this cell, it is expected that the role and scope of NGOs in West Bengal family welfare programs will be substantially increased.

Information Sharing

The Bank can also promote government-NGO relations by sponsoring meetings for dialogue and information sharing. In the **Sri Lanka Health and Family Planning** project, for example, joint training was provided for NGO and government staff in Information-Education-Communication techniques. In addition, a series of annual workshops was organized to bring government and NGO personnel together to discuss ongoing strategies and implementation plans.

Scaling Up and Scaling Down

Highly participatory NGOs tend to work on a small scale; experience suggests that some of their programs depend on staying small and resource intensive. But in some cases NGOs have established participatory processes that they have themselves extended to large programs or that have proved replicable by other organizations or by government agencies on a large scale. Various ap-

POINTERS II

proaches have been taken to enable successful NGO programs to be scaled up and "mainstreamed," where possible, without losing their essential participatory qualities and without individual NGOs having to grow to the point that they become hierarchical and bureaucratized. This may involve strengthening the capacity of NGOs, both through training and promoting NGO partnerships.

Scaling up may also involve training government staff in participatory methods and relaxing some government regulations. When working with governments to encourage NGO linkages, it is useful to consider that government agencies as well as the Bank may have to scale down in the sense of decentralizing and building flexibility and microvariability into their operations. This not only pushes decisionmaking down closer to the populations most affected (and in this sense is itself more participatory) but also makes it easier to work with regional and local NGOs.

The community support process in the **Balochistan Primary Education Program** is establishing new community schools for girls in remote rural villages. The process began in 1992 with a pilot project by a small national NGO whose community workers went door to door, urging parents to form village education committees, identify a potential female teacher, and select a site for a school. The success of the pilot led to full acceptance and ownership of the program by the government, which is now funding the program on a province-wide basis using International Development Association credit. Already, the NGO has succeeded in mobilizing community members to establish as many as 200 schools. Replicating the process on this scale and incorporating the schools and their teachers into the government system once the school has proved viable has depended on the willingness of the Ministry of Education to relax a number of its regulations, so that girls with as little as eighth grade education can qualify as teachers and receive training at home from mobile training teams.

Strengthening NGO Capacity

Encouraging NGO Partnership

For the Bank-financed **Improved Environmental Management and Advocacy** project in Indonesia, an international NGO teamed up with twelve Indonesian NGOs to strengthen the ability of local intermediaries to address the environmental consequences of pesticides. The international NGO assists local counterparts in developing primary learning approaches to educate local people about environmental problems and solutions. This collaborative NGO effort is a broad initiative to develop education and training programs for farmers, consumers, and province-level regulatory officials and also serves to transfer skills and knowledge among NGOs.

The goal of the **Uttar Pradesh Sodic Land Reclamation** project is to reclaim salt-affected lands using participatory management techniques that could serve as a model for replication more broadly in the future. Farmers' water management groups will be organized and community volunteers will be trained in technology transfer by small local NGOs. The staff of these grassroot NGOs will be trained in turn by larger intermediary NGOs with previous experience in participatory management.

Other projects, such as the **Bangladesh Participatory Forest Development** project, are using a similar structure in which advisory NGOs coordinate the implementation activities of small locally based NGOs. These projects are coordinated at the national level by a single organization that works directly with the government to ensure compatibility with national goals and policies.

POINTERS II

163

Providing Training

The Task Manager of the **Bangladesh Second Road Rehabilitation and Maintenance** project felt that for an NGO to act adequately as an intermediary between beneficiaries and government agencies, its staff should be trained specifically in the use of the Bank's resettlement guidelines and generally in land valuation and compensation.

Usually, training that builds NGO capacity is provided by a component for technical assistance within a large project or through a separate project. The **Ethiopian Social and Rehabilitation Development Fund** project treats proposals for training as it does proposals for other microproject components. Any community group or NGO that has an identified need for training is invited to submit a proposal. This fund has designed community development and microproject development training programs and has appointed a training and promotion officer.

Photo by Curt Carnemark

FINANCIAL INTERMEDIATION

This section looks at three methods that have been used in Bank-financed operations to give the poor a more active role in managing the resources intended to improve their economic security and well-being. The first involves fiscal decentralization to give municipalities and local governments more control over development funds and enable them in turn to support community-level development. The second involves social funds, which are an alternative mechanism for providing financial assistance for locally led initiatives. These approaches provide new ways to bring resources and control over them closer to the level at which they are being used. The third approach involves two-way reciprocal contracts, which form the basis for sustainable financial service systems.

Fiscal Decentralization

One of the most common ways to get resources to the local level is through municipal funds, matching grants, and community development funds that decentralize functions and money to existing line agencies and local governments. Under such arrangements, central governments allocate resources to municipalities or other institutions, which in turn fund many smaller projects. These subprojects are often prepared and controlled by communities, which contribute to cost-sharing through the donation of their labor and materials. Simple procurement procedures along with democratic and transparent project selection at the neighborhood and municipal levels contribute to the success of these types of funding arrangements. Through their ability to reach the neighborhood level and mobilize local resources, they remove a critical constraint to community action, the lack of financial resources.

The Bank's **Mexico Decentralization and Regional Development** project gives municipalities control over funding many local projects by providing them with annual block grants. Such grants are made through municipal solidarity funds, which are accounts created at the municipal and community levels to finance small community projects. They are intended to channel resources to the most deprived communities by democratizing project planning as well as decentralizing project financing. This signals a change in the destination of the resources from the line agencies to the municipalities and involved elected municipal officials jointly with the communities in project selection.

Numerous examples exist of fiscal decentralization. Not all involve local participation in decisionmaking, but most help to provide an enabling environment in which such participation becomes possible.

Social Funds

Social funds can provide funding to local organizations such as community-based groups, NGOs, and local governments in a more flexible, transparent, and rapid manner than line ministries. They are "demand-driven funding mechanisms." They do not identify projects in advance but instead respond to requests generated by local organizations. Social funds do not implement projects. They promote specific activities, appraise projects or subprojects for funding using strict selection criteria, supervise implementation, and monitor project effectiveness. Social funds have spread rapidly in developing countries since the **Bolivia Emergency Social Fund** was started in 1986; in 1994 the World Bank was supporting about thirty social funds.

Autonomy   Typically, social funds are set up as autonomous institutions that are transparent and have flexible funding, procurement, and disbursement procedures. Because they are autonomous, they are able to avoid political interference and respond directly to local needs. In some cases, a social fund is an autonomous governmental structure reporting directly to the president or prime minister. In other cases, such as the Agence D'Execution des Travaux d'Infrastructures Publiques (AGETIP) in Senegal, it is a private association contracted by the government.

The **Nepal Rural Water Supply and Sanitation (RWSS)** project uses an autonomous fund (RWSS-FUND) to support demand-driven, community-based water and sanitation initiatives. This fund is designed to be managed by a board with representatives from both the government and the private sector (NGOs). The board is autonomous and fully responsible for the fund's management. Money is provided by the Ministry of Finance through a simplified, block-grant release process.

In the **Albania Rural Poverty Alleviation** example, the Rural Development Fund was created by government decree as an autonomous agency because the existing government structure lacked the ability to work at the community level in a participatory manner. To fulfill its responsibilities for implementing both the pilot and full-scale Bank-assisted project, this fund was given administrative, financial, and technical autonomy as well as the authority to enter into contracts. One of the principal functions of the fund is to support

POINTERS II

Box 4.5. Designing a Social Fund

The following tips may be helpful to Task Managers responsible for designing a social fund.

- *Be clear about the objectives of a social fund* and the centrality of participation in realizing objectives. Designers must weigh the trade-offs between rapid disbursement and capacity building in beneficiary and intermediary organizations.
- *Refuse to fund nonparticipatory microprojects, and prioritize selection of microprojects according to the intensity of participation.* Ask how much local participation there has been in the processes of microproject identification, design, and planning and if the community is involved in implementation.
- *Encourage or mandate establishment of microproject management committees.* It may be necessary to require representation of women and other marginalized groups in the management committees.
- *Apply participatory data collection methods, such as participatory rural appraisal and beneficiary assessment (see Appendix I for descriptions), to monitor subprojects regularly.* Assessing 10 percent of subprojects a year may be a good target.
- *Provide for capacity building of intermediary and community organizations as early as possible.*
- *Develop a piloting phase* in which participatory mechanisms can be tested, the concept of participation introduced, and actors given time to learn.
- *Design flexible and transparent procurement and disbursement procedures.*
- *Deliver what has been promised.* Avoid delays in processing proposals and delivering services. Critically monitor the performance of the social fund.

Source: Alexandre Marc and Mary Schmidt. 1995. *Participation and Social Funds.* Participation Series, Environment Department Paper No. 4, World Bank, Washington, D.C.

---

work undertaken by village communities on the subproject for demand-responsive, rural infrastructure rehabilitation. The Rural Development Fund is governed by a Board of Trustees composed of the ministers of the relevant ministries such as agriculture, labor, and finance. It is chaired by the deputy prime minister of Albania.

Decentralized Operations

To operationalize the **Zambia Social Recovery Fund** to finance microprojects for rehabilitation of social service infrastructure, an office called the Microprojects Unit was set up within the Zambian presidency through which funds were channeled to local community organizations and NGOs. The special status of the Microprojects Unit allows it to hire personnel from outside the civil service and bypass the government bureaucracy.

This enables procedures to move quickly and allows the unit to deal directly with beneficiary communities. Communities prepare proposals for social service microprojects for which they contribute to total costs. On approval, the implementing organization sets up a bank account to receive direct, incremental dispersals from the Microprojects Unit, thereby cutting through typical bureaucratic delays and red tape. This has proved a quick and effective way of getting resources down to the local level and responding to varying demands and priorities among local communities. The channeling of funds to NGOs and local organizations has also increased the institutional ability of these organizations to undertake development activities and serve as instruments of participation.

In the **Albania Rural Poverty Alleviation** example, a social fund mechanism was used to provide funding for rural infrastructure rehabilitation. Infrastructure officers from the coordinating institution, the Rural Development Fund, are assigned to each district. They, along with engineers from the fund, work with local villages and assist them in preparing proposals for the one infrastructure rehabilitation project that represents their highest priority. Once a project is approved by the fund, the contractual partner for implementing the project becomes the commune (that is the corresponding local government unit). To fulfill the employment generation objective of this component, the commune, in turn, hires local villagers to work on the project. This approach has proved successful in delivering priority infrastructure to rural communities.

Sustainable Financial Systems

The preceding section examined ways to improve the effectiveness and impact of resources flowing from the government to the poor. In this section, we turn from *one-way grant* resource flows, which characterize most of the decentralization projects and social funds, to *two-way reciprocal contracts,* which are the basis for sustainable financial service systems.

Task Managers might want to know more about how to build sustainable financial service systems for poor men and women for two reasons. First, from the point of view of *financial sector development*, people who have not been integrated into the formal financial sector because of low income, gender, ethnic identity, or remote location often represent a large and potentially profitable market for institutions that can develop ways to reduce the costs and risks of serving them.

From the perspective of *poverty reduction*, the case is even more compelling. For the most vulnerable of the working poor, who may not be ready to take on debt, accessible savings can help maintain consumption over crisis periods and greatly improve economic security. Then, once some degree of economic security is attained, access to credit can help them move out of poverty by improving the productivity of their enterprises or creating new sources of livelihood.

Participation Continuum Participation occurs along a continuum. On one end are "beneficiaries," who are the recipients of services and resources. More and more successful projects, however, define participants as "clients" and invest in setting up timely feedback mechanisms to ensure they stay in touch with what their clients want. In these projects, "clients" are perceived as those who buy something (for example, financial services) and must agree to pay more than a symbolic fee for it. They also ensure that a clear contract exists with clients, which lets them know what

POINTERS II

Figure 4.1. The Participation Continuum

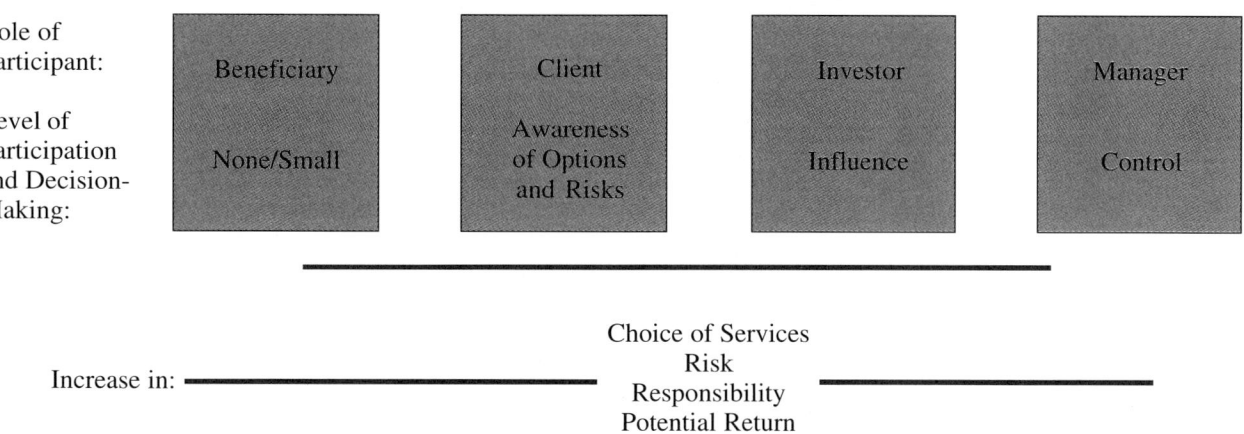

Role of Participant: Beneficiary | Client | Investor | Manager

Level of Participation and Decision-Making: None/Small | Awareness of Options and Risks | Influence | Control

Increase in: Choice of Services
Risk
Responsibility
Potential Return

Source: Lynn Bennett, Mike Goldberg, and Pam Hunte. *Group-Based Financial Systems: Exploring the Links between Performance and Participation.* Participation Series, Environment Department Paper (forthcoming), World Bank, Washington, D.C.

they must do to keep the services coming. The challenge is to devolve the decisionmaking power and control over resources to participants as "investors" or even "managers" who make strategic and operational decisions about how services are designed and delivered. But it is important to remember that many people are not willing or able to take on the additional risks and increased responsibilities associated with higher levels of self-management.

Overcoming Barriers

Building an appropriate system of financial intermediation that is accessible to poor people and yet sustainable for the lending institution can be a challenge. Overcoming the vulnerability imposed by continual reliance on subsidies (finance as charity) by establishing a market-based system (finance as business) that can operate on its own is not easy. In most cases, it is not something that can be fully achieved within the time frame of one or sometimes even a series of Bank lending operations. In some borrowing countries where barriers are created by remoteness, poor infrastructure, a stagnant or primarily subsistence economy, illiteracy, or social factors such as caste and gender, self-sustainable financial services may not be attainable for a long time.

Need for Intermediation

What is needed to build and support sustainable financial systems with the poor is a combination of financial and social intermediation. Mechanisms must be created to bridge the gaps created by poverty, illiteracy, gender, and remoteness. Local institutions must be built and nurtured, and skills and confidence of new low-income clients developed. This costs money and requires the help of intermediaries at local levels.

Group-Based Approaches

One of the most promising routes to sustainable financial intermediation is the use of local self-help groups. Although many local variations exist, the approach essentially involves identification and organization of local voluntary associations or self-help groups among disadvantaged populations. These groups are then *linked* with formal financial institutions or assisted in developing their own *parallel*, semiformal systems for financial intermediation.

Photo by Curt Carnemark

POINTERS II

Solidarity Groups One of the most successful—and certainly the best known—group-based financial service system for the poor is the **Grameen Bank** in Bangladesh. Grameen was established as a financial institution in 1983 to provide financial services to low-income rural households that had no access to formal sector programs. By 1993 Grameen Bank had served almost half of the villages in Bangladesh, lending $311 million and mobilizing $218 million in savings and deposits. Its total membership is more than 1.8 million, of whom 94 percent are women.

Grameen supports the formation of self-selecting "solidarity" groups of five people. Members receive small working capital loans backed only by the joint liability of other members. This means that even though the loans are given individually, default by any member blocks access to further credit for others in the group until they either prevail on the defaulter to pay or cover the debt themselves out of joint savings or a pooled contribution.

The loans are for twelve months with weekly installments, which makes accounting and repayment simple and easy for group members to understand. Members are also required to contribute to group savings and emergency funds on a regular basis. Many borrowers use the loans for petty trade, traditional agricultural processing, animal husbandry, and activities that borrowers know well. Reflecting its responsiveness to the vulnerability of its members to seasonal and other shocks, Grameen also lends for "consumption" purposes, such as medical care and food. Repayment for the program as a whole in 1993 was 96 percent.

Village Credit Committees In the **Albania Rural Poverty Alleviation** example, the dire economic situation made it imperative to inject cash into impoverished areas as quickly as possible by developing a credit delivery mechanism suitable to poor farmers. But the project designers did not stop with simply delivering the credit. They sought to *build a sustainable financial services system.* The villagers rejected the solidarity group approach (based on Grameen Bank) and chose to create a village credit fund in which the whole village is collectively responsible for repayment of individual loans. Each community elects a three-person village credit committee, which is responsible for selecting borrowers and ensuring that loans are repaid. Decisionmaking rests entirely at the local level and the village credit committee holds open meetings to evaluate community member loan applications. Expansion has been rapid with fifty-nine such committees established, more than 2,750 subloans made during the first two years of the project, and nearly 100 percent repayment.

Advantages of Group-Based Services Group-based approaches have several advantages to the financial intermediary: group liability is an effective collateral substitute, self-policing mechanisms can increase repayment rates and reduce lender risk, savings mobilization is often impressive and has proved an inexpensive source of loan capital, and administration and enforcement costs can be reduced. Group-based financial systems can in many situations effectively shift some of the costs and risks from the lending institution to the group.

From the client's perspective, groups may offer the only affordable way of gaining access to financial services. For landless men and women, group liability substitutes for physical or financial collateral; without it they could not obtain formal credit. The savings mobilized by groups are often re-lent to their members for emergencies, consumption, and similar purposes for which formal institutions are reluctant to lend. With regard to capacity building, group-

POINTERS II

169

based approaches can build solidarity, confidence, and financial management skills among members.

Advantages for Women

For women, one of the most important aspects of a group is that it provides a legitimate "social space" beyond the home and fosters a sense of solidarity that allows them to deal more freely with unfamiliar formal institutions and processes. Some evidence from Bank and other projects shows that women's groups perform better than men's groups in terms of repayment and longevity. One reason may be that in many societies women have few other financial opportunities and value them highly. Group membership may also have a personal and social value beyond its economic utility.

Characteristics of Successful Groups

Characteristics of strong groups include self-selection of members, literacy of at least a few group members, and membership of only one gender. Group enforcement of sanctions is strongest when a system for calling on outside assistance (usually from the NGO) is readily available to resolve serious conflicts. Most successful systems appear to be ones in which a large proportion of the lending capital is raised from group members' savings. Elements of groups that, contrary to general belief, do *not* appear to affect group performance include group size, leadership rotation, and the kind or frequency of group meetings.

Pitfalls of Groups

Groups are not a guarantee of success. Despite potential advantages, groups may face serious managerial problems. They may be costly to set up; corruption or control by powerful groups is a possibility; and minority groups or the most disadvantaged are often excluded. Nevertheless, the resiliency and popularity of many locally based, financial service organizations indicates that locally managed groups can improve their financial management practices and move toward sustainability through self-help efforts.

Building Capacity of Groups

It is critical to build up the human resources and local institutions needed to prepare groups to manage their own institutions or to enter into responsible business relationships with formal financial institutions. Ultimately, it is the cohesiveness and self-management capacity of the groups that enables them to bring down the costs of financial intermediation by reducing default through peer pressure and lowering the transaction costs banks incur in dealing with many small borrowers and savers.

To achieve this eventual efficiency gain and develop sustainable financial services for the poor, however, substantial up-front investments are needed to build the skills and systems that permit the group to take over most of the management of their own financial transactions eventually. Time-bound "infant industry" subsidies, such as building self-reliant groups through training group members in accounting skills, management skills, and use of management information systems, are also justified. Where government subsidies are *not* justified, however, is in supporting the price of financial services with artificially low interest rates for the end users.

CRAFTING RESPONSIVE INSTITUTIONS

Putting people first also requires changing the very ways in which government bureaucracies are accustomed to functioning. It requires different planning procedures, institutional arrangements, and measures for resource allocation. To put people's needs first, institutions must redefine responsibilities, reallocate staff resources, offer different incentives to staff, build in new mechanisms for learning and experimentation, and build outreach capacity by hiring new staff and retraining old.

Characteristics of Responsive Institutions

Delegating Authority
In the **Benin Health** example, the Ministry of Health gave the local health management committees decisionmaking power and control over resources. Each local health center (typically serving three to six villages) has its own management committee of six to eight people. Committee members are elected democratically; anyone may serve, provided that at least one member is a woman. The committee is directly involved in preparing the health center's annual budget for submission to the ministry. It is responsible for collecting and accounting for funds paid to the health center for services and drugs and also manages the procurement and inventory of drugs. Representatives of local committees serve on the board of the government's new drug procurement agency and on the government's central Health Sector Coordinating Committee, giving them a voice in national policy.

The success of **El Salvador's Community-Managed School Program (EDUCO)** depends on community involvement in public education. Each community is required to provide a building as a school for its children. Parents elect school board members for three-year terms. School board members, who are legally authorized to manage the schools, work with the Ministry of Education to establish annual budgets for the schools. Once the ministry transfers the agreed-on amount of money to the boards' bank accounts, the boards recruit, select, hire, pay, and manage the teachers and curricula. The boards and the teachers jointly allocate funds for teaching materials. Each local board monitors teacher performance and, if necessary, takes the necessary steps to fire teachers for whom poor performance or absenteeism is a problem. About 25 percent of schools in El Salvador now have such arrangements in their schools.

Flexibility
In the **Philippines Irrigation** example, it proved unrealistic to try to predict the amount of time needed to create local irrigation associations and ensure their full participation. It was found that preset targets tended to undermine the farmers' authority over the systems and, with it, their commitment. In view of this, the National Irrigation Administration persuaded the Bank to avoid setting specific, long-term targets for construction. Flexibility was achieved by developing work programs one year at a time, depending on the progress of the preceding year rather than rigidly scheduling work for the entire loan period. This flexibility allowed the National Irrigation Administration to spend more time building on existing irrigation associations instead of pressing to meet arbitrary targets for the creation of new ones.

Experimenting and Learning
In the **Rajasthan Watershed Development** project, the new challenge of implementing small, integrated watershed development forced staff from different disciplines to work together; the lack of prior experience even among senior officials created a general willingness to experiment with innovative approaches. Government field staff were told to "start with what you know, what you have resources for, and what people want." Staff were given the freedom to do small experiments and try whatever they thought might work. An enabling policy was

POINTERS II

that no penalties should be given for failed experiments and successful innovation would be rewarded. In this way, significant progress was made in developing area-specific technologies. Much of this progress came from interacting with local people and seeking out and using their indigenous practices.

In the **Cameroon Rural Community Microprojects**, the Ministry of Agriculture took a "learning" approach, allowing local committees in charge of approving loans to go slowly and learn from their mistakes in funding microprojects. The objective of the project was just as much on capacity building as it was on lending for microprojects. This flexibility and less structured pace allowed disbursements to be made slowly and allowed local people to learn valuable lessons and make adjustments to lending criteria as they went along. A marked improvement in the quality of microprojects and repayment rate after the first year demonstrated that local people had indeed improved their skills through the process of trial and error.

Accountability

An important factor in the success of the **Benin Health** example was the creation of a new governmental drug procurement agency, which exists as an autonomous agency responsible for procuring all drugs used in the country. As this was done poorly and corruptly in the past, the new agency is kept responsive and accountable to local communities through village representatives that sit on its board.

In the **Mexico Hydroelectric** example, accountability mechanisms were put into place during a reorganization of the national power company, CFE. A new, high-level Social Development Office was created that reported directly to the company management. In addition, each state government formed an independent *comité de concertacion* headed by the governor and consisting of different line agencies to review and assist with the resettlement plans. The National Indian Institute was asked to provide independent field monitoring of the project, and a senior, independent resettlement adviser was appointed to the office of the company president to conduct field reviews of the project. These mechanisms served two purposes: to channel information from the field directly to CFE's management and to keep CFE accountable and responsive through a public monitoring and review process.

In the **Nepal Irrigation Sector** program, farmer involvement in the selection of contractors provided a much-needed element of transparency in the mobilization and use of the Irrigation Department's financial resources. Farmer Irrigation Association oversight and ownership improved the quality of construction.

Multidisciplinary Approaches

To undertake participatory activities in Mexico's **Programa Integral para el Desarrollo Rural**, several local multidisciplinary teams consisting of sociologists, economists, planners, and various technical experts were put together to undertake collaborative planning with beneficiaries. This approach emphasized the linkage between the sociological and technical sides of the planning process.

In the **Mexico Hydroelectric** example, a new social development unit was created at the project level to introduce participatory approaches into project planning and decisionmaking. This institutional innovation brings together a four-celled resettlement team (planners, regional development workers, environmental specialists, and community organizers) with the head engineer in charge of construction. This multifunctional team creates a critical bridge between the technical and social sides of the project.

POINTERS II

Strengthening the Capacity of Government Institutions

Training As part of several forestry projects in **Nepal**, training programs are being conducted for forestry officials to facilitate greater communication and cooperation with rural forest users. Local officials have also been trained to watch for attempts by the wealthy to take control of forests from broadly based user groups and to focus on genuinely elected leaders of such groups.

In the **India Forestry** example, Forestry Department staff received training in participatory rural appraisal (see Appendix I) and other participatory approaches to prepare them to work in a collaborative manner with the village-based forest protection committees.

Providing Appropriate Incentives In the **Nigeria Women in Agriculture** example, to attract women agents into the extension service and increase their time spent interacting with women farmers in the field, the Women in Agriculture program offered incentives in the form of improved mobility, transportation, travel allowances, and higher salaries.

In the **Philippines Irrigation** example, National Irrigation Administration (NIA) employees receive bonuses when their decentralized cost centers break even or better. This means they must treat the farmers as valued customers whose payments for services are indispensable to NIA's existence. Such a system enables NIA agents to be responsive to the needs of their local clients. In addition, NIA's budget was linked to farmer contributions (that is irrigation service fees), whereas government subsidies were phased out. This structural change in the implementing agency helped to mainstream participation by helping to develop a strong service orientation, instilling client responsiveness and forcing agency employees to place a high value on farmer participation.

Developing Outreach Capacity In the **Nigeria Women in Agriculture** example, the Women in Agriculture program was set up within the existing state agricultural development projects, which was a very decentralized system. Each state agricultural development project has field offices staffed by local extension agents and has control over its budget and activities. The Federal Agricultural Coordinating Unit plays a coordinating role from the capital. To better respond to the needs of women farmers and increase the number of women extension agents in the field, the Ministry of Agriculture began a large-scale administrative "switch-over" during which a large cadre of existing home economic agents were redirected into the agricultural wing of the agricultural development projects to become Women in Agriculture field agents. Building on this existing human capital allowed a significant increase of field-level staff in the agricultural department with no net addition to the ranks of civil service.

In the **Tamil Nadu Integrated Nutrition** project, a cadre of community nutrition workers was created within the health outreach services of the Department of Social Welfare to disseminate information, raise awareness of better nutrition practices, and encourage the formation of women's groups to begin community-level action around health and other issues. The focal point of project activities was 9,000 community nutrition centers, each staffed by a local woman. Staffing criteria for this position required women who *(a)* were from the village, *(b)* were poorer than average but had well-nourished children, and *(c)* had an interest in health. Selected community nutrition workers were highly motivated and had good access to mothers. In choosing outreach staff for the community nutrition worker cadre, these qualities were given greater weight than education levels and qualifications.

POINTERS II

In the **Mexico Hydroelectric** example, the national power company, CFE, did not initially possess the skills or experience to manage a participatory resettlement program. To acquire this ability, they created new social and environmental units and recruited skilled personnel to run them. They also hired teams of young professionals with backgrounds in the social sciences, social work, and NGO activities and sent them out into the villages for three weeks out of every month to consult with villagers, answer questions, and record the concerns and priorities of communities on behalf of the company.

THE ENABLING ENVIRONMENT: LEGAL ISSUES

Laws and policies can create an enabling environment that facilitates—or at least does not impede—peoples' participation. Although individuals, groups, and agencies play key roles in initiating a process of "bottom-up" development, change can be facilitated if rules and regulations at both the national level and project level provide the freedom and incentives for people to participate in the design and implementation of development projects.

To ensure effective stakeholder participation in Bank-financed projects, sponsors and designers must examine the legal framework within which affected beneficiaries and communities operate to identify and address any constraints posed by the law. Three sorts of legal issues are important: *(a)* the right to information, *(b)* the right to organize and enter into contractual agreements, and *(c)* the impact of the borrower's financial and other regulations on communities.

Right to Information

Participation is a function of information through which people come to share a development vision, make choices, and manage activities. To achieve this, information must flow from governments and external supporters in ways that genuinely support people's informed participation. The objective of information sharing, therefore, is to ensure that all affected individuals or communities receive adequate information in a timely and meaningful manner. To attain this, the following questions are relevant:

Obligation to Disclose
- Is there an obligation on the part of the implementing unit to ensure that stakeholders are provided with adequate and relevant information?
- Is such information to be provided in a meaningful manner, that is, in a form that can be readily understood by relevant stakeholder groups?

Access to Information and Legal Remedy
- Is the mechanism for providing or requesting information accessible to all stakeholders? Is it a simple mechanism that can be used by all? For example, are stakeholders required to fill in complicated forms?
- Are there time and financial constraints that may discourage people from seeking information? Is there a significant delay between the request for information and the provision of information?
- Are there any cultural or social constraints for accessing this information? Do barriers exist that may inhibit women or other vulnerable segments of society? Are special measures required to reach potential participants who are poorly educated or illiterate? Is the information available in local languages and dialects?
- Do stakeholders have any legal remedy when their right to information is infringed?

Disseminating Information

Bank experience suggests that centralized offices may have problems disseminating information. In the **Sardar Sarovar** project, for example, information was available in an office near the dam site. But affected communities found this ineffective. It was costly, time consuming, and difficult to access the information. In addition, women who faced mobility problems or cultural constraints to travel were virtually cut off from information.

Information can be successfully disseminated to stakeholders in a number of ways. In the **Gambia Public Works and Employment** project, a community participation program is being developed that uses newspapers, radio, talk shows, leaflets, posters, and stickers to disseminate information. The Gambia experience reveals that taking into account literacy, language, scope, timing, and selection of themes sensitive to gender, age, and ethnicity is critical to channeling information flows to target audiences.

But sometimes newspapers, radio, television, and other forms of mass communication are not the most effective means of reaching the general public. Information can flow vigorously through local communication systems. This includes traditional entertainment such as song, dance, and community theater. The exchange of information can also be facilitated at traditional gathering places, such as village markets, religious meeting places, police stations, or marriage celebrations. If, on the other hand, these modes are ignored, such indigenous communication systems can transmit messages that oppose and undermine development efforts. In South Asia, such communication channels have in the past frequently carried negative rumors about the side effects of family planning methods, sometimes leading to the outright rejection of the contraceptives being introduced.

In the **Ethiopian Social and Rehabilitation Development Fund** project, a number of village-level workshops were held. Additionally, a number of NGOs and community facilitators who are respected by target communities were appointed and trained to disseminate information among communities. An effort is being made to recruit female promoters to improve the access of women's groups. In the expanded phase, it is expected that with the use of a mobile van, more effective dissemination of information can be achieved even in remote areas. In the **Guatemala Social Investment Fund**, field staff were recruited who spoke the local dialect and had a cultural background necessary to interact with the communities. Materials are also printed in the local languages.

Legal Literacy

The right to information is connected with the following issues of legal literacy:

- Are communities legally literate and aware of their rights?
- Is there a need to educate them?
- What institutional arrangements are necessary?

In the **Mexico Decentralization and Regional Development** project, illustrated brochures in Spanish were designed to communicate in a simple manner the economic opportunities afforded by the project as well as inform potential participants about the their rights and obligations.

Right to Organize

The second issue relates to the legal status of communities and groups and their internal organization. The objectives are to *(a)* design effective mechanisms for

POINTERS II

group participation, *(b)* ensure that legal standing of these groups is appropriate and enables them to interact effectively with external parties as required, and *(c)* ensure equitable relationships among group members and transparent processes for internal decisionmaking. Important questions include the following:

Formalizing Groups

- What are the available processes for formalizing groups so that they can participate in project-related activities?
- Are such processes complex or time consuming and beyond the scope of small community groups?
- Is such formalization necessary to receive public funds or enter into valid contracts?
- If there is no formal legislation or regulation, can project-specific arrangements be developed to achieve the same objectives?

Bank experience in this area is varied. In some cases NGOs and other groups may be reluctant or incapable of entering into a standard contractual agreement. In such cases, a memorandum of understanding or convention signed with the government or executing agency may be more appropriate. In the **India National Cataract Blindness Control** project, a participating NGO that was reluctant to take on the risk of contractual liability signed a memorandum of understanding defining it as an equal partner with the executing agency. According to specified terms, the NGO was under no formal obligation and would be paid for its services on verification of performance.

In the **Philippines Irrigation** example, the National Irrigation Administration persuaded the legislature to give legal recognition to the irrigation associations that provided them with authority over the operation and maintenance of the communal systems, legal water rights, and standing as corporate bodies with the Philippine Securities and Exchange Commission—which meant they could own property, make contracts, collect fees, and impose sanctions.

Ability to Receive Public Funds

A number of factors affect whether groups can engage in financial transactions. Important questions in this area include the following:

- Can the community group receive public funds?
- What are the requirements? Are such requirements complex, time consuming, or beyond the scope of small community groups?
- Does the community group have a separate legal identity?
- Can it enter into a valid contract on behalf of the members at large?

The **Uttar Pradesh Education** project permits informal groups to receive public funds upon compliance with certain specified conditions, including the collection of community contributions and the appointment of a headmaster. In the **Zambia Social Recovery Project,** however, the opening of a bank account and deposit of the community contribution is considered a satisfactory requirement to receive public funds.

In the **Mexico Municipal Funds** program, a component of the **Mexico Decentralization and Regional Development** project, government regulation permits groups to register as "solidarity committees" with the municipality, thereby giving them the right to receive public funds.

In the **Burundi Social Action** project, an intermediary with legal status, selected and approved by the community, is brought in to sign the contract on behalf of the community group.

Internal Regulations Where formal groups have legal standing, it may be important to examine their internal regulations or by-laws. The by-laws or internal regulations of the community group or entity should be developed by the group and are crucial in addressing some of these issues. Where community groups do not have the skills to identify issues and address them in the by-laws, assistance should be incorporated into project design. Appropriate questions include the following:

- Are the responsibilities and obligations of the members clearly defined?
- Do the internal regulations ensure that sharing of resources/profits is undertaken in an efficient and equitable fashion?
- If the project involves financial contributions by communities, is there a mechanism for ensuring that such contributions are provided in an equitable fashion? What constitutes community contribution? Can they contribute cash instead of labor?
- How are internal regulations drafted? How can they be amended?
- Is it possible to provide sample by-laws for different categories of project-related activities?
- Are records kept of such contributions to ensure that contributions are made by all beneficiaries in an equitable fashion?
- Are there any justifications for excusing specific households or individuals?

Representative and Accountable Groups Different kinds of questions relate to whether the groups so constituted are representative and accountable. To determine this, Task Managers may want to ask the following questions:

- Is there any restriction on membership to the group?
- Where the regulations are neutral, do they unintentionally have the effect of excluding women or other vulnerable sections of society?
- Can such unintended impacts be mitigated through the use of internal regulations or by-laws?
- Who makes the decisions? Is there provision for participatory decisionmaking processes?
- Are the leaders accountable to the larger group of members?
- Is there a possibility of introducing some form of mutual monitoring or peer pressure?

Impact of Borrower's Financial and Other Regulations

The third issue relates to the impact of the borrower's financial and other regulations on the ability of communities and groups to participate effectively in the project. The objective is to ensure that any potential bottlenecks created by the borrower's regulations are addressed well in advance and that NGOs, in particular, are not adversely constrained by government regulations. Because many of these restrictions are vested in law, the ability to modify them through project design may be limited. Some legal restrictions, however, can be interpreted in a flexible manner. Some potential issues follow:

Requirements for Competitive Bidding In many countries, national procurement regulations are not suitable for communities and NGOs involved in participatory projects. Borrowers' reluctance to decentralize fiscal control may also affect community-related procurement and disbursement. Often thresholds for competitive bidding, that is, the value of contracts that must be procured under competitive procedures) are set so low that even small contracts require bids that impose time-consuming and bureaucratic procedures on communities.

Some potential questions related to competitive bidding are:

- What are the mandatory processes for competitive bidding?
- Do they impede efforts by community groups to use competitive bidding?
- Are the threshold levels appropriate? Do they permit noncompetitive procedures when necessary?

In the **Uganda Alleviation of Poverty and Social Costs of Adjustment** project, any item more than $1,000 required approval by the Central Tender Board for Procurement and Disbursement. This tedious process caused serious delays and limited community involvement. In the **Guyana Health, Nutrition, Water, and Sanitation** project, community groups were allowed to procure their own goods through "local shopping" procedures, which required quotations from at least three qualified suppliers. This was found to be a burdensome requirement, because it was difficult to find even a single qualified supplier in some rural areas.

The traditional concept of competitive bidding may be not appropriate in cases in which community groups are contracted to undertake their own works. Often community groups invest in goods to be used by their own members; experience shows that, in such cases, there are built-in incentives for community groups to use their allotted resources efficiently. The experience with the **Mexico Municipal Funds** program, a component of the Mexico Decentralization and Regional Development project, for instance, has been that works implemented by the communities cost one-third to one-half less than works by traditional municipal administrators or contractors.

Prior Review of Contracts

The issue of prior review of publicly funded contracts—imposed by national legislation or sometimes by the Bank's procedures—has caused, in some instances, substantial delays and frustration during project implementation. To suit the needs for community-related procurement, requirements for prior review of contracts have been adapted in some projects.

The **Mexico Municipal Funds** program does not mandate prior review of contracts with communities; instead, a sample of projects are reviewed during or after implementation. Replacing prior reviews with strict ex-post reviews is done under the assumption that no disbursement will be made on contracts that violate principles set forth in the implementation guidelines. In the **Cameroon Food Security,** project contracts for goods and services above $50,000 require prior review. Because the majority of the community-related procurement subprojects are below $25,000, such a threshold level avoids the need for prior review in all cases.

Accounting and Auditing Requirements

Sometimes, participating groups, fearing that their autonomy is being threatened, may not want to reveal their accounts to the government. On the other hand, accounting transparency helps to reduce abuses and the government as well as the Bank have a right to insist on transparency of accounts in a Bank-financed project. The degree of information revealed by the participating group should meet the requirement of public scrutiny without compromising the independence of the group. A practice that has worked well in this context is that the government and the Bank are allowed to examine the accounts for that

POINTERS II

particular project but not all the NGO's accounts. In any case, the details of this should be agreed on to the mutual satisfaction of the government, NGO, and Bank at the outset of the project.

Key questions in this context include the following:

- Do the regulations require that the use of funds must be accounted for? If so, how, in what manner, and to whom?
- Do the regulations require that use of public funds be independently audited? If so, who is responsible?
- If the Auditor General's Office is responsible, can this task be delegated to a private entity?

In Zambia, for example, the auditor general is required to audit the use of public funds. This would require the NGO or community group receiving public funds to be audited by the auditor general's office. In some cases, however, it has been possible for the auditor general to delegate his powers to a private accounting firm to audit groups involved in project-related activities.

Processes for Disbursements   Sometimes government procedures and processes for disbursement can create delays. Experience has shown that delays in disbursement can significantly dampen community enthusiasm. In the **Colombia Integrated Rural Development** project, government procedures typically took 103 days to process disbursement requests. To overcome these problems, in some projects, especially those set up as social funds, the decree establishing the fund exempts its operations from the procurement and disbursement regulations in the country; thus, in the **Ethiopian Social and Rehabilitation Development Fund** project, the fund operates under its special procurement and disbursement guidelines specifically described in its operational manual. Appropriate questions in this context include the following:

- Are disbursement procedures for access to and utilizing funds transparent, efficient, and objective?
- Can steps be taken to keep government agencies out of the day-to-day affairs of community groups and NGOs?

Dispute Settlement Mechanisms   Dispute settlement is an important element for effective participation. A forum for presentation of grievances and the mechanisms for third-party settlement procedures are imperative for sustained development. A cursory examination of the formal dispute resolution systems in most countries reveals that access to remedies through the formal process is generally constrained. A large proportion of poor and disadvantaged people are legally illiterate; they have inadequate access to legal aid and do not have the economic resources to resort to the normally complex and sophisticated legal processes to seek remedies.

Many societies, however, have traditional methods of dispute resolution that are based on principles of mediation and conciliation. Project designers have attempted to make use of such indigenous methods of dispute resolution. In the **India Upper Krishna Irrigation II** and **Andhra Pradesh Irrigation II** projects, *lok adalats* or people's courts have been established to settle grievances of community groups that have been adversely affected by project activities. In the **Egypt Resource Management** example, such indigenous methods of dispute resolution have also been employed.

POINTERS II

The following questions are relevant to problems related to dispute settlement.

- Are existing formal dispute resolution mechanisms accessible, or are they lengthy and costly?
- Are there any customary dispute resolution mechanisms that communities can resort to?

METHODS AND TOOLS

Development practitioners use a wide variety of different methods, tailored to different tasks and situations, to support participatory development. This Appendix, set up as a reference guide, introduces the reader to ten methods that have been used in different development situations to achieve various objectives. These include: workshop-based and community-based methods for collaborative decisionmaking, methods for stakeholder consultation, and methods for incorporating participation and social analysis into project design.

The methods are first introduced in a matrix; then each is briefly described, including background, a step-by-step description, suggested further readings, and an example. Each method is compared and contrasted with the others and their advantages and disadvantages noted to help Task Managers choose those most useful to them. A glossary of available tools, many of which are components of the methods, follows the summaries. More details on both the methods and the tools can be found in the forthcoming Environment Department Paper *Methods and Tools for Social Assessment and Participation*.

Reading about participatory techniques will familiarize Bank staff and others with terminology and context, but learning from one's colleagues who have experience with these methods and tools is also helpful. Readers can call the Environment Department's Social Policy Division (ENVSP) to obtain an up-to-date list of Bank staff and consultants who are well versed in these methods and tools.

TYPES OF METHODS

Workshop-Based Methods
Collaborative decisionmaking often takes place in the context of stakeholder workshops. Sometimes called "action-planning workshops," they are used to bring stakeholders together to design development projects. The purpose of such workshops is to begin and sustain stakeholder collaboration and foster a "learning-by-doing" atmosphere. A trained facilitator guides stakeholders, who have diverse knowledge and interests, through a series of activities to build consensus. Appreciation-Influence-Control (AIC), Objectives-Oriented Project Planning (ZOPP), and TeamUp are three such methods.

Community-Based Methods
In many projects, Task Managers and project staff leave government centers and board rooms to undertake participatory work with local communities. Task Managers work with trained facilitators to draw on local knowledge and begin collaborative decisionmaking. In such settings, local people are the experts, whereas outsiders are facilitators of the techniques and are there to learn. The techniques energize people, tap local knowledge, and lead to clear priorities or action plans. Two such techniques (see Appendix I), participatory rural appraisal and SARAR (an acronym based on five attributes the approach seeks to build: self-esteem, associative strength, resourceful-

ness, action planning, and responsibility) use local materials and visual tools to bridge literacy, status, and cultural gaps.

Methods For Stakeholder Consultation

Beneficiary Assessment (BA) and Systematic Client Consultation (SCC) are techniques that focus on listening and consultation among a range of stakeholder groups. BA has been used throughout World Bank regions, in both projects and participatory poverty assessments (PPAs). SCC, which is used primarily by the Bank's Africa Region, is a set of related techniques intended to obtain client feedback and to make development interventions more responsive to demand. Both methods intend to serve clients better by making donors and service providers aware of client priorities, preferences, and feedback.

Methods for Social Analysis

Social factors and social impacts, including gender issues, should be a central part of all development planning and action, rather than "add-ons" that fit awkwardly with the universe of data to be considered. Social Assessment (SA) and Gender Analysis (GA) are methods that incorporate participation and social analysis into the project design process. These methods are also carried out in country economic and sector work to establish a broad framework for participation and identify priority areas for social analysis. Such methods evolved to meet the need to pay systematic attention to certain issues that traditionally had been overlooked by development planners. The SA methodology, which is described in this Appendix, has been designed specifically to assist Bank staff and reflects Bank procedures.

USING THE METHODS WELL

It would be misleading to claim that any tools or methods are inherently participatory or that they spontaneously encourage ownership and innovation among stakeholders. The participants in development planning and action—the users of these methods and tools—must be the ones who encourage and enable participation. The tools themselves facilitate learning, preparation, and creative application of knowledge. They make it easier for Task Managers and borrowers who are committed to participation to collaborate with a broad range of stakeholders in the selection, design, and implementation of development projects. These same methods, however, can also be implemented in a "top-down" manner, which merely pays lip service to participation. The ultimate responsibility for using these methods well, therefore, rests with the users and facilitators.

METHODS

TABLE A1.1. PARTICIPATORY METHODS AND TOOLS

Description	Comments

Collaborative Decisionmaking: Workshop-Based Methods

Appreciation-Influence-Control (AIC)

AIC is a workshop-based technique that encourages stakeholders to consider the social, political, and cultural factors along with technical and economic aspects that influence a given project or policy. AIC helps workshop participants identify a common purpose, encourages to recognize the range of stakeholders relevant to that purpose, and creates an enabling forum for stakeholders to pursue that purpose collaboratively. Activities focus on building appreciation through listening, influence through dialogue, and control through action.

Objectives-Oriented Project Planning (ZOPP)

ZOPP is a project planning technique that brings stakeholders to workshops to set priorities and plan for implementation and monitoring. The main output of ZOPP workshops is a project planning matrix. The purpose of ZOPP is to undertake participatory, objectives-oriented planning that spans the life of project or policy work, while building stakeholder team commitment and capacity with a series of workshops.

TeamUp

TeamUp builds on ZOPP but emphasizes team building. TeamUP uses a computer software package (PC/TeamUP) that guides stakeholders through team-oriented research, project design, planning, implementation, and evaluation. It enables teams to undertake participatory, objectives-oriented planning and action, while fostering a "learning-by-doing" atmosphere.

Strengths
- Encourages "social learning"
- Promotes ownership
- Produces a visual matrix of project plan
- Stakeholders establish rules of the game
- Stakeholders establish working relationships

Avoiding Potential Pitfalls
- Completed matrices should not be considered unchangeable.
- Workshops should be part of a plan that involves all stakeholders.
- Not all stakeholders are comfortable in workshop settings.
- Measures should be taken to give voice to less experienced public speakers.
- Choice of workshop location should be accessible to local stakeholders.

Collaborative Decisionmaking: Community-Based Methods

Participatory Rural Appraisal (PRA)

PRA is a label given to a growing family of participatory approaches and methods that emphasize local knowledge and enable local people to do their own appraisal, analysis, and planning. PRA uses group animation and exercises to facilitate information sharing, analysis, and action among stakeholders. Although originally developed for use in rural areas, PRA has been employed successfully in a variety of settings. The use of PRA enables development practitioners, government officials, and local people to work together on context-appropriate programs.

SARAR

This participatory approach, geared specifically to the training of local trainers/facilitators, builds on local knowledge and strengthens local capacity to assess, prioritize, plan, create, organize, and evaluate. The five attributes promoted by SARAR are: self-esteem, associative strengths, resourcefulness, action planning, and responsibility. SARAR's purpose is to (a) provide a multisectoral, multilevel approach to team building through training, (b) encourage participants to learn from local experience rather than from external experts, and (c) empower people at the community and agency levels to initiate action.

Strengths
- Based on interactive, often visual tools that enable participation regardless of literacy level
- Demystifies research and planning processes by drawing on everyday experience
- Participants feel empowered by their participation and the sense that their contributions are valued.

Avoiding Potential Pitfalls
- PRA or training alone does not provide local communities with decisionmaking authority or input into project management. These features must be built into the project.
- These techniques generate positive energy, which will quickly subside if it is not channeled into actual tasks and programs.
- Trained facilitators are necessary to guide and synthesize these exercises.

METHODS

(continued on next page)

TABLE A1.1. (CONTINUED)

Description	**Comments**

Methods for Stakeholder Consultation

Beneficiary Assessment (BA)

BA is a systematic investigation of the perceptions of beneficiaries and other stakeholders to ensure that their concerns are heard and incorporated into project and policy formulation. BA's general purposes are to (a) undertake systematic listening to "give voice" to poor and other hard-to-reach beneficiaries, thereby highlighting constraints to beneficiary participation and (b) obtain feedback on development interventions.

Systematic Client Consultation (SCC)

SCC refers to a group of methods used to improve communication among Bank staff, direct and indirect beneficiaries and stakeholders of Bank-financed projects, government agencies, and service providers so projects and policies are more demand-driven. SCC intends to (a) undertake systematic listening to clients' attitudes and preferences, (b) devise a process for continuous communication, and (c) act on the findings by incorporating client feedback into project design and procedures.

Strengths
- Systematic listening and consultation requires lengthier, repeated, and more meaningful interactions among stakeholders.
- BA and SCC are field-based, requiring project or program managers or their representatives to travel to communities and to become more aware of the realities of the field.

Avoiding Potential Pitfalls
- Listening and consultation alone do not lead to increased capacity or facilitation of client participation in decisionmaking or action.
- The effectiveness of these techniques often rests with the ability of the managers and their representatives to "translate" client needs and demands into operationally meaningful terms and activities.

Methods for Social Analysis

Social Assessment (SA)

SA is the systematic investigation of the social processes and factors that affect development impacts and results. Objectives of SA are to (a) identify key stakeholders and establish the appropriate framework for their participation, (b) ensure that project objectives and incentives for change are appropriate and acceptable to beneficiaries, (c) assess social impacts and risks, and (d) minimize or mitigate adverse impacts.

Gender Analysis (GA)

GA focuses on understanding and documenting the differences in gender roles, activities, needs, and opportunities in a given context. GA involves the disaggregation of quantitative data by gender. It highlights the different roles and learned behavior of men and women based on gender attributes, which vary across culture, class, ethnicity, income, education, and time; thus, GA does not treat women as a homogenous group nor gender attributes as immutable.

Strengths
- These methods provide a process for building information into plans and plans into action.
- Systematic social analysis identifies what communities think they need and sets up ways to communicate this back to implementing agencies.
- Flexible framework of GA and SA allows design to be consistent with project or policy components and goals.

Avoiding Potential Pitfalls
- Data collection and analysis must be focused on priority issues, rather than being general data collection exercises that are not necessarily tied to project or policy concerns.
- Involving experienced local consultants from a variety of disciplines builds in-country capacity for actionable social analysis.

METHODS

APPRECIATION-
INFLUENCE-CONTROL

COLLABORATIVE DECISIONMAKING:
WORKSHOP-BASED METHOD

"Appreciation-Influence-Control" (AIC) is both a philosophy and a model for action. The philosophy, anchored by the principle that power relationships are central to the process of organizing, was translated into a model for organizing development work by William E. Smith in the late 1970s and early 1980s. AIC is a workshop-based technique that encourages stakeholders to consider social, political, and cultural factors along with technical and economic aspects that influence a given project or policy. AIC (a) helps workshop participants identify a common purpose, (b) encourages participants to recognize the range of stakeholders relevant to that purpose, and (c) creates an enabling forum for stakeholders to pursue that purpose collaboratively. Activities focus on building appreciation through listening, influence through dialogue, and control through action.

AIC is a process that recognizes the centrality of power relationships in development projects and policies. Conferences that are part of the AIC process encourage stakeholders to consider social, political, and cultural factors in addition to technical and economic factors that influence the project or policy with which they are concerned. In other words, AIC facilitates recognition of "the big picture." This process has been implemented in a variety of sectors and settings, including local, regional, and national.

THE AIC PROCESS

In the development context, AIC proceeds along the following course: identifying the purpose to be served by a particular plan or intervention, recognizing the range of stakeholders whose needs are addressed by that purpose, and, through the AIC process, facilitating creation of a forum that empowers stakeholders to pursue that purpose collaboratively.

Through the AIC process of meetings, workshops, and activities (collectively referred to as the "conference" in AIC terms), stakeholders are encouraged to do the following:

- *Appreciate through listening.* Appreciate the realities and possibilities of the situation by taking a step back to gain perspective on the stakeholders and situation.
- *Influence through dialogue.* Explore the logical and strategic options for action as well as the subjective feelings and values that influence selection of strategies.

- *Control through action.* Enable the stakeholders to take responsibility for choosing a course of action freely, based on information brought to light in workshops, meetings, and activities.

AIC Philosophy in Practice

AIC was designed to break the patterns of "top-down" planning by stressing the following:

- *The value of small, heterogeneous groups.* Initially, when stakeholders are meeting, perhaps for the first time, heterogeneous, small groups allow for interaction and learning among people who tend not to interact in daily life. The objectives of these small groups is to interrupt the normal mood, thus opening participants to new ideas and different perspectives.
- *The value of homogenous groups.* Later on, when a strategy is generated for realizing the vision created during the appreciation phase, the power of homogenous groups of stakeholders, who share a common language, is harnessed for action. The objective of these groups is to consolidate the expertise of like stakeholders, each of whom has recently learned the perspectives of the other stakeholders at the conference.
- *The value of symbols.* Language and literacy differences can be a stumbling block, particularly at the beginning of a conference when participants are becoming familiar with each other's objectives. Participants often begin by creating nonverbal representations of their experience and understanding—drawings and pictures—to ease communication and to elicit creative thinking.
- *The value of the written word.* Agreements reached during sessions are promptly written up after the first workshop to clarify and create a common understanding of the elements of the plan. Seeing the groups' progress in writing helps participants to understand their individual responsibilities in context and to move forward on their commitments.
- *The importance of a strong facilitator.* The type of listening encouraged by AIC can be stressful for people who are used to taking immediate, decisive action. Similarly, certain stakeholders might not be accustomed to voicing their opinions. A skilled facilitator is trained in navigating around tough spots, guiding the entire group through new experiences, and stimulating open discussions and negotiation. The facilitator is a critical catalyst for setting the AIC conference in motion and for steering participants toward a conference closure that leads to action.

METHODS

185

REFERENCES

Kearns, James M. and Turid Sato. 1989. "New Practices for Development Professionals." *Development, The Journal of the Society for International Development.* No. 4.

Smith, William E. 1992. "Planning for the Electricity Sector in Colombia." In Marvin R. Weisbord, 1992. *Discovering Common Ground.* San Francisco: Bennett-Kohler Publications. pp. 171-187.

Smith, William E. 1991. *The AIC Model: Concepts and Practice.* Washington, D.C.: ODII.

Box A1.1. AIC Conference in Colombia Leads to Commitments and Action in the Energy Sector

Key stakeholders gathered for a three-day AIC conference in Santa Marta, Colombia. The AIC consultant, the Task Manager, and a third facilitator joined ministers, heads of utilities and their suppliers, mayors, congresspeople, opposition party members, interest groups, and others to design a plan to resuscitate the energy sector and to make commitments to carry out the plan. During the first day and a half of the conference, the "appreciative" phase, participants shared information, examined realities of the energy sector, and created group rapport that carried them through the conference. The AIC process encouraged participants to envision clear outcomes, make recommendations, and make commitments that would transform their conference plan into actions. Among the outcomes of the conference were:

- Collaboration between the task force and ministry to implement commitments
- Creation of an interim coordinating body and passage of legislation to support it
- Integration of the electricity and energy sectors
- Further Bank, Inter-American Development Bank, and Japanese Export-Import Bank support for an effort in which Colombian counterparts had shown their initiative to propose and commitment to meet various conditions.

The cost of this three-day AIC conference of approximately $30,000 was paid for in large part by the Colombians ($25,000). The Bank contributed the remaining $5,000.

METHODS

OBJECTIVES-ORIENTED PROJECT PLANNING (ZOPP) COLLABORATIVE

DECISIONMAKING:

WORKSHOP-BASED METHOD

ZOPP, from the German term "Zielorientierte Projektplanung," translates in English to "Objectives-Oriented Project Planning." ZOPP is a project planning and management method that encourages participatory planning and analysis throughout the project cycle with a series of stakeholder workshops. The technique requires stakeholders to come together in a series of workshops to set priorities and plan for implementation and monitoring. The main output of a ZOPP session is a project planning matrix, which stakeholders build together. The purpose of ZOPP is to undertake participatory, objectives-oriented planning that spans the life of project or policy work to build stakeholder team commitment and capacity with a series of workshops.

ZOPP is a process that relies heavily on two particular techniques—matrix building and stakeholder workshops—to encourage participatory planning and management of development work. ZOPP helps a project team create a project planning matrix (PPM), similar to a Logical Framework or LogFRAME, to provide in-depth analysis of project objectives, outputs, and activities. The PPM results from stakeholder workshops that are scheduled through the life of a project to encourage brainstorming, strategizing, information gathering, and consensus building among stakeholders.

THE PPM: PROCESS AND PRODUCT

The PPM is central to ZOPP-based project work because the process of building it relies on repeated, collaborative stakeholder input. In the stakeholder workshops in which the matrix is developed systematic attention is paid to five important issues:

- *Participation analysis.* Taking stock of the range of stakeholder identities, interests, biases, expectations, and concerns.
- *Problems.* Often made visually clear through a "problem tree," through which key problems the project is meant to address are identified, grouped, and prioritized and their causes and effects brought to light.
- *Objectives.* In a corresponding objectives tree, the desired solutions are articulated, clustered and prioritized.

- *Alternatives.* A project strategy is created by understanding the range of means for meeting objectives.
- *Assumptions.* These conditions are necessary for successful transformation of problems into secured objectives. Assumptions are systematically examined and arranged in the PPM.

Participants first review the variety of means available to achieve the project objective. The project planning matrix shows activities and results as well as the conditions necessary for achieving both. These conditions are important assumptions on which rest decisions about activities, location, timing, procurement, and so on. The information is organized along two axes that show (a) why the project is being undertaken and (b) what the project outputs are that signal success. The PPM thus systematically answers the following questions:

- Why does the project aim for this overall goal?
- What is the project purpose?
- What results/outputs will the project achieve?
- How will the project achieve these results/outputs?
- What external factors (assumptions) are important?
- How can achievement of the objectives be measured?
- Where are the means/sources of necessary data?
- What will the project cost?

ITERATIVE WORKSHOPS

ZOPP is not a one-shot exercise; the designers of the planning method envisioned strategic planning "phases," each of which requires a workshop that focuses on a fixed goal. In the workshops, participants analyze key issues throughout the project cycle. No set formula exists for a successful stakeholder workshop. In fact, each one is truly unique because it brings together a blend of people who have never before worked as a group and who need to create a common language to understand one another's widely divergent concerns. As described by its creators at GTZ, five distinct ZOPP phases, which run alongside the project cycle, can lead to a sound strategic project plan.

In the traditional conception of ZOPP, the first three of the five phases take place during project planning. The theory here is that extensive, earnest efforts to plan collaboratively prior to implementation increase the likelihood of smooth implementation and the degree of stakeholder ownership and readiness to work toward sustainability.

Collaboration is not "automatically" part of the ZOPP process. The project team, borrower, and stakeholders must commit to adopting a participatory stance for the

METHODS

overall project; otherwise, the ZOPP process is merely an organizing tool. During each planning phase of the ZOPP process, participants reinforce their commitment to include the diverse expertise and concerns of a variety of stakeholders.

APPLICATIONS IN BANK WORK

Objectives-oriented planning assumes that joint analysis and planning is necessary throughout the project cycle. If instituted early in the life of a project, ZOPP can provide a ready forum for extensive participation of diverse stakeholders. ZOPP is also a helpful approach to jump starting stalled project initiatives.

For a variety of reasons, promising projects have been known to falter unexpectedly in midstream. In these cases, ZOPP can be a powerful tool for reorganizing if stake-

holders' resolve to "save" the project is grounded in a broader commitment to collaboration.

In its initial form, ZOPP was created to be closely tied to the project cycle; hence, it has mostly been used in a variety of sector and country settings for project work. The two main component tools of ZOPP—the stakeholder workshop and the PPM—can also be used for the participatory planning of policy and economic sector work.

REFERENCES

Gesellschaft für Technische Zusammenarbeit (GTZ). 1991. *Methods and Instruments for Project Planning and Implementation.* Eschborn: Germany.

GTZ. 1988. *ZOPP (An Introduction to the Method).* Eschborn, Germany.

GTZ. 1988. *ZOPP in Brief.* Eschborn, Germany.

Box A1.2. Creating a Forum for Stakeholder Communication and Innovation

The Task Manager for an Industrial Efficiency and Pollution Control project for the Philippines took the initiative to create communication linkages among government, the Bank, industry, and nongovernmental organizations (NGOs) to establish a common Bank-borrower team approach to the project preparation process.

Through the local counterpart agency, the Task Manager organized a series of stakeholder meetings to further refine problem formulations and define the objectives for a project that had yet to be identified.

A ZOPP-based approach was used to bring together stakeholders who initially felt that their conflicting priorities would prevent them from reaching consensus on project objectives.

Not only did stakeholders achieve consensus on objectives and prioritization, but the communication linkages begun in the two-day workshop began a dialogue on systematically focusing on community-level demands to encourage participation and ownership at the local level.

METHODS

TEAMUP

COLLABORATIVE DECISIONMAKING: WORKSHOP-BASED METHOD

TeamUP is a flexible, team-based method for improving both the substance and process of project cycle management. It was developed to expand the benefits of ZOPP and to make it more accessible for institutionwide use. PC/TeamUP, a software package, automates the basic step-by-step methodology and guides stakeholders through team-oriented research, project design, planning, implementation, and evaluation.

The TeamUP method is an organized process for building high performance teams. It has two dimensions, *(a)* task functions, which assist stakeholders in planning, decisionmaking, and acting and *(b)* team building, which encourages stakeholders to collaborate as an effective work group.

The TeamUP method is a series of steps or modules designed to enable a group of individuals to perform essential management functions collaboratively. Typically, the team meets for a two-and-a-half- or five-day workshop. Software (PC/TeamUP) is available to facilitate the process. The software accommodates input from a broad range of stakeholders who stand to benefit or otherwise be affected by design or implementation decisions and adjusts as the range of stakeholders changes through the planning and implementation process.

TEAMUP AND ZOPP

TeamUP—developed in the late 1980s by the World Bank's Economic Development Institute and Team Technologies, Inc.—uses the basic ZOPP method and then expands it. TeamUP assumes that the past and future are two different sources on which to draw when designing and implementing project-related events. ZOPP, mainly concerned with anticipating and avoiding problem situations, looks to the past to understand the present. TeamUP, concerned with both problems and opportunities, looks to the past and the future to understand the possibilities that offer themselves to the present.

Furthermore, TeamUP adds depth to basic problem identification and design features by encouraging teams to anticipate implementation arrangements and inform the quality of their designs with these realities.

TWELVE BASIC STEPS

TeamUP's twelve core steps are arranged so that earlier steps help a team build identity and later steps help them take action.

- *Opening round.* In the opening round, stakeholders discuss their expectations for the team during the TeamUP workshop and beyond. What does each stakeholder hope to accomplish in the workshop?
- *Clarify representation.* Stakeholders define the interests each represents and set out roles that each will play. Who will act as the team manager? Who will be responsible for what?
- *Set norms.* "Rules of the game" are set out so that all team members have common expectations of how they can most effectively work together. How will consensus be measured? What will the protocol be during discussions? How will conflicts be resolved?
- *Identify client.* In this first action-oriented module, stakeholders establish who will benefit most if the objectives of the project are achieved. What is the total range of potential beneficiaries and negatively impacted groups?
- *Review history.* This is a team-building and action-oriented exercise to ensure that everyone at the meeting has equal footing. Is this a brand new project with no prior history? Are there applicable lessons from elsewhere? Have some team members worked together before?
- *Define mission.* What is the team's mission in the workshop? To prepare a project or a program? To develop a strategy for wider client participation? Furthermore, what is the mission of the project or program itself?
- *Define deliverables and assumptions.* In this module, the LogFRAME (see the glossary of tools at the end of this Appendix) is used to map out end products and necessary conditions in relationship to overall impact. What changes in behavior and environment will the project outcome inspire? Who will change and how? What are the assumptions on which these outcomes rest? Are these assumptions biased in any way? What if these assumptions do not prove to be true?
- *Clarify work plan.* Through the LogFRAME, team members define steps to move the project from idea to action. How will the intended deliverables become reality? In what order and with whose help? What tools and further plans are needed, and whose support is critical?
- *Define roles and responsibilities.* This module is designed to prepare the team to take action beyond the workshop by firming up how the work is broken down. Who will manage what aspects of fulfilling the objectives? Tools used in this module encourage people to identify specific tasks and take responsibility for following through with those tasks.

METHODS

- *Define learning system.* The team establishes a process to review what they have done and how the team has worked together. What have they learned from this experience? How will they carry what they have learned into the future of this project or program?
- *Establish budget.* Using performance budget planning tools, the team reviews the work plan and systematically attaches cost to each activity in the plan. Will this project or plan be feasible? Where should the team turn to secure financing? What are the possible sources of funding? Do budget estimates meet operational requirements? What further information is needed?
- *Implement and improve.* The conviction and wisdom of the team's plan is put to a series of tests. For example, the workshop facilitator will take on the role of devil's advocate to introduce obstacles that the

plan might face. What if certain assumptions turn out to be untrue? What if certain unforeseen events take place? Are contingency plans possible? Finally, a plan for future team workshops is set out.

REFERENCES

Cracknell, B. 1989. "Evaluating the Effectiveness of the Logical Framework System in Practice." *Project Appraisal* 4(3): 163-167.

McLean, D. 1988. *Logical Framework in Research Planning and Evaluation.* International Service of National Agricultural Research Working Paper No. 12. Washington, D.C.: ISNAR.

Team Technologies, Inc. 1991. *PC/LogFrame R&D Software and User Manual.* Chantilly, Virginia.

Box A1.3. Uganda, Private Sector Development Workshop

The World Bank provided assistance to the Uganda Manufacturers' Association and the Ministry of Finance and Economic Planning to organize a workshop, whose purpose was to (a) review survey results on 105 businesses and 265 private investors, (b) introduce a private sector development strategy to a broad constituency of private sector, government, and donor participants, (c) achieve agreement on fundamental elements, and (d) identify a private sector task force to begin preparation of a possible International Development Association-funded operation in this area.

The workshop design, based on the TeamUP approach, used public involvement methods for involving large numbers of stakeholders in building agreements about policy, strategy, and execution. The method integrated more than seventy participants in a series of small group discussions designed to identify issues, surface and resolve conflicts, and build understanding and initial agreement about a proposed project design. Summary responses from participants indicated they believed the workshop demonstrated the government's and Bank's commitment to a collaborative, demand-driven process.

PARTICIPATORY RURAL APPRAISAL

COLLABORATIVE DECISIONMAKING: COMMUNITY-BASED METHOD

Participatory rural appraisal (PRA) is a label given to a growing family of participatory approaches and methods that emphasize local knowledge and enable local people to make their own appraisal, analysis, and plans. PRA uses group animation and exercises to facilitate information sharing, analysis, and action among stakeholders. Although originally developed for use in rural areas, PRA has been employed successfully in a variety of settings. The purpose of PRA is to enable development practitioners, government officials, and local people to work together to plan context-appropriate programs.

Participatory rural appraisal evolved from rapid rural appraisal—a set of informal techniques used by development practitioners in rural areas to collect and analyze data. Rapid rural appraisal developed in the 1970s and 1980s in response to the perceived problems of outsiders missing or miscommunicating with local people in the context of development work. In PRA, data collection and analysis are undertaken by local people, with outsiders facilitating rather than controlling. PRA is an approach for shared learning between local people and outsiders, but the term is somewhat misleading. PRA techniques are equally applicable in urban settings and are not limited to assessment only. The same approach can be employed at every stage of the project cycle and in country economic and sector work.

KEY TENETS OF PRA

- *Participation.* Local people's input into PRA activities is essential to its value as a research and planning method and as a means for diffusing the participatory approach to development.
- *Teamwork.* To the extent that the validity of PRA data relies on informal interaction and brainstorming among those involved, it is best done by a team that includes local people with perspective and knowledge of the area's conditions, traditions, and social structure and either nationals or expatriates with a complementary mix of disciplinary backgrounds and experience. A well-balanced team will represent the diversity of socioeconomic, cultural, gender, and generational perspectives.
- *Flexibility.* PRA does not provide blueprints for its practitioners. The combination of techniques that is appropriate in a particular development context will be determined by such variables as the size and skill mix of the PRA team, the time and resources available, and the topic and location of the work.
- *Optimal ignorance.* To be efficient in terms of both time and money, PRA work intends to gather just enough information to make the necessary recommendations and decisions.
- *Triangulation.* PRA works with qualitative data. To ensure that information is valid and reliable, PRA teams follow the rule of thumb that at least three sources must be consulted or techniques must be used to investigate the same topics.

PRA TOOLS

PRA is an exercise in communication and transfer of knowledge. Regardless of whether it is carried out as part of project identification or appraisal or as part of country economic and sector work, the learning-by-doing and teamwork spirit of PRA requires transparent procedures. For that reason, a series of open meetings (an initial open meeting, final meeting, and follow-up meeting) generally frame the sequence of PRA activities. Other tools common in PRA are:

- Semistructured interviewing
- Focus group discussions
- Preference ranking
- Mapping and modeling
- Seasonal and historical diagramming.

ORGANIZING PRA

A typical PRA activity involves a team of people working for two to three weeks on workshop discussions, analyses, and fieldwork. Several organizational aspects should be considered:

- Logistical arrangements should consider nearby accommodations, arrangements for lunch for fieldwork days, sufficient vehicles, portable computers, funds to purchase refreshments for community meetings during the PRA, and supplies such as flip chart paper and markers.
- Training of team members may be required, particularly if the PRA has the second objective of training in addition to data collection.
- PRA results are influenced by the length of time allowed to conduct the exercise, scheduling and assignment of report writing, and critical analysis of all data, conclusions, and recommendations.

METHODS

191

- A PRA covering relatively few topics in a small area (perhaps two to four communities) should take between ten days and four weeks, but a PRA with a wider scope over a larger area can take several months. Allow five days for an introductory workshop if training is involved.
- Reports are best written immediately after the fieldwork period, based on notes from PRA team members. A preliminary report should be available within a week or so of the fieldwork, and the final report should be made available to all participants and the local institutions that were involved.

SEQUENCE OF TECHNIQUES

PRA techniques can be combined in a number of different ways, depending on the topic under investigation. Some general rules of thumb, however, are useful. Mapping and modeling are good techniques to start with because they involve several people, stimulate much discussion and enthusiasm, provide the PRA team with an overview of the area, and deal with noncontroversial information. Maps and models may lead to transect walks, perhaps accompanied by some of the people who have constructed the map. Wealth ranking is best done later in a PRA, once a degree of rapport has been established, given the relative sensitivity of this information.

The current situation can be shown using maps and models, but subsequent seasonal and historical diagramming exercises can reveal changes and trends, throughout a single year or over several years. Preference ranking is a good icebreaker at the beginning of a group interview and helps focus the discussion. Later, individual interviews can follow up on the different preferences among the group members and the reasons for these differences.

REFERENCES

Chambers, R. 1992. *Rural Appraisal: Rapid, Relaxed, and Participatory*. Institute of Development Studies Discussion Paper 311. Sussex: HELP.

International Institute for Environment and Development, Sustainable Agriculture Program. 1991-present. *RRA Notes* (now titled *PLA Notes*). United Kingdom.

McCracken, Jennifer A., Jules N. Pretty, and Gordon R. Conway. 1988. *An Introduction to Rapid Rural Appraisal for Agricultural Development*. London: International Institute for Environment and Development.

Theis, J. and H. Grady. 1991. *Participatory Rapid Appraisal for Community Development*. London: Save the Children Fund.

Box A1.4. Natural Resource Management in Burkina Faso

Prior to appraisal of this environmental management project, twenty pilot operations tested the PRA approach to determine which techniques suited the project's resources, topic, and location. Best practices were distilled without blueprint designs.

The result is a project based on a multitiered process in which communities design management plans with the help of multidisciplinary teams of technicians. This approach starts with awareness raising and trust building and proceeds to collaborative diagnosis, community organization, and plan design. Local government agreement, implementation, and participatory monitoring and evaluation follow.

Central and regional governments have come on board with this approach, endorsing administrative decentralization and reorganization and working for revisions of ambiguous land tenure laws. Both of these steps encourage local solutions to local problems and work for empowering people to manage natural resources in a sustainable way.

Source: The World Bank, Agriculture Technology and Services Division (AGRTN). October 1994. Agriculture Technology Notes. No. 6. Washington, D.C

SARAR

COLLABORATIVE DECISIONMAKING: COMMUNITY-BASED METHOD

SARAR is a participatory approach to training that builds on local knowledge and strengthens local ability to assess, prioritize, plan, create, organize, and evaluate. SARAR's purpose is to (a) provide a multisectoral, multilevel approach to team building through training, (b) encourage participants to learn from local experience rather than from external experts, and (c) empower people at the community and agency levels to initiate action. SARAR is a philosophy and practical approach to adult education that seeks to optimize people's ability to assess, prioritize, plan, self-organize, take initiatives, and shoulder management responsibilities. The acronym SARAR stands for five attributes or abilities that are critically important for achieving full and committed participation in development: self-esteem, associative strength, resourcefulness, action planning and responsibility for follow-through. SARAR is a highly experiential methodology that deliberately differs in style from conventional "top-down" methods. Its central strategy is group process; it begins with creating a relaxed and congenial atmosphere in which hierarchical differences are set aside.

The concept was first developed through field-based training of rural extension workers in Indonesia, India, and the Philippines in the early 1970s and in Latin America toward the end of the decade. In the mid-1980s the SARAR approach was applied to the water supply and sanitation sector in East and West Africa, Nepal, Indonesia, Mexico, and Bolivia. Initially, the focus of SARAR was primarily on local communities and field staff. In response to emerging needs and experience, the method has been broadened to include an institutional focus as well. SARAR has proved flexible in adapting to urban settings, although it was originally designed for rural use, and it has been applied across sectors, such as rural development, agricultural extension, health, and water and sanitation. It is now being adapted to wildlife conservation and utilization and HIV/AIDS-related education. SARAR is indeed directed toward whole communities, but it has proved to be especially useful in giving special attention to populations, such as women, whose input and needs are hard to assess with traditional development approaches.

SARAR's approach to group process combines generation of data with strengthening of group abilities to assess needs, identify priorities, establish goals, and design action plans to be implemented and monitored.

GENERATION OF DATA

The nuts and bolts of SARAR are a series of carefully developed, flexible activities. The activities are designed to draw out participants' own life experiences and bring to light local perspectives, feelings, values, and socially sensitive data. This data can be extremely valuable to project managers in establishing a partnership relationship with communities; thus, it is qualitatively different from data obtainable through conventional tools such as questionnaires.

The data-generating aspect of SARAR, however, is neither its main aim nor a discreet function to be used for extractive research purposes. The data-generating process is designed to set in motion a process of reflection, self-enhancement of positive values, and motivation to act. Data that grows out of the group activities becomes more meaningful when put at the service of decisions that underlie a plan of action. If activities are treated simply as a battery of data collection instruments to support management decisions, their use out of context can leave people confused, distrustful, and frustrated.

ACTIVITIES TO STRENGTHEN GROUP ABILITIES

SARAR activities fall into five categories:

- *Investigative.* Demystifying research by involving participants in data gathering and processing so they "own" the outputs and are committed to using them.
- *Creative.* Promoting fresh viewpoints and imaginative new solutions, liberating expressiveness and openness to change.
- *Analytic.* Engaging the mind in critical assessment of problems, identifying their causes and effects, categorizing and prioritizing them, and arriving at sound choices.
- *Planning.* Expanding the vision of what is possible; developing skills in goal setting and marshaling resources to achieve them; and managing, monitoring, and evaluating the outputs.
- *Informative.* Accessing the required information in an enjoyable way and using it for better decisionmaking in implementing a plan of action.

Each of the activities has been developed to be effective in a variety of circumstances. As a package of tools, they are designed to be multisensory so that they affect behavior in multiple ways. The intention is to

METHODS

193

foster creativity and involve the whole person, not just the intellect. Some SARAR activities, such as force field analysis, mapping, and gender and task analysis, are similar in focus and name to components of many methods for social assessment and participation. Some activities, such as pocket charts, story with a gap, flexiflans, and three-pile sorting cards, are unique to SARAR.

REFERENCES

Narayan, Deepa and Lyra Srinivasan. 1994. *Participatory Development Tool Kit*. Washington, D.C.: The World Bank.

Narayan, Deepa. 1993. *Participatory Evaluation*. World Bank Technical Paper Number 207. Washington, D.C.: The World Bank.

Srinivasan, Lyra. 1990. *Tools for Community Participation*. New York: PROWWESS, United Nations Development Programme.

Box A1.5. Stakeholders Identify Institutional Requirements of a Community-Management Approach in Indonesia

As part of preappraisal for the Water and Sanitation Project for Low-Income Communities, sixty senior government personnel from the provinces and the capital joined consultants and World Bank staff for a two-day workshop.

Using the SARAR approach, brief presentations were intermixed with hands-on activities; most work was done in small groups. Participants drew their personal visions of community management on large sheets of paper and presented and discussed them with one another. Participants then examined the roles and responsibilities that would be required to fulfill each vision. Using cards that list decisions that all water projects require and five levels of decisionmakers who might address them, participants discussed the decisions, procedures, and responsible actors needed to support each vision. Finally, participants explored the extent of capacity necessary at each level for community management.

The long, often heated discussions resulted in concurrence that the simpler the technology used—such as spring captures and improved wells—the more likely participants were to offer control and authority to community groups. A common vision about skills and training resulted in the decision to earmark 15 to 20 percent of project costs for capacity building in community management of water projects among decisionmakers at the community, subdistrict, district, and provincial levels as well as at the level of central government.

Source: Deepa Narayan. November 1995. Toward Participatory Research. World Bank Technical Paper No. 307. Washington, D.C.: The World Bank

BENEFICIARY ASSESSMENT

METHOD FOR STAKEHOLDER CONSULTATION

Beneficiary assessment (BA) involves systematic consultation with project beneficiaries and other stakeholders to help them identify and design development activities, signal any potential constraints to their participation, and obtain feedback on reactions to an intervention during implementation. BA is an investigation of the perceptions of a systematic sample of beneficiaries and other stakeholders to ensure that their concerns are heard and incorporated into project and policy formulation. The general purposes of a BA are to (a) undertake systematic listening, which "gives voice" to poor and other hard-to-reach beneficiaries, highlighting constraints to beneficiary participation, and (b) obtain feedback on interventions.

BA is a qualitative method of investigation and evaluation that relies primarily on three data collection techniques:

- In-depth conversational interviewing around key themes or topics
- Focus group discussions
- Direct observation and participant observation (in which the investigator lives in the community for a short time).

Interviewing and observation can be carried out with individual beneficiaries or with groups; BA work can take place in urban or rural settings. Focus groups are commonly used as a forum for interviewing a number of beneficiaries and for conducting institutional assessment done within a BA.

The BA approach is not meant to supplant quantitative surveys and other traditional methods for data gathering; rather it complements these methods with reliable and useful information on the sociocultural context and perceptions of a client population that will inform Task Managers and policymakers. BAs are approaches in which the participatory process can begin with systematic and continuous tracking of client attitudes from identification through preparation to implementation of a project.

Ordinarily, BAs are carried out by local people under the direction of a trained team leader or social scientist. The skill mix and number of staff varies according to the tools used and demographic characteristics of the beneficiary population; BAs often require an experienced focus group facilitator and participant-observer. From initial desk reviews of available information through field research to writing of the BA report, the entire BA process typically takes from four to six months. Ideally, this process is repeated in an iterative fashion throughout the life of the project. Recent BAs conducted by the Bank have cost between $50,000 and $100,000.

THE USES OF BA

- *Project Work.* BA helps to define problems from the point of view of the people who are affected by projects. Such knowledge improves project preparation and the monitoring of implementation. BAs can also help lay the foundation for participatory development work. With evidence that their ideas are being heard and respected, beneficiary populations are more likely to participate in development projects and take steps to improve their access to resources. BA is best used iteratively throughout the project cycle as a monitoring or supervision tool for evaluations. For example, three BAs were used for the mid-program evaluation of the Zambia Social Recovery Project to assess the success of the component funding microprojects in education and health. The BA approach has been instituted in some country work programs in Africa and South Asia as a management tool to improve quality.
- *Poverty assessments.* BAs provide qualitative input by focusing on the human factors that affect poverty, the incentives and constraints to behavior change, the reactions to service delivery and institutional responsiveness, and the importance of formal and informal safety nets. Specifically, BA work is done in connection with the consultative portion of a poverty assessment known as the participatory poverty assessment (PPA). When incorporated into poverty assessments, BA helps to ensure that poverty reduction strategies take into account the experience and concerns of the poor.

STEPS IN BENEFICIARY ASSESSMENT

- *Familiarization.* Technical specialists are selected to guide the BA project. Important problem areas are identified and reviewed using available information including interviews with key stakeholders such as donors, government, and local people. A guide for semistructured interviews is developed to cover key themes.
- *Study design.* Target populations are identified. An appropriate representative sampling framework is devised, and the issues to be explored (according to the objectives of the BA) are clearly delineated. A

METHODS

195

research group and team leader should also be designated.

- *Selection and orientation of local interviewers.* The research group helps select and train local men and women who are fluent in local language(s), good listeners, and skilled in recall and writing. The study team, including local interviewers, practices descriptive and accurate writing, note taking, awareness of and separation from preconceived notions, and data analysis.

- *Study.* BA work commonly includes interviews, focus group discussions, participant observation, and institutional analysis.

- *Preparation of the BA report.* The BA report includes recommendations that incorporate assessment findings into project design or sector work. The report should be reviewed by the interviewees to cross-check for accuracy.

BANK EXPERIENCE WITH BA

Between 1983-95, the BA approach has been used in forty-seven Bank-supported projects in twenty-seven countries and across six sectors. A 1993 review undertaken to assess the use of BA in Bank-supported projects found that BAs:

- Influenced policy and led to changes in project design through improved targeting, efficiency, and effectiveness of programs
- Informed policy with otherwise unavailable and/or new information
- Increased sustainability by providing operationally oriented feedback from the client population
- Gave voice to the poor by indicating what the poor see as problems and possible solutions
- Promoted dialogue, ownership, and commitment by involving all stakeholders in listening and consultation.

REFERENCES

Amelga, M. 1994. *A Review of Beneficiary Assessments Conducted by the Bank.* ENVSP Consultant Report. Washington, D.C.: The World Bank.

Salmen, Lawrence F. 1992. *Beneficiary Assessment: An Approach Described.* Working Paper No. 1. Technical Department. Africa Region. Washington, D.C.: The World Bank.

The World Bank, Africa Region, Southern Africa Department. September 1994. *Systematic Client Consultation.* Mimeo. Washington, D.C.

Box A1.6. Mali: Beneficiary Assessment in an Education Sector Project

A BA was done in Mali as part of an education project to try to understand why parents in rural areas did not send their children to school. Attendance for girls was especially low. The BA found that the costs of transportation and feeding the child at school plus the opportunity costs of losing the children's labor at home outweighed the benefits of a poor quality education with few prospects for finding a job.

These findings led to reformulation of policy to (a) reduce costs to beneficiaries by building schools in closer proximity, (b) increase attendance by designing a girl's component, and (c) train teachers to improve the relationship between parents and the school system.

METHODS

SYSTEMATIC CLIENT CONSULTATION

METHOD FOR STAKEHOLDER CONSULTATION

Systematic Client Consultation (SCC) refers to a group of methods used to improve communication among Bank staff, direct and indirect beneficiaries and stakeholders of Bank-financed projects, government agencies, and service providers so projects and policies are more demand driven. SCC endeavours to (a) *undertake systematic listening to clients' attitudes and preferences,* (b) *devise a process for continuous communication, and* (c) *act on the findings by incorporating client feedback into project design and procedures.*

SCC has been developed in the World Bank's Africa Region as a means for improving the sustainable development impact of their operations in the field. This approach emerged from the region's quality management strategy, which includes strengthening stakeholder commitment and systematic listening to beneficiaries. SCC emphasizes continuity in the process of learning and readjustment that is intended to make Bank-sponsored policies and projects more responsive to the needs and wishes of the countries they serve. It is a system for keeping a finger on the pulse of client reactions in the field so that Bank interventions are kept on target, even in contexts in which circumstances are subject to frequent change.

SCC recognizes that social research incorporates many dimensions and that the issues to be addressed determine which method is needed. Among the techniques used to carry out SCC are: firm surveys, sentinel community surveillance, beneficiary assessment, and participatory rural appraisal.

THE SCC THEORY

SCC is premised on the belief that information gathered must be analyzed, acted on, and reassessed; thus, SCC is based on:

- *Consultation.* Obtaining regular feedback from those involved with and affected by Bank-supported projects regarding the continuing validity of a project's goals and its effectiveness in meeting them.
- *Action.* Revising project designs and procedures on the basis of information gathered from clients.
- *Follow-up.* Assessing the impact of revisions and taking further action wherever necessary to make sure that client concerns are being addressed.

SCC IN PRACTICE: TEN STEPS

- *Laying the groundwork.* Before consulting with clients, staff must familiarize themselves with existing information, select information goals, and determine information needs in light of the overall project, sectoral, and country strategy.
- *Who does what.* SCC requires staff time throughout the life of the program, a local institution to carry out the consultations, an advisory committee (program managers, interviewers, government representatives, relevant civic associations, and other program partners), and institutional support from headquarters and the resident mission.
- *Establishing a budget.* In preparing a budget for SCCs, managers must consider the number of clients (individuals, households, businesses, focus groups, and so on) to be surveyed; the time period covered (usually the life of the project) and time required for preparation, fieldwork, and reporting; the number and periodicity of surveys (one consultation a year, three consultations with selected groups each year for five years, and so on); personnel requirements (interviewers, facilitators for focus groups, and participant-observers); training for interviewers; output (oral and written reports); and dissemination of findings.
- *Designing an information-tracking plan.* A project information-tracking plan should sequence a series of client polls at specific intervals throughout the life of the program; include mechanisms for information gathering, analysis, dissemination, responsive action, and evaluation; and be adjusted as the program progresses (sometimes targeting highly affected segments or other selected groups within the client population).
- *Identifying the target group.* In selecting the client target group, managers must identify those decisionmakers and officials whose assessment of the program is vital to its success; divide large client groups into smaller categories whose relation to the program can be more specifically defined; and identify clients who have current, factual information about project performance.
- *Designing data collection instruments.* In consulting with clients, field interviewers should be trained; interview guides and questionnaires should be pretested (questions should be as specific as possible and be largely confined to the clients' actual experience); clients should be asked to rate their concerns in order of priority and program services in order of importance and effectiveness; and clients should assess the effectiveness of any new measures taken.

METHODS

- *Putting client information to use.* Data supplied by clients can be used to help define economic strategies; set standards of program performance; adjust performance standards to accord with evolving public opinion; and direct resources and efforts to deal with issues the client community deems important.
- *Disseminating results.* To disseminate client feedback, the program must provide focused information on client perspectives; establish communication channels to stakeholders that will not require excessive staff time; and use brief, simple formats that make data easy to record and read.
- *Acting on client information.* In response to information gathered from client consultations, managers should establish mechanisms for relaying client comments to those who can affect policy changes; check the program's operational systems and procedures against clients' comments; ensure that the pro-

gram is oriented to deliver products and services with the characteristics that clients value; establish a mechanism for adjusting the program in response to client criticisms; and use client concerns as the basis for benchmarks for monitoring.
- *Follow-up.* This step repeats the actions in step 1, but this time asks clients about the efficacy of changes made to deal with issues identified during the last round of consultations.

REFERENCES

The World Bank, Africa Region. Southern Africa Department. September 1994. *Systematic Client Consultation.* Mimeo. Washington, D.C.

The World Bank, Africa Region. September 1994. *A Systematic Approach to Client Consultation.* Mimeo. Washington, D.C.

Box A1.7. Zambia: Outlook from the Field

In 1992 the Zambia Social Recovery Project launched a comprehensive client consultation program to find out what the intended beneficiaries thought of the project. The main technique used was beneficiary assessment. Local interviewers undertook three phases of consultations with community members, service providers, and key informants, individually or in focus groups.

In phase I of the SCC, beneficiaries rated local institutions that carried out welfare microprojects in the community. In phase II, beneficiaries assessed the community's role in these projects and its contribution in other social areas. In phase III, beneficiaries considered the project's and intermediary institution's overall impact on the community and ranked community problems and priorities.

The three phases of interviews provided information on community concerns and relative strengths and weaknesses of local institutions and committees. Specific problems with accountability, workmanship, and local government were identified and managers made recommendations for actions to address problems. In addition, the process enhanced local ability to undertake social research.

Source: The World Bank, Africa Region. September 1994. *A Systematic Approach to Client Consultation.* Washington, D.C.

SOCIAL ASSESSMENT

METHOD FOR SOCIAL ANALYSIS

Social Assessment (SA), a method developed by World Bank staff, provides an integrated framework for incorporating participation and social analysis into the Bank's operational and analytical work. Because there are many social variables that could potentially affect project impacts and success, SAs must be selective and strategic and focus on issues of operational relevance. Deciding what issues are critical and how they can be addressed requires consultation with stakeholders and other forms of data collection and analysis.

Gender, ethnicity, social impacts, and institutional capacity are among the social factors that need to be taken into account in development operations. In the past these factors have been analyzed separately with the result that some issues received attention whereas others were overlooked. Social assessment was developed by the Bank's Social Policy Thematic Team to provide a comprehensive, participatory framework for deciding what issues have priority for attention and how operationally useful information can be gathered and used. Because this method was developed by Bank staff, the steps in SA are consistent with Bank procedures and existing operational directives.

Social assessments are carried out in a project context to do the following:

- Identify key stakeholders and establish an appropriate framework for their participation in the project selection, design, and implementation.
- Ensure that project objectives and incentives for change are acceptable to the range of people intended to benefit and that gender and other social differences are reflected in project design.
- Assess the social impact of investment projects and, where adverse impacts are identified, determine how they can be overcome or at least substantially mitigated.
- Develop ability at the appropriate level to enable participation, resolve conflict, permit service delivery, and carry out mitigation measures as required.

ASSESSMENT DESIGN

SAs involve consultations with stakeholders and affected groups and other forms of data collection and analysis. Deciding how much work is needed, what information is required, and how it should be obtained depends primarily on the significance or complexity of the issues and the degree of participation that is needed to gain stakeholder ownership of and action on decisions that are made.

For example, where social factors are complex and social impacts or risks are significant, formal studies generally need to be carried out by consultants as part of project preparation. This does not mean that all problems can be solved in the project preparation process. Where there is considerable uncertainty due to lack of awareness, commitment, or capacity, social assessments can contribute to the design of projects that build on experience and respond to change.

The degree of stakeholder involvement needed also influences assessment design. In some cases stakeholders simply provided information and no further interaction was foreseen, but often projects are improved when issues are jointly assessed and agreed on or beneficiaries are given the responsibility for identifying problems and are empowered to find solutions. Where local participation in project design and implementation is expected, participatory data collection and analysis can help build trust and mutual understanding early in the project cycle.

The range of stakeholders in Bank-supported projects includes those negatively or positively affected by the outcome or those who can affect the outcome of a proposed intervention, including the following:

- *Government.* The Bank's most immediate client, the borrower, is the government, including the agencies responsible for project implementation.
- *Directly affected groups.* These include individuals, families, communities, or organizations that are project or policy beneficiaries. At-risk groups, such as the poor, landless, women, children, indigenous people, and minority groups, require particular attention.
- *Indirectly affected groups.* These include others with vested interests, including donors, nongovernmental organizations (NGOs), religious and community organizations, and private sector firms.

Social assessments may be carried out by a single social scientist who contacts key stakeholders and identifies and resolves issues or, where issues are more complex or more systematic participation is needed, by a consultant team that carries out social assessment as part of project preparation. SA can take place during all phases of the project cycle, but well-planned integration of social factors in operational work begins at identification.

COMMON QUESTIONS IN SA

- Who are the stakeholders? Are the objectives of the project consistent with their needs, interests, and capacities?

METHODS

- What social and cultural factors affect the ability of stakeholders to participate or benefit from the operations proposed?
- What is the impact of the project or program on the various stakeholders, particularly on women and vulnerable groups? What are the social risks (lack of commitment or capacity and incompatibility with existing conditions) that might affect the success of the project or program?

- What institutional arrangements are needed for participation and project delivery? Are there adequate plans for building the capacity required for each?

REFERENCES

The World Bank. May 10, 1994. *Social Assessment: Incorporating Participation and Social Analysis into the Bank's Operational Work.* Mimeo. Washington, D.C.

The World Bank. 1994. *Incorporating Social Assessment and Participation into Biodiversity Conservation Projects.* Mimeo. Washington, D.C.

Box A1.8. Morocco: Fez Medina Rehabilitation Project

This proposed project to rehabilitate the old city—called the medina—of Fez in Morocco includes components to upgrade infrastructure, open access roads, mitigate pollution from craft industries and workshops, and renovate residences and monument buildings to be consistent with the past but also to serve the present.

Early in project preparation, social scientists were recruited from universities in Fez to undertake a participatory and social assessment, which began with data collection on and consulting with a wide array of stakeholders. Government, religious and civic leaders, merchants, artisans, householders, renters, and many other ordinary citizens contributed ideas for possible elaboration into project components, worked toward consensus on interventions and strategy, and described the social dynamics of the city to assure a match among plans, aspirations, and local capacities.

The assessment process, which lasted four months and cost approximately $140,000, included stakeholder workshops, sample surveys, informal interviews, and focus group meetings. Three sets of workshops with fieldwork in between produced analyses and proposals that had been widely discussed by the time the assessment was complete.

The assessment produced ideas that had not been considered previously. Among them are: using the sites of buildings in ruins to provide social service centers, regulating encroachment by merchants into residential areas, disaggregating rehabilitation plans by neighborhood, allowing those displaced by access road construction to be rehoused in adjacent areas, and supporting craft associations in the medina and upgrading craft associations either in their present locations or, if necessary, by moving them in groups. By including residents in the decisionmaking process, the assessment also raised local interest in upgrading and maintenance of the medina.

GENDER ANALYSIS

METHOD FOR SOCIAL ANALYSIS

Gender analysis focuses on understanding and documenting the differences in gender roles, activities, needs, and opportunities in a given context. Gender analysis involves the disaggregation of quantitative data by gender. It highlights the different roles and learned behavior of men and women based on gender attributes. These vary across cultures, class, ethnicity, income, education, and time; thus, gender analysis does not treat women as a homogeneous group or gender attributes as immutable.

The concept of gender analysis arose from the need to mainstream women's interests while at the same time acknowledging that women could not be treated as a homogeneous group. It was realized that women's needs were better understood when viewed in relation to men's needs and roles and to their social, cultural, political, and economic context. Gender analysis thus takes into account women's roles in production, reproduction, and management of community and other activities. Changes in one may produce beneficial or detrimental effects in others.

Gender analysis is important in the formulation of country economic memoranda, country sector strategies, structural adjustment, country portfolio management, poverty assessments, environmental assessment, and in sector-specific project planning, monitoring, and evaluation; thus, many variants of policy and sector-specific gender analysis tools are available.

PURPOSE

Applied to development interventions, gender analysis helps *(a)* identify gender-based differences in access to resources to predict how different members of households, groups, and societies will participate in and be affected by planned development interventions, *(b)* permit planners to achieve the goals of effectiveness, efficiency, equity, and empowerment through designing policy reform and supportive program strategies, and *(c)* develop training packages to sensitize development staff on gender issues and training strategies for beneficiaries.

KEY CONCEPTS

- *Practical gender needs.* These relate to women's traditional gender roles and responsibilities and are derived from their concrete life experiences. For example, when asked what they need, women usually focus on immediate practical needs for food, water, shelter, health, and so on.
- *Strategic gender needs.* These generally address issues of equity and empowerment of women. The focus is on systemic factors that discriminate against women. This includes measuring the access of women, as a group compared with men, to resources and benefits, including laws and policies (such as owning property). Strategic gender needs are less easily identified than practical gender needs, but addressing these needs can be instrumental in moving toward equity and empowerment.
- *Intrahousehold dynamics.* The household is a system of resource allocation. All members of a household—men, women, and children—have different roles, skills, interests, needs, priorities, access, and control over resources. Any development intervention that affects one member of the household will positively or negatively affect all others; hence, it is important to understand these interdependent relationships, the rights, responsibilities, obligations, and patterns of interaction among household members.
- *Interhousehold relations.* Individuals and households belong to larger groupings (such as professional or religious groups or extended families) with whom they are involved in labor exchanges, flows of goods, and other alliances for survival. It is important to understand the social organization of these larger networks and the gender differences in roles, functions, and access.

KEY PRINCIPLES

Because gender planning is part of the overall planning process, the composition of the planning team, timing of data collection, tabling of issues, and integration of gender concerns into overall objectives is critical early in policy and project formulation.

- *Planning as a process.* Programs that intend to be gender responsive depend on flexible planning processes that are interactive, adjust objectives based on feedback, and enable beneficiaries to be active participants in the planning process.
- *Gender diagnosis.* Data collected should be organized to highlight key gender problems, underlying causes of problems for men and women, and the relationship between problems and causes.
- *Gender objectives.* Objectives clarify what gender problems will be addressed and what the practical and strategic goals are. It is important to negotiate

METHODS

consensus on objectives at policy, managerial, and working levels.

- *Gender strategy.* Clear operational strategies, which will be used to achieve stated objectives, must identify the incentives, budget, staff, training, and organizational strategies to achieve stated objectives.
- *Gender monitoring and evaluation.* Flexible planning requires gender monitoring and evaluation to enable adjustment to experience and to establish accountability of commitment to achieve gender-specific priorities.

GENDER ANALYSIS FRAMEWORK

Five major categories of information comprise gender analysis:

- Needs assessment
- Activities profile
- Resources, access, and control profile
- Benefits and incentives analysis
- Institutional constraints and opportunities.

The extent to which information is collected on particular issues depends on the nature of the problems being addressed and the quality and depth of information already available.

REFERENCES

Feldstein, Hilary Sims and Janice Jiggins (eds.). 1994. *Tools for the Field: Methodologies Handbook for Gender Analysis in Agriculture.* West Hartford: Kumarian Press.

Moser, Caroline O. N. 1993. *Gender Planning and Development: Theory, Practice, and Training.* London: Routledge.

Narayan, Deepa. November, 1995. *Toward Participatory Research.* World Bank Technical Paper No. 307. Washington, D.C.: The World Bank.

Wakeman, Wendy. 1995. *Gender Issues Sourcebook for Water and Sanitation.* UNDP-World Bank Water and Sanitation Program/PROWWESS. Washington, D.C.: The World Bank.

Box A1.9. Analyzing Gender Issues in the World Bank's Country Economic Memoranda: An Example from Uganda

This poverty profile illustrated the relevance of gender in assessing poverty and stressing the importance of incorporating gender concerns into the formulation and design of strategies for reducing poverty and promoting economic growth. The most pressing issues with respect to women's multiple roles, in relation to those of men are identified as the basis for the Bank's recommendations for raising the status and productivity of women. Among the problems cited are (a) women's lack of technology, inputs, and finance to carry out their agricultural tasks, (b) multiple household responsibilities without labor-saving technology, (c) low health and nutritional status, (c) low levels of literacy, and (d) laws and customs that impede women's access to credit, education, training, information, and medical care.

In response to these problems, the Ugandan government has adopted gender-responsive actions that will be undertaken as an interconnected package of mutually reinforcing measures.

Source: The World Bank. 1994. *Enhancing Women's Participation in Economic Development.* World Bank Policy Paper. Washington, D.C.

GLOSSARY OF TOOLS

Each of the methods described above is a combination of tools, held together by a guiding principle. Dozens of exercises exist to cultivate collaborative development planning and action. These are the tools with which social scientists and other development practitioners encourage and enable stakeholder participation. Some tools are designed to inspire creative solutions, others are used for investigative or analytic purposes. One tool might be useful for sharing or collecting information, whereas another is an activity for transferring that information into plans or actions. These brief descriptions are intended to provide the reader with a glossary of terminology that practitioners of participatory development use to describe the tools of their trade.

- *Access to resources.* A series of participatory exercises that allows development practitioners to collect information and raises awareness among beneficiaries about the ways in which access to resources varies according to gender and other important social variables. This user-friendly tool draws on the everyday experience of participants and is useful to men, women, trainers, project staff, and field-workers.

- *Analysis of tasks.* A gender analysis tool that raises community awareness about the distribution of domestic, market, and community activities according to gender and familiarizes planners with the degree of role flexibility that is associated with different tasks. Such information and awareness is necessary to prepare and execute development interventions that will benefit both men and women.

- *Focus group meetings.* Relatively low-cost, semistructured, small group (four to twelve participants plus a facilitator) consultations used to explore peoples' attitudes, feelings, or preferences, and to build consensus. Focus group work is a compromise between participant-observation, which is less controlled, lengthier, and more in-depth, and preset interviews, which are not likely to attend to participants' own concerns.

- *Force field analysis.* A tool similar to one called "Story With a Gap," which engages people to define and classify goals and to make sustainable plans by working on thorough "before and after" scenarios. Participants review the causes of problematic situations, consider the factors that influence the situation, think about solutions, and create alternative plans to achieve solutions. The tools are based on

diagrams or pictures, which minimize language and literacy differences and encourage creative thinking.

- *Health-seeking behavior.* A culturally sensitive tool for generation of data about health care and health-related activities. It produces qualitative data about the reasons behind certain practices as well as quantifiable information about beliefs and practices. This visual tool uses pictures to minimize language and literacy differences.

- *Logical Framework* or *LogFRAME.* A matrix that illustrates a summary of project design, emphasizing the results that are expected when a project is successfully completed. These results or outputs are presented in terms of objectively verifiable indicators. The Logical Framework approach to project planning, developed under that name by the U.S. Agency for International Development, has been adapted for use in participatory methods such as ZOPP (in which the tool is called a *project planning matrix*) and TeamUP.

- *Mapping.* A generic term for gathering in pictorial form baseline data on a variety of indicators. This is an excellent starting point for participatory work because it gets people involved in creating a visual output that can be used immediately to bridge verbal communication gaps and to generate lively discussion. Maps are useful as verification of secondary source information, as training and awareness-raising tools, for comparison, and for monitoring of change. Common types of maps include *health maps, institutional maps (Venn diagrams),* and *resource maps.*

- *Needs assessment.* A tool that draws out information about people's varied needs, raises participants' awareness of related issues, and provides a framework for prioritizing needs. This sort of tool is an integral part of gender analysis to develop an understanding of the particular needs of both men and women and to do comparative analysis.

- *Participant observation* is a fieldwork technique used by anthropologists and sociologists to collect qualitative and quantitative data that leads to an in-depth understanding of peoples' practices, motivations, and attitudes. Participant observation entails investigating the project background, studying the general characteristics of a beneficiary population, and living for an extended period among beneficiaries, during which interviews, observations, and analyses are recorded and discussed.

- *Pocket charts.* Investigative tools that use pictures as stimuli to encourage people to assess and analyze a given situation. Through a "voting' process, participants use the chart to draw attention to the complex elements of a development issue in an uncomplicated way. A major advantage of this tool is that it can be put together with whatever local materials are available.

- *Preference ranking.* Also called direct matrix ranking, an exercise in which people identify what they do and do not value about a class of objects (for example, tree species or cooking fuel types). Ranking allows participants to understand the reasons for local preferences and to see how values differ among local groups. Understanding preferences is critical for choosing appropriate and effective interventions.

- *Role playing.* Enables people to creatively remove themselves from their usual roles and perspectives to allow them to understand choices and decisions made by other people with other responsibilities. Ranging from a simple story with only a few characters to an elaborate street theater production, this tool can be used to acclimate a research team to a project setting, train trainers, and encourage community discussions about a particular development intervention.

- *Seasonal diagrams* or *seasonal calendars.* Show the major changes that affect a household, community, or region within a year, such as those associated with climate, crops, labor availability and demand, livestock, prices, and so on. Such diagrams highlight the times of constraints and opportunity, which can be critical information for planning and implementation.

- *Secondary data review.* Also called desk review, an inexpensive, initial inquiry that provides necessary contextual background. Sources include academic theses and dissertations, annual reports, archival materials, census data, life histories, maps, project documents, and so on.

- *Semistructured interviews.* Also called *conversational interviews,* interviews that are partially structured by a flexible interview guide with a limited number of preset questions. This kind of guide ensures that the interview remains focused on the development issue at hand while allowing enough conversation so that participants can introduce and discuss topics that are relevant to them. These tools are a deliberate departure from survey-type interviews with lengthy, predetermined questionnaires.

- *Sociocultural profiles.* Detailed descriptions of the social and cultural dimensions that in combination with technical, economic, and environmental dimensions serve as a basis for design and preparation of policy and project work. Profiles include data about the type of communities, demographic characteristics, economy and livelihood, land tenure and natural resource control, social organization, factors affecting access to power and resources, conflict resolution mechanisms, and values and perceptions. Together with a participa-

tion plan, the sociocultural profile helps ensure that proposed projects and policies are culturally and socially appropriate and potentially sustainable.

- *Surveys.* A sequence of focused, predetermined questions in a fixed order, often with predetermined, limited options for responses. Surveys can add value when they are used to identify development problems or objectives, narrow the focus or clarify the objectives of a project or policy, plan strategies for implementation, and monitor or evaluate participation. Among the survey instruments used in Bank work are *firm surveys, sentinel community surveillance, contingent valuation,* and *priority surveys.*

- *Tree diagrams.* Multipurpose, visual tools for narrowing and prioritizing problems, objectives, or decisions. Information is organized into a tree-like diagram that includes information on the main issue, relevant factors, and influences and outcomes of these factors. Tree diagrams are used to guide design and evaluation systems, to uncover and analyze the underlying causes of a particular problem, or to rank and measure objectives in relation to one another.

- *Village meetings.* Meetings with many uses in participatory development, including information sharing and group consultation, consensus building, prioritization and sequencing of interventions, and collaborative monitoring and evaluation. When multiple tools such as resource mapping, ranking, and focus groups have been used, village meetings are important venues for launching activities, evaluating progress, and gaining feedback on analysis.

- *Wealth ranking.* Also known as well-being ranking or vulnerability analysis, a technique for the rapid collection and analysis of specific data on social stratification at the community level. This visual tool minimizes literacy and language differences of participants as they consider factors such as ownership of or use rights to productive assets, life-cycle stage of members of the productive unit, relationship of the productive unit to locally powerful people, availability of labor, and indebtedness.

- *Workshops.* Structured group meetings at which a variety of key stakeholder groups, whose activities or influence affect a development issue or project, share knowledge and work toward a common vision. With the help of a workshop facilitator, participants undertake a series of activities designed to help them progress toward the development objective (consensus building, information sharing, prioritization of objectives, team building, and so on). In project as well as policy work, from preplanning to evaluation stages, stakeholder workshops are used to initiate, establish, and sustain collaboration.

METHODS

APPENDIX II

WORKING

PAPER SUMMARIES

The *Sourcebook* draws on the experience, talent, and contributions of more than 200 Bank staff and their colleagues. To produce background material for the *Sourcebook*, steering committees were established under the leadership of Bank participation practitioners, each of which prepared a draft paper of thirty to forty pages on participation in a specific area of the Bank's work.

Members of the steering committees shared their own experience, proposed further contacts and sources, and provided guidance on the content of the paper, reviewing and recommending changes to successive drafts. This process provoked thought and generated a wealth of information concerning participatory development practices.

The resulting papers provided material for the *Sourcebook;* chapter IV has also drawn on the practical information of these papers for the "how to" guidelines for Task Managers. The papers, which are being edited and published by the Environment Department as part of a Working Paper Series, present background information and provide an in-depth treatment of each topic to supplement the *Sourcebook*.

This Appendix provides summaries of twelve of the eighteen working papers. Copies of all working papers are available from the Environment Department, Social Policy Division, The World Bank, Washington DC 20433 (fax: 202-522-3247).

The topics covered and the authors of the eighteen working papers are as follows:

Bank-Supported Activities and Operational Tasks
- *Country economic and sector work:* Dan R. Aronson and Ellen Tynan
- *Poverty assessment:* Andrew Norton and Thomas Stephens
- *Project planning:* Jim Kearns and Jim Edgerton
- *Procurement and disbursement:* Gita Gopal and Alexandre Marc

Sectors
- *Agricultural extension:* Charles Antholt and Willem Zijp
- *Forest and conservation management:* Ajit Banerjee, Gabriel Campbell, Chona Cruz, Shelton Davis, and Augusta Molnar
- *Irrigation:* Ruth Meinzen-Dick, Andrew Manzardo, and Richard Reidinger
- *Water and sanitation:* Gabrielle Watson and N. Vijay Jagannathan
- *Education:* Nat J. Colletta and Gillian Perkins
- *Urban Projects:* Tova Solo
- *Social Funds:* Mary Schmidt and Alexandre Marc
- *Finance:* Lynn Bennett and Michael Goldberg

Cross Cutting Issues

- *Gender:* Michael Bamberger, Mark Blackden, and Abeba Taddese
- *Local government:* David Gow, John Frankenhoff with Jerry Silverman and Tim Campbell

- *Intermediary nongovernmental organizations (NGOs):* Tom Carroll, Mary Schmidt, and Tony Bebbington
- *Public sector management:* Malcolm Holmes and Anirudh Krishna
- *Community-based development:* Deepa Narayan
- *Indigenous peoples:* Shelton H. Davis and Lars T. Soeftestad

PARTICIPATION IN COUNTRY ECONOMIC AND SECTOR WORK

Using a participatory approach in the Bank's country economic and sector work may involve extra costs as well as some loss of control over the timing and quality of the work. Experience suggests, however, that these costs are more than offset by substantial benefits, including improvements in the Bank-borrower relationship, speedier acceptance of recommendations both by the Bank and the borrower, and increased in-country capacity for policy research and analysis.

The Bank's country economic and sector work (CESW) analyzes the situation of and prospects for borrowing countries and provides the framework for its lending programs and policy advice. Traditionally, CESW has been under the exclusive control and ownership of the Bank. Although well regarded for its technical standards, this work has also been criticized for failing at times to take sufficient account of social and political realities or for presenting borrowers with policy recommendations that they do not fully understand or cannot implement.

In addressing such concerns, agreement is emerging that CESW, like projects, benefits from the active participation of stakeholders. In a number of diverse cases, CESW has been undertaken in full collaboration and joint ownership with government. Often, as in the Morocco Women in Development Study, contributions have also been sought from experts and organizations outside government. In some cases, such as the Benin Transport Sector Strategy and the Guinea Health Sector Review, CESW has attempted to involve a broader range of stakeholder groups in the review process.

Making CESW participatory depends not just on the range of stakeholders consulted but on the depth of their involvement at various stages in the process. In practice, no process is fully participatory; nevertheless, Bank practitioners have found ways to share information and open the development dialogue with useful results both for members and for the Bank.

COSTS AND RISKS

It is important to be aware of the costs of doing CESW in a participatory way. Often, but not always, more time and money is required, including additional management work up front, to establish a participatory process. At the same time, changing the role of the Bank by adding other goals to that of technical excellence risks diluting the Bank's agenda and involves some loss of control over the schedule, methodology, and quality of the work.

BENEFITS

Although the number of participatory CESW exercises is still small, experience has demonstrated that participation can produce important benefits that more than compensate for the additional costs.

The Bank-Borrower Relationship

As a result of collaboration in CESW, communication between the Bank and the government can be improved and a sense of partnership developed with borrowers. The Bank gains better knowledge of and sensitivity to the client's circumstances. This was an important benefit, for example, of the participatory approach used in the Long-Term Perspective Study for Africa (see box A2.1). At the same time, greater transparency of Bank work increases the Bank's credibility within countries and among stakeholders.

Validity of Recommendations

The substance of the work benefits from a wider and deeper local knowledge, resulting in recommendations that are likely to be more valid and implementable. Country economic and sector strategy always involves a compromise between the best assessments of experts and the social and political interests operating in the sector. When the work is done in partnership, political and social questions can be raised, confronted, and integrated from the outset.

Acceptability of Recommendations

A given piece of CESW is successful only when its recommendations are adopted or at least incorporated into the debate on policy. By building ownership and consensus for policy formation and implementation in the course of the work itself, participatory CESW leads to speedier acceptance of recommendations by the Bank and borrower. Participation not only yields richer diagnoses of problems but also inspires and mobilizes the actors to follow through on the consensus that has been built.

Capacity Building

Participatory CESW increases in-country capacity for subsequent analysis in the same or new areas of concern. It treats CESW not just as a preparation for policy formulation and investment decisions but as a development activity itself, improving the capacity within member countries to take over the production of technically informed policies for themselves.

SUMMARIES

Box A2.1. Participation in the Long-Term Perspective Study for Africa

Sub-Saharan Africa: From Crisis to Sustainable Growth, A Long-Term Perspective Study was the last in a series of five major reports on Africa published by the World Bank in the 1980s. What distinguished this report from earlier ones was not only its broad scope and time horizon but also the participatory process by which it was organized. More than 300 people were consulted, of whom about two-thirds were Africans, including government officials, academics, development professionals, and representatives of the private sector and NGOs.

The Bank's Long-Term Perspective Study (LTPS) team made visits to fourteen African countries during a six-month period. During the trips, a group of LTPS African resident advisors was identified from among former high-level officials, academics, and development professionals. These were the major sources of background papers, country perspectives, inputs to the LTPS themes, reactions to the LTPS draft, and success stories. Through the World Bank office for liaison with the NGO community, the draft LTPS was circulated to a large number of NGO representatives. Drafts were also discussed at conferences and meetings of NGOs held outside Africa.

A five-day Workshop on Regional Integration and Cooperation was held at the Bank, bringing together more than three dozen participants from wide-ranging backgrounds including history, political science, economics, law, journalism, banking, business, and public service. The LTPS chapter on regional integration and cooperation drew heavily on the issues and themes discussed at this workshop. A few months later, in December 1988, the Arusha Conference brought together African contributors to the LTPS with donors and others to obtain input on whether the draft report was on the right track, its analysis valid, and its vision consistent with the Africans' long-term perspective for Africa. Following the conference, the LTPS team revised the draft report to reflect both the consensus and disagreement expressed by participants.

As a result of the participatory process and particularly the visits made to Africa by the LTPS team, the final report reflected some significant departures from earlier World Bank views. This was particularly true concerning the efficacy of adjustment lending in Africa. As participants in the process shared their views and experiences, the authors of the LTPS came to a new realization of the basic problems of African societies, the depth of the crisis, and the possibility of an alternative explanation to problems the continent faces. In short, what the LTPS team heard and saw in Africa through the participatory process led it to look beyond the adjustment optimism of the mid-1980s. The final report's content and messages reflected the new perspective gained through the process.

As a result, the LTPS study elicited strong support from the Africans, donor, and NGO communities, and United Nations and African regional organizations.

CONDITIONS FOR SUCCESS

Participatory CESW requires policymaking environments that are open to participation, enabling stakeholders to collaborate in defining the issues for analysis, gathering data, reviewing results, and deciding strategy and priorities. Task Managers, most of whom agree that the process is risky, messy, and potentially conflictual, have been creative in addressing each of these steps in a participatory way, adapting methods and style of participation to circumstances.

Building the Case for Participation

In some cases, participation in CESW has been in response to local conditions rather than a proactive choice of the Bank. In other cases, however, Bank staff have sought wider participation than the government partner expects. In these circumstances, building the case for participation depends on the experience of Task Managers in a given country and on their persis-

tence in developing good contacts within and outside the government.

Identifying Relevant Stakeholders

The search for relevant stakeholders must begin early in the participatory CESW exercise. Community organizations, professional groups, religious leaders, and individuals critical to the sector, can all be partners in the Bank's work; omitting early contact with them can reduce their willingness to cooperate.

Although identifying stakeholders is typically a fairly informal process, more deliberate procedures can ensure that a broad range of perspectives is covered and that participants are truly representative of the sectors or groups for which they speak. Successful methods have included field visits to help communities create committees of local villagers; open public meetings, often in several different cities and advertised in the newspaper; translation of draft documents and meeting proceedings into local languages; and inclusion of "opposition" nongovernmental organizations (NGOs), making work less comfortable in the early stages but creating the environment for further collaboration.

Task Managers stress that the Bank itself has an important role to play as a participant rather than a neutral party. The Bank team needs to argue its own positions as a stakeholder but from a posture of humility. Professional or at least neutral facilitators should chair workshops and roundtables so that the Bank team can play its stakeholder role and inject issues that it thinks are important.

Eliciting Stakeholders' Contributions

Consultation should begin early and broadly before the issues paper fixes the work program for the CESW exercise. Papers commissioned from the local research community, issues workshops, study panels, and open meetings can all point to themes that might not otherwise have appeared and highlight cultural and political points not normally raised in Bank discussions. In most countries, local consultants can make an important contribution. Consultative partners in setting the CESW agenda have also included development assistance organizations, NGOs, labor unions, and private business people.

Several strategies have been used to expand the stakeholder presence in data gathering and analysis, such as: establishing a task force of local experts; convening a general roundtable followed by a succession of retreats and workshops; contracting local consultants or university researchers, backed up by consultation with policy organizations, NGOs, unions, and trade associations; and, in some cases, setting up community committees and carrying out field interviews.

Avoiding Bias

Involving nontraditional partners in sector work puts extra emphasis on having clear and tight terms of reference for studies. Participatory CESW teams must also avoid co-opting local interest groups and maintain safeguards to ensure that potential sources of bias are recognized. For example, researchers can usually be counted on to emphasize the value of more detailed research, whereas NGOs stress greater reliance on their participation. Expert bias—the tendency for policymakers and the public to believe technical experts over stakeholders who are less articulate—is a recurring problem. The role of local team members is crucial in ensuring that diverse opinions are fairly represented and in preventing a dialogue from being hijacked by powerful or vocal parties.

The Role of the Bank

In the end, all policy choices, whether agreed on in the study or made afterward, must clearly be the responsibility of the borrower. The Bank's own policy or strat-

---

Box A2.2. Brazil: Creating Government Ownership

The Environment and Agriculture Division of the Bank's Brazil Department recently completed a major new study of management issues in agriculture, rural development, and natural resources. From the outset, the division and Task Manager were committed to doing a report that was rich in content and broad in impact, both on the Bank's lending program and on policy discussions in Brazil.

Following formal issues meetings within the Bank, the issues paper was drafted in Brazil. Two sets of Brazilian inputs were crucial. First, senior Brazilian agricultural economists were members of the CESW team. Second, a broadly based panel of experts drawn from politics, government departments, foundations, and universities across the country met in a two-day workshop to finalize the issues paper. They supplied more than thirty technical background papers and met again over a rough draft of the report. A government technical review followed.

Before the formal discussion of an early draft in the Bank, the CESW team translated the report into Portuguese and requested that the Ministry of Planning set up a cross-ministerial discussion of the draft. More than fifty officials attended, representing all the ministries involved. The workshop lasted three full days (with a half day devoted to each chapter). Most of the discussions and arguments around the table were among ministries, rather than with the Bank. The Ministry of Finance and Planning usually defended the Bank's recommendations against criticisms from the sectoral ministries, but the ministries generally agreed more than disagreed with the draft. By the end of the meeting, the executive secretary of the Ministry of Planning decided that he would try to adopt the same format for all CESW discussions. The intensity of the interaction, the fact that the Bank team was able to act only as a resource group, and the expressed pleasure with the format all indicate a high level of ownership of the results throughout the government.

After government clearance, the CESW team disseminated the report's findings at two research seminars outside government and published parts of it in a major Brazilian economics journal. Further seminars with farm groups, NGOs, and agroindustry representatives were to be held later.

SUMMARIES

Box A2.3. Benin: Confronting the Diverse Interests of Stakeholders

Both the Bank and the government of Benin supported a participatory process to prepare the country's first comprehensive transport sector strategy. Given the strength of the private sector in transportation, government ministries saw the wisdom of using participation to build commitment to the strategy. For the Bank, the goal was to build a strong foundation for future projects.

After initial preparation, a national workshop was held, attended by more than 120 people. Every ministry in the sector participated (finance, planning, transport, housing, and public works), as did various representatives of public enterprises and the National Assembly. The drivers union, the truckers syndicate, and the union for the freight-handling company were also included. Theme-focused working groups met on their own and with expert consultants, at which time participants began to enunciate their positions concerning possible regulatory revisions. The consultants were able to help establish areas of consensus and conflict even before beginning their own special studies.

Next, separate subsectoral study consultancy teams (each composed of international and local members) began their work. To ensure that their divergent findings would be aired fully rather than resolved within a single consultant's offices, the teams were led by consultants from different sources. Good coordination was needed to ensure the compatibility of findings as contradictions emerged.

After most of the studies had been completed, the Ministry of Public Works organized a second seminar to discuss the main conclusions. This time the range of participants was even broader, including other donors and groups of stakeholders that had been identified during the studies. Three days of intense and open discussion took place from 8:00 A.M. until 10:00 P.M. Study conclusions concerning privatization and price regulation were modified in what was by this time a well-informed policy debate. One local consultant helped work toward consensus; in the meanwhile, a foreign consultant worked to synthesize the debate and produce the final strategy.

After the government issued its draft strategy paper, a donor round table was held for a final debate involving eight ministers, members of the national assembly, donors, and consultants. The participatory process led to recommendations that were genuinely different from those the Bank and the government would have produced. Yet, the strength of the consensus in Benin has provided such momentum that the strategy conclusions have remained intact through the entire Bank review process.

egy within the economy remains, of course, the Bank's own prerogative to choose. As borrowing members gain stronger ability and confidence in initiating and informing their own policy debates, the Bank's comparative advantage will lie in providing a global frame of reference on a multitude of questions, including what works in building the capacity for transparent, participatory analysis.

* This note is based on the paper written by Dan R. Aronson. Contributors include Michael Azefor, Malcolm Bale, Kreszentia Duer, Sunita Gandhi, Charlotte Jones-Carroll, Peter Landell-Mills, Karen Lashman, Himelda Martinez, Bernard Peccoud, Robert Prouty, Lee Roberts, Helen Saxenian, Guilherme Sedlacek, Jerry M. Silverman, Susan Stout, Maurizia Tovo, Tom Tsui, and Bruna Vitagliano.

SUMMARIES

PARTICIPATION IN POVERTY ASSESSMENTS

The Bank's approach to country poverty assessments (PAs) is increasingly to stress the involvement of stakeholder groups with the aim of building in-country capacity to address the problems of the poor.* The participation of government and other institutional stakeholders in all aspects of the work increases sensitivity to poverty issues, improves analytical skills, and builds allegiance to the measures proposed for poverty reduction. In addition, conventional statistical analysis is complemented by qualitative information from participatory PAs (PPAs), which reveal concerns voiced by the poor. Some early lessons for Task Managers have already emerged from this experience.

RATIONALE

PAs are now an essential component in the Bank's country economic and sector work, contributing to the wider process of poverty-related analysis and the formulation of all aspects of country strategy. Making PAs participatory requires more time and resources but can yield important benefits.

Involving a range of stakeholders, including the poor themselves, can help the following:

- Improve understanding of the cultural, social, economic, and political dynamics that perpetuate poverty in a given country
- Ensure that strategies identified for poverty reduction reflect the real concerns voiced by the poor
- Promote ownership of the proposed solutions by a variety of stakeholders
- Build in-country institutional ability for ongoing analysis of poverty and the design of measures to reduce it.

A distinction is made between "participation in PAs," the subject of this paper, and PPAs. The latter has come to refer to the use of specific qualitative research techniques to discern the perceptions and attitudes of the poor themselves. PPAs, however, are only one component of the wider PA. This paper argues that most components of the PA, from defining the agenda and designing the research program through data gathering and analysis to report writing and formulating policy prescriptions, can benefit from broad stakeholder participation.

MAKING THE PA MORE PARTICIPATORY

The methods used to broaden stakeholder participation in PAs have varied enormously, depending on the time allowed, the funds available, the local research capacity, and the level of government interest in discussing poverty issues. It has also become clear since the initial flurry of PAs in 1993 that to increase participation Task Managers need somewhat more time and resources to complete PAs.

Involving Institutional Stakeholders

It is the institutional stakeholders, from senior government officials and a variety of actors in civil society to service providers and development workers at the community level, who are responsible for defining poverty reduction policies and for translating them into programs and services. The collaboration of these groups at each step of the PA helps to promote consensus, ownership, and commitment to the strategic conclusions among those whose support will be needed for effective implementation. It also helps to build the institutional capacity for ongoing, iterative policy analysis and formulation for poverty reduction.

So far, most institutional stakeholder involvement in Bank PAs has been limited to government officials and local researchers. Innovative approaches such as those used in Cameroon (see box A2.4), are needed to involve other actors, including opinion leaders, journalists, civic or religious leaders, public interest groups, and indigenous NGOs, in preparing the PA.

The scope for collaboration in defining the research agenda depends on political and institutional conditions in the country concerned. Especially in the early PAs, scope was also constrained by tight deadlines facing Task Managers for completing the work. Close consultation and agreement between the Bank and the government from the outset can reduce the risk of later misunderstandings and acrimony over politically sensitive issues, especially the controversial question of establishing a poverty profile and poverty line to serve as benchmarks against which progress can be measured.

Drawing as widely as possible on local skills and knowledge in the analytical work of the PA contributes to the quality of the conclusions. It also spreads the ownership base. Analytical studies and report writing have been contracted to local researchers and/or assigned to collaborative teams of Bank and local researchers. To broaden participation, Task Managers have also used workshops or retreats and established in-country task forces or steering committees.

Collaboration in formulating policy prescriptions can be more difficult; most Task Managers have faced the quandary of how best to reconcile the interests of senior officials and vocal stakeholders with the results of re-

SUMMARIES

search and analysis. The most PPAs in this respect have been those for Peru (see box A2.5) and Morocco: in each case, *(a)* the PA was presented as supporting research and analysis to help the government in the policy formulation process, *(b)* the government took full responsibility for preparing the policy document, discussing successive drafts with Bank staff before final publication, and *(c)* the Bank has integrated the government's poverty strategy in the lending program of the country department as a whole.

Incorporating the PPA

The participation of the poor and other groups through PPAs can contribute to the overall PA by complementing, informing, or validating the results of more conventional analysis based on household survey data and government statistics. To date, PPAs have been designed specifically to do the following:

- Enrich the poverty profile by illustrating local experience and understanding of poverty and vulnerability
- Improve understanding of the impact of public ex-

penditure by eliciting the perceptions of the poor on the accessibility and relevance of services
- Expand analysis of factor markets by illustrating the operation of constraints on disadvantaged social groups to realizing market-based opportunities
- Contribute to policy prescription on the economic and regulatory framework by demonstrating the impact of regulations on poor households and communities
- Support policy analysis of "social safety nets" by examining local experience of the operation of formal and informal safety net systems and the coping strategies used by the poor
- Assess the capacities of the poor to act independently through community organizations (box A2.6 provides an example from Kenya).

The participation of the poor has been elicited through various data gathering and consultative mechanisms. The main methodologies—beneficiary assessment and participatory rural appraisal—share many core techniques, including conversational and semistructured in-

---

Box A2.4. Broad Stakeholder Participation in Cameroon

Cameroon's PA was carried out with extensive Cameroonian participation and involved the National Statistical Office in preparing the poverty profile and the Centre for Nutrition Research in addressing food insecurity issues. The PPA was carried out by local NGOs and research institutes.

To share the research results and broaden participation in dialogue on the policy implications, a four-day technical workshop was sponsored by the government and the Bank with financial support from several key donors. Participants included representatives of donor agencies and some forty-five Cameroonians with interest in related research and civic or government activities from the government, university, research and advocacy groups, journalism, and NGOs. Women participants were funded by the United Nations Children's Fund. Despite the breadth of different interests represented. Some important areas of agreement emerged, including the potential benefits of decentralizing decisionmaking. By the end of four days, agreement was reached on the form the recommendations should take and considerable enthusiasm had been generated for the final report.

The workshop was followed by a one-day conference to provide wider exposure of the findings to both government and the general public. The immediate impact of this conference was to raise consciousness concerning poverty issues, generate widespread public interest and concern, and put poverty reduction higher on the public policy agenda.

Box A2.5. Policy Formulation in Peru

In the Peru PA, the Bank team opted to hold back on defining a poverty alleviation strategy and wait until the government produced their own strategy. Two things that helped this approach to work were that *(a)* most of the survey analysis had been done in Peru, making it easier for Peruvians to incorporate the results into a policy document and *(b)* government officials were aware that presentation of their strategy for poverty alleviation would be key to an effective Consultative Group meeting, which was to be hosted by the Bank to raise funds for social programs. Bank staff worked closely with government staff on drafts of the strategy. The resulting government document is quite strong, setting specific goals in several areas, and should serve as a good base for measuring progress in reducing poverty in Peru.

Box A2.6. PPA Highlights the Potential of Women's Groups in Kenya

The coping strategies of the poor (the vast majority of whom do not have access to credit) depend on diversifying their livelihoods and on the strength of their social networks and informal groups. Because their livelihoods are so diversified, no single employment program will reach the poor. The informal groups and associations, on the other hand, engage in a wide range of economic and social welfare activities. The PPA in Kenya highlighted the untapped potential of these groups to reach the poorer segments of society.

The PPA study estimated that at least 300,000 groups and associations exist in rural Kenya, including more than 23,000 registered women's groups. It found that every village had from five to seventeen different types of groups, and more than one active or defunct women's group. The following are some of the findings that emerged about these women's groups:

- During discussions of coping strategies at the individual, group, and community levels, women's self-help groups were mentioned frequently in every district. They were a particularly important part of the coping strategies of female-headed households.
- In addition to income generation, group objectives frequently included welfare activities: raising cash to pay school fees, meet hospital expenses, or assist with transport costs to bring the dead back to the villages for burial.
- Most groups levied membership fees and monthly contributions.
- Although the poor were excluded when membership fees were high, many groups targeted their activities specifically to assist the poor with food, school fees, and housing construction.
- Women's groups were often formed along clan or kinship lines and often had male members. Generally, they were supported by village men and the community at large.

Based on the findings of the PPA, proposals to reach the poor by strengthening women's groups include legal registration so that groups are eligible for credit, technical and business management training of group members, and extension of microenterprise credit to groups.

terviews, focus group interviews, and participant observation. Participatory rural appraisal (see Appendix I), which focuses on analysis at the community rather than household level, also uses thematic mapping, wealth and preference ranking, institutional diagramming, and other techniques by which participants generate their own analyses of key elements of their livelihoods.

The choice of methods has depended in practice on the particular experience of the Task Manager or supporting specialist, as well as on available resources and the role intended for the PPA within the overall PA. Achieving reasonable coverage for a national-scale beneficiary assessment to investigate a range of issues typically requires at least six to nine months work and a budget in the region of $50,000 to $100,000. Rapid appraisal, requiring less than one month of fieldwork, has been used in five of the seventeen countries in which PPAs have been undertaken.

Some early lessons have already emerged from this experience. In defining objectives of the PPA, the temptation exists to overload the agenda with a large number of questions important to the PA as a whole. Most Task Managers feel in retrospect that results of the PPA would have been richer if the research focus had been narrower. The PPA can provide an important new perspective on the issue of poverty, complementing but not substituting

for quantitative data. The key challenge is to integrate the two approaches within the PA framework, appreciating the limitations of each.

Identifying and selecting field sites and participants (a representative sample of "the poor") is a critical issue for the PPA, especially when societies and the communities within them are highly stratified. This can be approached either through participatory methods, using local perceptions of key groups for analysis, or through sampling based on household survey results. Researchers need to be clear about which they are using as results may differ.

There are good reasons for selecting a broad range of people, from different technical and institutional backgrounds, for the PPA research teams. Including NGO and government staff as well as academics broadens ownership and enables the team to draw on wider institutional experience. The more diverse the backgrounds of team members, however, the more vital is a rigorous training input to generate a unified and coherent approach.

Another lesson learned on the early PPAs is that it is easy to underestimate the time and skills required for analysis and synthesis of qualitative research material. Task Managers should plan for some of the analysis to be carried out in the field and also allow for inputs from experienced social scientists (from within or outside the Bank).

Box A2.7. Policy Impact of the Zambia PPA

In the case of the Zambia PPA, the impact on the PA was clearly strong especially on the action plan. Specific elements that influenced the action plan included the stress on rural infrastructure investments (roads and water) and on urban services (mainly water supply). Other parts of the PA that drew heavily on the findings of the PPA included the poverty profile (especially for community-based identification of the ultra-poor) and the chapter dealing with coping strategies, safety nets, and targeted interventions.

The Task Manager for the PA gave the following assessment of the overall impact of the Zambia PPA on policy formulation in Zambia to date:

- Government has been influenced by the priorities expressed by the poor in ranking exercises in the PPA (by reinforcing the current emphasis on agriculture and health, stressing the importance of rural infrastructure and environment issues to the poor, and emphasizing ongoing problems with the delivery of education services).
- The Ministry of Health has been using the results of the PPA and the PA extensively as a whole in policy development, for example one of the authors of the PPA has been participating in a committee looking into the issue of exemption from user fees for the poor.
- Observations from the PPA related to the timing of school fee payments (which coincide with the period of maximum seasonal stress for most rural communities) have contributed to ongoing work in the Ministry of Education on school fees; a new policy is in preparation that will address these issues.
- The very positive feedback from communities in the PPA on the functioning of the emergency safety net during the southern Africa drought of 1992 influenced policy recommendations on ongoing provision for the vulnerable in the PA.

Because the PPA is only one of the inputs influencing the recommendations of the PA, and because the PA document, in turn, is only one of the factors influencing actual policy change, it can be difficult to measure the policy impacts of specific PPAs. Nonetheless, policy relevance should be the guiding criterion in the design of methodology and process for the PPA. Evaluation by the country department of the impact of the Zambia PPA, as summarized in box A2.7, has found that the PPA strongly influenced both the conclusions of the PA, especially the action plan and national policy formulation.

Evaluation of the Zambian experience (the first national-scale PPA to be completed) also points to some measures that could have increased the value of the PPA in policy formulation: a stronger focus on the institutional mechanisms by which needs and problems could be resolved, completing the PPA earlier to allow for follow-up of the priority areas identified, and sharpening methods to investigate local perceptions on specific policy issues, such as food marketing.

This note is based on the paper written by Andrew Norton and Thomas Stephens. Contributors include John Clark, Hugo Diaz, Anne Doize, Ann Duncan, Jorge Garcia-Mujica, John Innes, Evangeline Javier, Polly Jones, Steen Jorgensen, Gibwa Kajubi, Sarah Keener, Qaiser Khan, Adriana de Leva, Claire Lucas, Alexandre Marc, Branko Milanovic, Deepa Narayan, Miria Pigato, Nicholas Prescott, Lawrence Salmen, Lynne Sherburne-Benz, Roger Sullivan, Maurizia Tovo, and Mark Woodward.

SUMMARIES

PARTICIPATION IN AGRICULTURAL EXTENSION

Putting responsibility in the hands of farmers to determine agricultural extension programs can make services more responsive to local conditions, more accountable, more effective and more sustainable.* To realize these benefits, the role of the public sector has to be redefined to permit multiple approaches that account for user diversity and to develop partnerships with farmer organizations, NGOs, and the private sector for service delivery.

RATIONALE

Project experience over the last twenty years has fueled debate concerning the role of public sector agricultural extension in strategies to increase agricultural productivity and alleviate rural poverty. The dominant approach in Bank-supported projects since the early 1980s—the training and visit system—has been to accelerate the adoption of new technology through intensive, regular interaction between government extension agents and selected "contact" farmers to disseminate a package of key agricultural messages. This approach has had some noteworthy successes and some failures. Although the system is intended to incorporate feedback from farmers, this is not always accomplished and the role of farmers as receivers of instructions is often passive. Consequently, the results of investment in training and visits have sometimes been disappointing and have been especially unsatisfactory regarding sustainability.

The most significant shortcomings of public agricultural extension in general have been (a) unresponsiveness to the variation in farmer needs, (b) lack of ownership by the intended beneficiaries, (c) failure to reach poor and women farmers, (d) limitations in the quality of field and technical staff, and (e) high and unsustainable public costs. Some of these problems have been eased by modifying the training and visit system, for example, by working with groups rather than individual farmers or by increasing reliance on radio and other mass media. Agricultural specialists increasingly recognize, however, that if extension is to meet the diverse needs of modern farming, a fundamental change of approach is called for toward educating and enabling farmers to define and solve their own problems and determine and take some responsibility for the extension services they require.

Agricultural extension in many countries is being reoriented to provide more demand-based and sustainable services, taking account of the diversity, perceptions, knowledge, and resources of users. The options governments are pursuing include full commercialization; devolving control to local government units; cost sharing between extensionists and farmers; contracting service delivery to private firms, NGOs, and/or technicians from cooperatives and farmers' organizations; and supporting farmers' self-help groups. Although Bank experience with these alternative approaches is still too new to permit systematic evaluation, evidence already exists of potential benefits and particular issues to be confronted in implementation.

BENEFITS

By making extension more demand driven and more accountable to farmers, participatory approaches can help to ensure that services are relevant and responsive to local conditions and meet the real needs of users.

When programs benefit from farmers' traditional knowledge as well as modern research, the risk of serious mistakes is greatly reduced. Examples of what can happen when the value of local knowledge is not appreciated include the aggressive promotion of maize by extensionists in Ethiopia to replace the indigenous grain *teff* despite skepticism and resistance from local farmers. Many Ethiopians suffered unnecessarily when maize proved less drought resistant and the crop failed; subsequent data also showed that *teff* provided superior food value. In Bali, after efforts in the 1970s to introduce the Green Revolution to rice cultivation had led to catastrophic pest damage, researchers learned that traditional local husbandry techniques were more efficient.

The opportunities for promoting technologies to improve farmer incomes are expanded through participatory, farmer-centered approaches to extension, which encourage a holistic perspective, shifting the focus of attention from simple production to the whole farm system. Farmer participation is essential, for example, in introducing integrated pest management, which requires farmers to invest effort and resources in techniques that are knowledge intensive. In Indonesia (see box A2.8), on-farm trials with substantial farmer involvement have proved the best means to ascertain and demonstrate the potential benefits of integrated pest management.

Participatory methods, often through NGOs, can also help to make the distribution of extension services more equitable. Proactive efforts are needed to ensure that opportunities for participation are open to all farmers, including the poor, indigenous peoples, and other marginalized groups. The importance of the role played by women in agricultural production is such that the widespread failure so far to reach women farmers through formal extension services has major repercussions for

SUMMARIES

Box A2.8. Integrated Pest Management in Indonesia

Integrated pest management (IPM) is an approach to crop protection based on the rationale that pest populations can be kept below economic injury levels with minimal or no recourse to chemical pesticides. The menu of IPM options is defined by agroecological, socioeconomic, and institutional factors. It involves developments of traditional crop management, such as crop rotations and intercrops, and includes the use of resistant varieties, biological control, and diagnostic techniques.

The Indonesia Integrated Pest Management project in Indonesia illustrates both the potential of this approach and its dependence on participatory extension.

After linking pest outbreaks in 1985 and 1986 to escalating use of pesticides, the government of Indonesia banned fifty-seven broad-spectrum pesticides for rice, gradually eliminated state subsidies on other pesticides, and instituted IPM as the national pest control strategy for rice. The IPM Farmer Field School was developed as the model for government extension agents and pest observers to train farmers in IPM.

The farmer field-school training approach represents a move away from conventional packet technologies in agricultural extension toward empowering farmers with knowledge and skills, using nonformal education methods and a field-based, experiential learning process. Farmers make their own decisions about crop management based on their experience, on local field and market conditions, and on basic IPM principles learned in farmer field-school training. These principles include weekly monitoring of pest levels, conserving the natural enemies of pests, sharing information, and coordinating control strategies with neighboring farmers.

Between 1987 and 1990 the volume of pesticides used on rice fell by more than 50 percent, whereas yields increased by about 15 percent. Farmers are testing and developing new IPM practices, including IPM for other crops, with the help of farmer trainers in their communities. NGO involvement has been encouraged to develop field school activities, new training components, and farmer networks, resulting in a wide exchange of ideas and resources and the spread of IPM farmer field schools from community to community. In 1993, $53 million was committed by the U.S. Agency for International Development and the government of Indonesia with support from the World Bank to a project to extend the use of IPM throughout the country.

---

national output and food security as well as social justice. The Nigeria Women in Agriculture Project (see box A2.9) illustrates the potential of the participatory approach to bring women into the national agricultural policy debate and local project management, as well as enabling them to improve their own productivity.

Making farmers influential and responsible clients rather than passive beneficiaries of the extension service improves sustainability—both of the benefits of investment in new technology and of the service itself. Participatory methods can increase farmer ownership of the technologies promoted by extension management, especially when the methods are developed, at least in part, by the clients themselves and are based on technologies that they have seen to be effective. At the same time, when the value of the service is clear to them, farmers are willing to contribute to its support, reducing dependence on public funds for meeting recurrent costs.

COSTS

A higher level of training and skills is needed if extension staff are to collaborate effectively with farmers, applying technical knowledge to site-specific socioeconomic and agronomic conditions, rather than delivering prepackaged messages. Agents also need training in participatory methods of working with farmers. Some of these additional costs can be offset by reductions in the number of staff needed, as farmers themselves take on more responsibilities, and the economies of "distance" methods (using mass media and modern information technology) are more fully exploited.

Additional time and resources are also needed to redefine and establish the institutional framework for participation, for example, to decentralize fiscal and administrative functions, to build collaborative partnerships, and to strengthen the capacity of NGOs and farmer organizations. On the part of the Bank, additional staff time is required for project preparation and supervision and resources are needed for participatory analysis during project design.

The costs of participation to farmers can be substantial, particularly in terms of their time. Where participatory programs depend on significant contributions of cash and/or labor from farmers, steps have to be taken to ensure that this does not exclude the poor from sharing in benefits.

KEY ELEMENTS

Key consideration in promoting participation in agricultural extension include the following:

Stakeholder Commitment

Broad consultation from the outset is needed to ensure sufficient commitment to change on the part of all stakeholder groups. Extension services that are participatory and accountable to farmers imply some loss of control for government central planners (and for Bank Task Managers). Even if the degree of control in setting specific targets and scheduling plans to meet these targets may sometimes be illusory, its symbolic loss can be strongly resisted. Vested interests in the existing extension bureaucracy can also present strong resistance. Farmers themselves may be skeptical of calls to contribute time, effort, or cash if their experience of extension in the past has been negative.

The Institutional Framework

There is no one institutional model for delivering participatory extension services. Some countries, such as Chile and Costa Rica (see box A2.10), are using the private sector to carry out what was traditionally a public sector activity; some are decentralizing and reorienting public sector agencies; and still others are working through NGOs and farmer organizations. A multi-institutional approach is common, recognizing that farmers get information from several different sources and that some organizations are more effective in reaching certain categories of farmers.

Defining and facilitating operational linkages at an early stage is crucial. This can be approached through stakeholder workshops during project preparation to discuss possible forms of partnerships and the allocation of responsibilities for implementation and support. Other key issues include: instituting incentives and mechanisms for accountability to farmers on the part of extensionists; identifying where legal and regulatory changes are needed; training staff in participatory methods; building the capacity of local farmer groups; and ensuring that local level institutions do not exclude some groups of farmers from participation.

Two-Way Communication

In adopting a learning process approach, the function of extension is not merely one of technology transfer but of ensuring effective two-way flows of information with the aim of empowering farmers through knowledge rather than issuing technical prescriptions. Methods available for listening to and establishing dialogue with farmers include beneficiary assessment, gender analysis, participatory rural appraisal and problem census. Joint problem solving and decisionmaking are achieved through workshops, round tables, public hearings, and farmer organizations.

Considerable potential exists for adapting the use of mass media and information technology to support participatory extension, channeling feedback from rural communities to researchers and extensionists as well as providing information to farmers. Farmer participation in designing and implementing mass media programs improves program quality and enhances the learning process.

Communication for technology transfer in agriculture is an extension methodology that combines the strengths of mass media dissemination and grassroots extension advisers. Focusing on behavioral change, the methodology involves gaining a thorough understand-

---

Box A2.9. Reaching Women Farmers in Nigeria

In Nigeria women were found to make up between 60 percent and 80 percent of the agricultural labor force, depending on the region, and to produce two-thirds of the country's food crops. As elsewhere in Africa, however, extension services focused on men and their farm production needs.

The Nigeria Women in Agriculture (WIA) project (see chapter II) was introduced to address this shortcoming in the extension system. Through a participatory, learning-by-doing approach, the project has succeeded in giving women a voice in the national policy reform process and in integrating women into the mainstream of agricultural extension and development initiatives in their localities.

Because of the shortage of women trained in agriculture, existing home economics agents have been retrained to become WIA agents. The formation of WIA farmer groups has facilitated the dissemination of agricultural innovations and provided women farmers with better access to farm inputs and credit than they would have as individuals. Assisted by WIA agents, women now participate through these groups in all aspects of subprojects, from identification to planning and implementation.

Project planning and replanning has been carried out through national workshops with representatives of WIA groupsæa process that both the Bank and the government have found to be effective in translating field knowledge into specific action for improving women's productivity in agriculture.

One of the greatest benefits of promoting participation in decisionmaking at both the local and national levels is found to be the momentum generated by the dynamism and resourcefulness of Nigerian women.

Box A2.10. Using the Private Sector in Latin America

As early as the 1920s, Chile began to replace public technical assistance to farmers with private services. Since 1990 extension to medium- and large-scale farmers in Chile has been executed by a private farmer's group and is now totally privately funded. The Agricultural Development Institute (INDAP) of the Ministry of Agriculture reaches a large number of small farmers through an extension program that is publicly funded and privately executed through private technology transfer firms. Community-based INDAP offices with community representatives select firms through competitive bidding and supervise and evaluate their performance. Farmers sign annual contracts with a firm and are expected to contribute up to 30 percent of program costs; if they are not satisfied with the service, they can decide as a group to ask INDAP for a change.

A recent project directed to the poorest and smallest farmers contains several innovations. Extension is to be provided by private sector firms and NGOs. To reduce dependence on the public sector, farmers graduate from a three-phase extension and credit program. Farmers will spend three to six years in the intensive phase I, which begins with individual visits. Phase II, to last for three years, will use a group approach and focus on managerial skills and marketing. Phase III is to be wholly farmer-financed, independent, extension support. As farmers graduate from the program, new farmers will join without any increase in INDAP's staff and budget.

Under a Bank-financed project in Costa Rica, a strategy has been devised to divest government gradually from extension. As the Ministry of Agriculture is reorganized, some extension personnel are to move to the private sector and government will provide training to private extensionists. The project intends to provide private technical assistance to small- and medium-scale producers through an Extension Voucher Pilot Program. Farmers will trade vouchers for individual and group technical assistance. Farmers are distinguished according to whether they require high- or low-intensity assistance. The extensionist is to indicate annually to the ministry which farmers should graduate from the program. At the end of the seven-year implementation period, all beneficiaries are expected to continue with purely private services.

ing of existing knowledge, attitudes, and practices in the target communities, before identifying potentially relevant technologies and testing communications options. Communication for technology transfer has been used successfully in Peru, Honduras, Indonesia, and Jordan, providing clear evidence that, when carefully tailored to specific conditions, mass media programming can magnify the impact of participatory extension cost effectively.

---

* This note is based on the paper written by Charles Antholt and Willem Zijp. Contributors include John Farrington, Malcolm Odell, Dennis Purcell, Franz Schorosch, Bachir Souhlal, Andrew Spurling, and Venkatachalam Venkatesan.

PARTICIPATION IN FOREST AND CONSERVATION MANAGEMENT

The participation of local communities and other stakeholders in managing forestry and conservation projects can help to improve forest productivity, alleviate poverty, increase environmental sustainability, and make rules governing forest access more enforceable. Introducing participatory management depends on government commitment and requires time and resources to develop consensus among stakeholders, establish new institutional arrangements, decentralize finance and administration, ensure appropriate rules and incentives for local involvement, and build organizational capacity at the local level.

Over the last decade, approaches to forest management and biodiversity conservation shifted fundamentally from a focus on centralized planning and management by government agencies to a more participatory approach that balances social, environmental, and economic objectives. Reflecting this shift, between 1991 and 1994, Bank investment in forestry projects classified as social and environmental increased from $834 million to $1.2 billion or 27 percent of all lending in the forestry sector.

Key differences between the two approaches are outlined in box A2.11. Under most centralized forest policies, large management units are oriented to a single-use objective (such as timber production or policing a conservation site) and the rights of local users are limited to low-value secondary products and temporary

Box A2.11. Contrasting Forest and Conservation Management Approaches

	Government Forestry and Conservation Projects	Participatory Projects
Objectives	Timber production or other single-use objective (for example, watershed protection and short-rotation fuelwood); protection of biodiversity paramount over other uses.	Usually multiple production and biodiversity conservation objectives involving all stake holders; developing local skills for forest and conservation management.
Scale	Large management units based on natural biophysical or political boundaries.	Micro-management units corresponding to self-selected or residential units.
Local Use Rights	Usually very limited and frequently ambiguous or temporary.	Extensive, clearly defined rights for local users.
Protection	Policing by forest service guards and fencing, often ineffective and expensive.	By local community, frequently using social fencing; higher local costs but low government costs; local accountability.
Typical Plan	Long rotation of even-aged stands for economies of scale in management and industrial supply; centralized management of protected areas and conservation sites.	Short rotation of uneven-aged stands designed to supply diverse products for continuous income and subsistence needs; community management.
Harvesting Contracts	Generally, large government contracts with administrative pricing mechanisms and subsidized supply arrangements.	Generally combine multiple household marketing arrangements with small-scale contracts for high-value products.
Technical Basis	Based on results of scientific research and single product optimization models.	Based on combination of traditional knowledge and use patterns with forest and conservation service guidance.
Planning Process	Centralized management planning process carried out by forest and conservation service staff.	Plans drawn up by community or household participants with guidance an d approval from forest an conservation service.
Plan Revisions	Generally, little flexibility in management prescriptions without cumbersome bureaucratic approvals.	Great flexibility in management prescriptions to adapt to changing conditions and needs.

SUMMARIES

concessions. In contrast, participatory forest projects are based on a broader valuation of forest resources, taking into account the multiple values of forests and the social and economic needs of local forest users. Access and use rights to forests—as well as conflicts arising among competing users—are locally defined and managed. The structure of incentives and the choice of technologies are geared to environmental sustainability over the long term.

BENEFITS

The benefits of using participatory approaches in forest and conservation management include the following:

Cooperation

In practice, one of the most compelling reasons for seeking the participation of forest users in managing forest resources has been the inability of governments to police forest areas effectively and enforce their own rules of access and use without local public support. When local communities and private companies share in the design, benefits, costs, and management responsibility of forestry projects, they have incentives to cooperate in enforcing rules on which they have themselves agreed.

Poverty Alleviation

The majority of the people who occupy forest areas or the agricultural fringes that surround them are poor and vulnerable populations. Many are indigenous or landless people who have migrated from other areas. Enabling these people to share in the benefits as well as the management of forest development and commercialization helps alleviate their poverty and diversify their sources of income.

Forest Productivity

With the benefit of local knowledge and participation, the value of nontimber forest products to different users for food, fiber, medicines, oils, and gums can be more fully exploited (see box A2.12). Indigenous productive technologies—applying knowledge based on close experience with local ecological conditions—can enrich scientific research and serve as potential sources of new products.

Sustainability

Although still seeking to generate economic benefits from forest resources, policymakers are increasingly aware of the important role played by forests in preserving biodiversity and protecting critical watersheds. Especially in regions with large and growing populations, participation is often the only viable way to conserve forest areas for sustainable use or for their environmental values as intact ecosystems.

COSTS AND LIMITATIONS

Participatory approaches have proved unworkable in some circumstances, including when (a) conflicts over forest resources are particularly intense, (b) forest resources are abundant in relation to a small, dispersed population in the forest vicinity, (c) powerful interests at the national level are opposed to policy reform in the sector or to decentralization of authority, or (d) extreme social inequalities at the local level reinforce the control of forest benefits by local elites.

Even in favorable circumstances, time and resources are needed to establish effective participatory processes. Costs are incurred in three broad areas: (a) identifying key stakeholders and creating the conditions for effective consultation, (b) establishing appropriate institutional

Box A2.12. Learning from Indigenous Practices to Increase Local Participation and Improve Forest Productivity

Using under-exploited tree and crop species in Africa. Trees in agroforestry systems in Africa provide many other products and services, such as food, fiber, medicines, oils, and gums, that are used by many indigenous groups (for example, *Elaeis guineensis* for oil, wine, thatch, and mulch; *Moringa oleifera* as edible flowers and leaves and fodder; and *Xylopia aethiopica* as a tobacco substitute and fuel in most of Kenya and the Farlo regions in Senegal). The annual harvestable production from leaves and fruits is about 300 kilograms per hectare in typical Sahel areas and more than 600 kilograms per hectare in the Sudano-Sahel.

Crop-livestock-fallow rotations. In the Zimbabwe and Haiti Bank-financed forestry projects, rotations of crop cultivation, grazing, and tree-shrub fallow are permitted as a result of documentation of indigenous crop-grazing systems. The rotations involve two or more subpopulations in the project site but often just one piece of land. Because lands are appropriated on the basis of kinship and ethnic affiliation, several families have user-rights to the land over a certain period of time. This multiple use arrangement encourages participation of other user groups.

arrangements, including intermediary organizations with the skills and incentives to address environmental and social objectives, and *(c)* building the organizational ability of local communities to manage large forest areas.

CONDITIONS FOR SUCCESS

Bank experience provides a number of lessons concerning the conditions for successful participation in forest and conservation management and the measures that have helped to establish these conditions, including the following:

Government Commitment

Success depends first and foremost on government commitment to broad stakeholder participation in determining forest sector and conservation objectives. Measures by Task Managers to facilitate policy dialogue have included: sponsoring international or regional meetings at the ministerial level, enabling policymakers to benefit from other countries' experience in devolving authority to forest users; holding donor meetings to coordinate initiatives and assist government in defining the agenda; using forest sector reviews and biodiversity conservation strategy work to begin policy discussions with decisionmakers and key stakeholders; and supporting preparation of issues papers by experts from stakeholder groups.

When government is actively involved in discussions with stakeholders, forest management reforms are easier to introduce. For example, the multisectoral stakeholder workshops held in Mexico and Zimbabwe were helpful in identifying key reforms in forest tenure policy, regulations on marketing of nonwood products, and delineation of protected areas for biodiversity conservation.

Decentralization

A wide range of different institutional arrangements—from private contractual agreements to joint public/private partnerships—has been used to devolve authority over forest management to the local level. In most cases, some restructuring of government agencies has been called for as well as changes in procurement and other administrative procedures.

Methods that ensure the availability of funds at the local level have included increasing private sector involvement by opening up lines of credit, underwriting private sector forestry investments, and endorsing joint contractual management of forests as in forestry projects in Indonesia, Zambia, the Philippines, Bangladesh, and Costa Rica. In other cases, direct funding to NGOs has proved the best means of delivering funds directly to communities. For example, under the Bank/Global Environment Facility-financed Conservation of Priority Protected Areas Project in the Philippines, a grant is made to a consortium of NGOs for implementation of conservation programs. Trust funds have proved useful, as in Bhutan and Uganda, when returns to investments occur over the long term.

Stakeholder Analysis and Consultation

Identifying and consulting stakeholders at the earliest possible stage is important not only for ensuring that all the important issues are addressed but also for strengthening commitment to implementing the necessary reforms. Gender analysis can be used to assess the different impacts of proposed policies on men and women, and measures can be taken to ensure that women share in decisionmaking and project benefits (see box A2.13).

Security of Tenure

Because of the long gestation period of forestry and conservation investments, security of tenure is particularly important as an incentive for community investment of time and resources. Existing regulations frequently restrict access and undermine local or indigenous claims to resources. Overlapping claims by government, different groups of forest users and industry, however, can make adjudicating tenure rights a complicated process. In Bank-financed projects in Nepal and India (see box A2.14), publicly endorsed written agreements have been instrumental in resolving tenure conflicts.

Equitable Rules and Incentives

Forestry projects have the best chance of succeeding when the costs and responsibilities of each stakeholder are closely related to rights and benefits. Arrangements for the sharing of costs, benefits, and management responsibilities as well as mechanisms for resolving conflicts among groups are most likely to motivate participation if they are widely understood and agreed on by all stakeholders through an open negotiating process. Special measures may be needed to ensure that women, indigenous groups, and landless households are not excluded.

Appropriate Technology

Appropriate forest management technologies provide important incentives for participation. The participation of local users is encouraged by an annual flow of income from nontimber products, such as agricultural intercrops, fodder, or thatch grass, and commercially valuable seeds or leaves. This can only occur in plantations with wider spacings and multitiered, more diverse tree and shrub

SUMMARIES

Box A2.13. Women's Participation in Bank-Financed Forestry Projects

Kenyan women participating in forest-sharing agreements. With the assistance of the international NGO CARE, the Kenya Forestry Development Project solicited the help of women in devising an agreement between the government and local users regarding distribution of agroforestry or intercrop benefits, because most of the village agroforestry lands were controlled by women. During project implementation, women were in charge of recording households that received harvest shares and they were key actors in resolving conflicts over forest benefits.

Indian women as members of forest protection committees. In the second West Bengal Forestry Project, the Bank worked with the state forestry agency and NGOs to permit and encourage the recording of women as forest protection committee members. This allowed women to participate fully in decisionmaking and thereby receive a more equitable share of timber harvests. When women were given responsibilities in these committees, the project gained wider support and spread rapidly to other villages.

Box A2.14. Tenure and Access to Forests in Nepal and India

The Bank-financed Nepal forestry project allowed user communities to take over forest management. Forest users received certificates ensuring long-term rights to forest benefits. The only control the Nepal state forestry agency retained over forests was through approval of village forest management plans. The project, however, had to reconcile the multiple and often conflicting rights to forests by local villagers before long-term tenure could be recognized.

In the Bank-financed second West Bengal Forestry Project in India, written agreements between the state and villages established ownership and user rights to forest protection committees. To maintain rights over forests, however, each committee had to provide evidence of sustainable forest use.

---

species than are found under conventional even-aged management. Technologies defined by the community on the basis of local knowledge are often more effective in terms of forest productivity and sustainability. Moreover, the entire community understands the management rules and has an incentive to monitor and enforce them.

Local Capacity

Most Bank and Global Environment Facility/Bank-financed forestry and biodiversity conservation projects involve a capacity-building component, often contracted to NGOs, to strengthen management capacity at the community level. The role of NGOs may include training of forest service staff and local leaders, village-level publicity and extension, developing microplanning tools and facilitating plan formulation, improving forest marketing information networks, facilitating the formation of women's groups and farm forestry associations, and technical support to forest product processing, energy alternatives, or village-based conservation inventories. One of the most effective tools for building local capacity is the study tour, enabling stakeholders to visit and question their counterparts on projects in which participatory management has already been established.

---

* *This note is based on the paper written by Ajit Banerjee, Gabriel Campbell, Maria C. Cruz, Shelton Davis, and Augusta Molnar. Contributors include Gloria Davis, Claudia Alderman, Bhuvan Bhatnagar, Daniel Gross, Asmeen Khan, William Magrath, Jessica Mott, Simon Rietbergen, Gotz Schreiber, Radha Singh, Jim Smyle, and Tom Wiens.*

PARTICIPATION IN THE IRRIGATION SECTOR

The irrigation sector provides a rich source of experiences and lessons in user participation. Participation by farmers in system design and management helps to ensure the sustainability of the system, reduce the public expenditure burden, and improve efficiency, equity, and standards of service. Mobilizing support at all levels and establishing the participatory process, however, involves costs; it also demands knowledge of the incentives facing each group of stakeholders and of the essential elements in building effective user organizations.

BENEFITS

Efforts to increase user participation have been spurred by poor performance in efficiency, equity, cost recovery, and accountability of many large irrigation systems managed by government agencies. Greater participation by farmers through water users associations has helped overcome many of these problems.

System Performance

The overriding reason for increasing participation in irrigation is to improve system performance. Clear gains in efficiency and standards of service are achieved when design and management of the irrigation system are transferred to farmers. System design benefits from local knowledge, and farmers have the means and incentives to minimize costs and improve services. For example, irrigation user associations can reduce labor costs by paying lower wages than government agencies; local farmers can provide closer supervision of staff than distant agency supervisors; and breakages are reduced when farmers feel a greater sense of ownership. In Senegal (see box A2.15), for instance, electricity requirements were reduced by half. Ultimately, as a result of more timely water delivery and repairs, farmers' yields are higher. In the Philippines (see box A2.16), dry-season rice yields increased by 12 percent and farmers' net income by 50 percent.

Public Expenditure

One of the most noted effects (although this has nothing to do with farmers' motives for participation) is the reduction in government staff and expenditure requirements caused by farmer management and contributions of cash, labor, and materials. Farmer associations have proved more effective collectors of user fees than government agencies. It is not unusual for farmers to be willing to pay more than the original user rates after transfer of the system to their control. Increased collection of fees, however, does not motivate farmer participation. Participation must also result in direct benefits to participants.

Box A2.15. Senegal: Creating Incentives for Farmer Participation

Early efforts in Senegal to transfer irrigation system management to farmers by establishing village units showed little success because of unclear plans, timetables, and provisions for transfer and because of the failure to provide control or incentives for the farmers.

Recognizing these problems, the 1990 Bank-assisted Irrigation IV Project required total transfer of operations and maintenance (O&M) to farmers as a precondition for financing rehabilitation works. Getting farmers to agree to take over these systems required considerable negotiation, particularly because they perceived existing irrigation fees as too high, let alone the additional costs and responsibilities of covering full O&M.

Increasing the control of farmers over irrigation services was the key factor that persuaded them to agree to assume responsibility for system management and cost recovery. Farmers demanded the right to hire their own staff, choosing agency operators only if they had performed well, and even then reducing their salaries from the full civil service package. Following the transfer to farmers of ownership of rehabilitated operating systems with their infrastructure, agency staff would be allowed to enter the schemes only with farmers' permission. To improve farmers' management capacity, manuals were prepared for each system; training in basic literacy as well as technical and financial skills for organizational leaders was incorporated. Farmers were willing to pay at least part of the training costs.

Although the long-term sustainability of the project is difficult to assess at this stage, the accomplishments to date are impressive. Before the transfer, assessed fees covered only 17 to 21 percent of maintenance and replacement costs; less than a quarter of these were actually collected. As a result, maintenance suffered, electricity often was not paid for, and system reliability was poor. After the transfer, farmers paid fees four times as high, covering full O&M and a replacement fund for capital. The benefit to the farmers was greatly improved irrigation reliability. Moreover, because they were able to monitor the pump operators and had an incentive to save on energy costs, electricity requirements were reduced by half. Savings to the government included huge reductions in agency staff costs, as farmers took over functions.

SUMMARIES

Box A2.16. Evidence from the Philippines

The first and best documented nationwide program to build in participation as a cornerstone of irrigation policy occurred in the Philippines. Beginning with a pilot project in 1976, the approach was expanded in 1980 to cover all communal systems and even extended to large national irrigation systems. The National Irrigation Authority has evolved from an agency primarily concerned with construction to one committed to developing and supporting the management capacities of farmer irrigation associations.

A 1993 study of three irrigation systems reported substantial improvements in performance after ownership and management responsibility were transferred to farmers: collection efficiency for service fees increased from 45 percent to 74 percent, recurrent maintenance costs were reduced by 60 percent and personnel costs by 44 percent, dry-season rice yields increased by 12 percent, and, taking costs and labor contributions into account, farmers' net income increased by 50 percent. These gains were most dramatic for tail-end farmers who saw major improvements in the equity of water delivery.

Sustainability

Building irrigation systems that are wanted, supported, and owned by users themselves provides the best assurance of sustainability. Physical and fiscal sustainability of the irrigation system beyond the project is enhanced when operation and maintenance costs are met from user fees rather than high levels of government subsidy.

Equity

More equitable organizational arrangements and water delivery have been noted when participatory approaches are followed. A contributing factor is the socioeconomic status of the leadership, which tends to be closer to that of the ordinary member, involving more tenants and small farmers than in nonparticipatory systems.

Spillover Effects

The transformation of water users from beneficiaries to partners in irrigation development can have a widespread impact as farmers become trained and organized. It can increase local ability to coordinate input supplies, for example, and to deal with other government agencies involved in rural development.

COSTS AND RISKS

Establishing user participation involves costs in mobilizing field staff, training, and organizing farmers and carrying out socioeconomic research. These additional costs, however, are usually offset by subsequent savings in construction costs and higher loan repayment rates.

A bigger problem can be the additional time needed to establish a participatory approach and get the project off the ground, especially in the absence of existing local institutions for cooperation. Developing farmer organizations is often a slow process, since less is under the project's control than when constructing dams or delivery structures. Once the participatory approach has been established, however, it is not unusual for participation actually to reduce the implementation period. The kinds of problems that typically delay the implementation of nonparticipatory irrigation projects, such as difficulties in negotiating rights of way or obstruction by farmers or local politicians may be avoided or solved through effective participatory processes.

CONDITIONS FOR SUCCESS

The success of participation efforts in the irrigation sectors depends on how well the project mobilizes support and builds effective farmers' organizations.

Mobilizing Support

User participation changes but does not eliminate the role of government agencies in irrigation development. Building support from policymakers and agency staff as well as farmers and other water users is essential for successful participatory projects and involves paying close attention to the incentives relevant to each group. The greatest receptivity to participation is often found in crisis situations, as was the case in Mexico (see box A2.17), when management problems or revenue drains are most apparent.

In building the confidence of policymakers and senior agency staff, pilot projects have been used effectively to demonstrate the capacity for farmer management, the potential improvement in system performance, and potential saving in government expenditure and improvement in cost recovery rates. Building alliances with supportive individuals in government has been facilitated by participatory economic and sector work, by enabling Task Managers to spend several years working in a country, and by supporting them with good social analysis.

Box A2.17. Mexico: Rapid Change in a Crisis Situation

Mexico experienced rapid and widespread incorporation of user participation in the irrigation sector. The objective was to make the national irrigation system financially self-sufficient as well as to obtain full cost recovery over time for major works already constructed. The cornerstone of this policy was the transfer of irrigation management to water user organizations.

Crisis situations in irrigation system financing and management provided the impetus for sweeping changes. By the end of the 1980s, an estimated 1.5 million of 6.1 million hectares of irrigated land went out of irrigated production because of lack of funding to complete infrastructure and for O&M. Bank management was influential in pointing out the need and direction for change; the Bank also provided a loan (cofinanced by the Inter-American Development Bank) for the Irrigation and Drainage Sector Project. The three pillars of this project were decentralization and transfer of irrigation districts to water user organizations, self-sufficiency in fee collection to cover full O&M costs, and efficiency in budget allocation.

The transfer is done in two stages. The first gives producers, organized in water user organizations (covering 5,000 to 18,000 hectares), responsibility for O&M of large lateral canals and drains. In the second, these organizations take responsibility for the main irrigation and drainage canals and the machinery and equipment required for O&M through the creation of an enterprise or *sociedad*. Farmer groups are set up as organizations, rather than less formal associations so that, under Mexican law, they can operate as legal entities and obtain loans. These organizations are meant to become financially self-sufficient through collection of water charges. Each organization hires a professional team to carry out O&M, including a manager and a group of water masters (one for approximately 3,000 hectares) and a chief of maintenance (all graduate engineers) as well as their support staff.

To educate farmers about the changes and persuade them to support the program, Mexico relied heavily on mass media campaigns prepared by communications specialists from the United Nations Food and Agriculture Organization (FAO), along with universities and industry. These were followed by detailed training of the farmer organization staff in, among other subjects, computer applications and use of maintenance machinery. Districts in the best financial condition were transferred first (after deferred maintenance was done) to ensure a successful start and build confidence.

The process of transferring management to farmers already has exceeded targets. Since 1991 thirty-three irrigation districts covering 2.3 million hectares have been transferred and an additional eleven districts are in process. O&M cost recovery rates have increased from 18 to 78 percent.

Project implementation rests ultimately with agency staff. Internalizing support for participation within irrigation agencies often involves structural changes to link agency budgets firmly to farmer contributions instead of government allocations and to promote a more service-oriented approach. Because agency staff typically come from engineering backgrounds and are not oriented toward dealing with farmers, incentives for them to support farmer participation need to be backed up by training programs. Study tours to farmer-managed irrigation districts can be particularly effective, not only for their demonstration effect but also in raising the prestige of participation, exposing staff to new possibilities, and creating a bond among participants.

The strongest opposition to farmer participation is often encountered at the field technical level, especially when civil service unions are strong. When field staff perceive the proposed changes as a threat to their jobs and livelihood, these vested interests can retard or even sabotage participatory projects. Clear directives are needed from policymakers, supported by performance measures linked to bonuses and promotions, to encourage greater accountability to the farmers. The new ethos can only develop gradually. Sudden cuts in the status quo should be avoided, and the composition of staff allowed to change gradually.

Building Effective Farmers Organizations

Teams of trained specialists acting as community organizers have proved to be the most successful catalysts in participatory irrigation projects. Wherever possible, existing organizational capacity should be built on, as in Nepal (see box A2.18), for example. In cases of very hierarchical social structure and inequitable distribution of assets, it may be unrealistic to expect fully democratic local organizations. To control vested interests, the varying incentives of different categories of farmers should be identified and accounted for in project design (for example, in defining water rights), along with the resulting problems of achieving collective action.

Appropriate incentives are needed if farmers are actively to support the user associations that are essential channels for participation and to assume the additional costs in time, materials, and fees (as experience in Pakistan has demonstrated). The most important of these in-

SUMMARIES

Box A2.18. Nepal: Building on Traditional Strengths

Nepal has a long tradition of direct farmer participation and cooperation in irrigation development. About 70,000 farmer-managed irrigation schemes, ranging in size from very small to thousands of hectares, account for 70-80 percent of the country's irrigation. In general these systems achieve high levels of performance over long periods of time without government cost or involvement. Such systems, however, are frequently damaged by landslides and floods beyond the capability of farmers to repair alone; most can be improved substantially with modern materials and construction techniques.

The Bank's irrigation line of credit was designed to assist these schemes by building on the farmers' traditional capability to organize and cooperate together. To participate under the irrigation line of credit, farmers had to form legal farmer irrigation associations, agree ahead of time to contribute to capital costs, pay full O&M costs, and maintain full control and responsibility for all decisions regarding their irrigation schemes. Such stringent requirements had never been attempted before under a Bank-supported project in Nepal. But in practice these requirements simply formalized the farmers' traditional mode of irrigation development and provided an avenue for Bank assistance that would strengthen rather than destroy the traditional farmer institutions. The irrigation line of credit approach proved highly successful, has become strongly demand driven, and is now being expanded to government-managed projects.

centives are improved irrigation services and a voice in management decisions through a user organization that is fully accountable to its members. The support of farmers is most likely to be sustained and organizational capacity developed when they are involved from the beginning in decisions on system design and their organization has full ownership and management control of the system. It is essential, for example, that specialized staff be selected by and accountable to the farmer organization, even if they have been trained by government agencies.

To be successful, farmer organizations must interact constructively with government agencies and technical experts. This relationship works best when consistent rules and procedures are established and supported by government regulation for the turnover of responsibility to farmers throughout the project or sector. Building the necessary organizational capacity for this turnover involves training farmers for a variety of new functions, including basic literacy, accounting, how to hold meetings, how to deal with agencies with legal regulations, possibly even computer applications, and water management and operation of equipment.

Fundamental to meeting all these conditions is a strong and transparent legal framework for the organization from the outset, providing farmers with rights and benefits as well as duties and responsibilities. This framework should also be flexible enough to allow farmers to evolve their own organizational structure and to permit the organization's responsibilities to grow in line with its capacity.

PARTICIPATION IN THE WATER AND SANITATION SECTOR

The participation of users in designing and implementing projects and managing water and sanitation (W&S) services is now being built into Bank-funded projects with the aim of increasing efficiency, equity, and cost recovery and facilitating the extension of service coverage to poor communities.* Success depends on establishing the necessary institutional arrangements for participation and project delivery. In addition, Task Managers have to spend more time in the field, and adapt Bank procedures to support appropriate models for financing and procurement.

CHALLENGES FOR THE SECTOR

Prior to the last decade, the business practices of W&S utilities hardly ever involved consumers in decision-making or management. More recently, with concern that agencies are still failing to reach more than a billion of the poorest in developing countries, moving people center stage in W&S projects has become an important theme.

Despite massive investments between 1980 and 1990—the International Drinking Water Supply and Sanitation Decade—the needs of rural and urban poor are still largely unmet by formal public services, whereas in many areas private vendors charge ten to a thousand times the official tariff rates. Pervasive inefficiency on the part of overstaffed agencies providing subsidized urban services has resulted in financially unsustainable services that benefit only a small portion of the population.

At the same time, competing user needs have not been well balanced; many water resource interventions—large dams and irrigation projects in particular—have misallocated water resources and caused social and environmental disruption.

To increase responsiveness to user needs, improve cost recovery and service management, and incorporate financial, environmental, and social concerns into project design and management, services should be based on demand.

THE ROLE OF PARTICIPATION

Participation plays a central role in meeting these challenges. An example from Kenya (see box A2.19) shows how involving users in the design and management of W&S services provides a means of revealing demand and ensuring that services match what people want, are willing to pay for, and will strive to maintain. The rationale for user participation is summarized as follows:

- User participation makes services and service providers more responsive and accountable to beneficiaries.
- Cost recovery and the sustainability of services improves when technology choices and services correspond with what users want and are willing to pay for.
- Management of services is more effective when institutional arrangements are tailored to local practices.

Demand-based approaches can also help resolve conflicts over water resource allocation among competing sectoral uses. Increased participation by primary stakeholders, whether through consultation or through the purchase of water rights in regulated water markets, helps ensure that choices are anchored in demand and not unduly influenced by contractors, consultants, and other secondary stakeholders.

Most of the experience with participatory W&S projects so far has been gained by NGOs and, with a few notable exceptions, mostly on a small, experimental scale. Although stakeholder participation is well accepted in the Bank's work in this sector and is seen as especially vital in extending services to the poorest communities, participatory W&S projects are relatively new, mostly either still under implementation or in preparation. Much is yet to be learned about ways to optimize participation in large projects, but a number of important lessons are already emerging.

CONDITIONS FOR SUCCESS

Promoting the participation of water users is not equally appropriate and feasible in all W&S projects. It is better suited to the provision of feeder than trunk infrastructure. Adverse political and institutional conditions may make it difficult to establish participatory processes. In the poorest countries in which capacity is weak, the cost of expatriate facilitators to promote institutional intermediation may also be high.

The critical question is to understand what rules and institutional arrangements are useful in supporting stakeholder participation in the sector and under what circumstances they are appropriate.

Working with Governments and Sector Agencies

Support from higher levels of government is essential to the success of demand-driven projects. It was crucial, for example, in overcoming line agency resistance to plans for beneficiary participation through an autonomous fund for rural W&S projects in Nepal. Cultivating national level support for participation in W&S can be tackled from two ends: by country economic and sector work, through which support is generated before projects

Box A2.19. Community Mobilization for Sanitation in Kenya

The village of Maina is an informal settlement within the boundaries of Nyahururu town in Kenya, where the Danish International Aid Agency executed a sewerage house connection project between 1988 and 1991. In the first year of the project, a trunk sewer and a few lateral sewers were constructed without any participation by the residents. The consequences were predictable: villagers did not understand the project motives and resisted collaborating with project teams when the plans indicated that the layout of some plots would be altered to make room for roads, storm drains, and toilet units. Villager apprehensions were based on a valid concern that engineering plans would result in large-scale alterations to existing houses and structures.

A review mission by the Danish International Aid Agency in 1989 recommended that, before any further investments were made, the physical plan be revised with community participation. A site committee was formed, involving residents in the process of determining what the project components would be. Extension workers with government ministries and staff from a leading Kenyan NGO were selected as facilitators. The results were striking. Communities began mobilizing labor and materials for construction and also began participating in O&M of constructed facilities.

By the time the project came to an end, the community groups with support from the NGO had charted a completely different course for the project and were able to engage the municipal council in a productive dialogue on where and when other infrastructural facilities such as roads, a police station, and a post office should be located within the village.

are begun, or through individual participatory projects, whose lessons change sectoral policies at the national level. When consensus or political support at the national level is weak, it may be easier to begin by demonstrating the move from projects to policy work. Most of the demand-driven projects reviewed in this paper, however, emerged from earlier sector work that laid the basis for and created interest in trying this new approach.

Finding agencies capable of carrying out participatory projects may be difficult. Several strategies have been used in cases in which the sector agency is not qualified or interested in involving primary stakeholders more actively: *(a)* using multiple agencies in project implementation, *(b)* cultivating reformers within the larger resistant agencies, *(c)* bypassing the agency by creating a new agency or fund, and *(d)* designing the project to include an expanded range of secondary stakeholders as partner organizations to prevent capture of project benefits by water utility staff and contractors.

Each of these approaches has its own drawbacks (an example is described in box A2.20) and in all cases the challenge remains to persuade engineers trained in applying industrial country standards to consider alternative technologies, leave their drawing boards, and consult with primary stakeholders. Investment in training staff in community participation by itself cannot remedy the situation unless career rewards are linked with success in implementing demand-based projects. Lower-level staff often have more accepting attitudes toward community involvement and are better equipped to interact with poor beneficiaries. Staff with experience from other agencies involved in extension work can also adapt easily to an intermediary role between consumers and W&S service providers; in a project in Brazil, for example (see box A2.21), responsibility for rural water has been placed with the public health agency with good results.

In Bank-funded projects in which existing sector agencies have had few qualified community mobiliza-

Box A2.20. The Risks of a Multi-Agency Approach

In a rural water project in a country in Asia, the central government did not provide adequate resources to the department of local government responsible for setting up rural water associations with community involvement. The public works department, on the other hand, received its budget allocations on schedule and went ahead procuring well-drilling materials before communities had been consulted on what sorts of facilities they wanted and were willing to pay for. In response to political pressure from provincial politicians, the public works department distributed budget allocations evenly over all the provinces, spreading project investments too thinly. The project was driven by drilling companies and politicians rather than, as envisaged in the project, by the community-based rural water associations. These pitfalls could probably have been avoided if community participation had been established before the hardware was procured.

SUMMARIES

Box A2.21. Learning about Participation Models

The PROSANEAR, a Brazil water and sanitation project for low-income communities, is being implemented in several states in Brazil. Each state water company has been free to incorporate participation, using its own procedures. In practical terms, what has emerged are models of participation that differ depending on how the water company and the project design consultants worked out the "rules of the game."

In the *engineer-activist model,* the engineering consultant was also a dedicated social activist. The rules permitted beneficiaries to negotiate a wide range of topics with the state water company, such as levels of service, physical layouts, sequencing between water supply and sanitation investments, prices, billing, and so on.

In the *participation specialist model,* professional community participation facilitators work jointly with design teams led by engineers. In one variant of the model, the water company decides on engineering design in advance and allows communities to negotiate the organization of billing, assignment of operational responsibilities, and group contributions of labor. In the other variant, negotiations are restricted to assigning O&M responsibilities among the beneficiaries, user groups, and the water company.

In the *hygiene education model,* health educators focus on a more conventional set of interventions intended to change knowledge, attitudes, and practices, rather than iteratively working out or negotiating any aspect of service provision. The assumption of this model is that there is no need to build any explicit negotiation mechanism into the choice of service level.

The extent of conflict has been greatest in the participation specialist model and nil in the hygiene education model. Per capita investment costs were highest in the hygiene education model. After project construction is completed, it will be possible to evaluate the effect of each of these models on service sustainability.

tion staff, specialists hired as project consultants have added up to 10 percent to total investment costs. The best outcome in terms of community participation, beneficiary satisfaction, and per capita costs for water and sewerage resulted from having the detailed engineering design done jointly under one bid by consulting teams consisting of engineers and community participation specialists.

Designing Stakeholder Participation

Most projects set up community councils or water user associations, through which beneficiaries can influence deci-

Box A2.22. Tips for Task Managers of Water and Sanitation Projects

- *Financing and Procurement.* Standard bulk procurement procedures are rarely appropriate for demand-driven projects. Alternatives include *(a)* direct procurement by communities or agencies from prequalified, small construction firms and consulting engineers, using a schedule of standard materials and labor costs; *(b)* multiple procurement procedures, depending on the size of the project; and *(c)* geographic clustering of subprojects to allow limited packaging of specific elements.
- *Project Preparation.* Sector work can help clear the way for participatory projects. An essential part of preparation is the time spent by Task Managers in the field. Especially at this learning stage for the Bank and borrower countries, preparation and supervision of participatory water and sanitation projects require more financial resources and staff time than conventional projects.
- *Supervision, Monitoring, and Evaluation.* Monitoring, evaluation, and fine tuning of project design becomes an iterative, consultative process, involving Task Managers, sectoral counterparts, project managers, and beneficiaries. Personal field visits by Task Managers are essential. Staff time for supervision in participatory water and sanitation projects has varied from twenty to forty-five weeks a year.
- *Mobilizing Additional Resources.* Task Managers have mobilized extra funding for preparation from the Japanese Trust Fund, Japanese Grant Facility, and Project Preparation Fund. Bilaterals, the United Nations Children's Fund, regional development banks, and local and international NGOs working in the country have been useful sources of experience, information, and innovative approaches.
- *The Role of Consultants.* Almost all projects involve consultants promoting participation in some capacity. The key issue is how the community participation specialist and the engineering design specialist can be encouraged to coordinate their efforts. One solution is to invite bids proposing both together, forcing consultants to form consortia of engineers and social activists.

sions concerning the sort of service to be provided, play a role in project implementation, and channel their contributions of cash, labor, and materials. Long-term community participation in O&M of systems may also be sought, although this is more difficult and experience is still limited.

Project design must allow time to discover workable structures. Flexibility in community-level project design allows institutional arrangements to be adjusted as needed to match what community members feel comfortable with. It also permits changes to be proposed by beneficiaries during the course of project implementation in rules and procedures, management structures, assignment of responsibilities among alternative organizations or firms, or the kind of service to be provided.

Demand-driven projects allow beneficiary communities choice over the type and level of W&S service they want, based on their needs, priorities, and financial situations. To make informed decisions, they must receive sufficient information about options, their respective costs, and other implications. The range of service options may be limited by settlement density, resource avail-

ability, and hydrological or geographic factors. Typically, however, a number of options exist; the key factor is motivating the engineering staff to be innovative in searching these out.

To limit the influence of local elites, effective beneficiary participation also requires accountable leaders who make decisions on the basis of transparent rules. In Paraguay the combination of easily understood program rules and clear information about costs and benefits has produced an effective rural sanitation program for larger villages. The government's sanitation agency offers the program to any community that can set up a committee and supply 15 percent of the investment costs. The community repays another 15 percent in cash or labor and materials at the time of implementation and a further 30 percent over ten years, contributing to 60 percent cost recovery for capital costs. The community is expected to cover 100 percent of operational costs. The success of this program in terms of cost recovery and the effectiveness of local organizations owes much to the clear rules for entry and for division of responsibilities.

This note is based on the paper written by Gabrielle Watson and N. Vijay Jagannathan. Contributors include Balint Almassy, Alexander E. Bakalian, Jannik Boesen, Niel Boyle, John Briscoe, Louis Chang, Lea Donaldson, Mike Garn, Efraim Jiminez, Farin Kemper, Xavier Legarin, Abel Mejia, Vicente Paquero, George Plant, Lars Rasmussen, Geoffrey Read, Carlo Rietveld, Robert Roche, Gerhard Tschannerl, Anthony van Vugt, Albert Wright, Rekha Dayal, Peter Lochery, and Mukami Kariuki.

PARTICIPATION IN THE EDUCATION AND TRAINING SECTOR

Operations in the education sector can be greatly improved by increasing stakeholder participation of government officials, education professionals, local communities, and the private sector.* Such participation can increase the relevance and quality of education, improve ownership, build consensus, help to reach remote and disadvantaged groups, mobilize additional resources, and build institutional capacity. Participatory operations involve risks and costs, however, and certain preconditions are necessary for success.

POTENTIAL BENEFITS

Many Bank-assisted and other education projects have promoted the participation of stakeholders from government officials and education professionals to community members, parents, students, and employers in design and implementation. Such participation can contribute in a variety of ways to meeting the challenges facing education systems in developing countries: improving quality, promoting equitable enrollment, and controlling soaring public costs.

Improving the Relevance and Quality of Education

In a sector in which demand is often poorly understood, a fundamental rationale for increased stakeholder participation is to improve the relevance, effectiveness, and sustainability of projects by ensuring that learning programs match the needs of the populations they are serving.

Efforts to make the provision of *basic education* more responsive to community needs have included education vouchers for families, fund transfers to school boards, and various models of school- or community-based management. Colombia's Escuela Nueva program (see box A2.23) and the Balochistan community support process (see box A2.24) provide two examples. The involvement of parents and other community members in decisionmaking has, in many cases, made the curriculum, teaching materials, and school calendar more appropriate to local conditions and improved teacher and student attendance rates. The result has been to boost morale, reduce drop out and repeater rates, improve achievement scores, and expand enrollment demand.

Nonformal education has had a relatively long history of student and community participation. Programs have proved more effective in terms of attendance rates, learning achievements, and behavioral change when learners help identify their needs, design and manage learning programs, and participate in developing learning materials. Not only are such programs more relevant to the knowledge and interests of the students, but also the participatory activities themselves support the learning process.

Similarly, the motivation and achievement of students in *vocational and higher education* have been enhanced when students and community-based organizations participate in designing and managing programs to meet their needs. In these sectors, the participation of private sector employers has been particularly important for improving technical standards and linking training to real employment opportunities.

Box A2.23. Student and Community Participation in Colombia

Colombia's Escuela Nueva program was created in the mid-1970s to overcome curriculum, training, and administrative deficiencies in multigrade rural schools. The program incorporates a number of innovative components, including participation of students in school government and community participation in designing and supporting the school curriculum.

In each learning task, self-instruction books guide students to identify examples, cultural elements from their own experience, and local materials to be accumulated in the learning centers. Teachers are encouraged to organize meetings with parents and discuss the material prepared by the students. Children also participate in health, sanitation, and nutrition activities. In this way, the school gradually becomes a resource center for teachers, for agencies operating in other sectors, and eventually for the community itself.

In addition, Escuela Nueva children are introduced to civic and democratic life through student councils. Students organize into committees to take care of discipline, cleaning, maintenance, sports, school garden, newspaper, and library. They also cooperate in the instructional process by helping slower students. This is seen as an essential part of the curriculum as it creates linkages between the school and the community.

Evaluation of the program, which has expanded rapidly to some 20,000 schools, suggests that educational achievement and civic behavior compare favorably with the output of traditional schools at similar costs per pupil.

SUMMARIES

Box A2.24. Mobilizing Community Support to Primary Schools in Pakistan

The community support program in primary education in Balochistan, a province in Pakistan, provides a remarkable example of what can be achieved in adverse conditions through participatory methods.

Beginning with a pilot project in 1992, the community support program has already succeeded in establishing 198 new community girls schools in remote rural villages that had no government school and no tradition of parental involvement in schools. Enrollment of girls is 100 percent in many of these villages with high attendance rates.

To begin the participatory process, community workers went door to door, urging parents to form an association. In each of the villages, education committees have been created that are responsible for selecting a site for the school, identifying potential teachers, and monitoring teacher attendance and student enrollment.

A local girl, educated at least to the eighth grade, has been identified and trained as teacher for each school. After she demonstrates her commitment by teaching for three months on a voluntary basis, mobile teacher-training teams are sent to her home village to provide intensive three-month pedagogical training. This home training is needed because of cultural barriers that prevent girls from traveling far. Following the training, the teacher becomes a government employee: government rules, which normally require teachers to have matriculated, have been stretched to accommodate the program.

The pilot project resulted from the initiative of a Pakistani consultant. The Bank Task Manager, with whom she discussed her plans, recognized the potential of this approach and was able to organize U.S. Agency for International Development funding for the pilot. The consultant subsequently formed a small NGO to qualify for funding from other sources, which now include local and international NGOs, USAID, the United Nations Children's Fund, and the government of Balochistan through a World Bank loan.

At the project preparation stage, when the pilot was tried, there was no way of knowing if the approach would work or not. The success of the pilot led to full acceptance and ownership of the program by the government, and the government itself is now funding the program on a province-wide basis using International Development Association credit. Because of the experimental nature of the project, World Bank support to the program has only been possible through the new lending approach, which supports the entire primary education program rather than selected components.

Building Ownership and Consensus

In a sector as socially, politically, and culturally sensitive as education, stakeholder involvement in policy dialogue helps to define the values on which policy is based and to develop consensus between competing interest groups. It also helps to ensure that proposed changes have the understanding and support of all the groups on whom successful implementation will depend.

In some cases in which major policy reform has been envisaged, education commissions have elicited relevant information and views from many sections of society. Techniques for facilitating dialogue among stakeholders in policy or project design have included focus groups, workshops, conferences, and, as in Botswana, innovative use of video technology. The Philippines (see box A2.25) is one of several countries in which Economic Development Institute workshops have been the catalyst for participatory education sector work.

Box A2.25. Building Borrower Commitment in the Philippines

The participatory process used in education sector work in the Philippines is reported to have called for much more time and patience on the part of Bank staff than would have been the case with a more traditional Bank approach, but it is hoped it will pay off in terms of government commitment.

This work started with an Economic Development Institute workshop, focusing attention on the characteristics of effective schools, how schools improve, why schools were not working well, and what the priorities of reform should be. This was followed by another national seminar on the same subject. Broad stakeholder involvement was promoted through a participatory workshop for project design (the ZOPP methodology) that included forty people from each broad geographic zone. From these participants and other stakeholders, a team was selected to draft a national implementation plan. Having secured ownership in the sector, the exercise is now being extended to the central agencies in which the decision to borrow or not ultimately lies.

Reaching Disadvantaged Groups

Participatory methods have often been successful where formal education systems have proved least effective in serving the needs of girls (see box A2.24), remote communities, and marginalized groups. Participatory social research, as used in The Gambia to investigate the reasons for low attendance of girls in primary schools (see box A2.26), can help identify the policy measures needed to counteract the bias against disadvantaged groups. Expertise in bringing educational opportunities to the poorest communities and in promoting the education of women is found in NGOs that have experience in working with community-based organizations and the necessary flexibility to adopt participatory methods.

Mobilizing Resources

The experience of participation through cost sharing in education has been mixed. Efforts to generate community contributions of cash, materials, or labor to school construction, for example, have tended to be most successful in remote areas where the influence of central government bureaucracy is weak. They have been least successful when communities have not participated in decisions concerning location, design, construction, school management, or education priorities. The support of parents and other community members through fees or voluntary contributions is motivated by their having a voice in such decisions and confidence in the value to them of the school or program.

Building Institutional Capacity

As in other sectors, participation by stakeholders in designing and managing programs in the education sector can also yield substantial long-term benefits beyond the individual project by strengthening the institutional capacity for sustained development. The process of participation empowers individuals and enhances their ability to contribute to the wider development process as new skills are learned and new norms adopted. Although these external benefits are difficult to measure, they can be inferred from many of the project reviews.

COSTS AND RISKS

Evidence in the education sector suggests that higher initial costs may be incurred in participatory projects to carry out the necessary social research and community work and to disseminate information or organize workshops. Furthermore, project costs may be understated when the opportunity cost of voluntary time and effort is high. These additional costs, however, are generally offset by subsequent gains in efficiency.

Box A2.26. Participatory Research in The Gambia Uncovers Reasons for Low Enrollment and High Dropout

An innovative approach was used in this survey to gain better understanding of the reasons for low enrollment and high dropout rates of girls in primary education in the Gambia. In addition to conventional survey methods (including questionnaires in schools, teacher interviews, and parent focus interviews), the techniques of participatory rural appraisal (PRA) were adapted to education to counteract the bias against disadvantaged groups and provide a voice to people who are not usually heard.

Thirteen local researchers, including statisticians, Ministry of Education staff, and teenage girls (to interview their peers) were trained in PRA methods. After trials in three villages, the team carried out a series of projects in seven villages and seven urban schools. Focus group discussions were held, at which community members were asked to explain their problems and how education related to those problems. Villagers constructed matrices of community and educational problems, drew seasonal diagrams on income and expenditure, constructed social-educational "maps" of the village, identified households with girls of school age, and provided a wealth of socioeconomic information.

One of the most startling results was the discovery that one-quarter of all the school-age girls (those who were pregnant, married, or about to be married) had remained "hidden" from enrollment statistics, because they had not been counted by villagers in the initial census. Costs to parents, including indirect costs and the coincidence of school fee payments with the season of lowest income, were seen as the biggest problems associated with education. As a result of this research, various measures have been introduced, including a change in the timing of fee payments.

The work was followed up by a second project, working with two rural communities to examine practical, community-based solutions to the problems identified in the first project and to assess available community resources for implementing such solutions. Options deemed by the community to have the highest chance of success were included in a community action plan. Women in one of the villages, for example, decided to start a communal farm and devote half the income from sales of farm produce toward school costs for girls.

There is some risk that the allocation of costs may be inequitable or place an excessive burden on the poor in participatory projects in which substantial community contributions are sought. For example, even the contribution of labor in school construction has been found to be beyond the means of some of the poorest communities. Estimating the ability and willingness of communities or individuals to share in costs needs to be approached on a case-by-case basis in the context of equity objectives.

Difficulties that have been encountered in participatory projects include delays in implementation and dependence on charismatic project leaders. The risk of abuse by individuals, local elites, or interest groups also has to be borne in mind, as does the potential for misuse of funds.

Commitment to a process of dialogue among groups of stakeholders involves its own risks, which must all be taken into account: the timing and possibility of reaching consensus are uncertain; political conflicts are liable to be exposed; and the risk exists of generating social unrest by raising unrealistic expectations among participants.

These costs and difficulties notwithstanding, the risks of expensive failure in participatory projects are judged smaller than in a typical, "top-down" education project, in which lack of sustainability may not be recognized until after significant investment is complete.

Conditions for Success

The most important preconditions for success in participatory projects are political will on the part of central government and commitment by key actors. In cases of weak political will, support for participatory approaches has been generated by sustaining dialogue and demonstrating potential benefits through pilot projects.

Institutional conditions may make participation more or less difficult to achieve, whereas simple scarcity of management and communication skills may be the main constraint to increasing participation in some of the poorest countries. It is often necessary, therefore, to build an education or training component into a participatory project in any sector to overcome skill shortages. Information sharing and dialogue are also important to success; in demand-driven education projects, communities must have access to the best possible information on technical options, costs, benefits, and opportunities.

Because of the need to respond flexibly to developments as the project evolves, making education projects participatory calls for additional skills and greater tolerance of uncertainty on the part of the Task Manager; it also puts a greater onus on the quality of project preparation, clarification of objectives, and project supervision.

Task Managers who are promoting participation in education projects say that success depends on attention to the following critical elements:

- Early stakeholder analysis and involvement
- Information sharing and dialogue among stakeholders
- Flexibility in the funding, timing, and scale of projects
- Institution strengthening
- Appropriate systems of monitoring and evaluation, and mechanisms for ensuring accountability.

---

* This note is based on the paper written by Nat J. Colletta and Gillian Perkins. Contributors include Sarbani Chakraborty, Mae Chu Chang, Francoise Delannoy, Ward Heneveld, Eileen Kane, Samuel Lieberman, Paud Murphy, Makha Hdau, Robert Prouty, Alcyone Saliba, Lawrence Salmen, Yogendra Saran, and Don Winkler.

PARTICIPATION IN SOCIAL FUNDS

The newest Bank-supported social funds are designed explicitly to increase the participation of beneficiaries in identifying and managing microprojects with the aim of making project activities more relevant and sustainable.* Features that support participation are built into the design of the funds' management structure and the microproject cycle. Additional time, management, and training resources are needed to assess and build the necessary capacity of local organizations; special measures may be called for to enable the most marginalized groups to participate.

Social funds have spread rapidly in developing countries since the well-known Bolivia Emergency Social Fund was launched in 1987. The first large-scale funds were designed as temporary institutions to mitigate the adverse impact of structural adjustment by creating employment and delivering emergency social programs. As objectives have evolved over time, funds are now also used more generally to support development in the social sectors and poverty reduction at the local level.

Social funds are typically set up as autonomous institutions to provide funding to local organizations (community-based organizations, NGOs, or local governments) in a more rapid, flexible, and transparent manner than line ministries. The funds do not themselves identify or implement microprojects; instead, they respond to requests generated by local groups, appraise projects for funding, supervise implementation of projects, and monitor their effectiveness.

Because most social funds have been temporary and because they have not provided for recurrent costs, fund managers have often faced difficulties in sustaining large numbers of dispersed microprojects. Strategies to involve beneficiaries in cost sharing were developed initially in response to these difficulties. Currently the World Bank is funding about thirty projects to support social funds; the newest of these, including the Gambia Social Recovery Fund and the Ethiopian Social and Rehabilitation Development Fund, are designed explicitly to increase beneficiary participation in microproject identification and management as well as costs.

BENEFITS

The involvement of beneficiaries in consultation, cost sharing, and decisionmaking can improve the outcomes of Bank-supported social funds by ensuring that the microproject is relevant to beneficiary needs and by generating commitment to sustaining project activities and benefits beyond the life of the fund.

Increasingly, beneficiary participation is also sought as an end for two primary reasons. First, when communities are given the responsibility and ability to identify, implement, and supervise microprojects, they are better prepared to involve themselves in future development activities. Second, social funds can serve as models for participatory processes, demonstrating to governments and other intermediaries the feasibility and utility of participatory approaches.

COSTS

Promoting participation in social funds involves costs as well as benefits. Building the ability of beneficiaries to assume responsibilities throughout the microproject cycle can increase management and training costs as more staff and equipment are needed to reach beneficiaries and to build organizational capacity. Some of these expenses can be absorbed by the microproject, but it is likely that some will have to be covered by the social fund.

In addition, social fund managers face two potential conflicts: *(a)* the conflict between the need for rapid microproject implementation and the time required for consultation and capacity building and *(b)* because demand is expressed first by communities with the skills necessary to prepare proposals and gain access to the fund, the demand-driven nature of social funds may have to be supplemented by special measures to enable the poorest and most marginalized among intended beneficiaries to participate.

Because the implications of these trade-offs are so important, fund designers must clarify and integrate priorities from the outset.

BUILDING PARTICIPATION INTO FUND DESIGN

In promoting participation in social funds, Task Managers must consider how to involve all stakeholders, how participatory elements of temporary funds will be ultimately transferred to government ministries, how to enhance participation at every stage of the microproject cycle and how to evaluate implementing and community organizations.

Stakeholder Groups

The participation of all stakeholder groups in social fund design—central and sectoral ministries, the NGO community, municipalities and local governments, as well as community-based organizations and beneficiaries—builds ownership and commitment to beneficiary participation among all parties on whom implementation will depend.

In preparing the Armenia Social Investment Fund, efforts to cultivate wider government support included conducting seminars for senior government officials, taking them to the field to observe beneficiary participation firsthand, involving them in targeting selection, and sharing reports with them. To support consensus building, national debates involving parliaments, the press, and NGO communities were promoted prior to establishing social funds in Zambia, Guatemala, and Honduras. In Albania and Armenia, pilot phases were used to introduce and demonstrate the concept of participation.

Appropriate tactics for disseminating information on social funds are outlined in box A2.27.

Institutional Structures

When the fund is intended to be a temporary institution, design must incorporate mechanisms for transferring the participatory elements to regular government ministries. The Bolivia Emergency Social Fund developed a program for training ministry staff in management information and cost control systems during microproject appraisal and execution; this training will be extended to cover appraisal and monitoring procedures. Similarly, the Ethiopian Social and Rehabilitation Development Fund project is training local government staff to work with communities in a participatory way.

Decentralization of fund management to regional offices encourages managers to pay greater attention to participation-related issues, although it may also expose them to local political pressure. Regional offices have been established or are planned for fund management in eight countries (including Mexico, see box A2.28), sometimes for purely logistical reasons but sometimes to decentralize responsibility for consulting with communities and for contracts with local organizations.

Beneficiary participation in project activities is best promoted by assigning full-time staff to multidisciplinary teams. In Guyana, for example, a multidisciplinary team is able to integrate services needed by the community, while continuity is ensured by having the same team appraise, supervise, and evaluate a microproject.

The Microproject Cycle

At every stage of the microproject cycle, strategies can be employed to enhance participation. For example, in identifying target groups, participatory data collection techniques (including beneficiary assessment and participatory rural appraisal [see Appendix I]) have been used to enable communities themselves to identify the neediest.

Piloting can help point to adjustments needed in promotional strategies. In Ethiopia, it was learned in the pilot phase that cultural and time constraints and illiteracy had prevented women's groups from submitting proposals; as a result, in the next phase of the fund, promotional activities will target more women's groups and preference will be given to females in hiring community organizers.

Clear and well-publicized microproject selection criteria that "measure" participation can be used to signal to all stakeholders the fund's commitment to beneficiary participation. Such an approach, prioritizing microproject selection according to intensity of participation, is planned in The Gambia.

Box A2.27. Tips for a Successful Social Fund Media Campaign

Media campaigns should be designed to increase the awareness of the population and the direct beneficiaries of the social fund, sensitize and encourage community participation, improve a continuous dialogue with beneficiaries, and maintain the flow of information about the running of the social fund. Tactics that have proved successful include the following:

- Consulting government agencies and NGOs that have run media campaigns to determine the optimal strategy to reach the bulk of the population. Use of written media, such as newspapers and leaflets, mainly reaches the literate, who may be a minority of the population.
- Using visual media such as posters and stickers to promote themes similar to those broadcast on radio or in other media
- Disseminating information through institutions, individuals, and avenues that are accepted and integrated into daily cultural practices (such as traditional singers and dramas). This reduces the potential mistrust of the messages communicated.
- Using radio spots on popular music radio stations to reach urban youth who tend to lose interest in more traditional channels
- Linking themes among different outlets to reinforce messages
- Enabling communities to express their own ideas, such as through radio phone-in programs.

Box A2.28. Mexico: Flexibility at the Regional Level

The National Indigenous Institute of Mexico and its regional Indigenous Coordinating Centers, which are in remote zones, launched the Funds for the Development of Indigenous Peoples in 1990.

The Indigenous Coordinating Centers requested that each indigenous organization or community interested in receiving funds send representatives to regional assemblies organized throughout the country. At these assemblies, the organizations elected five- to nine-member leadership councils, which in turn were formed into subcommissions to oversee the administrative, financial, and technical aspects of the funds.

Once formed, the National Indigenous Institute transferred funds to the Funds for the Development of Indigenous Peoples, which then received, appraised, and approved loan requests from indigenous organizations for productive projects, which these organizations designed and their members implemented.

When beneficiaries, especially marginalized groups, are to take responsibility for preparing projects, documents can be simplified and funding provided for technical assistance to help community groups prepare proposals and carry out technical feasibility studies. In addition to training, one of the ways to prepare beneficiaries for a role in microproject implementation or supervision is to ensure that they are involved from the earliest stages of the microproject cycle, enabling them to learn about the technical aspects of the project. In particular, project design needs to take account of the technical capabilities of the community.

Various approaches have been used by managers both to monitor and evaluate microprojects in a participatory manner and to monitor participation itself. The Zambia Social Recovery Project has conducted three beneficiary assessments to date (see box A2.29), using participatory research tools to gather qualitative and quantitative data.

Box A2.29. Zambia: Beneficiary Assessment in a Social Fund

Phase II of the beneficiary assessment conducted for the Zambia Social Recovery Fund employed conversational interviews, participant observations, and focus group discussions. The combination of these research tools with a multidisciplinary research team from the Rural Development Studies Bureau of the University of Zambia helped to remove biases, strengthen the quantitative data base, and obtain qualitative information.

The specific objectives of the study were to identify, examine, and assess the factors affecting project implementation and community participation. Such factors included: the allocation of responsibility for maintenance, the perceived impacts and benefits of projects, the views of beneficiaries and project committee managers on the performance of the Microprojects Unit and regional office, and governance issues such as transparency and accountability.

Key findings on community and intermediary organizations were as follows:

* In a minority of cases, communities had no say in the selection of the project committee.
* The average female representation on project committees was less than 20 percent. Among the factors explaining this were social attitudes and women's lack of time due to other duties.
* Factors constraining community participation included the following:
  * Lack of transparency and accountability (54 percent of projects)
  * Domination of the committee by one or two individuals or an NGO (16.7 percent)
  * Other agencies doing the work and the committee being ornamental (7.5 percent)
  * Contracting builders from outside rather than within the project area
* Mobilization was constrained by suspected misuse of funds and materials.

Donor funds in three projects discouraged cash and labor contributions as it was felt that donor funding was sufficient and that sacrifices should not be made by the poverty-stricken community.

The findings of this assessment led to specific recommendations and actions to improve fund administration and increase community participation. Actions included: improvements in accountability procedures, development of a bookkeeping module for the project committee training manual, confirmation of community cash and in-kind contributions as mandatory conditions for Microprojects Unit support, strengthening of regional offices to speed communication and disbursement, simplification of application forms, and initiation of project launch workshops in communities to ensure information dissemination.

SUMMARIES

Box A2.30. Characteristics of Intermediaries That Successfully Support Participation

- Participation is an institutional objective.
- Field presence
- Staff incentives and training that support participation
- Iterative planning in consultation with local communities
- "Bottom-up" accountability mechanisms
- Contributions of cash, labor, raw material, or local facilities by local communities, which make the communities clients of the intermediary.
- Horizontal and vertical linkages to other institutions
- The agency has prior experience in the community in which the microproject is to be implemented and is aware of local conditions.
- The community/beneficiaries have a positive perception of the agency.
- The agency and its personnel have a keen understanding of and sensitivity to issues concerning women and minorities and toward the environment.
- The philosophy of the agency on community participation is reflected in other microprojects it has undertaken, and the strategy for participation in the present proposal is in line with the fund's strategy.

The beneficiary assessment can be integrated as a permanent mechanism by, for example, assessing 10 percent of completed microprojects every year. In Guatemala, annual monitoring procedures stipulate that interviews be carried out in communities that have not submitted proposals as well as those that have to identify problems in communicating fund goals and to ascertain how and by whom decisions are reached.

Intermediary and Community Organizations

Because of the important roles delegated to intermediary organizations, it is becoming common to allocate resources at the initial stages of a social fund for assessing and strengthening their capacities in terms of both development effectiveness and beneficiary representation. Implementing agencies are evaluated during regular appraisal of a microproject on the basis of selection criteria (see box A2.30), which also serve to highlight where training is needed for capacity building. In addition, assessment after the fact during impact assessment studies or annual and mid-term evaluations is designed to yield lessons for future fund strategy and mechanisms.

The capacity of community organizations may be assessed as early as the targeting stage, as in Bolivia; more often this is done at the time of microproject appraisal. Providing training for community organizations can empower beneficiaries to identify and prioritize their needs and to develop strategies to meet them. The key to such training is to make it community-centered rather than project-centered, avoiding a "top-down," expert approach and respecting indigenous knowledge.

This note is based on the paper written by Mary Schmidt and Alexandre Marc. Contributors include Alan Carroll, Constance Corbett, Shelton Davis, Abdou Salem Drabo, Nuria Homedes, Steen Jorgensen, Robert Maurer, Maria Nowak, Amolo Ng'Weno, Dan Owen, Leslie Pean, Anna Sant'Anna, David Steel, Julie van Domelen, and Grace Yabrudy.

GENDER ISSUES IN PARTICIPATION

The equal participation of men and women in policymaking, economic and sectoral analysis, and project design and management may be impeded by cultural and legal constraints against women's participation and by women's relative lack of time and mobility caused by their workload and multiple roles. If participatory development is to benefit from women's contributions and meet the particular needs of women, a range of strategic and practical measures must be taken to overcome these barriers.

WHY A PROACTIVE APPROACH IS NEEDED

Experience in participatory development has made clear that, unless specific steps are taken to ensure the equal participation of men and women, women are often excluded. As a result, projects fail to benefit from women's contributions and fail to meet the particular needs and interests of women. A World Bank evaluation of 121 rural water supply projects, for example, found that even in a sector in which women carried the greater share of responsibility, they appeared to benefit little from the 83 percent of water projects that had not been specifically designed to involve women.

The causes are deeply embedded in social and legal institutions. Men and women play different roles, have different needs, and face different constraints in responding to macroeconomic or sectoral policy changes and to the specific opportunities and limitations provided by particular projects and programs. Systemic gender biases often exist in the form of the following:

- Laws and customs that impede women's access to property ownership, credit, productive inputs, employment, education, information, or medical care
- Customs, beliefs, and attitudes that confine women mostly to the domestic sphere
- Women's workload, which imposes severe time burdens on them

Imbalances in the division of labor between men and women and in access to education and productive resources have important implications, not only for equity, but also for economic output, productivity, food security, fertility, and child welfare. They also profoundly affect men's and women's different capacities and incentives to participate in economic and social development.

Overcoming these systemic biases requires a proactive approach. In the long run, the equal participation of men and women depends on strategic measures—policy and institutional changes—to tackle the root causes of gender inequalities and remove the constraints to women's involvement in public life. Examples of such measures in Bank-supported programs include: legal reforms granting women equal rights to land tenure and ownership in Honduras (a condition for tranche release under the Honduras Agricultural Sector Adjustment Credit), incentives to encourage the enrollment of more girls in secondary schools in Bangladesh, and efforts to make government agencies more accountable to women in El Salvador. In addition, a variety of practical measures, taking account of existing gender-based constraints, can facilitate the participation of women in specific projects or activities.

ADDRESSING GENDER ISSUES

Surprisingly few developing countries systematically gather and report statistics disaggregated by sex or carry out systematic gender analysis. The first step toward incorporating gender issues in the policymaking process and determining appropriate measures for strengthening women's participation is to obtain good information on gender roles, existing institutions, and the constraints operating against women's participation through a combination of quantitative surveys and qualitative social assessments. To be effective, assessments must be designed specifically to elicit the views of women. Often, gender awareness training is needed for facilitators or interviewers.

At the Policy Level

Gender issues are receiving more attention in the Bank's country economic and sector work, which provides the framework for its policy advice. It is still rare, however, even in participatory sector work, for women's participation to be sought explicitly in carrying out this work. The Morocco Women in Development Sector Strategy (see box A2.31) provides a model for involving women in policy work, which could well be replicated in other sectors and countries.

Women in Development assessments (which were completed for forty countries in the five years prior to 1994) and recent PAs that were designed expressly to yield gender-differentiated data (see box A2.32) have usually involved less intense participation by women. Nonetheless, they have produced valuable gender analysis and policy proposals for enhancing women's ability to contribute to and participate in the development process.

Box A2.31. Involving Women in Policy Work

In the Morocco Women in Development Sector Strategy, poor rural and urban women were given the opportunity to articulate their needs and priorities through a participatory rural appraisal process that provoked discussion among community members about development and gender issues and sought their views in formulating national policy objectives.

The women's concerns and priorities differed from those of the men and from those of other stakeholder groups. First and foremost, before progress could be made on other objectives, was the need to reduce women's daily burdens through measures such as easing their access to fuel and water, introducing collective ovens for bread baking, and improving health care. Second were measures to improve their incomes, for which women viewed agricultural extension services and access to credit as most important. Third were measures needed to secure the future, including female education and strengthening community-based institutions. The group interactions helped men to understand how the constraints on women affect the family and the village as a whole. The collective solutions that emerged were supported by men as well as women.

The new perspectives gained from the participatory rural appraisal surveys were applied in defining the recommended program of action.

The crucial next step, which is starting to receive more attention, is integrating the results of this work into the Bank's country assistance strategies. The 1993 country economic memorandum for Uganda, for example, was combined with the PA and highlighted the economic and social implications of various forms of gender discrimination. The poverty profile was supplemented by the results of a rapid poverty appraisal soliciting the opinions of rural men and women. In response to the problems identified, the Ugandan government is giving priority to reforms, including legal reforms, that will raise the incomes and status of women.

At the Institutional Level

Designing and implementing gender-responsive policies effectively depends on developing appropriate institutional capacity, including changes in the responsible public agencies. When sociocultural constraints are severe, promoting separate units within government ministries to provide segregated women's services may be the only workable strategy. This tends to result, however, in limited, small women's programs that are peripheral to mainstream activities. With sufficient general awareness of gender differences and inequities, it is possible to move to a gender approach, incorporating gender in mainstream programs, instituting incentives to create responsiveness to gender differences, and making line agencies accountable to both men and women clients.

In El Salvador, for example, public agencies are moving away from a segregated strategy to a more systematic gender approach. The National Center for Agricultural and Forestry Technology eliminated its women's program in 1994. It is taking steps to incorporate gender systematically into planning, monitoring, training, extension, and research and has modified its organizational structure to ensure that gender issues are addressed effectively. Since putting these institutional changes into effect, the National Center for Agricultural and Forestry Technology has been able to increase the participation of women in its extension programs. Other agencies are following the center's lead. The government is now supporting an initiative, to be funded by the Bank's Institutional Development Fund, to promote public sector capacity building and accountability in gender.

When public agencies are not responsive to the particular needs of women and when cultural constraints inhibit women from voicing their opinions freely, women's groups at the community level and the regional or national NGOs that are supporting them play a particularly important role. Strengthening the capacity of these organizations increases women's ability to find ways of meeting their own needs and of contributing to community development. For example, the poverty assessment in Kenya highlighted the importance of the many rural women's self-help groups in the coping strategies of the poor. Proposals to strengthen these groups, based on the findings of this assessment, include legal registration so that groups are eligible for credit, technical and business management training of group members, and the extension of microenterprise credit to the groups.

At the Project Level

If both men and women are to participate, gender issues need to be addressed from the outset, gender constraints identified, and steps taken as in the Togo Urban Development Project (see box A2.33) to ensure that the perspective and concerns of women are incorporated fully in project design.

Box A2.32. Addressing Gender Issues in Poverty Assessments

Poverty assessments, through quantitative survey methods as well as qualitative methods used in the participatory poverty assessment component, can provide important information on gender differences in labor force participation, coping mechanisms, and how men and women perceive poverty and ways to reduce it. Some of the most recent poverty assessments have been designed explicitly to generate gender-specific data on a wide range of questions.

In the *participatory poverty assessment in Cameroon,* 50 percent of the interviewers and 50 percent of those interviewed were women. The resulting information was fully integrated in the subsequent analysis and recommendations with strong policy implications. For example, women in Cameroon were found to be shouldering most of the burden of producing and marketing food. One of the specific actions proposed for improving food security was to target small-scale women farmers with a "productivity package" of critical agricultural inputs. The poverty assessment confirmed the heavy workload of women. As a result, urgent action was recommended to give women access to transport and time- and labor-saving technology to allow them the opportunity to develop their own skills and participate in community projects.

The *Zambia poverty assessment* also focused on collecting sex-disaggregated data related to the division of labor and the implications of time constraints on female labor. Most poor households in rural Zambia were found to be headed by men, using traditional technologies and practicing gender-specific labor allocation, which put extreme pressure on women's time, especially in the peak months of planting and harvesting. In modeling rural household behavior, the study estimated that the value of crop production per household member more than doubled when labor was allocated on a gender-neutral basis.

Appropriate measures vary depending on the particular social and political context, the exact nature of the constraints operating against women, and the kind of activity in which their participation is sought. Constraints affecting women more than men may include any combination of legal or cultural obstacles, time constraints, lack of access to information, illiteracy, lack of transport, or lack of access to finance. The following are some examples of the approaches taken to facilitate women's participation in recent Bank-supported projects.

When the obstacles to women's participation are severe, a case can be made for targeting women's needs and designing projects exclusively for women as in the Women in Agriculture Project in Nigeria and the Women in Development Project in The Gambia. Integration of women's activities into mainstream programs can occur once the environment for their participation has been created.

In some cases, the representation of women has been ensured by making it mandatory. Under the Yemen Education Sector Adjustment Program, for example, it was specified that at least one-third of the workshop participants should be women. Similarly, in the Benin Health Services Project, it was stipulated that each village health committee must include at least one mother.

Working through separate, women-only groups is often the preferred option; depending on cultural conditions, few alternatives may exist. In the Phalombe Rural Development Project in Malawi, women opted for their own women-only farmers' groups instead of mixed sex groups. They felt freer to discuss and develop their ideas

Box A2.33. Gender Awareness in Project Design

In designing the Togo Urban Development Project, gender awareness was explicitly incorporated in the participatory process. Initial studies revealed that women had almost exclusive responsibility at the household level for maintaining a sanitary environment, providing water, managing waste, and promoting family health. They also found that knowledge of the links among health, clean water, and hygiene was extremely limited.

During the preappraisal mission, the first two meetings with community elders, held in the chief's compound, included no women, so the Bank team suggested holding a separate meeting at which the women could articulate their priorities and concerns. The following day the chief's wife chaired a meeting attended by about fifty women from the community. The same questions were asked of them as of the men; a local consultant served as translator and intermediary. Their main concerns, which differed from those of the men, were: men's unemployment; the need for market upgrading, including standpipes, latrines, and central play space for children; access to drinking water; access to finance and credit; and training in management, hygiene, health, and literacy. The women's agenda was fully incorporated in the final project design, which included employment generation through labor-intensive public works and a training program in environmental management geared to the needs of a largely illiterate and mostly female population.

with extension workers. Also, having better repayment rates than men, they preferred to obtain credit in women-only clubs. In the Matruh Resource Management Project in Egypt, when no women showed up at the public PRA sessions, parallel women-only sessions were held to ensure that the project design reflected women's as well as men's views.

Whether women meet with men or on their own, their workload often makes it more difficult for them to attend meetings. As their domestic responsibilities often require them to stay close to home, lack of mobility and shortage of time may be constraints. Various practical measures, from providing child care facilities to installing standpipes that reduce the time spent in fetching water, can make it easier for women to attend meetings or training sessions. In particular, the choice of time and place for meetings must take account of women's schedules (see box A2.34) and the availability of safe transport.

Similarly, special measures may be needed to ensure that women have equal access to project information and are not prevented from communicating their concerns or participating in decisionmaking by illiteracy or relative lack of education. This may involve, for example, targeting women in promotional campaigns, training project staff in gender awareness, hiring female community workers, ensuring that meetings are conducted in the local dialect, or finding creative ways (akin to the techniques used in participatory rural appraisal) for illiterate women to take responsibility for project monitoring and evaluation.

For instance, after the initial promotional campaign for the pilot phase of the Ethiopian Social and Rehabilitation Development Fund project, it was learned that women were not submitting proposals. In the next phase, therefore, promotional activities are targeting more women's groups, community organizers are being sensitized to the important role played by women, and more women are being hired as community organizers. A particularly successful technique for disseminating information in the Gambia Women in Development Project has been to train women in operating video cameras and in other methods of documenting their activities to share and exchange information with other women.

Box A2.34. Enabling Women to Attend Meetings

In the Nigeria Women in Agriculture Project, specific steps were taken to reduce the conflicts in women's schedules and facilitate regular attendance at meetings. Each group meets on the same day at the same time and place, reminders about the meetings are posted at highly visible and accessible locations, and, if the scheduled day conflicts with a market day, the women are consulted in advance and an alternative time agreed on. Consequently, women rarely face the problem of not knowing where and when the meetings are held. The meeting site is selected after the Women in Agriculture agent has introduced herself and the purpose of her visit to the village head. She, in turn, informs household heads who then give their permission for wives to attend meetings.

---

* This note is based on the paper written by Michael Bamberger, Mark Blackden, and Abeba Taddese. Contributors include Jerri Dell, Lynn Bennett, and Elizabeth Morris-Hughes.

SUMMARIES

PARTICIPATION AND INTERMEDIARY NGOS

NGOs can be effective intermediaries in Bank-funded projects that depend on participation and capacity building at the community level. Successful collaboration depends on identifying an organization with appropriate characteristics and involving its staff in decisionmaking from as early as possible in the project cycle.* Steps must be taken to prevent Bank or government requirements from undermining the participatory orientation of the NGO and, where necessary, to strengthen NGO capacity, encourage cooperation among NGOs, and support communication between NGOs and government.

THE INTERMEDIARY ROLE

As Bank-lending operations increasingly emphasize poverty reduction, investment in human resources, and environmental management, more and more Bank-supported projects depend on participation and capacity building at the community level. Participatory community-based development depends in turn on intermediary organizations with the specialized skills and experience to provide links between community-level institutions on the one hand and national institutions and the Bank on the other. The intermediary functions include facilitating communication between project beneficiaries and government; helping to identify and voice community needs; supporting participation and group formation; training and building the capacity of community groups; and channeling resources to the community level.

This bridging role may be filled in different ways, depending on institutional circumstances and the nature of the particular project. Line agencies or local government units may be restructured and reoriented to fill the role of community facilitators. Alternatively, the needed services may be contracted out to the private sector, multilateral or bilateral agencies, NGOs, or a combination of these. Often, the strongest grassroot links, most capable and dedicated community workers, and greatest experience in reaching disadvantaged groups through innovative participatory methods are found in NGOs.

Not all NGOs are participatory and not all Bank-NGO collaboration has been with the purpose of promoting participation. Until recently, the Bank looked to NGOs primarily for capability in service delivery. In approximately two-thirds of projects approved in recent years, however, the promotion of beneficiary participation was cited as the main rationale for seeking NGO involvement. For the Task Manager, the key issues are

(a) identifying an organization that is willing to collaborate and whose capacity and orientation match the specific task at hand and then *(b)* ensuring that the influence of the Bank is to support rather than undermine the participatory character and capacity of the NGO.

IDENTIFYING PARTICIPATORY NGOS

The term "NGO" encompasses a broad array of different organizations, varying enormously according to their purpose, philosophy, sectoral expertise, and scope of activities. A distinction is made between operational NGOs, which are engaged primarily in designing and implementing projects, and advocacy NGOs, whose main purpose is to defend or promote a specific cause. Some NGOs engage in both types of activity. Advocacy NGOs, such as those defending the rights of indigenous peoples, may perform an important intermediary role in supplying information and facilitating communication and consultation. Generally, however, Bank-NGO collaboration on specific projects is more likely to involve operational intermediaries.

NGOs vary greatly in the extent to which they ensure beneficiary participation within their own programs. At one extreme are NGOs whose orientation and competence are very similar to the private sector firms with whom they compete for contracts in project implementation or service delivery. Such NGOs may be efficient (and in strong demand) as service deliverers but are oriented to meeting the requirements of bureaucratic funding agencies and are unlikely to use participatory processes. At the other extreme are participatory NGOs that see themselves exclusively as enablers and capacity builders and refuse to compromise their objectives or independence by collaborating in official programs. A minority of exceptionally effective NGOs combine a high level of competence in service delivery and in community capacity building. The Aga Khan Rural Development Program in Pakistan provides an example of what can be achieved by such organizations, committed to "bottom-up" planning and combining strong technical expertise with effective institution building at the village level. Using infrastructure projects as the catalyst for institution building, this program reached 38,000 households and created 110 women's groups within four years.

An organization serves the interests of those to whom it is accountable. In this respect, national- or regional-level membership NGOs, including federations of grassroot organizations or cooperatives, trade unions, peasant unions, or ethnic groups can be valuable partners in projects requiring broad participation (although women and marginalized groups are not always well represented). One difficulty, however, can be that they are often more politically embroiled and subject to state regulation. Among NGOs that are not membership based, accountability to client communities, for example, through community contributions of cash, labor, materials, or facilities, is an important indicator of an organization's participatory effectiveness. Nonparticipatory NGOs tend to regard community members purely as beneficiaries and the funding agencies as their clients.

Specific criteria for selecting an NGO in terms of technical and operational capacity, outreach potential, skills in community capacity building, and knowledge of conditions in target communities need to be matched to the specific task at hand. Guidelines for assessing the participatory effectiveness of an NGO are summarized in box A2.35. Assessment should be based on the NGO's proven track record as well as its stated objectives. Paper credentials and financial or organizational strength are often less important than dedication, commitment, and enthusiasm.

OPERATIONAL CHALLENGES

Several operational challenges face Task Managers in working with NGOs in the participatory process, including supporting the participatory orientation of NGOs, permitting flexibility in the scale and timing of implementation, enhancing NGO capacity, and strengthening NGO-government linkages.

Supporting the Participatory Process

A paradox confronting the Task Manager is that the qualities that make NGOs participatory and therefore attractive as intermediaries are incompatible with many government, donor, and Bank requirements. One of the major constraints to group formation and capacity building

is donor or government pressure to disburse and deliver services quickly. Unless procedures are made more flexible and both the Bank and the government are committed to supporting participatory processes, the NGO is pressed into a service delivery rather than capacity-building role. This has happened in a number of Bank-funded projects, including Liberia's Second Education Project. Under this project, schools were constructed rapidly and at low cost. No attention was given, however, to supporting the intermediary NGO in building community ownership of schools, and planning for maintenance. As a result, many schools deteriorated and some went unused. Similarly, in the Zambia Squatter Upgrading Project, it was agreed in principle to pursue long-term community development goals by promoting active beneficiary participation. A stipulation was included, however, in the final agreement that, if the collective self-help approach to be used by the two intermediary NGOs interfered with the predetermined project schedule, then contractors would be employed to carry out the work.

Creative Task Managers have found ways to ensure that they support rather than undermine the participatory strengths of NGO partners by introducing mechanisms that permit revisions in project priorities, greater flexibility in the timing and scale of implementation, and alternative procurement procedures, or that allow NGOs to design and implement their own programs.

Consultation from the outset concerning development objectives can help resolve the tension between the short-term project focus of the Bank or government and the long-term community development goals of NGOs. The most successful cases of Bank-NGO collaboration have involved mutual transparency and shared decisionmaking from early in the project cycle. If NGOs are to participate in a Bank-financed project in a significant way, it is important that they have a say as early as possible in the design of the project and in defining the terms of their involvement.

Box A2.35. Indicators of Participatory Effectiveness in Intermediary NGOs

- A flat management structure with decentralized authority
- Organizational structures at the community level to which funding and/or other decisions are delegated
- Use of iterative planning, involving consultation with local communities
- Contributions of cash, labor, raw materials, or local facilities by community members and organizations, making them clients rather than beneficiaries of the NGO
- Staff recruitment criteria, incentives, and training that support participation
- Strong field presence outside metropolitan areas with high proportion of staff of local origin
- Community leaders and members have a positive perception of the NGO
- Turnover of client groups as they "graduate" over time and intensive field attention transferred to new groups

---

The Question of Scale

Highly participatory NGOs tend to work on a very small scale; some of their programs depend on staying small and resource-intensive. In other cases, NGOs have established participatory processes that they have themselves extended to large programs or that have proved replicable by other organizations or government agencies on a large scale. Various approaches have been used to enable successful NGO programs to be scaled up and "mainstreamed," where possible, without losing their essential participatory qualities and without individual NGOs having to grow to the point that they become hierarchical and bureaucratized. This may involve strengthening the capacity of NGOs, both through training and through promoting NGO partnerships among NGOs.

Scaling up may also involve training government staff in participatory methods and relaxing some government regulations. When working with governments to encourage NGO linkages, it is useful to consider that government agencies, as well as the Bank, may have to scale down in the sense of decentralizing and building flexibility and microvariability into their operations. This not only pushes decisionmaking down closer to the populations most affected (and is in this sense itself more participatory) but also makes it easier to work with regional and local NGOs. The community support process under the Balochistan Primary Education Program (see box A2.36) illustrates how flexibility on the part of government can allow an innovative pilot project by a small NGO to be expanded successfully and linked into government programs.

Enhancing NGO Capacity

Training of NGO staff is often needed to ensure that the institutional capacity of an NGO partner matches the scope and demands of the project. Although it is difficult to generalize for the sector as a whole, common areas of weakness in NGOs are limited financial and management expertise, limited number of staff with training and experience in community mobilization, lack of technical capacity, limited coverage in terms of scale or area, concentration in urban centers, lack of communication or coordination with other organizations (including government agencies), and limited understanding of the broader social and economic context in which they are working. Because institutional gaps can be difficult to foresee, it is important to build flexibility into the provision of training.

As the examples in box A2.37 demonstrate, facilitating cooperation and partnerships among NGOs can be a highly effective means of organizing training, as well as enabling small organizations to contribute to large-scale projects and developing the capacity of the local NGO sector as a whole.

Strengthening NGO-Government Linkages

Relationships between government and NGOs vary greatly between countries (and between NGOs) on the basis of historical, political, and ideological differences. Simple lack of communication, however, is often responsible for mistrust and misunderstanding about the other's objectives, concerns, and constraints. The Bank can help to promote state-NGO communication by sponsoring joint training, workshops, and conferences in advance of project appraisal and, in particular, by including both government and NGOs as stakeholders in project design.

A number of Bank-supported projects (the West Bengal Population Project, for example) have also led to the creation of NGO liaison units in government.

Box A2.36. Mainstreaming a Successful Participatory Process

The Community Support Process, included in the *Balochistan Primary Education Program,* is establishing new community girls' schools in remote rural villages. The process began in 1992 with a pilot project by a small national NGO whose community workers went door to door, urging parents to form village education committees, identify a potential female teacher, and select a site for a school. The success of the pilot led to full acceptance and ownership of the program by the government, which is now funding the program on a province-wide basis using International Development Association credit. Because of the experimental nature of the project, Bank support has only been possible through the new lending approach that supports the entire primary education program rather than selected components.

So far, the NGO has succeeded in mobilizing community members to establish 200 schools. Replicating the process on this scale and incorporating the schools and their teachers into the government system once the school has proved viable has depended on the willingness of the Ministry of Education to relax a number of its regulations, so that girls with as little as an eighth-grade education can qualify as teachers and can receive training at home by mobile training teams.

Box A2.37. Encouraging NGO Partnerships

In the *Benin Food Security Project,* partnerships were encouraged between stronger, larger NGOs and weaker, newer NGOs to stimulate the transfer of methodologies and technology. This project began as a pilot, which involved international NGOs and a few Beninese NGOs. After two years of the pilot experience, NGOs were brought together with government and donors at a workshop to design a new project based on the pilot phase. One of the findings at the workshop was that geographic concentration in the capital isolated many large NGOs from target communities. International NGOs had the human and financial resources to submit competitive proposals to be included in project activities; they often, however, had the least recent or direct experience with potential client communities. Where local NGOs lacked transport to access project areas, international NGOs had the necessary equipment and staff but lacked the local contacts. At the workshop, consensus was reached to modify the project in several ways, including creating incentives for NGOs to establish field offices in the project area, giving regional offices the authority to approve microprojects and disburse funds, and requiring international NGOs to partner local NGOs to facilitate technology transfer and information sharing.

For the Bank-financed *Improved Environmental Management and Advocacy Project* in Indonesia, an international NGO teamed up with twelve Indonesian NGOs to strengthen the ability of local intermediaries to address the environmental consequences of pesticides. The international NGO assists local counterparts in developing primary learning approaches to educate local people about environmental problems and solutions. This collaborative NGO effort is a broad initiative to develop education and training programs for farmers, consumers, and province-level regulatory officials. It also serves to transfer skills and knowledge among NGOs.

The goal of the *Uttar Pradesh Sodic Land Reclamation Project* is to reclaim salt-affected lands using participatory management techniques that could serve as a model to be replicated more broadly in the future. Farmers' water management groups will be organized and community volunteers will be trained in technology transfer by small local NGOs. The staff of these grassroots NGOs will be trained in turn by larger intermediary NGOs with previous experience in participatory management.

Other projects, such as the *Participatory Forest Development Project* for Bangladesh, are using a similar structure in which advisory NGOs coordinate the implementation activities of small, locally based NGOs. These projects are coordinated at the national level by a single organization that works directly with the government to ensure compatibility with national goals and policies.

---

* *This note is based on the paper written by Thomas Carroll, Mary Schmidt, and Tony Bebbington. Contributors include John Delion, Christopher Gibbs, John Hall, Janet Koch, Xavier Legrain, Philip Moeller, Gallus Mukami, Stanley Scheyer, Susan Stout, and Thomas Wiens.*

DESIGNING COMMUNITY-BASED DEVELOPMENT

When properly designed, community-based programs can be highly effective in managing natural resources, providing basic infrastructure or ensuring primary social services. Participation in community-based development depends on reversing control and accountability from central authorities to community organizations. Successful design requires tapping into local needs, understanding and building on the strengths of existing institutions, and defining the changes needed in intermediary implementing agencies to support community action.

COSTS AND BENEFITS

Two persistent myths exist about community-based programs: that they cost more than conventional programs and that they take longer. Additional costs may be incurred at the outset in building capacity at the local level. These costs, however, are significant only when community-level organizations have been so eroded that substantial time and resources have to be devoted to capacity building. Even when initial costs are high, they are more than offset by subsequent gains.

Evidence increasingly indicates that, *when the institutional framework is right,* participatory community-based programs actually cost less (see box A2.38) and are quicker to implement. In Bank-funded projects, the typical pattern has been a slow build-up period, when time is invested in community organization and setting the rules for interaction, followed by speedy disbursements.

Once the participatory process is established, the benefits of community-based development include increased efficiency and cost effectiveness. Furthermore, when the success of projects depends heavily on changes in behavior at the community level, promoting participation in community-based programs may be the only means of meeting objectives. The examples in box A2.39 indicate the

---

Box A2.38. Does Participatory Community-Based Development Cost More?

In Pakistan's Orangi Pilot Project, which provided sewerage facilities to nearly 1 million people in a poor area of Karachi, costs were one-eighth of conventional sewerage provided by city authorities. This was due to changes in technical design and the elimination of payoffs to intermediaries.

In Brazil's water and sanitation project for low-income communities (PROSENEAR), a ceiling of $120 per capita has been imposed on sanitation expenditures. Within this cost limit, engineers and community development experts are encouraged to work with communities to devise the most appropriate solutions. Through this process, projects have been designed for as little as $50 per capita.

Box A2.39. Community Participation Yields Significant Results

In Gujarat, India, during the 1980s, an average of 18,000 forest offenses were recorded annually: 10,000 cases of timber theft, 2,000 illegal grazing, 700 fires, and 5,300 other offenses. Twenty forestry officials were killed in confrontations with communities and offenders; assaults on forestry officials were frequent. In response, an experiment in joint management with communities was begun by the conservator. This included community meetings, widely publicized creation of forest protection committees, and profit sharing of 25 percent of timber returns with local groups. As a result, conflicts between officials and community groups diminished, community groups assumed responsibility for patrolling forests, and productivity of land and returns to villages increased sharply. In one year, one village of eighty-eight households harvested and sold 12 tons of firewood, 50 tons of fodder, and other forest products, while also planting and protecting teak and bamboo trees.

In Côte d'Ivoire, a national rural water supply program established community water groups that managed maintenance of 13,500 water points and reduced breakdown rates from 50 percent to 11 percent at one-third the cost. The shift to community-level maintenance was managed by taking away the responsibility for rural water supply from the sector agency, supporting private sector involvement in spare parts distribution, retraining technicians, and signing contracts with village groups and the water directorate. The results were sustained in those villages that had high demand for the rehabilitated water point and in which well-functioning community organizations already existed.

In Tamil Nadu, India, a community-based nutrition outreach program in 9,000 villages resulted in a one-third decline in severe malnutrition. A group of twenty women interested in health issues was hired in each village as part-time community workers accountable to the community. The women's groups, formed initially to "spread the word," subsequently branched off and started food production activities on their own. Earlier programs focusing only on the creation of health infrastructure were unable to make any difference in the nutritional status of children.

potential benefits of a community-based approach in three broad areas—managing natural resources, providing basic infrastructure, and ensuring primary social services.

CONDITIONS FOR SUCCESS

From time immemorial, communities have organized themselves to take care of collective and individual needs. Why then have so many attempts at getting people to participate and take responsibility for community-based development failed in the last fifty years? Experience provides some clear lessons about what works and what does not work in community-based development. Prominent among the failures have been attempts to achieve results on a wide scale through the infusion of external management, funds, and technology, controlled from distant places. A fundamental prerequisite of successful participatory programs at the community level is *the reversal of control and accountability* from central authorities to the community level.

Experience also points to a series of common elements in the design of successful programs. The first ingredients are knowledge and understanding of local needs and of the existing network of social interaction at the household, group, and community levels. This knowledge provides the basis for defining the changes needed, both in existing local organizations and in external agencies, to meet specified objectives.

Changes at the Community Level

If a community group is to function successfully, several criteria must be met: the group must address a felt need and a common interest; the benefits to individuals of participating in the group must outweigh the costs; the group should be embedded in the existing social organization; it must have the capacity, leadership, knowledge, and skills to manage the task; and it must own and enforce its own rules and regulations. Whether strengthening or modifying existing organizations or establishing new ones, steps need to be taken to ensure that these conditions are in place.

What may seem an obvious point but is often neglected is that a group functions only because it is *addressing a felt need of its members*. A fundamental design flaw in a natural resource management project in the Philippines, for example, was the assumption that upland farmers were interested in forest management. In contrast, the need to solve what is perceived as an urgent problem may bring different class and power groups together. In South India, for example, the entire village manages community-based irrigation systems and has developed a monitoring system to discourage water theft. Groups continue to function as long as the benefits of participation to their members continue to outweigh the costs (see box A2.40); hence, project design must be based on knowledge of community demand and must ensure that incentives for participation are in place.

In any community, inherited networks of organized reciprocity and solidarity form the basis for individual trust and cooperation. New community-based programs need to use and build on this existing stock of social capital and, wherever possible, to *work through existing organizations*. In Nepal, for example, when government policy prescribed the creation of farmers associations, assistant overseers found many informal groups of farmers organized around irrigation systems. Rather than creating new organizations, these existing groups were encouraged to register themselves as official farmers associations.

Sometimes, notably when existing social organization is highly inequitable, creating new groups is the only means of promoting the participation of disadvantaged people. Many successful projects that specifically target women or the poor have formed special organizations such as the Grameen Bank, the Self-Employed Women's Association of India, and women's farmer groups in Ni-

---

Box A2.40. The Benefits Must Outweigh the Costs

In the Philippines, farmers actually negotiated an increase in their irrigation fees because they had worked out a formula with the irrigation agency through which they would benefit from imposing and managing the collection of higher fees.

If the group does not undertake new tasks as old ones are accomplished, there is no new benefit flow and the costs begin to outweigh benefits. In Indonesia, water user groups that took on new tasks and provided additional benefits (such as individual household toilets and food security) continued to thrive, whereas others that did not functioned at a low level or not at all.

In Pakistan, 14,000 water user associations were hurriedly created to become active in water course improvements. When construction was completed, however, the associations did not move on to broader irrigation management tasks because they saw neither a purpose nor a benefit to continued existence. Instead, they reverted back to the traditional *warabandi* system, which was already well established and hence involved lower transaction costs.

Box A2.41. Checklist of Steps in Designing Large-Scale Projects

- Clarify and prioritize objectives. Link objectives to outputs.
- Identify the key stakeholders at the community and agency levels. Assess their capacity and interests.
- Assess (do not assume) demand, bearing in mind that demand is influenced by the confidence people have in the service provider.
- Establish eligibility criteria for community groups, so that communities can select themselves for projects, rather than projects selecting communities.
- Structure subsidies that do not distort demand.
- Restructure fund release to support demand.
- Learn by doing, adjusting plans annually on the basis of experience.
- Invest in strengthening social organization to increase local participation in decisionmaking.
- Institute participatory monitoring and evaluation with feedback loops.
- Redefine procurement rules to support community-level procurement where appropriate.

---

geria and the Gambia. These new organizations are the creation of their members, drawing as much as possible on what is already in place. Attempts to speed up a community development process by circumventing existing institutions and investing in new externally designed organizations have frequently failed in their aims. They also carry the danger of undermining existing institutions, diminishing the ability of community members to cooperate and organize effectively for other purposes.

An important reason for building on indigenous principles of organization is that, to be effective, a group must own and enforce its own rules defining membership criteria; the allocation of responsibilities, contributions, and benefits; and the mechanisms for ensuring accountability and resolving conflicts. If these rules are dictated from outside, people do not feel obliged to follow them, free riding becomes common, conflicts escalate, and the group becomes ineffective (see box A2.40).

Depending on the tasks the group is designed to manage and the existing capacity of the group, *investment in training* may be needed over a period of several years to build the necessary management and technical skills. Groups have failed because too much was expected of them too soon without supportive training.

Changes in Implementing Agencies

Designing an appropriate outreach strategy to support the community development process often involves difficult *changes in the structure and orientation of the implementing agencies.* The technical personnel in engineering agencies are commonly reluctant and ineffective community organizers. Merely adding more community workers makes no difference unless the overall incentive environment rewards staff for responsiveness to clients and support to community workers. Incentives

for performance are easier to institute when agencies are required to be financially viable, have autonomy to manage themselves, and have control over hiring and firing of staff.

An alternative to restructuring existing agencies is to *contract out the needed services* to NGOs (as in rural water supply in Kenya), the private sector (in agriculture in Malaysia), other government agencies (public health workers for a water and sanitation project in Brazil), or multilateral or bilateral agencies (the United Nations Children's Fund in low-income housing in Guatemala). In Mexico, the national water authority has an in-house group of senior social scientists and communication specialists who design the strategy for community outreach, applied research, and communications. This is then subcontracted to the private sector.

The choice of *outreach approach needs to match the goals of the program.* The extension approach, in which the field agent acts primarily as a channel of information and inputs and remains accountable to the agency rather than the community group, is not appropriate when the objective is community initiative and responsibility for management. When the success of a program hinges on participation through strong local groups, an empowerment approach is called for in which the field agent is a community organizer acting in liaison with technical agencies. It may be essential to introduce female agents to ensure the participation of women.

The role of the agency and its relationship with community groups needs to be supported by appropriate *changes in legislation.* Key issues include the mandate of agencies, funding mechanisms, accountability systems, the registration requirements and legal status of community groups, and use and tenure rights over assets (particularly over natural resources). Many rules and regulations may also need to be changed—from the required

Box A2.42. Shared Control and Benefits: CAMPFIRE in Zimbabwe

The incentive for Zimbabwe to protect its wildlife resources is high. Wildlife activities such as safari hunting, game cropping, tourism, and live animal sales contribute more than $250 million annually to Zimbabwe's national economy. Most wildlife, however, is outside parks on tribal or communally owned land. The Department of National Parks and Wildlife Management has recognized that wildlife resources will only be conserved if private and communal landowners derive economic benefit from protection of the resource and are given responsibility for conservation and management. The return of benefits to local communities from wildlife resources is the basis of Zimbabwe's Communal Areas Management Programme for Indigenous Resources (CAMPFIRE).

Using the CAMPFIRE approach and philosophy, the Chikwarakwara community of approximately 150 households in the remote Beirbridge area of Zimbabwe has taken over proprietorial management authority for wildlife resources from the district council. After a series of negotiations focusing on community membership, household definition, and revenue-sharing procedures, the council devolved management responsibilities and access to revenues derived from safari-hunting activities to the community. The benefits accrued to the community as a result of this responsibility have included a new school, a new grinding mill, and a Z$200 cash payment to each household. The council has benefited through an 11.7 percent levy, and the central government has benefited through an increase in taxable revenues.

The CAMPFIRE approach has not worked when communities have not been involved in rule formulation or when sharing of benefits with communities is minimal. In Nyaminyami District in the Zambezi Valley, for example, inequities exist in the distribution of benefits and in the management responsibilities among the district council, ward, and villages. The basic issue of whether the Nyaminyami Wildlife Trust, which was created by the district council to develop institutional capacity for wildlife management, should be an income earner at the district level or a grassroot wildlife management program has yet to be resolved.

qualifications for community workers, teachers, or health educators, for example, to procurement rules.

Implementing the institutional and legislative changes necessary to support large community-based programs inevitably meets resistance from powerful vested interests and needs *strong political support* to see it through. Many Bank-supported projects that implement institutional reform are led by reform-minded senior civil servants with access to the country's top political leaders.

---

* This note is based on the paper written by Deepa Narayan. Contributors include Maria C. Cruz, Jean Delion, Jim Edgerton, Steven Holtzman, Pierre Landell Mills, Kathryn McPhail, Lant Pritchett, and Julie Viloria.

PARTICIPATION AND INDIGENOUS PEOPLE

The characteristics of indigenous groups make participatory approaches especially critical to safeguarding their interests in the development process. Such approaches, recognizing the right of indigenous peoples to participate actively in planning their own futures, are supported by major donors and international organizations, including the World Bank, but have proved difficult to implement. They call for changes in attitudes, policies, and legislation to address the key issues: recognizing rights to land and natural resources, ensuring culturally appropriate procedures for consultation and communication, and building on the strengths of traditional lifestyles and institutions.

WHY SUPPORT PARTICIPATION?

Indigenous or tribal people, numbering at least 250 million throughout 70 different countries, have often been on the losing end of the development process. In many cases, their resources have been exploited for the benefit of other groups in society; in many countries they are the poorest of the poor. Often they experience political and economic discrimination and are perceived as backward or primitive.

Even when development policies and programs have been designed specifically to improve the welfare of indigenous peoples, the approach has usually been paternalistic, seeking their cultural assimilation and ignoring the strengths of indigenous institutions and knowledge (including environmental knowledge). This, in turn, can contribute to worsening poverty, social marginalization, and ethnic resistance.

The characteristics that distinguish indigenous peoples include their strong attachment to the land; dependence on renewable natural resources, subsistence practices, distinct languages, and cultures; historical identities as distinct peoples; and, often, mistrust of outsiders. For development institutions and planners, the challenge is how to incorporate such diversity of culture, language, ecological adaptation, and history into development planning. Cultural barriers make it especially difficult for the outsider to communicate with indigenous groups, understand their institutions, or discern their needs.

In these circumstances, the participation of indigenous people in planning and managing their own development is a means of safeguarding their interests in the development process. The past decade has seen growing recognition of the rights of indigenous peoples, supported by international legal instruments, to decide their own priorities for the development or use of their lands and other resources and to exercise control over their own economic, social, and cultural development.

At the same time, from a practical point of view, a participatory approach to indigenous development is a means of improving the quality of projects. In communities whose institutions, leadership patterns, and lifestyles are not well understood by outsiders, participation can ensure that projects and services are relevant to perceived needs and sustainable through indigenous institutions. To be effective, programs must be undertaken in partnership with indigenous peoples, rather than planned for them or carried out among them.

KEY ELEMENTS IN A PARTICIPATORY APPROACH

Although the need for a participatory approach is now widely accepted by international development agencies, it is difficult to implement. Obstacles include existing national policy and legislative frameworks, widespread prejudices, a tendency on the part of outside NGOs to control rather than facilitate, and a lack of development planning and management skills on the part of indigenous peoples themselves.

In Bank-supported operations, the challenge is typically confronted in two contexts. The first is in mandatory environmental assessments or indigenous peoples' development plans, intended to identify and mitigate potentially adverse effects of Bank-supported projects on the livelihoods of indigenous peoples. The second is in a new generation of Bank-funded projects in which indigenous peoples are the primary beneficiaries. Critical issues for the Task Manager on these new projects are outlined here:

The Legal and Policy Framework

Government willingness to devolve some degree of autonomy in decisionmaking to indigenous communities is a precondition of successful projects. Judgments must then be made on the need for legislative or policy reforms to support such participation in the decisionmaking process. Many of the line agencies or ministries responsible for relationships with indigenous people are weak. They lack professionally trained staff and often take a paternalistic approach. In these cases, reforms are needed before a participatory project can succeed. Local and regional elites may also impede authentic indigenous participation, even where an adequate legislative and policy framework exists (see box A2.43).

SUMMARIES

251

Box A2.43. The Politics of Indigenous Participation

Projects that incorporate indigenous consultation and participation need to take into account ongoing and complex political situations. Without a good understanding of these dynamics, even the most well-designed projects can lead to unforeseen turmoil and frustration. An example is the Indigenous Peoples Component of the Bank-funded Eastern Lowlands Natural Resource Management and Agricultural Development Project in Bolivia.

The purpose of the Indigenous Peoples Component is to provide land tenure security and other services to several Ayoreo and Chiquitano Indian communities in the Eastern Lowlands. Originally prepared in a highly participatory manner by a regional Indian federation in collaboration with a non-Indian technical assistance NGO, the component encountered political obstacles when implementation was due to begin.

The precipitating event for these problems was a protest march by the Indian federation, calling for more indigenous control over forest resources. This soon escalated into a major confrontation between the federation and the regional development corporation (the project implementing agency) over who should have control of the component. The Bank found itself in the unenviable position of trying to negotiate differences between the two bodies, many of which predated the protest march. Unable to find a solution after long meetings, the Bank accepted the redesign of the component, which regrettably reduced the power of the indigenous federation and put more power into the hands of an implementing unit within the regional corporation.

Colombia is one of the countries to have set an example in establishing a legal and policy framework that supports indigenous participation. Although Colombia maintains a special office within the ministry that deals with indigenous matters, the country's constitution recognizes the rights of indigenous communities to control their lands and natural resources and their internal political affairs. Each recognized indigenous community has its own council with the power to decide on the use of the community's land and resources, resolve internal disputes, and negotiate health, education, and other programs with regional development corporations and the national government. Recent Colombian legislation also provides for the direct transfer of government resources to these councils for projects that they design and execute.

Rights to Land and Natural Resources

Despite some recent progress, legal recognition of the customary rights of indigenous peoples to their ancestral lands is often lacking; many development programs have to deal with the question of indigenous land tenure security and natural resource rights.

Bank legal staff and lawyers within client countries can help Task Managers through the complexities of national land, resource, and environmental legislation as it relates to indigenous peoples. In the Laos Forest Management and Conservation Project, for example, one of the Bank's lawyers reviewed national forestry and land legislation relating to the customary rights of ethnic minorities in upland villages. This review provided the Bank with the necessary information to raise the subject with the government and to include provisions in the project for recognizing and regularizing customary land rights.

The Bank has also had experience, for example, in the Philippines and Brazil, in improving the institutional capacity of the government agencies responsible for the titling of indigenous lands. This experience has demonstrated the benefits to be gained from indigenous participation in physical mapping and land demarcation.

Culturally Appropriate Communication

In designing consultation and communication procedures with indigenous peoples, several special aspects need to be taken into account: their distinct languages, their traditional means of transmitting knowledge and values, and their mistrust of outsiders.

The language issue is central, because few indigenous people, especially women or elders, speak the national language fluently; hence, consultations need to be held in the vernacular language with the help of skilled interpreters. Development strategies for indigenous education (see box A2.44) also need to take into account the traditional importance of legends, folk tales, and proverbs for the oral transmission of knowledge and culture. Modern schooling of indigenous children has proved more effective when it includes instruction in both vernacular and national languages and when it is bicultural or multicultural in content.

Effective communication depends heavily on the element of trust. Through historical experience, indigenous people have learned to be cautious of "benevolent" outsiders, be they missionaries, government officials, teachers, or anthropologists. Those individuals or organizations that have been able to gain their trust have usually

Box A2.44. Community Participation in Bilingual Education

Although ethnic Vietnamese constitute the bulk of Viet Nam's population, there are fifty-three ethnic minorities living mostly in the mountain areas. The Bank-funded Primary Education Project contains a special Ethnic Minorities Education Component, which will finance a comprehensive package of educational inputs to minority children. This package, premised on the importance of the vernacular language and of community participation, consists of policy measures, pedagogical activities, provision of physical facilities, and institution building. To implement the component, existing province- and local-level committees will be involved in teacher training, textbook production, and maintenance of local schools.

Similarly, in the Second Primary Education Project in Mexico, the use of bilingual school teachers and pedagogical materials in the vernacular languages is combined with a strong element of community participation. Such participation is linked to the country's overall poverty alleviation program and includes the involvement of community committees, municipal education councils, parents associations, and school councils.

done so through long years of contact, learning, and respect for their languages and cultures. If such individuals or organizations can be brought into the project preparation process, a much better chance exists for introducing culturally acceptable mechanisms for consultation and participation.

Building on Traditional Strengths

The traditional lifestyles of indigenous peoples involve subsistence strategies that use locally available natural resources to satisfy their basic needs, while maintaining a balance with their environment. Many unfortunate examples of programs for indigenous development exist that have undermined these traditional subsistence strategies without providing socially and ecologically viable alternatives. The most successful programs with indigenous peoples, such as the West Bengal Joint Forestry Management Program (see box A2.45), are those that take traditional environmental knowledge and livelihood systems as the given basis on which to build new knowledge, technologies, and economic activities.

Similarly, the most successful projects are building on existing institutions, instead of creating new ones to deal with specific development tasks. In the Matruh Natural Resource Management Project, for example, among the Bedouin of Western Egypt, using the *bayt*—the Bedouin local lineage group—as the basis for project activities has inspired the confidence of the Bedouin population, including Bedouin women. As a result, it has avoided many of the pitfalls of earlier projects that attempted to introduce Western-style cooperatives.

Social assessments in which community members participate as partners rather than mere informants are used to improve understanding of the indigenous social structure and institutions on which to base development strategies and to assist the communities in determining how best to adapt their institutions to new purposes. Social assessment techniques can also reveal the existence of conflicts with implications for participation, for example, between traditional and modern institutions or sources of authority.

As in any other social groups, strengthening the capacities of indigenous peoples (see box A2.46) to evaluate options and implement their own development programs requires training in basic skills and technical assistance in areas such as management, topography, for-

Box A2.45. Tribal Women and Forestry

The West Bengal Joint Forestry Management Program is considered to be a model of participatory forest management. One of its most important aspects is the way in which tribal women, their traditional environmental knowledge, and their livelihood strategies have been incorporated into the program. In most areas, the recognition of the rights of tribal women to collect and market leaves of Sal and Kendu trees has been the major incentive that has led to the program's economic and institutional success.

In the village of Pukuria, women gather the leaves for six months of each year for the purpose of making plates, some 700,000 of which are exported monthly by the village. Minor forest products represent the primary occupation and most important source of income for Pukuria's tribal women. Given the low investment costs for reestablishing Sal forest productivity, combined with the benefits of protecting the upper ridge tracts where forests are located, this system seems to have considerable potential for increasing employment and income-earning opportunities, while reducing soil erosion levels.

Box A2.46. Investing in Capacity Strengthening

Promoting training and strengthening capacity may be one of the best investments for the economic development of indigenous communities. The Bank's Latin American and Caribbean Region's Environment Unit (LATEN), for example, has launched a program to assist indigenous organizations in the following activities: defining their own development strategies and proposals; strengthening their institutional structures in areas such as personnel management, training programs, budgeting, and finance; and improving their negotiating skills to finance their own development proposals.

The program is financed through grants to government agencies and/or indigenous organizations from the Bank's Institutional Development Fund; thus far, programs have been designed or are under preparation in ten countries. Each training program contains a consulting seminar, a series of workshops, a monitoring and evaluation system, and an evaluation seminar. Many of the seminars take place in the regions in which indigenous people live; all of them focus on indigenous values, cultures, and philosophies, as well as modern management and development planning skills.

estry, agriculture, marketing, and community health care. It also, however, involves promoting and strengthening traditional systems, for example, of natural resource management and medicine. Some of the best experiences with capacity strengthening have come from exchanges among indigenous peoples themselves. For example, in Latin American countries, NGOs have facilitated workshops in which indigenous peoples from different tribes and linguistic groups exchange experiences about land protection, mapping, and natural resource management.

Direct Funding

Many of the first-generation Bank-supported projects with indigenous peoples allocated funds to the national government agencies responsible for indigenous development. The typical result was expansion of the government agency concerned without much direct benefit to the indigenous communities. In Brazil, for example, where the Bank promoted large investments in increasing the staff and infrastructure of the National Indian Foundation, the impact was minimal in such important areas as natural resource protection, indigenous health, and community economic development.

In more recent projects, therefore, the goal is for funds to be controlled and managed by indigenous people themselves, preceded by the necessary capacity building. Group-based lending schemes, in which groups rather than individuals are responsible for protection against default in repayments, have proved adaptable to the finance needs of poor indigenous populations, as the principle of joint liability is often an important element in traditional systems of social control. These lending schemes increase the self-confidence of their members and demonstrate the ability of indigenous populations to participate in the development process.

This note is based on the paper written by Shelton H. Davis and Lars T. Soeftestad. Resource people in the Bank include Dan Aronson, Michael Cernea, Gloria Davis, Concepcion Del Castillo, Charles di Leva, Cyprian Fisiy, Mary Lisbeth Gonzalez, Scott Guggenheim, Kristine Ivarsdotter, Alf Jerve, Hemanta Mishra, Albert Ninio, Harry Patrinos, William Partridge, Stan Peabody, Ellen Schaengold, and Jorge Uquillas.

INDEX

B

C

D

E

F